Indira Falk Gesink is Associate Professor of History at Baldwin-Wallace College in Berea, Ohio. She received her Ph.D. in History from Washington University in St. Louis, Missouri, in 2000 and lived in Egypt in 1995–96 and 1998.

LIBRARY OF MODERN RELIGION

1. *Returning to Religion: Why a Secular Age is Haunted by Faith*
Jonathan Benthall
978 1 84511 718 4

2. *Knowing the Unknowable: Science and Religions on God and the Universe*
John Bowker [Ed]
978 1 84511 757 3

3. *Sufism Today: Heritage and Tradition in the Global Community*
Catharina Raudvere & Leif Stenberg [Eds.]
978 1 84511 762 7

4. *Apocalyptic Islam and Iranian Shi'ism*
Abbas Amanat
978 1 84511 124 3

5. *Global Pentecostalism: Encounters with Other Religious Traditions*
David Westerlund
978 1 84511 877 8

6. *Dying for Faith: Religiously Motivated Violence in the Contemporary World*
Madawi Al-Rasheed & Marat Shterin [Eds.]
978 1 84511 686 6

7. *The Hindu Erotic: Exploring Hinduism and Sexuality*
David Smith
978 1 84511 361 2

8. *The Power of Tantra: Religion, Sexuality and the Politics of South Asian Studies*
Hugh B. Urban
978 1 84511 873 0

9. *Jewish Identities in Iran:*
Resistance and Conversion to Islam and the Baha'i Faith
Mehrdad Amanat
978 1 84511 891 4

10. *Islamic Reform and Conservatism:*
Al-Azhar and the Evolution of Modern Sunni Islam
Indira Falk Gesink
978 1 84511 936 2

11. *Muslim Women's Rituals: Authority and Gender in the Islamic World*
Catharina Raudvere and Margaret Rausch
978 1 84511 643 9

ISLAMIC REFORM AND CONSERVATISM

Al-Azhar and the Evolution of
Modern Sunni Islam

Indira Falk Gesink

TAURIS ACADEMIC STUDIES
an imprint of
I.B. Tauris Publishers
LONDON • NEW YORK

To
my parents,
Dr. Arthur E. Falk and Dr. Nancy Auer Falk,
For raising me to the academic life,
and
Dr. David Ede,
For teaching me to see the edges of my boxes
and think outside them.

Published in 2010 by Tauris Academic Studies, an imprint of I.B.Tauris & Co Ltd
6 Salem Road, London W2 4BU
175 Fifth Avenue, New York NY 10010
www.ibtauris.com

Distributed in the United States and Canada Exclusively by Palgrave Macmillan
175 Fifth Avenue, New York NY 10010

Library of Modern Religion 10

ISBN: 978 1 84511 936 2

A full CIP record for this book is available from the British Library
A full CIP record for this book is available from the Library of Congress

Library of Congress catalog card: available

Printed and bound in India by Replika Press Pvt. Ltd.
from camera-ready copy edited and supplied by the author

CONTENTS

Acknowledgments   vii

Note on Transliteration   viii

1. Introduction   1

2. Religion and the State: Al-Azhar During Muhammad 'Ali's Rule   9

3. Order and Disorder: The Evolving Critique of Madrasa
   Education (1834–1870)   37

4. Progress, Nationalism, and the Negative Construction of
   al-Azhar 'Ulama (1870–1882)   59

5. A Conservative Defense of Taqlid   89

6. Efficiency, Mission, and the Meaning of 'Ilm (1882–1899)   111

7. The Syrian Riwaq Cholera Riot   143

8. Muhammad 'Abduh and Ijtihad   165

9. Who Reformed al-Azhar?   197

10. Conclusions   231

Notes   237

Selected Bibliography   279

Index   293

ACKNOWLEDGMENTS

I could not have completed this book without help. Grants from the National Security Education Program (1995–1996) and the American Research Center in Egypt (1998) supported my research in Egypt. Fellowships from Washington University in St. Louis, Missouri, and summer grants as well as a Research and Publications Grant from Baldwin-Wallace College in Berea, Ohio, funded the writing process. Many colleagues and friends contributed ideas or read various chapters of the manuscript, including Engin D. Akarli, Ana de Freitas Boe, Derek Hirst, Ahmet Karamustafa, Victor LeVine, M. Nabil Nofal, Timothy Parsons, Mark Pegg, Christopher L. Pepus, Mustafa Ramadan, Steven Siry, Laura Westhoff, and last but not least, my parents, Arthur and Nancy Falk. I am particularly indebted to Kenneth Cuno and David Commins, who read and commented on the final manuscript, and to my husband, Greg, without whose patience and support the book would not exist. All errors are my own.

NOTE ON TRANSLITERATION

I use a simplified transliteration system for Arabic and Turkish words, in which *q* stands for *qaf*, *gh* for *ghayn*, *dh* for *dhal*, and so on. I leave out diacritical marks except for the ' for *'ayn* and ' for initial *hamza*, and drop the *h* for *ta marbuta* and the final *hamza* of frequently used terms, such as *'ulama'*. I retain Anglicized spellings and plurals for certain words (Cairo for *al-Qahira*, fatwas for *fatawa*) and render names of Ottoman Egyptian administrators in their common Arabicized forms. Colloquial Arabic phrases are rendered phonetically to clearly distinguish them from phrases in classical Arabic.

1

INTRODUCTION

Picture this scene: Just across the street from the Khan al-Khalili, Cairo's medieval commercial district, overtopped by brick apartment buildings and surrounded by the rush of human activity, a student leads a reading group on a medieval theology text. He stands under a portico in al-Azhar mosque and madrasa complex, one of the most august institutions of Sunni Islamic education. The student presides as if he were a teacher, using written commentaries by other authors to interpret and evaluate the text's meaning. It is not unusual for advanced students to teach, but the faculty considers the ideas in this text controversial and has not taught them for several decades. A high-ranking professor sees the student and challenges his authority to teach such controversial subjects. The student replies that he knows the material and is willing to be examined on the spot if necessary. The student, Muhammad 'Abduh, goes on to become a pioneering journalist, a revolutionary, an educational reformer, and finally the most influential legal authority of his time. Years later, 'Abduh remembers exchanges like this with bitterness. He tells a journalist that the teaching methods used at that school harmed his intellect and that he spent years sweeping his mind clean of the school's influences, without total success.[1] He perceives his society as struggling to free itself from intellectual fetters of the past, crippled by its leading scholars' unwillingness to accept new ideas or contemplate controversial ones, and as a result unable to effectively counter European imperial control. Using the newly flourishing Arabic journalism that he and other reformers pioneered, he relentlessly pillories those whose authority depends on upholding the status quo. His professor, Muhammad 'Ilish, and other leaders of al-Azhar's scholarly community respond that the primary threat to Islamic society is internal division and that 'Abduh's proposed solutions would further divide and weaken it.

'Abduh employed the incident recounted above in a campaign to reform al-Azhar and its pedagogical traditions, courses, and administrative techniques. That campaign for reform stood at the center of an intellectual battle between so-called modernists and conservatives, the effects of which reverberated throughout the Islamic world. Both Western and Muslim scholars reproduced only the modernists' side of the story. In the course of the debate, the modernists depicted the Islamic legal tradition as stagnant and in need of revival. They also altered the meaning and usage of certain legal mechanisms, leading to the development of lay legal interpretation. The modernists originally intended lay interpretation to strengthen Muslims' faith, but today, it has freed Sunni Muslims to draw their own conclusions from the Qur'an and hadith rather than bowing to legal scholars' interpretations. It has also conventionally been accepted that conservative scholars succeeded in blocking reforms at al-Azhar, although the modernist vision of reform ultimately won over the literate public and spread around the world, inspiring Muslim revivalist movements from Indonesia to Turkey. However, a close look at the process of al-Azhar's reforms suggests that conservatives actually accomplished them.

This sounds like a petty academic debate or a struggle between forces of modernity and tradition in which we know exactly who is on what side and which side is good. It is not. Muhammad 'Abduh and the other actors in this drama stood on the cusp of a new era. The conceptual boundaries that their debates constructed did not exist before, nor did the nation that their arguments described. Further, the religion that their educational and legal reforms articulated was distinctly more personal and less communitarian than that of their predecessors. Thus these debates constitute a critical juncture in the evolution of modern Sunni Islam.

Today al-Azhar University is the most influential voice of establishment Sunni Islam. During the ages of Islamic power, al-Azhar was known for the breadth of its scholars' specializations, offering training in all four schools of Sunni law as well as various theoretical sciences. Its endowments provided stipends for scholars as well as free education, lodgings, and daily bread rations for thousands of students. Its fame was due in part to its historical stature as the second oldest continually existing university in the world. It was founded in 969 CE during the reign of the Fatimid caliph al-Mu'izz and commenced teaching activities in 975.[2] However, during the nineteenth century, al-Azhar madrasa was by most accounts an administrative mess. Reformers described its crumbling edifices, the squalor of the mostly impoverished students residing in its courtyards and loggias, the declining relevance of the subject matter its scholars taught, and rioting by students who distrusted government attempts to intervene. Even during this low period, al-Azhar attracted students from all over the Islamic world and returned those students to their countries as teachers, preachers, prayer leaders, and jurisconsults.

Beginning in the 1830s, because of al-Azhar's local and global importance, some religious scholars and government officials began to call for its reform, for the government to impose methods of administrative order learned from Europe, and for the scholars to teach modern sciences that would aid the cause of progress and allow Muslims to combat European subjugation. Ottoman and European imperial control of Egypt imbued these efforts with political danger.

Al-Azhar's teaching faculty had an ambivalent relationship with Muhammad 'Ali Pasha, the Ottoman governor from 1805 to 1848. Muhammad 'Ali had embarked on a massive scheme to centralize administration of state finances and land tenure arrangements, develop a professional military, and create a system of military schools that would produce bureaucrats and officers. Because this entailed both infringements on the financial independence of religious institutions and competition for students, educational reformers were often suspected of collaborating with the state against the interests of the scholars. In the mid-1860s, French and British creditors began to have increasing influence over Egypt and its elite, culminating in the British occupation of the country in 1882 and the establishment of the Veiled Protectorate. Educational reformers now became the darlings of European Orientalists, an association that further tainted their efforts. Reforming al-Azhar also had deep social implications: The reformers' models of progress threatened the integrity of religious knowledge, the authority of the religious scholars ('ulama) as interpreters of that knowledge, and the underpinnings of the Islamic legal system. The reform of religious education in Egypt therefore did not just happen. It was—and had to be—a negotiated product that both preserved key elements of the existing system of knowledge transmission and allowed reformers and their opponents to participate equally.

Since the Prophet Muhammad began to gather followers, what constitutes Islam has been to some extent constructed by believers. Islam today is marked by widespread contestation of religious authority and fragmentation of the umma, the worldwide community of Muslims. In the twentieth century, the dissemination of printed texts, increasing availability of education, and rising literacy rates delivered interpretation of religious texts into the hands of individuals, leading to the proliferation of divergent readings.[3] Lay interpretation provided a tool to those who wished to use Islam to subvert arbitrary rule by an authoritarian state, even if they then moved to subject Muslims to an equally arbitrary authoritarian religious rule forged out of their own interpretations of revelatory texts. The origins of these contemporary trends lie within the nineteenth-century arguments for reform of al-Azhar.

Adequate attention has not been paid to the ways in which nineteenth-century educational reformers subtly encouraged lay legal interpretation. Similarly, no one has examined the views of those who opposed widening the franchise of legal interpretation, chiefly because the sources most readily accessible to scholars were Arabic journals and newspapers owned by a relatively small coterie of intellectuals, most of whom opposed overt processes of colonization but accepted to some extent the content of the European modernizing project. The views of these reformist intellectuals passed down into the canon of authoritative Orientalist works on Islamic intellectual and social history, while the views of their opponents were set aside.

Terminology

It is difficult to categorize the participants in these debates. Orientalist scholarship—and even reflections on Islam informed by Orientalist sources, such as those of Friedrich Nietzsche and Michel Foucault—has tended to assume that Islam is a uniform, static, and collective entity, imbued with characteristics that were binary opposites to those of Europe.[4] Previous scholarship on al-Azhar has also been marked by Orientalism, with its rigid categorization of the participants into reformers (those who wanted to change and become modern and were thus more open to or at least more accepting of European sensibilities) and opponents of reform (those who were not). Globally influential reformers such as Jamal al-Din al-Afghani and Muhammad 'Abduh, who have even been described as the Luthers and Calvins of modern Islamic history,[5] have received by far the most scholarly attention, and scholars have accepted at face value reformers' characterizations of their opponents as recalcitrant reactionaries and obstacles to progress. Fascinated with the modernizing reformers, historians ignored the writings of the reformers' opponents, and neglect consigned them to untouched shelves in the archives, where they were lost to public memory. I am convinced that developments people collectively decide to ignore must be as—or even more—informative about human social change than those with which we appear obsessed. With the help of grants from the National Security Education Program (1995–1996) and the American Research Center in Egypt (1998), I have sought out and found nonmodernist views in multiple forms: a collection of fatwas by conservative legal scholar Muhammad 'Ilish; letters of conservative Shaykh al-Azhar Salim al-Bishri; reports in nationalist newspapers, colloquial journals, and ephemeral broadsheets; and committee reports on the processes of curricular reform.

I undertook this project out of an interest in discarded histories. I do not defend the conservatives. I merely wanted to restore their voices to the debate. It became clear to me early on that "they"—the opponents to reform—were not clearly distinct from the assumed "us"—the reformers. Reformers and opponents are not exclusive categories and should not be essentialized. Essentialisms are approximations at best—ultimately, they are incapable of explaining variation and change in a population. We have long understood that essentialism is inadequate for the life sciences, and that it is more appropriate to think in terms of population genetics: to think of populations as collections of interbreeding (or in this case, intellectually interacting) individuals.[6] Ideas, like genetic characteristics, can appear as recessive traits where they are not expected. The reformers and conservatives did not hold mutually exclusive sets of ideas but rather interacted and accepted portions of one another's arguments.

To continue with biological metaphors, one could also understand the participants in these debates as cultural hybrids. Some of them mimic European customs even as they try to circumvent European colonial influence; some clothe legal change in invented traditions; some stand with one foot in a discourse of Egyptian secular nationalism and the other in Ottoman Pan-Islamism. Their writings shift across cultural and temporal divides, defy definition, and in the process articulate an era.[7] It is too simple to describe the debaters as mere agents of conceptual colonization or defenders of tradition. That would fetishize a putative "pure" precontact culture as a foil for the insidious evil of the colonial culture. Rather, all these debaters worked together as agents of hybridization, sculptors of the new cultural forms Islam would inhabit in the twentieth century.

For clarity, however, I still need terminology to refer to individuals in the aggregate. It seems appropriate to name people as they named themselves. The well-known reformers often called themselves muslihun (reformers) or muhaddithun (modernists). They did not yet use the term "salafi" by which 'Abduh and his followers are sometimes known now. Because they became part of an intellectual lineage today known as Islamic Modernism, I have called them modernist reformers. These self-identified reformers consistently promoted curricular and administrative change at al-Azhar, often using European Utilitarian models of educational reform. Those who resisted aspects of reform were usually called muhafizun, when polite terms were used. The root "h-f-z" connotes protection of something, as in memorization of a text to preserve the knowledge it contains; so it seems reasonably appropriate to translate this term as "conservative." However, the conservatives only rarely named themselves—they seemed not to conceive of themselves as a political grouping requiring a name other than "Muslims." That refusal to name themselves was in itself a strategy of power: to allow the modernist reformers to box themselves in with self-definition and so exclude themselves from the normative group. The conservatives tended to share a more amorphous set of characteristics, including support for the pedagogical traditions of the madrasa, the separation of religious and temporal authority (especially over education), the unity and stability of the community, and taqlid. However, although individuals in these groups depicted themselves as standing on the edges of a clear cultural divide, that clarity was often rhetorical.

Themes

Underlying the narrative of this book are four themes. First, both the Arabic and Orientalist historiographical traditions of the Azhar reform debates used mainly modernist sources and focused particularly on Muhammad 'Abduh and the Islamic modernist party. In the resulting narrative, conservative religious scholars became opponents to reform and enemies of social progress. I reintroduce the conservative perspective, which depicts modernist reformers as agents of conceptual colonization of the madrasa and the Islamic legal tradition, bent on destroying the position of the religious scholars as intermediaries between people and their sacred texts. The result, the conservatives felt, would be chaos—in an era when Muslims desperately needed to remain unified to face imperial aggression.

Second, the Azhar debates produced an invented tradition of a stagnant Islamic law, which passed via modernist contacts with Orientalists into authoritative scholarship and current understanding of Islamic law and society. An essential part of the battle took place in the field of legal methodology. The modernists promoted "revived" use of ijtihad, a method of legal reasoning that involved derivation of new legal principles or rulings from original sources. The conservatives promoted taqlid, or adherence to established precedent. A pervasive theme of the modernist campaign for ijtihad was an assertion that ijtihad's practice was believed to have ceased and that it needed to be revived. This was not wholly accurate; ijtihad was still being used in certain circumstances. However, conservative scholars such as Muhammad 'Ilish countered by claiming that, indeed, ijtihad of the type modernists advocated had ceased, and its revived use would lead to moral confusion among the masses. This invented tradition of the cessation of ijtihad and a concomitant socio-legal stagnation was passed down via the modernist domination of journalism and contacts with Orientalists into Orientalist authoritative scholarship and into current understanding of Islamic law and society.

Third, the campaign to revive ijtihad was actually a campaign to change its definition: from a legal method restricted to use by highly trained jurists to a principle of intellectual investigation. Taqlid was equated with intellectual laziness and social stagnation. This campaign encouraged laymen to proceed directly to the primary sacred texts of the religion. Modernists believed that Muslims would uncover in those texts the true meaning of Islam, which to them had been covered up by centuries of juristic explanation and obfuscation. Ijtihad is today understood by many as something anyone with a good understanding of Arabic and a copy of the Qur'an can do. That has led not only to the undermining of scholars' authority but also to the proliferation of interpretations, including politically motivated ones used by groups like Hamas, the Egyptian Islamic Jihad, and al-Qaida, interpretations that legitimate violence against authoritarian governments, against innocents, and even against other Muslims. It has also led to the widespread belief that any public figure, no matter what his training, may issue legitimate fatwas.

Finally, throughout the book I have tied these developments to the progress of the reforms at al-Azhar. Chapters 2 and 3 detail the conditions of al-Azhar in the 1800s and how reformers constructed a narrative of decline. The traditional narrative of the reform debates tells how the conservatives stalled the good efforts of reformers like Hasan al-'Attar and Muhammad 'Abduh, eventually defeating them. Conservatives did not eschew reform or play a purely preservative role; they took an active role in modifying modernist ideas to make them culturally acceptable and eventually came—in history though not in memory—to craft the vision of modern Islam that animated the reform process.

The Azhar reform debate took place at a critical juncture in Egyptian history, a liminal time during which Egypt was first not quite totally under Ottoman control and then not quite totally under British control. Egypt as a nation was in the process of becoming. The participants in these debates were struggling to articulate that nation—its characteristics, its primary identities, its objectives, and its definitions of progress, stability, and community. In the process, they made indelible imprints on the contemporary form of Sunni Islam; they helped to define the present; they articulated an era.

2

RELIGION AND THE STATE: AL-AZHAR DURING MUHAMMAD 'ALI'S RULE

The famous scholar and mystic al-Ghazali once warned that religious scholarship and politics do not mix well. According to a hadith, "There is a circle of Hell uniquely reserved for 'ulama who visit kings." Political influence warps views and corrupts jurisprudence; legal opinions are given to please and obtain favors rather than to direct rulers to the straight path of Islam. In Egypt, this basic philosophy led to the development of religious institutions that were theoretically independent of the corruptive effects of political intrusion. The government was not secular, and religious personnel did involve themselves in matters of government. However, it was understood that the provision of justice and legal advice was best done from a position that governing authorities could not directly undermine if they disapproved of the justice or advice offered.[1] Decades of financial deprivation in the late eighteenth century, and state centralization efforts in the nineteenth century that utilized 'ulama, journalists, and bureaucrats trained in Europe, challenged this separation of powers. Most scholars saw educational reformers as furthering the intrusive power of the state. This set up a conflictual relationship between the state and religious institutions that persisted until the twentieth century, and produced a complex spectrum of engagement among the 'ulama that cannot be wholly captured in the dichotomy of reformer and resister.

The Perception of Decline:
Mamluk Warfare and the Awqaf

A combination of warfare, corruption, and bureaucratic centralization in the late eighteenth and early nineteenth centuries led to the implosion of Egypt's religious educational system and challenged the authority and independence of the 'ulama. Historically, Egypt's religious institutions had been funded primarily through awqaf (singular waqf). A waqf is an endowment of revenues from agricultural land or commercial property for the support of various religious and charitable purposes, including mosques, public kitchens, hospitals, public wells or cisterns, and educational institutions. A waqf was supposed to endure "until God inherits the earth," or until the end of time, and it was supposed to be immune from seizure and exempt from taxation. However, although Egypt was technically under the suzerainty of the Ottoman Empire, as it had been since 1517, Egypt's affairs were administered by the Mamluk amirs, local notables who claimed descent from slave aristocrats of the Mamluk Empire (1249–1517).[2] The Mamluk amirs were in almost constant warfare with one another. Many amirs sought to protect their property from seizure in the event of their deaths, often by willing much of it to their wives or by designating it as waqf.

During this time, the most powerful 'ulama filled power vacuums or served in key ways to hold the fabric of the Mamluk political order together. The 'ulama divided themselves into three groups. The distinguished elders occupied official administrative and symbolic positions within the educational and Sufi hierarchies, and represented the Egyptian subjects to their Mamluk and Ottoman rulers: as local administrators; as financial administrators; as creditors; as tax collectors; as guardians of families, houses, and wealth; as judges, teachers, notaries, and preachers; and in general as guarantors that God's command be carried out in society.[3] The historian 'Abd al-Rahman al-Jabarti, a scholar himself and an eyewitness to many of the events he described, attested to the public respect accorded these 'ulama and sufi shaykhs by the Mamluks and public alike.[4] 'Ulama elders also often had common interests and alliances with various Mamluk families, who often provided economic opportunities that made some of them extremely wealthy. Their offices also put them in charge of extensive awqaf, the revenues of which were intended for use in performance of the office. For example, al-Azhar awqaf controlled by the Shaykh al-Azhar (the rector) were the most extensive and lucrative in Egypt. Holders of high office also received stipends as waqf administrators as well as cash allocations from awqaf, and tended to invest in urban properties, tax farms, and domestic and foreign trade. Furthermore, the great 'ulama were better able to protect their wealth than other wealthy segments of society because 'ulama were immune from taxes, forced loans, and confiscation of property.[5]

Mid-level 'ulama usually taught at al-Azhar or lesser madaris (singular: madrasa), or served as jurisconsults or judges. Their incomes were sufficient for their families' livelihood. Warring Mamluk amirs often tried to preserve their wealth from seizure by willing much of it to their wives, or establishing trusts that would ensure income for their families. 'Ulama advised and represented those wives if they had to defend their property rights in court, and supervised the trusts, from which they could receive significant income.[6]

The lesser 'ulama, who depended upon the charitable services provided by waqf-supported religious institutions, such as bread rations and stipends for scholars, were devastated by the reduction of these services. Moreover, in the late 1700s, while warfare disrupted trade routes and collection of tax revenues, a lengthy drought crippled the economy. The water level of the annual Nile floods remained low for decades, until at least 1802, impoverishing artisans, traders, and schools in rural areas.[7] Warring Mamluk amirs and embezzling supervisors also siphoned off revenues from al-Azhar's religious endowments, to the extent that student provisions were occasionally withheld, causing students to riot.[8] All of this contributed to the impoverishment of the lesser 'ulama.

Muhammad 'Ali and Ottoman Centralization Efforts

In 1798, Napoleon invaded and occupied northern Egypt, and established a ruling council composed of Egyptian 'ulama. When the French decamped, Egypt remained under the sovereignty of the Ottoman Empire. In 1805, the 'ulama of Cairo nominated a new Ottoman governor, Muhammad 'Ali Pasha (r. 1805–1848). Muhammad 'Ali's main concern was to create a provincial military capable of protecting Ottoman realms against the predations of the Europeans. Like the Ottoman sultans of that time, he adopted models of military reform that were based on the best recent example of military success—in his case, the model of the Napoleonic army.

When Napoleon was finally defeated in 1815, a surplus of French military experts entered the world market, many finding employment in Egypt. Muhammad 'Ali set about organizing a massive military force, which entailed converting diverse parts of the society into a manageable, economically productive machine. Unlike the foreign military aristocracies and temporary levies of the past, this military force was, from 1822 on, a professional force conscripted from native Egyptians. Muhammad 'Ali also built a factory system to supply the military with European-style equipment and a school system to provide the military and factory system with properly trained personnel, while subjecting the entire country to a gradually progressive economic reorganization that ensured availability of surplus for use in the factories and for export to fund the development projects. Muhammad 'Ali corresponded with Jeremy Bentham and sent students, including his son Ibrahim, to study the factories and educational systems of Europe.[9]

Although Muhammad 'Ali's centralization projects were not exactly new, some having been attempted earlier by powerful Mamluk amirs,[10] they challenged in significant ways the authority of the 'ulama and also affected the financial health of the religious institutions. The initial effects of these developments were to alienate 'ulama at all levels of social strata, and to divide them between supporters of centralization efforts and opponents seeking to retain al-Ghazali's ideal of a separate space for juridical authority.

These centralization efforts included gradual replacement of tax farmers with bureaucratic tax administration, and remanding of agricultural awqaf lands to state supervision, beginning in 1809. By 1814, these efforts were largely complete.[11] In 1846, Muhammad 'Ali issued a decree preventing any further agricultural land from being alienated from taxation through endowment as waqf.[12] He did promise to maintain both individual and institutional beneficiaries of existing awqaf,[13] but this still interfered with 'ulama sources of wealth[14] and increased the friction between 'ulama who were political purists and those who supported Muhammad 'Ali.

More importantly, state waqf supervision contributed to the financial problems the madaris were already facing due to warfare, drought, and corruption. The state now bore responsibility for paying out revenues to the awqaf's beneficiaries. The more popular mosques, including al-Azhar, were to be maintained and their former supervisors compensated. State subsidies to the madaris appeared as a regular part of Muhammad 'Ali's budget until 1833. Smaller institutions, however, he closed.[15]

Historians concluded that the 'ulama developed an attitude of entrenchment whereby they opposed nearly anything that Muhammad 'Ali did that intruded into their domains. However, 'ulama whose finances were not totally dependent upon special appointments or land holdings often retained their wealth; some who sought to influence the governor did succeed; and some even founded scholarly dynasties that persisted into the twentieth century. Muhammad 'Ali moved directly only against those who challenged his authority and resisted bureaucratization.[16]

The Azhari 'ulama had been subject to the political machinations of the Mamluk amirs before him, but not to this degree.[17] Muhammad 'Ali and his descendants now subjected higher-level religious offices to state control, placing in them men who were receptive to the European models of education and reform. Consequently, those 'ulama who achieved high office through the governor's good graces were increasingly alienated from their colleagues. Also, the divisions among the 'ulama reflected badly in the public eye. Many ordinary Egyptians regarded Muhammad 'Ali as an oppressor, and although this view was not universal, the fact that some 'ulama acquiesced in his rule devalued their social capital.[18] Al-Jabarti reported that people insulted 'ulama in public for their apparent hypocrisy.[19]

Some 'ulama also came to perceive Muhammad 'Ali as subordinating the interests of religious institutions to pecuniary concerns. For example, in November of 1810, Muhammad 'Ali debated whether he should tax waqf lands. He consulted a group of 'ulama elders, including the Shaykh al-Azhar. One of the governor's officers suggested that the 'ulama might be willing to give up their traditional tax exemptions. The Shaykh al-Azhar choked and called the officer an "evil man." Muhammad 'Ali then suggested, as an alternative, taxing lands set aside for provisioning the poor. The 'ulama responded that taxing these lands would ruin the institutions they supported. Muhammad 'Ali argued that he would only tax lands the awqaf of which no longer functioned, since the mosques they served were already in ruins. Some of the 'ulama then insisted that it was his fault if waqf supervisors were insufficiently motivated to use waqf revenues correctly and thus caused the ruin of their mosques.[20]

Muhammad 'Ali decreed that agricultural waqf lands were taxable in 1812. Immediately some 'ulama predicted the ruin of the mosques. Muhammad 'Ali responded that none of the mosques wholly dependent on waqf revenues were in good repair anyway, and that he would ensure that ruined mosques were given sufficient means for their repair.[21] In 1813, the 'ulama addressed complaints about the poor condition of mosques to Ibrahim Pasha, Muhammad 'Ali's son and governor of Upper Egypt. He wrote:

> I have inspected the mosques and found them in ruins, while the supervisors gobble up the revenues! The treasury has a better claim [to the revenues] than they do! . . . Those mosques that I found in a good

state of repair I have provided with sufficient income and more. I have found some mosques endowed with vast lands but in ruins and not in use. . . . [22]

In contrast, the historian al-Jabarti claimed that Muhammad 'Ali's waqf centralization immediately destroyed smaller religious institutions and the 'ulama who worked at them. By 1815, only a year after state control had been established over awqaf, they were producing little wealth for the religious institutions, and many katatib (plural form of kuttab, elementary-level Qur'an schools) were in ruins. He implied that the government had failed to allocate them adequate revenues. In fairness, given previous reports of drought and abuse of funds, the revenues from waqf lands had probably been at minimal levels for much longer than one year—and perhaps the awqaf were not by that time generating enough funds to pay for repair of the decaying rural mosques and schools. Nevertheless, al-Jabarti portrayed the problem as an intentional result of Muhammad 'Ali's policies.[23]

Foreign visitors' descriptions of the conditions of mosques corroborate 'ulama complaints of generally reduced financial circumstances, but do not prove that these circumstances were due to state supervision of the awqaf. The *Description de l'Egypte* stated that at the turn of the century, most 'ulama subsisted on incomes derived from gifts from patrons, fees for various services, and small waqf allowances, which were not cash payments but bread allotments (some 5,600 ardabbs of grain annually were distributed to 'ulama and students through administrative shaykhs). There were no salaries per se. It appears, then, that the majority were already poor when Muhammad 'Ali removed their wealthier colleagues from positions as waqf supervisors.[24]

As for the effects on al-Azhar, a visitor to Cairo in 1828–1829 and 1830 remarked that the number of students at al-Azhar had temporarily decreased as a result of waqf centralization.[25] In 1834, the British Orientalist Edward Lane wrote that al-Azhar had lost

the greater portion of the property which it possessed: nothing but the expenses of necessary repairs and the salaries of its principal officers, are provided by the government. The professors . . . receive no salaries. Unless they inherit property, or have relations to maintain them, they have no regular means of subsistence but teaching in private houses, copying books, &c.; but they sometimes receive presents from the wealthy. . . . Since the confiscation of the lands which

belonged to the Azhar, the number of that class of students to whom
no endowed riwaq [dormitory] is appropriated has very much
decreased. The number of students, including all classes except the
blind, is (as I am informed by one of the professors) about one thousand five hundred.

Lane also noted that the 'ulama differed as to the number of students studying at al-Azhar. Some claimed there were more than three thousand students: "it varies very much at different times."[26]

There is little direct evidence that al-Azhar's state of disrepair was due
solely to the state's assumption of awqaf control and not also to decades of
reduced waqf revenues and neglect.[27] Direct evidence that government payments to al-Azhar and other larger mosques were insufficient to cover their
day-to-day operating expenses has not yet been found, and historian Mine
Ener has shown that the state Ministry of Awqaf continued to provide assistance to the poor of al-Azhar through the 1840s.[28] According to Felix Mengin, in the 1820s, al-Azhar was receiving some 3,800 pounds of bread every
other day, oil for lamps, and monthly student stipends, which the shaykhs
of each administrative unit distributed. The whole endeavor amounted to
630,000 piasters annually, "partly furnished by the government, and partly
arising from the rent of houses, shops, and warehouses, bequeathed to the
charity by pious individuals"—in other words, in the 1820s al-Azhar was
still receiving income from awqaf.

James Augustine St. John wrote, after visiting the mosque in the late
1840s, that "though less flourishing than formerly, this establishment is
still considerable." More flourishing times referred to the traveler Van
Egmont's egregiously exaggerated claim that al-Azhar had once supported
40,000 employees and beneficiaries.[29] All told, the sum of these reports
suggests that al-Azhar did receive both an allowance from the state and
revenues from various private awqaf, from at least the 1820s to the late
1840s.

Furthermore, evidence suggests that 'ulama or agents of Muhammad
'Ali's successors deliberately spread rumors of the centralization's terrible
effect upon the religious institutions. Florence Nightingale mentioned, in
1850, that upon being guided through al-Azhar mosque, she was informed
that Muhammad 'Ali had taken

possession of all the lands of the Azhar (among the other mosques),
and consequently of all the salaries of the ulama, or learned men, so

that they now receive nothing, but are obliged to maintain themselves by private lessons. . . . The poor students must also get their living as they can . . . since this great confiscation, their number has, of course, diminished.[30]

According to Ehud Toledano, 'Abbas Pasha (r. 1848–1854), Muhammad 'Ali's grandson and successor, may have wanted to spread such ideas as a way of distinguishing his own practice from Muhammad 'Ali's relatively poor relations with the 'ulama.[31] It may also be useful to consider that the period of state sequestration of waqf revenues lasted at most forty-four years, from 1814 to 1858, when the Land Law allowed institutions to resume receiving revenues from their awqaf.[32]

Whatever the true cause, the financial deprivations did have some negative impact on al-Azhar. In 1883, the Comité de Conservation noted that "the principal parts of the edifice are propped up and need reconstruction"; a photograph from the 1880s showed the facade of the outer courtyard walled up between the columns; and a civil servant, 'Ali Mubarak, documented repairs at that time. Perhaps more significantly, smaller mosques and schools were downsized or closed, which would have left 'ulama who worked at them and students who depended on waqf stipends without means of subsistence. Those who could not be absorbed into other professions migrated to institutions that still offered hope of a livelihood. In 1806, a Spanish traveler had been disappointed that the floors of al-Azhar were covered with mats rather than carpets, so that the "vermin" of the poor could be washed off. In the early 1830s, Edward Lane described al-Azhar as a haven for the poor and homeless. In the 1840s, most of the homeless in Cairo sheltered overnight at al-Azhar. J. A. St. John noted during his visit in 1845 that a number of indigents who were not students lay asleep on mats throughout the mosque, and that the mosque's funds supported a greater number, at least 2,000, who were students. These also slept in the mosque. By 1846, al-Azhar's enrollment records showed 7,403 students, double the estimated numbers at the beginning of the century and four times more than Edward Lane's figures.[33] In 1850, Florence Nightingale's guide told her that the number of students had decreased, but she described the main court of the mosque as crowded in a manner utterly unlike the other mosques she had seen, its occupants "making . . . a most tremendous noise." Nevertheless, the portico in which lessons were being read was silent, except for the voices of the 'ulama leaning against their pillars and the scratching of students writing on their slates as they sat in neat circles on the ground.[34]

In the decades after Muhammad 'Ali's fiscal centralization, the population of 'ulama and students at al-Azhar and other larger madaris, such as the Ahmadi in Tanta, gradually swelled with 'ulama from closed institutions and new students who would have ordinarily attended smaller schools. These larger institutions became the most important refuges for destitute 'ulama, students, and other beneficiaries of the mosques' various services. Gradually, the populations of impoverished students and dependent 'ulama increased, stretching the available revenues and contributing to 'ulama resentment of Muhammad 'Ali.

The Halqa

The swelling student population posed an even more fundamental challenge: It threatened to undermine the pedagogical traditions of Islamic education and the religious authority of the scholars. A madrasa is literally a "place of study"; in this context, it refers to a school established to teach fiqh (Islamic jurisprudence) and its various preparatory and ancillary disciplines. Madaris were at that time usually but not always attached to a mosque, which might also provide lodgings and food. Teaching scholars were known as shaykhs, a title of respect given also to elders and headmen. The shaykhs did not hold courses as we understand them. The shaykhs would claim an area, either in al-Azhar itself or in a nearby mosque, in front of a pillar or other recognizable architectural feature. Students would gather around them in a halqa, or circle, to listen as the professor dissected a written text. The sessions, and the system of education, became known as the halqa.

Teaching in the halqa meant reading texts: The instructor would read a text aloud, explain its grammatical points, and draw the students' attention to possible interpretations, engaging them in a dialectical process. Knowledge was understood to be embodied in texts that had to be read aloud to be given concrete meaning. Written Arabic does not always note short vowels. Meanings signified by various combinations of written root consonants remain fluid, resonating with the meanings of surrounding combinations of consonants, until given voice by a speaker/interpreter. For example, the Arabic root 'ayn-lam-mim may mean "he taught" when pronounced 'allama, "learned ones" or "scholars" when pronounced 'ulama, "instruction" when pronounced with a prefixed t, ta'lim. The pronunciation 'ilm can mean "discursive knowledge" or "science" depending on the suggestion of surrounding words. Dependence on oral pronunciation echoed the transmission of religious texts in Islamic history, which originated in oral transmission and later, after being written down, still needed to be read aloud.

Authorial intention could not be recaptured unless there was an unbroken chain of oral readings stretching back to the originator of the text or early recipients of it. Thus the authority of religious knowledge was bound up with the process of transmission, the understanding of the potentialities of written words that underlay that process, and the interests of the human beings who were vehicles of transmission.[35] It is significant that the act of teaching was almost always referred to as qira'a (reading or reciting).

The halqa system followed its own logic of authority and order patterned on the hierarchy of textual interpretation. Just as an original text stood above the commentaries made of it in that hierarchy, and the commentaries above the super-commentaries, students began their studies with the ultimate original text, the Qur'an, and went on to hadith and its ancillary studies. They moved on to subjects that were, in essence, elaborations upon these basic sources or vehicles of exegesis, such as the principles of theology and jurisprudence. Finally, if judged capable, they were allowed to enter specialized studies in a particular madhhab, a legal school or rite. To function effectively as a means for training qualified legal personnel and religious scholars, the halqa system required that the 'ulama maintain a personal connection with the students, so that the professor "instructs, confronts, and disciplines each student individually."[36] Each level of study required that the student master certain preparatory texts and explicative skills, and, while students could move from one professor to another according to their preferences, as long as the number of students studying with each professor was manageable, professors were still able to ensure that no student went on to read a text to his own circle until he was adequately prepared. Once a student had mastered a text with a professor, the professor would write him a letter called an ijaza that listed the text's transmission from author to explicator and permitted the student to read that text to his own circle of students. This established each ijaza recipient as a link in a putative chain of knowledge transmission that stretched back to the first generation of Muslims, thereby reinforcing the authority of religious knowledge as something derived from oral transmission and spoken mediation of the text. Descriptions of students' activities during lessons suggest that many of them made their own copies of the text in question, adding their own notes as interlinear commentaries and marginal glosses, and gathered together later to compare notes and help one another memorize relevant materials by reading aloud.[37]

Anthropologist Dale F. Eickelman suggests further that the professor introduced his students into the social contexts in which they would progress from simple "mnemonic possession" of a text to fahm, or under-standing. Understanding a text may not have implied being able to inter-pret it beyond explication of grammatical points. Since interpretation sug-gested departure from the transmission of the author's intent, understanding meant ability to deploy knowledge socially, by quoting appropriate texts during conversation or when preparing legal opinions. Professors' social behavior and status thus also formed part of the educa-tional process for students, as professors would introduce students into higher social circles and demonstrate how the knowledge they were learn-ing should be displayed.[38]

In practice, however, renowned institutions like al-Azhar attracted many who were not students in the technical sense. Anyone wishing to add to his knowledge of religion was welcome to listen to a reading and glean from it what value he could. These ephemeral listeners did not proceed through les-sons according to the logic of the system; they came to hear famous schol-ars read, or to hear a famous text read.[39] They could sleep in the mosque loggias or courtyards if necessary. This made it difficult to define who real-ly was a student, because the Arabic word *talib* simply meant anyone who sought knowledge. This was a significant issue for the madaris because it became difficult to tell who qualified for bread rations provided by the awqaf. This would also become a significant issue for the state, because madrasa students were exempt from conscription.

Competition from the Military School System

In the 1810s to the 1840s, as the populations of large madaris swelled, Muhammad 'Ali built his own educational system to serve his military. Tra-ditionally, technical or vocational education had not been within the purview of religious education, although religious scholars might read texts on theoretical science or mathematics with their students.

Muhammad 'Ali's concerns in developing military education in Egypt were to improve his army and achieve a higher standard of administrative efficiency in his government.[40] Hence he was interested in acquiring knowl-edge of European and Ottoman military and administrative practices and of the sciences, technologies, and industries required to support a European-style centralized military system.[41] Because the subjects he desired his schools to teach were not among those regularly cultivated by Egyptian scholars, Muhammad 'Ali initially imported European advisors to train his troops and teach in his schools, although he intended eventually to replace the foreigners with their own trainees.[42]

Even before Muhammad 'Ali had fully formed his plans for military and administrative reform, he had begun sending student missions to European cities "to see for themselves what was lacking in the country and what the Westerners had to give and teach." It was customary for scholars to travel to different countries seeking the specialized knowledge of different regions, but these early missions were different in that the state sent students specifically to Europe to learn technical subjects: military science and engineering (1809), printing (1809 and 1815), and ship-building and mechanics (1809 and 1818).[43] Later mission students (1826–1879) studied a variety of European sciences and political subjects.[44] When the military schools were established, it was clear that the subjects they taught were not within al-Azhar's purview. The War School (1824) taught drawing, French, tactics, arithmetic, geometry, infantry exercises, and gunnery. The School of Music (1824) taught bugling and trumpeting. There was also a School of Medicine (1827), a Veterinary School (1827), a School of Maternity for midwives (1831), and Schools of Irrigation (1831), Industry (1831), Artillery (1831), and Engineering (1831).[45]

Al-Azhar offered an elementary religious education and also trained specialists in Arabic, theology, and law. The elementary students read the Qur'an and texts on hadith (sayings of the Prophet and his Companions), tafsir (Qur'anic exegesis), tawhid (monotheistic theology), usul al-din (sources or roots of religion, theology), fiqh (jurisprudence), Arabic grammar, and logic. Students of Arabic language would study the Qur'an, hadith, exegesis, morphology, syntax, expressions, style, and rhetoric. Theology students read texts in exegesis, hadith, theology, monotheistic theology, jurisprudence, and logic. Law students read texts in exegesis, hadith, and jurisprudence. Although a great variety of subjects had been offered at al-Azhar before the 1830s, by mid-century when the military schools were at their height, al-Azhar no longer offered sciences, languages other than Arabic, or mathematics. Therefore, the only military schools that overlapped with the religious schools' offerings were the High School (1826), which taught Arabic but also sciences, and the School of Translation (1836), which taught Arabic as well as other languages.[46] Moreover, the military schools served an objective fundamentally different from that of religious schools like al-Azhar.

However, the student missions to Europe and the military schools would eventually impinge upon al-Azhar's interests. First, al-Azhar students filled the majority of the later missions, probably because al-Azhar was the only school that offered the level of training required for higher education.[47]

Second, the demand for primary education was increasing, because the military schools required some level of elementary education beyond the basic reading and writing skills learned in religious primary schools. Al-Azhar, overburdened already, could not fulfill this demand. So Muhammad 'Ali established a number of primary schools, stating that they were to supplement the religious primary schools and replace those that had decayed or disappeared as a result of the waqf reforms. Instructors from al-Azhar staffed the military primary schools, but tacitly acknowledged that the technical subjects of the higher military schools were within the purview of foreign and government-educated teachers.[48]

Moreover, al-Azhar and other religious schools had traditionally trained many of Egypt's government ministers, clerks, judges, jurists, and teachers. The new schools offered an alternative for administrative education, and their students began to take over jobs previously filled by al-Azhar graduates. Those jobs that remained exclusively the preserve of 'ulama, such as Arabic language teaching in the primary schools (until 1872), were neither lucrative nor prestigious. This would become a serious problem, because the number of students attending al-Azhar continued to grow throughout the nineteenth century, while their opportunities for employment shrank. By the early 1900s, even administrative posts at al-Azhar were filled by graduates of military schools trained to serve in the government bureaucracy. Hence in addition to the loss of their political roles as mediators, the 'ulama were also being displaced from other traditional areas of employment by a new class of technocrats in an environment of state control.[49]

Pedagogical Challenge

In 1847, Muhammad 'Ali issued orders to create national schools in Cairo based on the Lancaster model of instruction. This was a rule-based model intended to create maximum efficiency in the classroom. Students were to follow written rules that governed all aspects of their personal appearance, demeanor in class, and progress through the lessons. Lessons were written on boards along the walls. Students moved from easy to harder lessons; monitors herded them from one lesson station to the next; and instructors tested the students by means of written orders: "Face front" and "show slates."[50] While it is difficult to tell whether the military schools followed this model, they were at least intended to disseminate knowledge as sets of instructions, of written language as conveyor of those instructions, and of authority as diffused rather than located in an authoritative reader of a text.

There were also immediate practical consequences to the development of a separate, nonreligious track of administrative education. For example, al-Azhar had no curriculum in the sense of a formal plan of offerings. Student demand and availability of ijaza-holding 'ulama determined texts to be read. As Muhammad 'Ali's school system grew, demand for texts on theoretical science and mathematics at al-Azhar declined, and the 'ulama who read texts in those areas went into the military school system.[51] Students who wanted to study something other than Islamic jurisprudence or Arabic grammar and literature could turn to the military schools for their training, and would finish their studies more quickly than they would have done at al-Azhar, where mastery of a text could take years. Hence, when Muhammad 'Ali's schools were at their greatest number in the 1830s, the readings offered by al-Azhar were narrowing by the logic of lessening demand to purely religious and ancillary subjects—while at that very time, reformers within al-Azhar began agitating for greater access to scientific education and broader training for students at religious schools.

There were practical reasons for locating administrative education outside religious schools. If Muhammad 'Ali had forced the faculty at al-Azhar to accept the expanded curriculum that technical administrative education would have required, he would have broken with the principle that al-Azhar's curriculum was solely the province of the 'ulama themselves to determine—that is, that religious matters should be left to religious experts and should not be subject to coercive political concerns. Furthermore, he would have had to supplement al-Azhar's faculty with non-Azhari-trained teachers, as Azhari expertise did not include all the desired subjects. This most 'ulama were unwilling to accept.[52] More importantly, they would have had to accommodate a method of teaching that used words simply to communicate an author's meaning, and did not require the mediation of an authoritative speaker, something that was alien to the halqa system.

One of the key differences between these two systems of education is in the nature of communication between instructors and students. The model of education suggested for the military schools was implicitly coercive, while the halqa model was contractual, empowering not only the teacher but also the students. According to philosopher of language H. P. Grice, meaning is conveyed in oral communication when one intends to induce a belief in an audience and when the audience recognizes in one's utterance or behavior the intent to mean what one wants the utterance or behavior to mean. This is relevant to halqa education because the students—here, the audience—are empowered by the teacher's need for them to participate in recognizing his intent. Meaning is to some extent under the control of the audience.[53] In any conversation, an implicit contract exists, speaker with listener, that is renewed instant by instant. It is noncoercive in the sense that the audience may opt not to participate, even invisibly, by dissenting silently or simply ceasing to pay attention. The teacher is also empowered, given a willing student, because he has a significant degree of control over what the student learns, since the teacher need not proceed with the lesson until satisfied with the student's progress. The asymmetry of power implied by this is corrected by the possibility of losing confirmation of a teacher's status when a student ceases to acknowledge it.

The Utilitarian models impose asymmetry of power and eliminate the contractual correction. Mass education also relies to a greater extent on learning directly from textbooks, which requires that teachers find less direct methods to monitor student learning, such as examinations, which again impose asymmetry and eliminate the correction. From the perspective of a nineteenth-century madrasa teacher, direct textbook learning is also potentially dangerous. The knowledge being learned was of such pivotal importance, since incorrect information could damage one's possibility of entering Paradise, that the incomplete control of a textbook over a student's mind and the possibility of erroneous understanding were first steps into the abyss of unbelief and social chaos.

After 1809, Muhammad 'Ali began to replace 'ulama who disapproved of him with those who had accepted the new understandings of language and knowledge, some of whom were Azhari-trained 'ulama themselves. There appeared now a new phenomenon: Bureaucratic 'ulama—who, because of their training at al-Azhar, were usually considered members of the independent religious establishment—were now being seen as agents of a hostile epistemological invasion. When these bureaucratic 'ulama began to criticize the halqa system in favor of the efficient methods used in Muhammad 'Ali's military schools, some independent 'ulama suspected them of ulterior motives and took aim at their political and social vulnerabilities in order to destroy their credibility.[54]

An Early Critique: Shaykh Hasan al-'Attar

The first nineteenth-century critic of education at al-Azhar was the 'alim Hasan al-'Attar. Shaykh al-'Attar mentored a generation of reformist journalists and translators, and therefore was indirectly responsible for the transformation of Egyptian intellectual culture in the nineteenth century.[55]

However, as Shaykh al-Azhar, or rector (1830–1834), he felt isolated from and victimized by the other 'ulama.[56]

Hasan al-'Attar was born in Cairo, of Maghribi parentage, around 1766. He entered al-Azhar at the elementary level and continued his higher education there. During the French occupation (1798–1801), Shaykh al-'Attar taught French savants Arabic, shared information about science and literature with them, and became convinced that Egyptians must study Western scientific methods. Between 1803 and 1810 he studied geometry, medicine, anatomy, theology, and Turkish in Istanbul and Albania. He continued his studies in Syria while teaching medicine and anatomy as well as jurisprudence and hadith. When al-'Attar returned in 1813 to Egypt, his lectures on al-Baydawi's book of Qur'an interpretation were exceptionally well-attended. It was said that 'ulama elders even abandoned their own classes whenever he came to teach, so that they could attend his lessons, and two of his contemporaries testified to his intelligence and popularity.[57]

Nevertheless, Shaykh al-'Attar's writings reveal a deep rift between him and some of his colleagues, which plagued him throughout his life. After al-'Attar's experiences in Istanbul and Syria, he felt stifled at al-Azhar. Between 1828 and 1830, al-'Attar wrote a supercommentary on the *Jam' al-jawami'*, a book on the fundamentals of theology, in which he offered a critique of Azhari education. The book was reprinted several times and became a standard text at al-Azhar.[58] His complaints were simple:

> We have limited ourselves to the study of narrow, derivative books composed by recent authors, which we repeat throughout life, and we do not permit ourselves to study anything else, as if true knowledge is contained within them. When we receive a question on theology that is not found in them, we dispose of it [by saying] that it is of the philosophers' debate . . . or a literary point from among the topics that have been disproved.[59]

Al-'Attar also complained that although there were many translations of foreign books containing valuable knowledge of new inventions and developments in biology, engineering, and military arts, his colleagues did not read them.[60] This, he pointed out, had not always been the case; Azhari 'ulama had previously been curious about books that contradicted their own doctrines and had even read the Torah and other non-Muslim scriptures. He further lamented that the 'ulama of his time limited themselves to transmitting and commenting upon the works of past great scholars.[61] At the end of both passages, he wrote: "These are the sighs of an oppressed heart." By the end of the 1820s, al-'Attar was doing his most serious teaching at home, outside what he perceived as the constrained atmosphere of al-Azhar,[62] and it is apparent from his later writings that he never felt fully assimilated into Azhari society. The subjects he wanted to study had fallen under the purview of the military schools; there was limited demand for them among Azhari students. Also, al-'Attar did not seem to appreciate that the act of commentary, which provided justification for the pronunciations of the words and explored the ramifications of alternate vowelizations, was an essential part of transmission. Peter Gran has suggested that al-'Attar, in fact, subscribed to a new idea of writing.

Al-'Attar wrote a manual on insha', or composition of letters, for secretaries of the War School. Gran argues that al-'Attar gave insha' new meaning: expository writing that used expressions precisely and accurately so that the author's meaning was clear to a reader. This, he thought, would be especially useful for writers preparing materials for the military schools.[63]

Al-'Attar's examples in his *al-Insha'* were not earth-shatteringly different from what had gone before. His meaning was embedded within layers of literary allusions, rhymes, poetic patterning of morphology, and colorful praises for the recipient, and clearly echo the flowery and poetic style of past insha' masters. However, al-'Attar's letters do not subordinate meaning to form as was typical in older examples—the meaning is readily apparent to the reader.[64] This had profound implications: Al-'Attar's superlative use of this genre challenged his contemporaries to subordinate form to meaning.

Some medieval scientists and philosophers had used a highly metaphorical style to protect themselves from those who would persecute them for their unorthodox ideas and also to protect unprepared readers from accidentally acquiring arcane and possibly harmful knowledge. Books written in such a style required expert interpretation and explication, a task for which Azharis were explicitly trained. Al-'Attar thereby challenged the 'ulama's position as bulwarks between the unprepared reader and the kinds of knowledge that, if misunderstood, could lead them astray. Finally, al-'Attar's comments about "derivative" works may have insulted his contemporaries, whose commentaries were not simply discussions of grammar and morphology, but often served as vehicles (or covers) for much innovative thought. In short, al-'Attar's use of insha' constituted a potential challenge to the authority of the 'ulama.

Al-'Attar's position was even more ambiguous because of his personal association with Muhammad 'Ali. Al-'Attar had been friends with 'Abd al-Rahman Sami Pasha, personal secretary to Muhammad 'Ali's son Ibrahim, who had secured al-'Attar's introduction to Muhammad 'Ali.[65] In 1828, Muhammad 'Ali gave al-'Attar a government position as editor of *al-Waqa'i' al-Misriyya*, a newly created official government circular, which would be published in Arabic and Turkish versions and would summarize government decisions and daily news. This circular would be sent to government bureaus throughout Egypt, thereby informing officials of the achievements of the new regime as well as conditions in Egypt and the surrounding countries.[66] The appointment indicated Muhammad 'Ali's high regard for al-'Attar. Two years later, Muhammad 'Ali elevated al-'Attar to the highest position of authority at al-Azhar, that of the Shaykh al-Azhar. The Azharis' own candidate for the position was Shaykh al-Quwaysini, a blind man known for his piety, his fairness in adjudicating disputes, and his great knowledge of theology and jurisprudence.[67] However, Shaykh al-Quwaysini refused the position on account of his blindness.[68]

Shaykh al-'Attar complicated his position by refusing to adhere to accepted juridical precedents.[69] For example, he sided with Muhammad 'Ali against his colleagues on a particularly thorny issue regarding the Medical School. Muhammad 'Ali had asked the 'ulama for advice (a fatwa) as to whether dissection of human corpses should be allowed in the Medical School. They ruled that dissection was not permitted. Because a fatwa is only legal advice and is not binding on the petitioner, Muhammad 'Ali was able to ignore it and seek other 'ulama who would give him a more favorable ruling. He did so, and al-'Attar gave him a fatwa explicitly supporting the practice of dissection.[70] This was not merely a political favor, which would have been considered highly unethical: Al-'Attar's ruling was consistent with his stance on dissection generally. In 1814 Hasan al-'Attar had written a treatise describing dissection as it was then practiced in Europe and in Istanbul, in which he stated that the empirical study of anatomy was one of the sciences by which one discovered the "wonders of Creation and the masterful skill of God."[71] In 1832, Shaykh al-'Attar praised Clot Bey, the French director of the School of Medicine, whose requests to do autopsies had brought the issue of human dissection into the realm of public debate, and publicly supported the School of Medicine in an address to the graduating class.[72]

The problem with this was that for many 'ulama, adherence to juristic precedent, or taqlid, defined the boundaries of the Sunni Islamic community. By contravening precedent, al-'Attar was placing himself beyond the margins of that community. So he was an outsider, and a threat, in several potent ways. And consequently, some 'ulama refused to accept his authority as Shaykh al-Azhar.

For example, on one occasion, al-'Attar appointed a fellow Maghribi, a friend, to the office of Shaykh of the Maghribi riwaq. Al-Quwaysini, al-'Attar's rival for the office of Shaykh al-Azhar, was said to have plotted with others to exile al-'Attar's appointee to prevent him from taking office. In another incident, al-'Attar suffered a petty prank. The shaykhs had convened to discuss various matters at the Citadel. One of them stole al-'Attar's sandals. Shaykh Mustafa al-'Arusi, who would later become a Shaykh al-Azhar himself, then sent al-'Attar's servant and mule home so that al-'Attar would be forced to either walk home barefoot at night or admit his humiliation publicly by calling for a servant to retrieve his mule and fetch a new pair of shoes.[73]

These humiliations isolated al-'Attar and inspired him to write a scathing condemnation of his colleagues:

> [W]hen people die, they are followed by voracious animals and attacking monsters. If we have relations with them, they will ravish us; if we stay away from them, they slander us. So we have no safety from them. Either we are with them or not with them. I say that may that time be praised which comes to me and makes pleasant the day so that I may sit alone in my chair away from these voracious monsters, who have no humanity in them, neither for this world nor for the one to come. . . . I wish that I myself could withdraw and refuse entirely to see mankind, as if I were on top of some tall mountain. For when I became Shaykh al-Azhar, toward the end of my life, I forgot even the scholarship in which I had spent my life, until my eyes finally grew weak. I do not see anything but enemies wearing the clothes of friends. [I see] only arrogant, wily, malicious tricksters who are laying traps for me . . . and my destruction stares me in the eye. O! my God, protect me from those who want to injure me, and stand between them and me. O! my God . . . save me from their treachery. For I sense that many of those who smile at me would never hesitate if they were given the chance to drink my blood. God is my guardian, for indeed, before I entered this position, I had not known there were human beings like these. May God protect me from them.[74]

The shaykhs' apparent disrespect for al-'Attar followed him to his grave. His biographer reported that upon al-'Attar's death, Shaykh al-Quwaysini declared that his heirs had no rights to his property because his son was a minor and his wife a slave, who had no rights even to the disposition of her own body. There followed repeated incidents in which al-'Attar's books were removed from the house and put into the Maghribi riwaq library and other personal libraries, until Muhammad 'Ali decreed that 'ulama were no longer allowed to enter al-'Attar's house.[75]

Al-'Attar's situation as Shaykh al-Azhar was impossible. From his opponents' point of view, he was an illegally appointed, unqualified Shaykh representing the interests of a governor who was blamed for financially decimating religious institutions and for advocating methods of writing and pedagogy that would destroy the authority of the 'ulama and sever their chains of knowledge transmission. It is no wonder that al-'Attar did not try to push reforms at al-Azhar.

Because of the fragmentary nature of Shaykh Hasan al-'Attar's biography, it is difficult to determine with any certainty where he absorbed the Utilitarian ideal of writing as communication, of exposure of authorial intent. Yet it is his belief in this ideal and his desire to re-expand the readings offered at al-Azhar that led historians to label him the first Azhar reformer or first Islamic modernist.[76]

Al-'Attar's Protégé: Shaykh Rifa'a al-Tahtawi

Shaykh al-'Attar died in office in late 1834 and was succeeded by al-Quwaysini. In subsequent decades, al-'Attar's students and other like-minded government bureaucrats would develop the critique of religious education in a political setting more favorable to reform. Al-'Attar's relative success as a mentor occasioned the rise of a second generation of reformers, many of whom became prominent in government-sponsored translation bureaus and as journalists. The most famous of these was Shaykh Rifa'a al-Tahtawi.[77] Al-Tahtawi's first sustained critique of al-Azhar education followed themes that al-'Attar had outlined: a revival of the Islamic tradition of scientific endeavor, re-expansion of al-Azhar's curriculum, and creation of a clear Arabic writing style suitable for transmission of technical subject matter to a literate lay public.

While Shaykh al-'Attar was serving as the editor of *al-Waqa'i' al-Misriyya* and teaching at al-Azhar, Muhammad 'Ali had asked him to recommend from among the Azhari 'ulama an imam for one of the student missions. Al-'Attar chose Rifa'a al-Tahtawi. At age twenty-five, al-Tahtawi had already been at al-Azhar for eight years, studying history, literature, geography, and astronomy with Shaykh al-'Attar.[78] He was very poor, because his family had been hard hit by Muhammad 'Ali's confiscation of their tax farms, and so he was forced to seek employment.[79] After six years of study, in 1824, he had begun teaching books in hadith, logic, rhetoric, and prosody, and had been appointed as an imam in Muhammad 'Ali's army.[80] In 1826, Shaykh al-Tahtawi went to Paris as imam to the military student mission, where he spent five years studying physics, geometry, mathematics, astronomy, geography, European history, and political philosophy. He had an affinity for the French language, and his French instructor suggested that he do translations, the manuscripts of which he took back with him to Egypt. Among the works he translated was the "ethnography" of Georg Bernhard Depping, which taught that undeveloped or uncivilized peoples were such largely because of "indolence." Depping's ideas were to influence al-Tahtawi profoundly. Al-Tahtawi also developed a special interest in the works of the philosophes, particularly Jean-Jacques Rousseau's *Social Contract*.[81] He returned to Egypt in 1831 and published his most famous book, *Takhlis al-ibriz fi talkhis Bariz* [A golden nugget on the essence of Paris], in 1834.

The *Takhlis* was essentially a description of al-Tahtawi's experience of Paris. It was also al-Tahtawi's first work of educational criticism. In several instances al-Tahtawi praised the French educational system, implicitly comparing it with the Egyptian madaris. For example, al-Tahtawi's description of the French system of elementary instruction in reading explained that French children began to read by first learning words for things that children knew through their everyday experience, such as cat and canary. Then they learned to read basic adages and instructions for good behavior such as "Obey thy mother and father," and eventually they progressed to more "important" books.[82]

In order to understand how this passage would be interpreted by Azhari readers, this description must be viewed against the backdrop of Azhari instruction in reading. At al-Azhar, as well as in the katatib that were the mainstay of Egyptian primary education, a young student's first textbook was the Qur'an. The student's first experience in reading Arabic, therefore, was not linked to his childhood experience, but rather to a complex religious scripture the language of which was, while beautifully poetic and grammatically instructive, also archaic and grammatically unfamiliar. Consistent with the Arabic relationship between words and meanings, Qur'an teachers laid heavy emphasis upon memorization of the text, because memorization could aid the student in relating letters to sounds in lieu of comprehension.[83] Learning the appropriate vowelizations for a word was more important at this stage than learning the word's meaning.

Most children never went beyond this phase in their education. Those who did, including most native Egyptians at al-Azhar, would progress to a class on grammar. They would not learn to employ grammatical codes as French children did; rather, they learned to vowelize consonants and endow them with meaning. Grammar was taught as nahw and sarf. Nahw connotes "modes of sameness" and is usually translated as "syntax." Sarf refers to the different arrangements of vowels, or movements, around root consonants. It connotes "modes of difference," and is usually translated as "morphology."[84] However, the texts read with the students were often complex medieval treatises definitely not geared to children's capabilities. For example, al-Azhar elementary grammar courses used Ibn Ajrum's *Kitab al-Ajrumiyya* until the twentieth century. It stated "Speech is a composite utterance conveying by convention a meaning; its parts are three: noun, verb, and particle. . . . As for the noun, it is known by genitive case, nunation, a preceding alif and lam [the definite article]. . . ."[85] The use of this work was so widespread that the word for grammar in Egyptian colloquial Arabic is agrumiyya. We can imagine the bewilderment of the beginner upon being presented with such a text. One student reported:

> I began by reading the commentary of al-Kafrawi on the [*Kitab al-*]*Ajrumiyya* in the Ahmadi Mosque in Tanta and I spent a year and a half without understanding a thing because of the dreadfulness of the method of instruction. The teachers would assail us with grammatical and jurisprudential terminology that we did not understand, and they did not take care to explain their meanings to those who did not know them. And so I began to despair of success and fled.[86]

Classes were not categorized by difficulty, and shaykhs apparently paid little attention to the fact that their students included youngsters and casual listeners as well as near-adepts,[87] addressing themselves to their primary coteries of advanced students. Some students reported that no one learned anything in their first year. Another student remarked that learning Arabic was like learning a foreign language, which, since Egypt's colloquial dialect was substantially different, it was.[88] Seen against the context of Egyptian pedagogical practice, al-Tahtawi's description of French reading instruction constituted an implicit critique of the halqa system and a challenge to 'ulama authority.

Al-Tahtawi also developed al-'Attar's critique of the scholarly Arabic writing style. For example, in a description of the French writing style, he said:

[W]hat has allowed the French to progress in the sciences and arts is the easiness of their language . . . for their language does not require much cultivation in order to learn it. Any person who has the disposition and good aptitude can, after learning it, read any book. . . . And if the instructor wants to teach a book he never has to decipher any of its expressions, because the expressions are clear in and of themselves. . . . The person reading one of [the Arabic] books in one of the sciences must apply to it all the tools of the language and scrutinize its expressions as well as he can. And he will come away with an interpretation very far in meaning from its literal appearance. . . . [T]he books of the French . . . do not require commentaries or glosses except rarely . . . as the text itself is sufficient for one to understand its meaning at first glance.[89]

Al-Tahtawi contended that the Arabic writing style of his time was highly alliterative, reverberating with like-sounding words and use of adjacent roots of similar connotation, and highly metaphorical, and that therefore it was best suited to poetry, literature, and the explication of revelation and miracles. As an example, al-Tahtawi pointed out that many Arabic books on science were written in verse, in which more attention was paid to the way the words sounded than the information that they conveyed. This had the effect of limiting acquisition of knowledge to those who could interpret the texts and their audiences. It prevented wider dissemination and retarded social advancement. Without clear, communicative writing, sciences in particular could not be explained to the public, and therefore, the public could not benefit from them. The directness of French writing and the efficiency of the French educational system allowed for a greater literacy on the part of the French people, even their children, boys and girls, which in turn allowed them to read and respond to reports of events and discoveries that could improve their lives or otherwise affect them beneficially. Literacy and increased access to scientific ideas through clear writing, therefore, would produce social progress.

Here lay a key point, for al-Tahtawi implied that versification of texts resulted from the nature of the language itself.[90] There is an element of misdirection here, such that readers unfamiliar with the context of the halqa system received from his account an image of a stagnating literary tradition, in which writing was intentionally and unjustifiably obtuse. The charge of intentionality was deserved in cases where writers employed metaphor to protect themselves and to protect their readers from acquiring dangerous knowledge. However, despite the importance of oral mediation of words in some Arabic textual traditions, much contemporary Arabic writing was intended to communicate meaning clearly upon a cursory reading (al-Jabarti's history is a case in point), and the versification and alliteration that al-Tahtawi found so contrary to European written style often functioned as mnemonic aids for readers. Thus the subtext to al-Tahtawi's statements was misleading. Al-Tahtawi had made the first steps toward fabricating the past and creating an image of historical stagnation—here, centered around the inefficiencies of Arabic writing that prevented progress.[91]

Al-Tahtawi also took up al-'Attar's call for the diversification of Egyptian education. In his description of the French libraries, museums, observatories, and scholarly associations, he advocated government sponsorship of scientific institutions, which suggests that he supported Muhammad 'Ali's activities in promoting scientific instruction.[92] Elsewhere his support was more explicitly stated: "As Egypt has now adopted the bases of civilization [tamaddun] and education according to the fashion of European countries, she has precedence over and is more entitled to the varieties of ornament and industry her ancestors left her [i.e., Egypt's heritage of past scientific achievement]."

Al-Tahtawi went on to imply that it was this scientific tradition, inherited from Egypt, that Napoleon used to achieve his victories. However, he said, science had declined in the very land of its birth. By repossessing her scientific heritage, Egypt could once again achieve strength and prominence. To al-Tahtawi, his task, and that of all the mission students, was to acquire French learning and propagate it within the realm of Islam.[93] He quoted at length and in apparent approval the recommendations for the promotion of Egypt's development suggested by Edmé-François Jomard, supervisor of Muhammad 'Ali's missions to France. These recommendations included cultivation of the natural sciences, mathematics, medicine, and the uses of electricity.[94]

Al-Tahtawi's earliest educational critique can therefore be seen as a development of a number of Hasan al-'Attar's positions. These include the simplification of Arabic style (both to improve elementary education and to promote new, foreign, or scientific ideas), the adaptation of the curriculum to emphasize more sciences, and a general revival of the Islamic tradition of scientific endeavor. Both his and his mentor's reformism can be tied to the educational reforms of Muhammad 'Ali as well as to educational trends outside Egypt. Al-Tahtawi probably did not intend overt polemics. His time in France coincided with fervor over educational reform that would culminate in the universalization of free, secular primary education. He was passing on to literate Egyptians what he perceived as the most advanced ideas in education.[95] Nevertheless, al-Tahtawi had begun the process of inventing a history of decline, which he would refine and develop over the years.

This earliest of his critiques was contemporary with the end of Hasan al-'Attar's term of office as Shaykh al-Azhar and the events that followed his death. Shaykh al-'Attar, still alive at the time the *Takhlis* was published, had written a short introduction praising it.[96] The public's reception, however, is harder to piece together.

Like his troubled mentor's term as Shaykh al-Azhar, Shaykh al-Tahtawi's activities were unfavorably marked by his association with the government.[97] He was both a product of Muhammad 'Ali's student missions and a government employee. Many mission students absorbed European attitudes and adopted their dress, such that upon their return they no longer felt comfortable in traditional Egyptian society. Sometimes not even Muhammad 'Ali appreciated the subjects they had spent so long acquiring; one student of civil administration, on being questioned by Muhammad 'Ali after his return, told him he had studied "government affairs." Muhammad 'Ali exclaimed, "What! You are not going to get mixed up in the administration! What a waste of time! It is I who govern. Go to Cairo and translate military works."[98] Many mission students found themselves employed in areas in which they had no training. Mission students assigned to government positions were resented as usurpers by others who laid claim to that privilege: Ottoman administrators, European advisors, and the 'ulama.[99]

Although Shaykh al-Tahtawi had apparently not suffered the same degree of cultural dislocation as some of the mission students did, he was nevertheless associated with them.[100] Furthermore, immediately upon his return to Egypt in 1831, he was appointed chief translator for the School of Medicine, beginning a long career in government service. The first work he published, tellingly, was Depping's *Aperçu historique sur les moeurs et coutumes des nations*—suggesting to his contemporaries that their inferiority to the French was due to their nonindustrious natures.[101] For his translation of Conrad Malte-Brun's eight-volume *Précis de la géographie universelle,* Muhammad 'Ali promoted him to the rank of commander.[102] In 1833 he transferred to the Artillery School, where he translated several works on military science and engineering. Thus despite his Azhari training, al-Tahtawi was thoroughly associated with Muhammad 'Ali and his military projects. His position was more tenable than al-'Attar's because he was never appointed to a position of direct authority over al-Azhar. In fact, there is very little evidence that al-Tahtawi experienced opposition because of his critical attitude toward madrasa pedagogy until after 1837, when his assignments began to directly threaten the interests of the 'ulama.

The source most often quoted in describing 'ulama reception of the *Takhlis* is from a single incident Edward Lane reported in a footnote to his translation of the *One Thousand and One Nights*. On 27 October 1834, Lane was sitting in the shop in the Khan al-Khalili that sold books printed at the government press. It was his custom to visit the shop during the biweekly auctions, so as to observe the "amusing scene." On this day, he met

> a man of a very respectable and intelligent appearance, applying for a copy of the sheykh Rifa'ah's account of his visit to France, lately print-ed at Boolak. Asking what were the general contents of this book, a person present answered him, that the author relates his voyage from Alexandria to Marseilles; how he got drunk on board the ship, and was tied to the mast and flogged; that he ate pork in the land of infi-delity and obstinacy, and that it is most excellent meat; how he was delighted with the French girls, and how superior they are in charms to the women of Egypt; and, having qualified himself, by every accomplishment, for an eminent place in Hell, returned to his native country. This was an ironical quizz on the sheykh Rifa'ah, for his strict, conscientious adherence to the precepts of El-Islam during his voyage, and his residence in France.[103]

This quotation is frequently and erroneously cited in support of the claim that the 'ulama disliked either al-Tahtawi or his book. First, it is unclear from the passage whether any of the persons involved in this dialogue are shaykhs, so we cannot assume that they reflect Azhari opinion of Rifa'a al-Tahtawi. Second, Lane says this comment was "an ironical quizz"—a joke. The joker was playing on al-Tahtawi's reputation for piety. The passage is therefore evidence against its usual interpretation, namely, that the shaykhs were jealous of al-Tahtawi's relatively high favor with Muhammad 'Ali, and that his *Takhlis* was "poorly received among conservatives at al-Azhar and elsewhere."[104]

To the contrary, the presence of an applicant for al-Tahtawi's book indi-cates that at least some people were buying it. Furthermore, Lane went on to say that the applicant for the book had cataracts, and Lane suggested that he go to Clot Bey, the French director of Muhammad 'Ali's School of Med-icine, for treatment. The applicant demurred and "said that he was afraid to go to the hospital; for he had heard that many patients there were killed and boiled, to make skeletons: he afterwards, however, on my assuring him that his fears were groundless, promised to go."[105] The applicant's fears of the French-run hospital reveal that the market for the book did not consist solely of those who already supported European science and Muhammad 'Ali's schools. Furthermore, the *Takhlis* sold so well that it was reprinted three more times in the nineteenth century in Egypt alone,[106] and in 1840 Bulaq Press published an even more popular Turkish edition, which Muhammad 'Ali had distributed to all his officials and sent to Istanbul.[107]

Conclusion

The effects of the eighteenth-century predations and Muhammad 'Ali's centralization process on the religious educational systems of Egypt were complex. One effect was a gradual process of financial deprivation and physical neglect, not wholly due to Muhammad 'Ali's reorganization of land-tenure arrangements, which ruined small institutions and concentrated the populations of waqf-dependent 'ulama and students at larger ones. This concentration strained the already stretched resources of these larger mosques and madaris, and contributed to 'ulama perceptions of relative impoverishment. Another effect was a reification of existing divisions between 'ulama elders who were willing to serve government interests and those who insisted that the ethics of religious scholarship mandated that the state have no administrative power over religious institutions.[108] The creation of a military school system that offered scientific subjects and administrative training resulted in the narrowing of al-Azhar's offerings to religious, legal, and ancillary subjects, created a class of technocrats who began to displace madrasa-trained employees from civil service positions, and challenged the pedagogical foundations of 'ulama authority. 'Ulama who had absorbed the Utilitarian ideals of efficient communication and education laid the blame for Egypt's failure to match European progress (as they saw it) at the door of the other 'ulama.

The whole subsequent debate over reform of al-Azhar is inscribed by negotiations of power: the resistance posed by defenders of the contractual space enclosed by the halqa circle against the spread of noncontractual efficiency-driven pedagogies. The 'ulama made use of their own networks of authority to maintain that space: For example, some, the historian al-Jabarti among them, propagated the image of Muhammad 'Ali preying upon the religious institutions. Some offered explanations to foreign travelers, whose reports of course corroborated 'ulama claims that Muhammad

'Ali was systematically ruining religious institutions and undermining the authority of the 'ulama. Some harassed 'ulama who overtly allied themselves with Muhammad 'Ali.

The military-school 'ulama found themselves mired in paradox. Al-'Attar's stated desire was to expand Azharis' interests, but it was his patron's creation of a military school system that had contracted al-Azhar's offerings. Also, al-'Attar's acquiescence to Muhammad 'Ali's authority also circumscribed his power to act, and the expansion of that authority was a proximate cause of the problem he wished to remedy. Those who would have reformed al-Azhar had enmeshed themselves in a political paradox: Their affiliations simultaneously created an object of action (reform of religious education) and excluded them from acting upon it. Thus their challenges could be met without resorting to an ideological defense.[109]

3

ORDER AND DISORDER: THE EVOLVING CRITIQUE OF MADRASA EDUCATION (1834–1870)

In the mid-nineteenth century, the population of madrasa residents doubled. Under this pressure, the reserve and quietude of the madrasa noted by Florence Nightingale disintegrated. Al-Azhar already had problems with crime and public image. In the late 1790s, an Azhari shaykh ran an extortion ring out of the Sa'idi riwaq, the living quarters for students from southern Egypt. Students apparently assisted him. In January of 1810, students were implicated in counterfeiting of piaster coins, which then became known as "Azhari money." In January of 1812, sons of influential Azhari shaykhs hid in the courtyard and mugged passersby, and several prostitutes were expelled from the Azhar Quarter. This "gave rise to much gossip about the people of al-Azhar and its environs." According to al-Jabarti, even the lowest classes attributed to al-Azhar "every vice and evil" and accused its people of spreading sin.[1] There were two al-Azhars in the public mind: one of the 'ulama elders and teaching shaykhs to whom people appealed for help and came for authoritative readings of texts, and one of impoverished scholars and students and an occasional charlatan, who depended on charity for subsistence. As one of the few remaining large schools that still received waqf revenues and government subsidies, al-Azhar had become a magnet for the impoverished. The madaris had always been refuges for the poor because of the services they offered, and religious schooling was the best opportunity for a poor son of peasants to achieve upward social mobility.[2] But the disturbances and violence of the mid-nineteenth century were of a different order, and added to public perceptions that the noble Azhar hid a dark poverty-stricken underbelly. The indigent population of al-Azhar continued to rise, leading to several incidents that created a climate of doubt about the ability of existing administrative and pedagogical methods to deal with the new problems, and a concomitant willingness to accept centralized control by a Shaykh al-Azhar who himself was increasingly linked to the authority of the state. Some historians consider this a period of 'ulama re-entrenchment after the assaults of Muhammad 'Ali.[3] On the contrary, this period continued state school encroachment on al-Azhar's territory and state attempts to engineer control of the institution by the Ottoman legal rite. State intervention prepared the ground for modernist reformers' attempts to impose European models of reform, which overcrowding and disorder made the 'ulama willing to accept.

The critiques of religious education referred to in chapter 2 were written in the heyday of Muhammad 'Ali's power, when the military schools were growing. After 1840, however, Muhammad 'Ali's power was deteriorating, and his schools, too, began to suffer from lack of financial support. Muhammad 'Ali's seizure of Syria in 1831 earned him the ire of the Ottoman sultan, whose British-Ottoman coalition defeated Muhammad 'Ali in 1840. The subsequent Treaty of London required him to reduce the size of his army from its maximum of 400,000 to 18,000 troops, while offering in conciliation the assurance that Muhammad 'Ali's progeny would serve as hereditary viceroys of Egypt.[4] Although the actual reduction was far less drastic, it still resulted in abandonment of much of Muhammad 'Ali's economic program, which had been directed toward military development.[5]

Because Muhammad 'Ali's military schools had existed to train officers and administrative personnel for the armies and related manufactories, the downsizing of the military and factory system ended the military schools' raison d'être.[6] As the 1840s wore on, Muhammad 'Ali closed most of the military schools and reorganized the remaining schools under a civilian Department of Schools with a much tighter budget. According to Heyworth-Dunne, the budget cuts undermined the administrative structure of the schools. School administrators became lax, and accountants' positions were auctioned off to the highest bidders. Although some schools, such as al-Tahtawi's School of Languages, survived after 1840, most were closed by 1849.[7]

The Interest of the State

The liquidation of most military schools redirected government attention toward the madaris. Since the few remaining military schools could afford to support few students, it became apparent that the madaris would produce the majority of Egypt's clerks, legal personnel, and teachers for some time to come. Because the religious schools were independently administered, they were simply given more money, in hopes that their administrators could then afford to make improvements. Meanwhile, the remaining military schools were reorganized. Graduates of Muhammad 'Ali's student missions and military schools oversaw this reorganization. This fact had a crucial impact on the path that the debate over madrasa reform would later take, as it allowed Muhammad 'Ali's groomed reformers unprecedented access to positions of determinative authority over the entire Egyptian educational system. These reformers began a campaign against the halqa system.

One of those trusted with reorganizing the military schools was Shaykh Rifa'a al-Tahtawi, who was continuing his efforts to disseminate scientific ideas by publishing books on various subjects not taught at al-Azhar, such as world geography, Newtonian physics, and astronomy.[8] Al-Tahtawi was given the opportunity to present his views to a much wider audience when he became general editor of *al-Waqa'i' al-Misriyya,* Muhammad 'Ali's news circular, a model for later newspapers.[9] Al-Tahtawi's literary endeavors also included the translation of European works. As director of Muhammad 'Ali's School of Languages and Accountancy after 1837, al-Tahtawi published some twenty translations on various subjects, including geography, history, and military science. Moreover, he directed or supervised approximately 2,000 student translations: histories of the ancient and medieval world, histories of European kings, and Charles-Louis de Secondat, Baron de Montesquieu's *Considérations sur les causes de la grandeur des romains et de leur décadence.*[10]

Al-Tahtawi's activities were at first only supplementary to the madrasa system, much as the early military schools had been. But in 1837, he established a government School of Islamic Law and Jurisprudence, in violation of the madaris' tacit monopoly on the training of legal personnel. This school was attached to the School of Languages and Accounting, over which al-Tahtawi had assumed control earlier that year. The School of Islamic Law and Jurisprudence trained jurists of the Hanafi madhhab, the official legal school of the Ottoman government. Madhabib are the legal schools within Islam. There are four Sunni madhabib: Hanafi, Hanbali, Maliki, and Shafi'i. Al-Azhar offered specialization in all four major Sunni legal schools. The new school's faculty was composed of al-Azhar shaykhs, but the students, unlike their counterparts at al-Azhar, studied as a main part of their curriculum foreign languages, history, geography, mathematics, and French law. Whereas previous military schools had taught only medicine, technology, foreign languages, and administration, subjects considered secondary at al-Azhar, this school represented a frontal attack on the Azhari sphere of knowledge. If the military school students needed expertise in fiqh (jurisprudence), ordinarily they would have also studied at al-Azhar; this school suggested that al-Azhar could not provide the needed expertise in an efficient time frame, and also that Hanafi legal experts might need a broader perspective than they could get at al-Azhar. Furthermore, the fact that the state sponsored this school suggests a desire to control the transfer of knowledge, to channel the students into useful fields. The lengthy Socratic repartee of the halqa was not really relevant to the needs of the state. Also, the names and subsequent careers of the teachers suggest that they, like al-Tahtawi, straddled the uncomfortable fence between government and religious employment. Some of the 'ulama who taught there became estranged from al-Azhar.[11]

In part, this new effort to extend the influence of the state grew out of the agendas of Muhammad 'Ali's successors. However, because the 1840 Treaty of London had given Muhammad 'Ali's family nearly independent powers in Egypt, each successive khedive, or "lord" of Egypt, was free to pursue his own concerns. Ibrahim (r. 1848) closed most military schools, due to the decreasing needs of the downsized armies.[12] Khedives 'Abbas Hilmi I (r. 1848–1854) and Sa'id (r. 1854–1863) favored leaving education to the 'ulama. Khedive Isma'il (r. 1863–1879) supported the construction of a new civil school system. The fortunes of the state-sponsored 'ulama rose and fell with the succession of khedives.

Khedive 'Abbas, a pious Ottoman ruler who disapproved of his predecessors' fast-paced European-model reform, lavished his attention on the religious institutions. In August 1849, 'Abbas reversed Muhammad 'Ali's 1846 prohibition against endowing certain types of land as awqaf. This returned to the 'ulama their chief means of protecting their agricultural lands from the state. In 1851, 'Abbas reopened Muhammad 'Ali's defunct waqf administration (closed in 1838) to supervise private endowments, many of which benefited religious institutions. In 1852, 'Abbas himself endowed awqaf to support the new Citadel mosque. Hence there began between 1850 and 1860 a financial revival of the religious institutions.[13]

'Abbas also paid attention to the concerns of the 'ulama. In 1850 he demoted al-Tahtawi, who had developed a reputation as a critic of Azhari legal education, and sent him to the Sudan to head a primary school.[14]

'Abbas then, in 1851, closed al-Tahtawi's School of Islamic Law and Jurisprudence, along with the attached School of Languages and Accountancy. 'Abbas also had a poor opinion of *al-Waqa'i' al-Misriyya;* he cared little
for the translation of European texts, so al-Tahtawi remained persona non
grata until after 'Abbas's death in 1854. In 1855, 'Abbas's successor, Sa'id,
recalled al-Tahtawi from the Sudan and appointed him supervisor of the
War School, the translation bureau, the school of accountancy, the school
of civil engineering and the inspectorate of the building department.[15]

Conscription and Sanctuary

Madaris often served as sanctuaries for those who sought to escape conscription. In 1854, Sa'id involved Egypt in the Crimean War. Changes to
state conscription policy had grave consequences for al-Azhar, which was
otherwise left to its own devices. Muhammad 'Ali and his successors
Ibrahim and 'Abbas had continued to draft peasants into the military after
it was downsized. Although conscription was lighter under 'Abbas's rule
than under Muhammad 'Ali's, 'Abbas still maintained a force of approximately 100,000 troops who usually served in public works projects or in the
Sudan. Sa'id had reformed the state conscription policy to lighten the burden on peasants, making the draft an annual drive and extending it to
include non-Muslims and sons of village headmen. But in 1853, just before
the Crimean War, Sa'id prepared to send some 20,000 troops to aid the sultan in his battle against the Russians, and the numbers drafted into the military sharply increased.[16] So did the numbers of men seeking to escape conscription. Numerous accounts of draft dodging can be found in European
travel narratives from this period. This affected al-Azhar because madrasa
students were exempt from conscription, and so men seeking to escape military service flocked to the religious schools, especially schools whose
finances had weathered the depredations of the Mamluks and Muhammad
'Ali's centralization.[17]

During this time, al-Azhar's student population increased dramatical-
ly, overwhelming the mosque's administrative system. At the turn of the
century there had been forty to sixty teachers at al-Azhar and between
1,500 and 3,000 students. By 1846, there were 7,403 students. After
Egypt's Crimean War conscription efforts ended in 1855, numbers
declined again, to 5,940. By 1865, enrollment had further decreased to
2,817. In 1867, there were 221 teachers and 4,712 students. By 1873,
only six years later, there were 314 teachers and 9,441 students. In 1876,
there were 325 teachers and 10,780 students.[18] It was this flood of

students that began to undermine al-Azhar's own pedagogical techniques of order and authority and made French techniques so appealing to the reformers.[19]

The population of Cairo was also increasing rapidly during this time, due in part to the training of draftees and to extensive public works projects. Most rural migrants to the city found lodgings with relatives or in cheap inns, but those who did not were taken in by local mosques. Most of these latter sheltered at al-Azhar, where they could sleep in relative safety in its open courts and porticos.[20] The erosion of al-Azhar's order became apparent as the inundation of the mosque led to disturbances. In 1847, Shaykh Ibrahim al-Bajuri had been appointed Shaykh al-Azhar at the age of sixty-four. He was so popular that even Khedive 'Abbas had attended his readings. Nonetheless, by Sa'id's time, the aging shaykh was unable to cope with the increasingly large and fractious student body. So many villagers were fleeing to al-Azhar to avoid conscription that two village headmen came to al-Azhar to seek villagers posing as students. Under the hierarchical administrative system that Muhammad 'Ali had set up, village headmen were held responsible for local administrative tasks such as collecting taxes, policing the village environs, and filling quotas for corvée labor and military service. If they failed at these tasks, they could be subjected to as many as 300 lashes or lengthy imprisonment—and if their district supervisors failed to enforce the quotas, they could be caned. Thus these men may have been quite insistent that the errant "students" return with them. Upon hearing their demands, Shaykh al-Bajuri berated the headmen and ordered that they be beaten. The students pounced upon the men with "sandals, fists, and canes," killing one of them.[21]

In another incident in 1853, students from the Maghribi riwaq claimed that Shaykh al-Bajuri had withheld their bread rations, and they physically assaulted him. The shaykh tried to have the students seized, but they ganged up on him. To quell the uprising, Shaykh al-Bajuri was forced to call upon government forces, resulting in the closure of the Maghribi riwaq and the exile of four students.[22] 'Ulama blamed the newcomers from rural areas, who were not accustomed to the social norms of the madrasa. However, if students such as the Maghribis whose daily bread rations were provided via waqf funds did not receive these because of revenue or grain shortages, hunger and fear may also have contributed. It thus appears that, despite financial gains, al-Azhar's increasing student population stretched its resources and undermined the ability of prevailing social norms to influence student behavior.

Sa'id, who was not inclined toward unrequested intervention in Azhari affairs, did not pressure the madrasa for reform. Instead, he addressed madrasa financial conditions. In 1858, Sa'id's Land Law ended state agricultural monopolies and allowed the religious institutions to resume receiving revenues from their old public awqaf.[23] Salim Pasha and Princess Zaynab, a daughter of Muhammad 'Ali, both established awqaf that eventually yielded 7,000 Egyptian pounds (£E) a year for al-Azhar. It was nevertheless not enough to address the increasing financial pressures on al-Azhar. In fact, the reality of al-Azhar's overburdened finances and administrative infrastructure clashed with Azharis' expectations that conditions at the madrasa would now improve, creating an explosive situation.

Matters came to a head in 1858,[24] when students from the Sa'id (southern Egypt), then one of the poorest regions, fought with Syrians over sitting spaces in their classes. The Syrians wielded canes and clubs against their attackers, and the Sa'idis responded, resulting in a fierce fight. The Sa'idis drove the Syrians into their riwaq and held them captive there. An Azhari shaykh sought the help of influential Syrian merchants, who called in the prefect of Cairo and an Albanian army unit to quell the riot. The Sa'idis defeated the Albanians, and more soldiers had to be called in. The soldiers entered al-Azhar's courtyard armed and booted, violating the sanctity of the mosque and causing a general uproar. As a result of this conflict, some thirty students were arrested and imprisoned for twenty days, and three of their shaykhs were also detained.[25]

At the time of the crisis, Khedive Sa'id was in the Hijaz. In his absence, a regency council of four ministers governed the country. This included Sa'id's successor, Isma'il. The regency council intervened by removing Shaykh al-Bajuri from de facto leadership: The council ordered Shaykh Mustafa al-'Arusi (who had in his younger days persecuted Shaykh Hasan al-'Attar) to have al-Azhar 'ulama elect four deputies to administer al-Azhar in al-Bajuri's place. Shaykh Mustafa al-'Arusi was to head the deputies' council. Mustafa al-'Arusi was not elected but was rather a government appointee. This suggests someone on the regency council was already trying to maneuver a candidate into position to assume the office of Shaykh al-Azhar upon al-Bajuri's death.[26]

'Ali Pasha Mubarak (1824–1893)

Al-Bajuri died in 1861, but the deputies' council continued to administer al-Azhar until 1864–1865, after Isma'il came to the throne. This provided

a point of entry for extension of state authority. Fervor for change and efficiency permeated the political ethos of the 1860s, and, as in earlier decades,
literate sentiment throughout the Ottoman Empire favored European models of reform.[27]

An observer remarked that in Egypt itself, "the whole nation was occupied with [reforming education]."[28] The new governor Isma'il (who had
bribed the Ottoman sultan to recognize his title of khedive, or "lord") also
embraced this ethos. He was enamored of both French and Ottoman
models of reform, and was said to have proclaimed that Egypt "is no longer
in Africa; it is now in Europe."[29] He imparted to Egypt's cities a superficially European appearance: demolishing houses to permit the construction of
straight boulevards lined with majestic Parisian-style apartments and store-
fronts, locating government offices and schools according to a European
urban logic at the center of the network of outwardly radiating streets, and
encouraging wealthy notables to construct homes in the European style.
Egypt was to be physically remade, enframed, to reflect an assumed pre-
existent concept of order, an order that was more easily inspectable, mar-
ketable, controllable.[30]

Khedive Isma'il also developed a new school system, based on the framework provided by Muhammad 'Ali's military schools but with a new purpose. These were more intentionally civil schools, designed to serve the larger interests of the state and its people. Rather than simply training military
and administrative personnel, these schools produced industrious citizens.
To supervise his civil schools, Isma'il chose veteran bureaucrat Shaykh
Rifa'a al-Tahtawi and 'Ali Mubarak, a bureaucrat whom Khedive 'Abbas had
favored.[31]

'Ali Mubarak had attended a military primary school and then the
School of Engineering. In 1844–1849 he was sent to the Egyptian School
in Paris, where he studied military engineering. This school was organized
on the model of military discipline: The day was compartmentalized into
discrete units, each reserved for a particular activity—5:15 A.M. reveille and
inspection, 5:15–6:45 study, 6:45–7:45 breakfast, and so on. Likewise, the
school assigned individuals to classrooms, seats, and ranks, and defined correct behavior, infractions, and punishments. Supervision was constant.[32] In
Egypt from 1849 to 1855, Mubarak taught at the School of Artillery,
directed the Egyptian Polytechnic, supervised the School of Engineering,
and helped with the creation of a centralized school for the best students
(1,696 in all) of the old military system, for which he chose students, teachers, and books.[33]

Upon Khedive 'Abbas's death, 'Ali Mubarak abruptly lost favor. In 1855, Khedive Sa'id expelled him from government service and inducted him into an army unit serving in the Crimea, while al-Tahtawi was recalled from the Sudan.[34]

Khedive Isma'il retrieved 'Ali Mubarak in 1863 and immediately appointed him supervisor of the Delta Barrage. In 1867, Mubarak once again found himself in Paris, where he toured Paris school buildings; examined the schools' curricula, pedagogy, and textbooks; and admired the order, industry, and earnestness of the French—so different, he later wrote, from the shouting, fractious Egyptians. The difference, he concluded, was the result of the orderly system of French education, which imparted to the children "elementary rules of discipline." When he returned a few weeks later, Isma'il made Mubarak the deputy minister of education, as well as supervisor of railways, education, and public works. In 1869, Isma'il gave him control of the waqf ministry, through which many schools and public works were funded; in 1871 he named Mubarak supervisor of the Department of Education.[35]

'Ali Mubarak's philosophy of education was distinctly different from that of the madrasa. According to Mubarak, the shaykhs organized their courses around explication of a single book which students memorized, paying more attention to "understanding expressions and deciphering grammatical constructions" than to understanding and application. He quoted a saying that expressed Azhari attitudes toward acquisition of knowledge: "Man hafaza al-mutun haza al-funun" (One who memorizes the texts possesses the arts). Mubarak also asserted that the Azhari 'ulama taught no history, geography, or philosophy, which they viewed as a waste of time, and only a little mathematics, and they labeled those who valued such subjects unbelievers.[36] Mubarak thus viewed the training offered at al-Azhar with a jaundiced eye, declaring: "They teach books there, not knowledge."[37] Indeed, Azharis were taught to replicate and explicate books whose authority was dependent upon reproduction of the original meanings, just as with Qur'anic verses and hadith. Mubarak's knowledge was not dependent upon the author's reading: Mathematical equations could be reproduced without an author's, or teacher's, presence with exactly the same results. Books were not the same as the abstract knowledge which a reader was supposed to be able to extract from them, and not having had a madrasa education himself, he did not perceive the necessity for religious knowledge to be linked via a continuous chain of readers to its originators.

Likewise, Mubarak, having accepted the rigid French structures of class-room discipline as constituting order, and assuming that such order was necessary for the imparting of knowledge, noted the structural disorder of al-Azhar. In Paris, Mubarak had admired the efficiency of locating all administration in a single place, so in Cairo he centralized his various offices in one palace, where he could also make daily inspections of schools nearby. In contrast, al-Azhar had no such centralized administration. According to Mubarak, al-Azhar was only theoretically controlled by its Shaykh al-Azhar; in reality, dozens of shaykhs of individual riwaqs and legal schools administered it with no formal system of student registration or formal schedule of supervision. Shaykhs were not responsible for knowing whether their students were present or absent, lazy or diligent, and there were no formal examinations.[38] There were constant conflicts between students of different regions and legal schools.[39] Although Mubarak's criticism was delivered in a descriptive rather than polemic tone, it nonetheless stood in vivid contrast to the rigorous order and streamlined efficiency of the French schools.

The disorder of al-Azhar was not solely due to the apparent absence of organization. Even accounting for exaggeration, it is clear that al-Azhar was overcrowded with students. Mubarak claimed that the poorer students, mostly native Egyptians, lived in squalor (they were the largest ethnic group; the awqaf established for them therefore had to be spread the fur-thest). The Sa'idis' goats slept with them and accompanied them to class, and students suffered from lice and scabies. Furthermore, he stated, the area in which classes were held was so packed that it was impossible to walk through it. Students shoved and pushed one another in competition for seats and made an incredible din, and the smell of their bodies in the sum-mer was unbearable. According to the then-popular theories of miasmic contagion, crowding was unhygienic and could even cause disease.[40]

This negative perception of al-Azhar permeated the bureaucracy. Mubarak was but one of hundreds of government employees who had been trained in Muhammad 'Ali's schools and in Paris. There were now second-generation disseminators of European educational techniques as well. At the School of Languages and Accountancy alone, al-Tahtawi trained more than sixty-five students who were employed in various government offices.[41] To them, al-Azhar's condition was inexcusable and inimical to the process of learning.

Writers such as Mubarak and al-Tahtawi promoted the efficiency of print dissemination of knowledge, which, if the writing was suitably clear, did not require the intensive mediation of an 'alim interpreter or transmitter. But print dissemination without the oral mediation of a teacher/transmitter isolated the audience from the speaker, removed students from personalized connection with their teachers,[42] and severed the text from its author's intent. This was what government reformers failed to recognize in their attempts to interpose Utilitarian models of education between the authors of religious texts and their audiences. Moreover, they assumed efficiency could not be achieved under indigenous models of education and did not view accepting external models as disempowering the religious establishment.

The ethos of bureaucratic reform blinded them to the historical context in which madrasa education had developed. Al-Azhar's system of knowledge dissemination had its logic in the Arabic alphabet, in which short vowels were not written but supplied by oral readers. At al-Azhar, the 'ulama recited books to their students, who memorized them and made their own annotated copies, which they might use as a basis for their own classes if they became teachers. This contributed to the relatively voluminous production of commentaries and glosses, which had served for centuries as means of simplifying, abridging, or expanding upon original texts.[43]

Encoding Surveillance

The disturbances at al-Azhar in the late 1850s lent credence to critics. At that time, al-Azhar was still the primary supplier of Egypt's teachers and legal personnel, and Khedive Isma'il apparently believed that improving their training was an important step in transforming the country.[44] One might assume that Isma'il's fascination with European order and appearances would alienate him from the Azhar 'ulama, but that was not the case. A devout Muslim, Isma'il was genuinely concerned about the state of higher religious education and the moral leadership of his people. He was on good terms with the 'ulama, made grants of money to them and to specific institutions, and began physical renovations at al-Azhar. Some 'ulama believed him to exemplify the "true Muslim ruler."[45]

Isma'il could well afford to invest in 'ulama confidence, because Egypt's fortunes were by then on the rise due to rising international demand for Egypt's staple crop, cotton, and a tenfold increase in income from cotton sales.[46] From the number of grants Isma'il made to various religious concerns, it appears that a decent portion of Egypt's new wealth made its way into the religious institutions. Most Azharis certainly held Isma'il in higher regard than they had Muhammad 'Ali. They did not object when their benevolent Muslim viceroy appointed Al-'Arusi Shaykh al-Azhar, bypassing the usual selection process whereby 'ulama offered up their own candidate for state approval. Thus agents of state authority controlled the mechanisms by which reforms could be implemented at al-Azhar.

By all accounts, Shaykh al-Azhar Mustafa al-'Arusi was an awe-inspiring figure, revered by students and professors alike. Both his father and his grandfather had been Shaykh al-Azhar before him. Al-'Arusi was obsessed with the eradication of bid'a, activities that he and other 'ulama regarded as unacceptably divergent from orthodox practice, such as begging for coins in exchange for recitation of the Qur'an and teaching in al-Azhar without permission.[47] Ideas or technologies that originated with political enemies were sometimes labeled bid'a as well, although such things were just as often overlooked.

Al-'Arusi did not regard the French models of pedagogical order as bid'a. Shaykh al-'Arusi's reform code, promulgated in 1865, was concerned with administrative, sanitary, and pedagogical order, and thus addressed the same issues that Mubarak had criticized. The new code formalized the supervisory hierarchy of the madrasa and the authority of the Shaykh al-Azhar, which now was to approximate the position of headmaster in a civil school. For example, the code required 'ulama to obtain the Shaykh al-Azhar's permission before teaching a new book, stipulated that no 'alim could teach a book unless he was sufficiently qualified to do so and understood the book himself, and instructed professors to teach in a clear and simple manner and to make sure that the students understood the lessons. It reminded riwaq shaykhs of their responsibility to distribute student rations fairly, and demanded that the 'ulama practice good hygiene, demonstrate upright morals, and behave with decorum.

More controversial was imposition of yearly final examinations, those ubiquitous tools of normalizing surveillance. Although the exam would remain oral, as were existing informal procedures for advancement, the process was to be universalized and enforced. This challenged previous practice that allowed students the freedom to advance from one class to another and change classes without censure. Moreover, it removed the shaykh's authority to determine when a student was ready to assume teaching duties and gave that authority to the Shaykh al-Azhar.

The new code also abrogated conventional seating arrangements in the teaching areas of the mosque. Previously, each madhhab, or legal school, had been allotted a certain number of columns, which senior shaykhs within the madhhab then apportioned to teachers.

Figure 3.1 A large halqa, c. 1900. *(Source:* **Muhammad 'Abd al-Gawad,** *Hayat al-mujawir fi al-Jami' al Ahmadi* **[Cairo: Matba'at al-I'timad, 1947]: 183.)**

Teachers then stood (Figure 3.1) or sat (Figure 3.2) by their columns and held their readings. Each madhhab had a monopoly over a certain number of columns, and if the membership of one madhhab decreased, its shaykhs would simply allow new teachers to take up the extra columns rather than allow other madhahib (plural form of madhhab) to appropriate them. Madhahib whose numbers increased thus suffered a shortage of columns. The new program ended the madhahib's monopolies over column apportionment and stated that the Shaykh al-Azhar would allot vacant columns to only the most worthy candidates without regard to their madhahib.[48]

To understand why this change would have encountered opposition, one must imagine the dashed hopes of middle-aged Azhari 'ulama who had waited years for a senior professor of their madhhab to die or retire so that they could finally teach within the sanctified precincts of al-Azhar. Many Azhari 'ulama did not have a column within al-Azhar but instead held their halqas at lesser mosques or in their homes. The acquisition of a column was roughly equivalent in conferred status and security to the rank of full professor. With the change to the new system, those 'ulama of lesser talents saw their dreams of teaching within al-Azhar evaporate.

Figure 3.2   A small halqa, c. 1900. *(Source:* Muhammad 'Abd al-Gawad, *Hayat al-mujawir fi al-Jami' al Ahmadi* [Cairo: Matba'at al-I'timad, 1947]: 181.)

Ethnic rivalries may also have entered into this matter, because in many cases those from a particular region all belonged to the same legal school. Sa'idis and Maghribis, for example, were nearly all of the Maliki madhhab, whereas the Syrians tended to be Hanafis. Given the ethnic tensions of the era and al-Azhar's history of inter-madhhab conflicts, some 'ulama may have suspected that the Shaykh al-Azhar, who was a Shafi'i, would favor the Shafi'is in his redistribution of columns. Previous Shaykh al-Azhars, including al-'Arusi's predecessor, had been accused of favoring those of their own madhahib, so precedents did exist.

Had it been implemented, Shaykh al-Azhar al-'Arusi's reform program would have effectively concentrated power within the Shaykh al-Azhar's hands and established a formal hierarchy of supervision. Al-'Arusi also acceded in the code to Isma'il's request that geometry, physics, music, and history be offered as electives.[49] But the code was not implemented. According to a government order that announced al-'Arusi's deposition, the 'ulama turned against him and petitioned Khedive Isma'il to have him removed from office. It is not surprising that they petitioned Isma'il to remove him. However, it is surprising that they asked Isma'il to appoint a new Shaykh al-Azhar, thus giving up the privilege of choosing their own Shaykh al-Azhar.[50] The petition itself holds some clues to this puzzle.

As Marsot has noted, the names of the signatories suggest collusion between Isma'il and the 'ulama. The petition was signed by the shaykhs of the riwaqs; by the Hanafi Mufti, Shaykh Muhammad al-'Abbasi al-Mahdi, who was a close confidant of the khedive; and by the tutor of Isma'il's sons.[51] The tutor would already have passed Isma'il's scrutiny, by virtue of his position, and thus was probably himself sympathetic to French models of order. But why then would these two ask for the removal of a reformist Shaykh al-Azhar? There had been Ottoman pressure to appoint only Hanafis to official juristic positions. The Shaykh al-Azhar was not a juristic position, however, and furthermore, there were 101 Shafi'i shaykhs at al-Azhar, and only forty-two Hanafis. Azhari objections to al-'Arusi's code may have been such that al-'Arusi's presence as Shaykh al-Azhar was an obstacle in the path of Isma'il's plans for al-Azhar. However, the official decree announcing al-'Arusi's deposition says only, rather vaguely, that "the 'ulama had turned their hearts from him."[52]

The shaykhs of the riwaqs also stood to gain from the deal. Their support for Shaykh al-'Abbasi's candidacy may have reflected a growing belief that a new model of order was necessary, if only to deal with the growing numbers of students. Or perhaps, if authority was to be centralized in the Shaykh al-Azhar's hands, they simply did not want al-'Arusi—or any shaykh of the Shafi'i madhhab—to be the Shaykh al-Azhar.

As for Khedive Isma'il, it was apparent that the reforms could not succeed without support from Azharis themselves. The shaykhs' petition offered him a way to assert control over the political avenues of reform while still respecting 'ulama sensibilities.[53] With support from Isma'il and from a growing number of efficiency-oriented bureaucrats (notably 'Ali Mubarak, who had been named deputy minister of education in 1867 and supervisor of the Ministry of Education in 1871, and Shaykh al-Tahtawi, who was editor of *Rawdat al-madaris,* a new periodical on education published by the Ministry of Education, in 1871), the new Shaykh al-Azhar was able to implement most of the reforms that al-'Arusi had planned.

The new Shaykh al-Azhar, Muhammad al-'Abbasi al-Mahdi, was a scion of a well-known 'alim family, as his predecessor Mustafa al-'Arusi had been. Muhammad al-Mahdi's father had been Muhammad Amin al-Mahdi, Hanafi Mufti under Muhammad 'Ali, his grandfather Shaykh

Muhammad al-Mahdi. He was known as al-'Abbasi to distinguish him from his illustrious forebears. Initially popular and well-liked, he was also the Grand Mufti of the Hanafi madhhab and the first to hold the title of Mufti al-Diyar al-Misriyya, Grand Mufti of Egypt. Representatives of the Shafi'i madhhab had held the office of Shaykh al-Azhar for 145 years; no Hanafi ever had.[54]

The Hanafi madhhab was the official legal school of the Ottoman government and thus of Isma'il's government. In 1839, the Ottoman government had decreed that official jurisprudence should be performed using specified texts, all of which were Hanafi. Employees of the shari'a courts, therefore, had to rule according to the Hanafi legal school.[55] By the 1860s, more Azhari students were registering as Hanafis than ever before, reflecting growing awareness that the government, which was still the largest employer of Azhari graduates, had to hire Hanafis. Thus Isma'il and the leading shaykhs felt that the Hanafis should take on a more prominent leadership position at al-Azhar, replacing the Shafi'is who had dominated the office.

There are no records of disturbances among the students over the appointment of a Hanafi as Shaykh al-Azhar in 1870, but the Shafi'i 'ulama did register their protest. They refused to appoint a new head for their madhhab, and insisted that they would leave the office vacant until it could be again filled by a Shaykh al-Azhar. However, in the early part of the 1870s, Shaykh al-'Abbasi was able to use Isma'il's support to repair his relationship with his Azhari colleagues. He convinced Isma'il to restore the annual bestowals of kasawi al-tashrif upon the 'ulama, a practice which had ceased with the mid-century suspension of state subsidization. Kasawi al-tashrif, literally meaning "robes of honor," could also entail other gifts, including cash.[56]

Shaykh al-'Abbasi and Isma'il established a fund for 'ulama kasawi that provided £E 897.36 annually. Isma'il gave the Shaykh al-Azhar the right to distribute the monies to thirty-eight deserving Azhar 'ulama according to a specific formula. He could give two shaykhs £E 30.867 each, three shaykhs £E 27, eight shaykhs £E 24, six £E 21, four £E 15, and ten £E 12. He also gave non-Azhari 'ulama annual awards. This took some of the sting from al-'Abbasi's subsequent implementation of the unpopular column reapportionment plan.[57] This introduced salary schedules, implying an official categorization and separation of individual talents into ranks and supplanting the column as an indicator of rank, in which all column holders were relatively equal in status. But because the 'ulama were relatively underpaid, this salary schedule gave Shaykh al-'Abbasi a broad base of support.[58] Isma'il also made private gifts to leading 'ulama whose financial situations were particularly poor.[59] Al-'Abbasi's association with the new grants thus bolstered his status. For these and other reasons, Shaykh al-Azhar Muhammad al-'Abbasi was able to implement a series of codes that encompassed many of the reforms Shaykh Mustafa al-'Arusi had originally envisioned.

Al-'Abbasi implemented the Examination Code, the first of the nineteenth-century reform codes, in 1872. Historians have hailed this law as the first step or first phase in the reform of al-Azhar. It was also the first program to successfully impose European techniques of surveillance and normalization on an Egyptian madrasa. The 1872 code stated that students could acquire "the 'alimiyya degree," and thus be certified as an 'alim, only by passing an examination, which would be given by a committee of 'ulama selected by the Shaykh al-Azhar. Successful examinees would be assigned one of three ranks according to their performance on the exam, and the results would be made public. Those who achieved the first rank would receive a kiswa al-tashrif from the khedive. The code also stipulated eleven subjects in which students would be examined: jurisprudence, principles and texts of religion, the theology of monotheism, hadith, Qur'anic exegesis, grammar, morphology, three kinds of rhetoric, and logic.[60] This had the effect of establishing a curriculum, something that previously had never formally existed.

Why did the 'ulama accept this imposition? Problematic effects of the code did not materialize right away, and at the time of its appearance, the examination served a purpose that few 'ulama would publicly oppose. It prevented imposters from teaching at al-Azhar.

Order and Legitimacy

Arab historians who wrote that conservative Azharis reacted immediately and negatively to the 1872 code were viewing the reform movement in retrospect, some from the point of view of the 1890s, some from the twentieth century. By the 1900s, there did exist both a relatively coherent conservative front within al-Azhar and a number of people who opposed specific reforms. It appears that the Arab historians conflated the existence of anti-European conservatism and opposition to reform codes and projected the existence of an organized conservative opposition from their present onto their construction of the past.[61]

As stated previously, it was a long-standing tradition in Egypt that 'ulama and madrasa students were exempted from military conscription.

This courtesy was also extended to exemption from conscription for labor in local public works projects. Therefore, when the time came for village and neighborhood leaders to round people up for, say, dredging irrigation canals or clearing refuse from bridge supports, some men would claim to be madrasa students. To bolster these claims, some even persuaded legitimate al-Azhar 'ulama to write them fake certificates that "proved" they were students. The men then took refuge in the mosque.[62] Some men took advantage of these certificates, which permitted them the right to teach the text for which they had supposedly received the certificate. To the horror of legitimate 'ulama, this sometimes resulted in imposters reading texts to circles of listeners. In the flood season, by necessity an off-season for farmers, al-Azhar became crowded with men seeking refuge from labor gangs: "One could see there students who were over sixty years old and 'ulama who knew nothing of learning except the names of the subjects."[63] The imposters might even receive compensation for their services, doubling their assault upon the authority of legitimate teachers by fraudulently accepting money from al-Azhar's already overburdened awqaf. This was a violation of the conditions set by al-Azhar's awqaf for the support of religious scholars and necessitated immediate correction.[64] Furthermore, the imposters' ignorance constituted a threat to the chains of transmission that ensured integrity of religious knowledge, and to the public's confidence in the 'ulama as repositories and interpreters of that knowledge.

Shaykh al-'Abbasi and the committee that formulated the 1872 code intended it to put an end to the writing of fake certificates. The new law specified examination of anyone who wanted to teach at al-Azhar. The examination conferred the 'alimiyya degree, which was now to be accepted as the sole certification for teaching.[65] If all students had to be examined in eleven subjects by a special, handpicked committee in order to get their certificates, it would be extremely difficult for an imposter to gain fake certification. Given the reasoning behind this law, then, we can understand why the majority of the 'ulama would support it.

Conclusion

Previous scholarship considered the period between the death of Shaykh Hasan al-'Attar and the rise of Shaykh Muhammad al-'Abbasi al-Mahdi as one of conservative re-entrenchment after 'ulama sufferings at the hands of Muhammad 'Ali. Rather, it was a foundational period, during which 'ulama took the first steps toward hybridizing European models of efficiency with the halqa system.

There is similarity between the historical conditions in Egypt at the time and the conditions under which Utilitarian models of education were developed in Europe. Michel Foucault described the development of modern society as an accommodation to population growth and the need to create new mechanisms of power to control the results of that growth. These new mechanisms involved the diffusion of micro-power networks, such that the exercise of power and conditioning of individual behavior gradually came to be associated less with force exercised by a central authority figure and more with the unseen mesh of social mores, the observing public, and the societally molded and disciplined self. He used Jeremy Bentham's Panopticon as metaphor and example. The Panopticon was a hollow multistoried penitentiary, with cells arranged so that inmates would always be backlit by external light and always in view of a central supervisory tower. The inmates could not see the supervisor (who could be a member of the public), but they knew they could be observed at any time, so they disciplined themselves; they themselves were co-opted as supervisors. In a panoptic society, individuals would be constantly exposed to supervision, examination, classification, analysis, placement on a spectrum of normality, and penitentiary discipline, all intended to normalize them. The gaze of the supervisor would be everywhere—in workplaces, hospitals, educational systems, in the military, in the justice system. Likewise, the social sciences would render individuals as objects of knowledge (subjects of studies, of analyses, on minds, bodies, and aggregates) and by implication, objects of a normalizing process that creates productive, nationalist citizens. Like the inmates, citizens of a panoptic society cannot see the supervisor because he is at once the whole public and the self, enmeshed within a complex arrangement of power- and knowledge-producing disciplines that are so embedded in the society that they are impossible to escape. These citizens are conditioned without exercise of force.

Foucault asserted that this nexus of power/knowledge relationships evolved out of a conjunction of several historical trends. Eighteenth-century demographic changes in Europe brought massive numbers of people to the city and into educational systems, hospital systems, and militaries. These were often "floating" populations: workers or others not attached to property or localities and thus not easily taxed or controlled. The developing capitalist economy had also to deal with the increased numbers in the workforce and increasingly complex forms of investment. The floating populations and capitalist endeavors could not be controlled by existing feudal or monarchical methods of supervision and punishment—they all had to be channeled into useful functions, and thus a new system of control based on maximizing utility had to be developed. Populations had to be broken out of socially horizontal alliances, trained as individuals within a vertically hierarchical pyramid in which they would be subject to surveillance and discipline, and then channeled toward maximum productivity and efficiency. At the same time, there developed democratic government and a juridical system based on recognition of equal individual rights and liberties, the liberating effects of which were checked by the nonegalitarian and hierarchical influence of micro-power.[66]

In Egypt, the mid-nineteenth century saw increases in urban floating populations and more complex forms of investment capitalism side by side with state centralization of land tenure, taxation, and conscription. While centralized control remained the rule in Egypt, Mitchell has demonstrated admirably how panoptic mechanisms embedded in pedagogy, civic architecture, and writing practices were absorbed and transmitted by Egyptian elites, especially al-Tahtawi and 'Ali Mubarak.[67] However, one must separate panopticism from the implication that it is insidious, controlling, even evil. It is problematic to say, for example, that panoptic methods of sanitation are evil, and that reformers' imposition of them upon Egyptians was not in some way beneficial.

The collapse of Muhammad 'Ali's military school system in the 1840s redirected government attention to the madaris, which were between the 1840s and 1870s the main source of trained personnel for government positions. During this period, specialists trained in Parisian schools, who had absorbed as norms of educational order the disciplinary methods of French military education, continued to train translators, journalists, and teachers for government employment and to publish their ideas, influencing the literate elite and future government employees and encouraging an interventionist disciplinary sentiment within influential circles. Under Governor Sa'id, high quotas for conscription and rural immigration into cities led to large floating populations of draft dodgers and indigent dependents at al-Azhar, undercutting its delicate network of behavior controls on the students and straining its already overburdened finances. When bread allotments for Maghribi students were interrupted, students assaulted an elderly Shaykh al-Azhar, necessitating armed intervention. This attracted the intense scrutiny of Mubarak, who penned a vehement criticism of madrasa education, focusing on al-Azhar's pedagogical methods and administration and contributing to an image of the madrasa, and the 'alim, in decline. The disturbances also provided an excuse for benevolent state intervention, via the appointment of two Shaykh al-Azhars, and their promulgation of reform codes modeled on the military order of French schools. The overcrowding and violence also led the Azhari 'ulama to acquiesce to the application of European models of order to the madrasa, as long as that order served to protect their authority. As a result, ranks were formalized and supervisory techniques to certify acquisition of those ranks established. The bodies of the fractious 'ulama, once horizontally cohesive within madhhabs, were now vertically divided and rendered at least theoretically docile. Further partitions of rank and manipulations of the new salary schedules would later serve to factionalize the 'ulama and convince segments of them to accept further reforms. Also, as a result of the new curriculum, students began to focus on the required subjects rather than exploring their own interests. Since al-Azhar's offerings were determined by student requests for subjects, those subjects not required for the exams started to languish.[68] Continuing the paradox that trapped Shaykh al-'Attar, just as the reformers were beginning to demand that religious scholars have training in natural sciences, mathematics, geography, and languages, al-Azhar's course offerings were again contracting. Thus the abridgment of the curriculum occasioned by competition with Muhammad 'Ali's military schools now accelerated, and the curriculum and examination procedure would eventually lead to standardization, normalization, and canonization of religious knowledge.

However, just as unionism mitigated the rage of the working classes upon which Marx counted for his proletarian revolution, so have microcontracts mitigated the networks of micro-control through which panopticism influences individuals. Social/scientific and federal collection of information about us, for example, is subject to right-to-privacy laws and the practice of informed consent. The halqa system, with its implied contractualism, would also mitigate the effects of panoptic efficiency. What would eventually emerge from these efforts was not conceptual colonization, but a hybrid.

4

PROGRESS, NATIONALISM, AND THE NEGATIVE CONSTRUCTION OF AL-AZHAR 'ULAMA (1870–1882)

The decade of the 1870s was marked by increasing acceptance of European educational techniques on the part of both the Azhari 'ulama and agents of the Egyptian state. In part, this was the result of an unrelenting campaign by a group of journalists whose education and influence permitted them to redefine and promote for Egyptian Muslim society the concepts of progress and community-as-nation and to suggest what manner of education best suited those concepts. After 1870, the campaign involved a parody of 'ulama conservatism that served as antithesis for the journalists' definition of progress. Conservative 'ulama became for the reformers their Other, that foil against which they defined themselves. Throughout this chapter, I emphasize the continuing critique of al-Azhar education, as laid out by Shaykh Rifa'a al-Tahtawi, the Persian-born activist Jamal al-Din al-Afghani, and al-Afghani's students, and their campaign to lay the blame for al-Azhar's disorder upon the 'ulama and their pedagogical and scholastic traditions. Underlying that critique was a redefinition of the legal methodologies of ijtihad and taqlid: Taqlid was recast as a cause of social stagnation and ijtihad as a mechanism of social growth. The integrity of legal theory was suborned under nationalist rhetoric. Furthermore, reformers taught that the meaning of the Qur'an was inherently present in the text, so ijtihad was something any educated Muslim could do. This redefinition would change the world.

Shaykh Rifa'a Rafi' al-Tahtawi:
". . . all knowledge is beneficial . . ."

Egypt's literate population was growing in the last decades of the nineteenth century, as was the production of printed materials in Arabic. The Azhari 'ulama produced volumes of books, but as their mechanisms of knowledge transmission required an unbroken chain of informed oral transmitters, many 'ulama did not see a need to print their books for mass audiences. Books were also relatively expensive. Journals and newspapers were the reading materials of choice: Newsprint was easy to read, and newspapers were cheap. Writers could also make a living producing articles for periodicals.[1] There now arose a few 'ulama and bureaucrats, notably Shaykh Rifa'a al-Tahtawi and Sayyid Jamal al-Din al-Afghani, who perceived journalism as something more—a means of transforming a people—and they taught a generation of Egyptian journalists to pursue that objective. As the public turned increasingly to print for information, and as rulers encouraged them to do so,[2] people became more critical of the halqa system and 'ulama who emphasized the orality of true knowledge.

In the 1840s, al-Tahtawi had made an abortive attempt to introduce science writing into the official newsletter *al-Waqa'i' al-Misriyya*. The first Arabic presses in Egypt were owned and operated by the government, intended mainly to provide news, official propaganda, translations of European works, and textbooks to government bureaucrats and other functionaries. With Isma'il's 1863 accession to the throne of Egypt, however, things changed. The literate public had become accustomed to the dissemination of printed information, although most periodicals available to Egyptians were still printed in French, Italian, or Turkish. Isma'il supported publication of specialized journals in medicine, military science, and education. In 1870, Isma'il's Minister of Education, 'Ali Mubarak, appointed al-Tahtawi chief supervisor of the new journal of the Ministry of Education, *Rawdat al-madaris* [Garden of schools].[3]

From the first, Isma'il and 'Ali Mubarak had envisioned *Rawdat al-madaris* as a vehicle for the teaching of science and reading as well as religious matters.[4] It also included articles on the meaning of progress and the means for national advancement, some of which launched the now decades-old critique of religious education in new directions.

Al-Tahtawi claimed that applied sciences had declined in popularity among the 'ulama of Egypt for several reasons. These sciences, which were known as al-hikma al-'amaliyya wa al-tara'iq al-ma'ashiyya (practical wisdom and means of livelihood), had long carried for certain Sunni 'ulama the stigma of the Hellenistic philosophies from which they had originated.[5] In the eighteenth century, applied sciences such as medicine were considered trades and were not given much academic study. Other subjects derived from the Hellenistic tradition, such as logic, had been incorporated into Ash'ari theology and thence into the corpus of madrasa education. Even then, logic and hikma were only taught after the sunset prayers and seem to have been the smallest classes; the most important classes were taught between sunrise and midday.[6]

The 'ulama had additional reasons for preferring religious or legal studies to hikma. Many of the 'ulama were supported by madrasa awqaf. The documents establishing the endowments usually specified minutely what expenses could be paid from waqf revenues,[7] sometimes including the subjects that could be taught by the recipients of waqf charities. The subjects specified were almost invariably branches of the religious, legal, or linguistic sciences. Therefore the 'ulama had economic incentives to study the funded subjects.

"Useful knowledge"

According to al-Tahtawi, the restrictions against study of applied and rational sciences were derived from a prophetic saying. Muhammad had once said that a man's actions could be continued after his death by leaving behind him one of three things: alms, an upright son, or knowledge by which one benefits ('ilm yuntafa'u bihi). Previously, beneficial knowledge had been understood as meaning religious knowledge, in the sense that someone would benefit spiritually from it. Thus only religious sciences had been cultivated. Al-Tahtawi contended that the Arabic phrase al-'ilm al-nafi', beneficial knowledge, in no way excluded knowledge that was beneficial in a material sense, because all knowledge benefited the community of Muslims (milla): agriculture, manufacturing, and other practical fields.[8] This was not a mere adoption of English Utilitarian concepts of useful knowledge, for English Utilitarianism was at heart inspired by individualism. Al-Tahtawi's benefit accrued to the community as a whole in accordance with early nineteenth-century Ottoman interpretations of the concept of maslaha as public good.[9]

Furthermore, since 'ilm (learning or knowledge) had been redefined as including the vocational and applied sciences, so would 'ulama—those who are learned—also have to be redefined. In al-Tahtawi's time, the word 'ulama had been understood as designating all learned men, but primarily religious scholars and Sufi shaykhs. Within the larger designation there had been subspecializations: a mutakallim was a specialist in kalam, or dialectical theology; a muhaddith was a specialist in hadith, or the sayings of the Prophet and his Companions; an usuli was a specialist in usul al-fiqh, the principles of jurisprudence; and a hakim was a specialist in hikma, medical and anatomical studies derived from Greek science and philosophy. Al-Tahtawi distinguished between 'ulama, by which he meant learned men in general, and umana' al-din, by which he meant those to whom religion is entrusted or the guarantors of religion. Al-Tahtawi was not trying to develop a terminology of secular versus religious subjects; it was rather a more inclusive terminology that incorporated contemporary subject matter under the general heading "useful knowledge."[10] Al-Tahtawi also wanted to defend his assertion that religious scholars had traditionally studied trade subjects—he used the term *'ulama al-shari'a* to designate legal scholars, but said even these 'ulama include within their ranks some who studied applied sciences and other things "needed by the state." Ultimately, he said, all 'ulama, scientists included, deserved respect for fulfilling functions that were essential to the nation.[11]

Yet what al-Tahtawi proposed was still a partitioning of knowledge, and a formalization of that partition through framing terminology. If he did not intend it to be also a hierarchical ranking of types of knowledge, it nevertheless became so. For the "guarantors of religion" and the "legal scholars" were not fulfilling their functions adequately. Al-Tahtawi accused them of restricting themselves to the study of Arabic linguistics. Subjects such as linguistics were merely tools for "unlocking the door to true knowledge," but they had been elevated to ends in themselves.[12] Texts on religious and legal matters were being studied only as sources for interesting grammatical problems, the potential import of their contents forgotten.

Taqlid, Ittiba', and Ijtihad

According to al-Tahtawi, all of these faults of the educational system were due to the importance of taqlid and ittiba' to the 'ulama. Taqlid and ittiba' are legal terms that denote a legal scholar's practice of following the accepted ruling of his madhhab on a particular matter. One who practices ittiba' follows the ruling of his madhhab with full knowledge of the reasoning and evidence upon which the ruling was based. Taqlid, on the other hand, could be understood to mean the practice of following that ruling without knowing the underlying argument. According to some jurists, taqlid was a restriction upon those who were not qualified to derive independent judgments from the sources of law.[13]

Al-Tahtawi did not find ittiba' sufficient to resolve what he saw as the stultification of jurisprudence. He promoted ijtihad, the derivation of independent informed rulings, which was the methodological opposite of taqlid. During the first few centuries of Islam, jurists had been called upon to resolve novel matters in ways that agreed with the spirit of the Qur'an and hadith. When Muhammad asked his governor of Yemen what he would do if the judgments he sought were not to be found in the Qur'an or hadith, the governor replied, "I will strive [sa ajtahidu] diligently, without sparing any effort, to form an opinion." Muhammad indicated approval. Likewise, the caliph 'Umar told a judge that if the answers he sought were not in the Qur'an or hadith, he should "follow [his] own judgment independently."[14] Ijtihad continued to be synonymous with the informed opinion of a jurist (ijtihad al-ra'y) until the eighth century CE, when jurists began to resolve matters by means of analogy (qiyas) and to discover general principles by means of inductive reasoning that could be applied to new cases. Ijtihad referred to the process of exerting one's utmost effort in both development of derivational principles (usul) and applying those principles to the texts. The problem inherent in ijtihad was twofold: If a mufti (jurisconsult) performed ijtihad rather than a qadi (judge), the result of his efforts was merely an opinion—an opinion binding neither on other jurists nor on petitioners—and subject to change. Furthermore, ijtihad was an inherently subjective process. Unless the opinion reached the status of a general rule by means of ijma' (communal consensus), there was no way to ensure that the rulings of individual jurists agreed in any meaningful way. Muftis could not reach a confirmed consensus upon which qadis could base binding judicial rulings within a reasonable degree of conformity. It was possible to resolve a legal question by using any number of legitimate but mutually contradictory precedents. In other words, there was no way to reach the point of rule of law.[15] Thus some early jurists were understandably eager to limit ijtihad's use.

Some jurists, notably al-Shafi'i (d. 820), the eponymous Imam of the Shafi'i madhhab, stated that ijtihad was performed via qiyas.[16] Al-Shafi'i clearly ranked qiyas below the hadith in terms of the authority of the rulings they could yield. Al-Shafi'i also outlined the four usul al-fiqh, the basic sources and hermeneutical principles of Islamic jurisprudence, as they are now conventionally understood. The subordinate place of qiyas in this ranking can be clearly seen. The first and most authoritative source was the Qur'an, which yielded unambiguous verses (qat'iyyat), the meanings of which were clear and therefore were the most authoritative sources of law, and ambiguous verses (zanniyyat), the meanings of which were open to interpretation. The second most authoritative source was the sunna, or the normative principles drawn from the hadith, sayings of the Prophet and the members of his early community. Of these, the most authoritative were those that could be traced to the Prophet himself. Hadith were also classified as sound or weak, according to an elaborate tradition of hadith criticism. The hadith were initially transmitted orally along with a list or chain of previous transmitters, and scholars examined the chains of transmission for gaps or untrustworthy transmitters. Generally, those that were multiply transmitted and had no gaps or weak transmitters were sound; those that were singly transmitted, had gaps in transmission, or had immoral transmitters were considered weak. Some jurists, and later schools of thought, accepted only sound hadith; others accepted even weak ones as preferable to qiyas as a source of law. The third root of jurisprudence was ijma', or communal consensus. Originally defined as the consensus of the entire community, this later came to be understood as the consensus of scholars within a locality, and even later, the consensus of jurists in a particular madhhab. Ijma', however, was a crucial element of jurisprudence. According to a hadith, Muhammad once said that his community could not agree on something in error. Thus if the community could come to consensus on the validity of a legal ruling, it must truly be valid. Ijma' therefore could elevate a ruling reached via human reasoning to the status of an unambiguous verse of the Qur'an. The fourth and least reliable source was qiyas, analogy, since it relied heavily upon (potentially flawed) human reasoning.

However, because ijtihad as qiyas was still considered legitimate, the problem of legal indeterminacy remained. Al-Shafi'i did show concern for this, in that he suggested that only scholars who could distinguish between general guidelines and specific prescriptions in the Qur'an should be permitted to engage in jurisprudence.[17] Gradually, jurists coalesced into more or less coherent schools of thought, based on the hermeneutics and rulings produced by eminent scholars like al-Shafi'i. These schools of thought were named after their founders, the Sunni Imams: the Hanafi madhhab, which followed Abu Hanifa (d. 765), the Maliki madhhab, which followed Malik ibn Anas (d. 796), the Shafi'i madhhab, which followed al-Shafi'i (d. 820), and the Hanbali madhhab, which followed Ahmad ibn Hanbal (d. 855).[18]

Mohammad Fadel's study of the Maliki madhhab suggests that, by processes of ijma' and by coalescing into madhahib, the results of generations of legal thought and analysis were whittled down until the madhhab had a more or less cohesive body of authoritative rules from which to derive

judgments, a kind of "codified common law."[19] However, independent ijtihad within the madhhab remained a problem, because even an individual
practitioner of ijtihad might have taken different positions during his lifetime. Thus the unlimited practice of ijtihad threatened the integrity of
authoritative law. Eventually there accumulated a body of authoritative rulings upon which influential jurists within the madhahib could agree, and
gradually jurists began to bind themselves and their juniors to these accepted rulings, limiting jurists' rights to perform ijtihad. By the 1300s, some
jurists had begun to argue that only the most knowledgeable 'ulama should
be allowed to perform ijtihad at all, and some held that there were no more
'ulama with the great learning and inspiration required to perform ijtihad
beyond certain limits, as the founders of the four main madhahib had
done.[20] While certain modes of ijtihad continued to be practiced, generally within the boundaries of madhhab rules,[21] acceptable rules gradually
came to be associated with the consensus of the madhhab rather than the
opinion of mujtahid, or a practitioner of ijtihad (plural mujtahidun). Some
'ulama even claimed that the "gate of ijtihad" was closed; that independent
ijtihad was no longer to be performed.[22] After the 1300s, with some excep-
tions, it came to be expected that the majority of legal scholars as well as
ordinary Muslims would adhere to taqlid—that is, that they would base
their judgments upon the accepted rulings of their madhahib.

According to the historical record, high-ranking scholars continued to
perform limited ijtihad to adjudicate novel cases, but independent ijtihad
of the type exercised by the founders of the law schools was generally considered to have ceased. The need for consensus within the juridical community, at the very least on legitimate sources and derivational principles,
meant that only the lesser degrees of ijtihad could be permitted, and the
franchise for lesser degrees had to be limited as much as possible. Even highly qualified mujtahidun were expected to follow the hermeneutical principles outlined by the madhhab founders and a strict hierarchy of acceptable
rulings in cases that had already been addressed.[23] Nevertheless, research in
the last decade has demonstrated that no consensus ever existed on the "closure of the gate of ijtihad."[24]

Claims of consensus, however, did exist. They served different purposes
in different historical contexts. For the formative period of the shari'a, Wael
Hallaq proposed that closure rhetoric was adopted by groups that rejected
qiyas in favor of taqlid and literalist interpretations of the hadith; similarly,
Leonard Binder suggested that ijtihad was given up out of opposition to
rationalist methodologies, such as the Shi'i principle of 'aql (reason used in

deriving legal rulings). According to Frank Vogel, for Hanafi 'ulama of the 'Abbasid era, the claim that ijtihad had ceased was a conscious attempt to ensure that their version of fiqh (jurisprudence) would survive and compete against contending principles, such as siyasa (statecraft), in the 'Abbasid legal system. Thus it may have been a political move to preserve the power and authority of the 'ulama and their fiqh against that of the state and its siyasa.[25] Muhammad Iqbal wrote that 'ulama claimed closure to strengthen the legal system's ability to define and unite the community against Mu'tazili rationalism, Sufi methods of symbolic exegesis, and in the thirteenth century, the social and political disruptions caused by the Mongol invasions. According to Muhammad Fadel, for Maliki jurists of the fourteenth century, closure was a logical solution to the problem of legal indeterminacy. And as Wael Hallaq, Lutz Wiederhold, and Aaron Spevack have pointed out, some claims of ijtihad's cessation were due to differences of opinion as to what ijtihad actually was. If a jurist understood ijtihad to mean the jurist's search for a solution to a difficult legal question, he might allow it. On the other hand, if he understood ijtihad to mean independent reasoning or derivation of new hermeneutical principles, he might not.[26] Given the variation in jurists' local and temporal circumstances, there may be any number of valid explanations for jurists' attempts to restrict ijtihad, or, conversely, to promote it.

Al-Tahtawi did not provide a historical explanation for the waning of ijtihad; he simply asserted that it had become accepted in Egypt that no mujtahidun existed. In fact, there were qualified jurists who appear to have performed functions analogous to ijtihad, but al-Tahtawi did not recognize them as mujtahidun. Most jurists did adhere to a hierarchy of madhhab rulings; that is, they practiced taqlid.[27] Thus al-Tahtawi would argue not just for utilization of ijtihad but for the reopening of its gate.

New Social Meanings for Taqlid and Ijtihad

Al-Tahtawi claimed that taqlid caused social stagnation. He perceived taqlid as more than just a method of legal derivation, but as a principle underlying a mind-set fundamentally different from his own, the principle that everything new is harmful and that one's ancestors have accomplished all that is good. Within the mind-set based on taqlid, the established rules of the madhahib contained everything a scholar would need to answer legal questions, the highest point of civilization was a Golden Age of the distant past, and innovation was dangerous because it departed from inherited truths. Thus taqlid, according to al-Tahtawi, was not just a juridical prac-

tice; taqlid also represented a worldview fundamentally opposed to progress, the foundation of a decaying civilization. And the 'ulama were guilty
of preserving taqlid. This opinion expressed al-Tahtawi's hybridized Orientalism: His implicit acceptance of European concepts of progress was
embedded in his critique of Islamic juridical discourse, using the conventional format of a review of prevailing opinions.

According to al-Tahtawi, the solution to the problem would be to reopen
the gate of ijtihad and to reexamine and reinterpret the Qur'an and hadith.
Ijtihad would be necessary if Muslims were to adapt to the changing circumstances of their society. Al-Tahtawi himself had performed ijtihad in his
reinterpretation of the hadith about beneficial knowledge, in order to
defend the study of the applied sciences he felt were so critical to the material revival of the Muslim community. In al-Tahtawi's written views and in
his use of the term, ijtihad also became more than a method of legal derivation; it became a mechanism for creating social change.

Al-Tahtawi made some of his most influential arguments for a return to
ijtihad in the government-supported journal *Rawdat al-madaris*. In an article published early in the first year of the journal's existence, al-Tahtawi
appealed to the readers on behalf of ijtihad. He wrote that it is a natural goal
of the human being to become educated, and of the educated man to seek
extensive knowledge and some kind of permanent place in collective human
memory. He pointed out that men have throughout history achieved places
in human memory not only by having good morals, but also by acquiring
knowledge: "Being remembered for knowledge is one of the highest perfec-
tions." Extensive knowledge was especially important for an educated man:

> [T]here is nothing more misleading than half a legal theorist, nothing
> more ungrammatical than half a grammarian, nothing more ignorant
> than half a jurist, nothing more deadly than half a physician, and
> nothing more irrational than half a rationalist. The first corrupts reli-
> gions, the second corrupts the language, the third corrupts legal judg-
> ments, the fourth corrupts bodies, and the fifth corrupts legal
> principles.[28]

According to al-Tahtawi, those who performed ijtihad in the past had
always been those with the highest degrees of learning, and for their efforts
they had often earned a place among those who were well remembered for
the extensiveness of their knowledge. The mujtahidun were those who
expended their effort, jahd, in deriving laws from the Qur'an and hadith,

and therefore had always been important to the Muslim community. If they had not done this work, the community would have languished.[29] Thus al-Tahtawi implicitly connected derivation of laws from the Qur'an and Sunna with social growth.

Furthermore, the critics of ijtihad claimed that ijtihad introduced innovations into the faith that were not justified by the Qur'an or hadith. This, he said, was false, because the mujtahidun performed ijtihad exclusively to derive laws regarding things not mentioned in the Qur'an and sunna. According to the Prophet, that which was new was not necessarily harmful, unless God had expressly forbidden it. In the past, mujtahidun had used the Prophet's explanations of the Qur'an much as their own works were used by commoners, as an explanatory supplement. Contemporary mujtahidun would, like their illustrious predecessors, also be guided by the texts of the Prophet's traditions: "Using his word [as guide] we will not inadvertently subvert anything in the Qur'an."[30]

Al-Tahtawi concluded that the Muslim community still needed people to explain and comment upon the religious sources and that it was necessary to revive ijtihad in order to renew religion.[31] Both al-Tahtawi's call for the study of sciences and his revival of ijtihad were tied to the idea that following the ideas of one's predecessors (taqlid and ittiba') would lead to social stagnation. Thus in a book supplement that was attached to the sixth issue of *Rawdat al-madaris,* he criticized the practice of uncritically accepting the interpretations of the Qur'an and hadith that had been made by the first generations of Muslims (the salaf). Not only should ijtihad be revived for the resolution of new problems; it should also be employed in a complete reexamination of accepted interpretations of the religious sources: "[F]or there may be discovered in the words of Prophecy that which would not have occurred to the Companions [of the Prophet]."[32] Al-Tahtawi's twenty-four-page supplement, entitled *al-Qawl al-sadid fi al-ijtihad wa al-tajdid* (Forthright speech on ijtihad and renewal) (1870), appears on the surface to be a carefully worded, mildly argumentative explanation of the opinions of respected legal authorities on the viability of ijtihad and taqlid. However, al-Tahtawi's subtextual argument was that while some 'ulama claimed the gate of ijtihad was closed, the practice of ijtihad had not in fact ceased and would not, therefore, be dangerous to the faith.

Al-Tahtawi followed standard models of scholarly discussion of ijtihad, first explaining how different scholars and madhahib delineated ranks of mujtahidun. He explained that the Shafi'i madhhab recognized only three ranks, while the Hanafis recognized seven ranks. According to al-Tahtawi,

Shafi'i scholars recognized the first-ranked al-mujtahid al-mustaqill or independent mujtahid, which he said was also called the al-mujtahid al-mutlaq,
the absolute or unrestricted mujtahid; the second-ranked al-mujtahid al-
muntasib or al-mujtahid al-madhhab, who was qualified to derive rulings
according to the rules laid down by his madhhab's founder; and the third-
ranked al-mujtahid al-fatwa, who was qualified to perform tarjih, the eval-
uation of the relative accuracy of conflicting madhhab opinions.[33] In failing to distinguish between the independent and unrestricted mujtahidun,
al-Tahtawi was obscuring an important point. Jalal al-Din al-Suyuti
(d. 1505), whose ranking al-Tahtawi was summarizing, clearly distinguished between the independent mujtahidun such as the four founders of
the Sunni law schools, who derived not only novel judgments but also
devised the hermeneutical structures other jurists used to derive judgments,
and the unrestricted mujtahidun such as he himself, who derived novel rulings from the sources within the confines of existing madhhab hermeneutics.[34] Failing to make that distinction would make it easier for al-Tahtawi
to claim that his contemporaries did acknowledge living mujtahidun of the
first rank.

He did acknowledge that al-Subki (1327–1369 CE), who claimed in a
letter to a Syrian leader to be "the undeniable unrestricted mujtahid of the
world," seemed to occupy an intermediate rank between the independent
and madhhab-affiliated mujtahidun, which al-Tahtawi called "al-mujtahid
al-mutlaq al-muntasib." This rank applied to jurists who sometimes applied
the rules of the independent mujtahidun and sometimes transgressed them.
He also said that some jurists behaved as independent mujtahidun on some
issues and as affiliated mujtahidun on others.[35]

Al-Tahtawi also acknowledged that there were muqallidun, practitioners
of taqlid, who had achieved some fame. He was careful to point out that the
issue as to whether ijtihad was still being practiced was far from dead, even
among the Shafi'is. "Some of them said that the first rank independent
mujtahid, who derives rulings from the Book and the Sunna, ceased to exist
after about 300 years, but [Jalal al-Din] al-Suyuti [d. 1505] claimed its continuation until the last days."[36] Also, some scholars claimed that even ijtihad al-fatwa ceased to be practiced after the death of al-Nawawi (d. 1273),
but others contended that Shihab al-Din al-Ramli (d. 1563) and Ibn Hajar
al-Haytami (d. 1566) were more than mere muqallidun. Al-Tahtawi argued
that they used tarjih and in the opinion of some were thus mujtahidun.[37]

Al-Tahtawi then went on to explain and compare the equivalent seven
ranks of the Hanafis: The first rank were the mujtahidun fi shar', those who

had standardized the sources of jurisprudence and developed hermeneutical systems for derivation of laws from the sources.[38] Of these there were only a few, notably the four eponymous founders of the Sunni madhabib. The second rank were the mujtahidun fi al-madhhab, recognized as the followers of Abu Hanifa, the founder of the Hanafi madhhab, who were qualified to derive judgments from the sources according to the rules for derivation that Abu Hanifa had established. These mujtahidun sometimes differed from Abu Hanifa in the conclusions they drew, but they followed his methods of derivation. The third rank were mujtahidun who dealt with matters that had not been discussed by the founder of their madhhab but did not contradict his judgments on other matters. The fourth rank were muqallidun who practiced takhrij, which to al-Tahtawi meant exegesis and verification of sources and dealing with matters on which the accepted judgment had more than one possible interpretation.[39] The fifth rank were muqallidun who practiced tarjih, who were capable of evaluating the relative validity and social benefit of different madhhab opinions. The sixth rank were muqallidun who were able to distinguish between weak and strong judgments. The Ottoman jurist from whom al-Tahtawi was quoting, Ahmad Ibn Kamal Pasha (d. 1533), noted that recent scholars had achieved this sixth rank. The seventh rank were the muqallidun who were incapable of even "distinguishing the fat from the meager," or distinguishing valid opinions from weak ones.[40]

As a Shafi'i scholar in a Hanafi state, al-Tahtawi apparently felt it was sufficient to discuss only Shafi'i and Hanafi rankings of mujtahidun and muqallidun. Al-Tahtawi then took up the question that was central to his argument: Was the current era devoid of mujtahidun? Was the door of ijtihad truly closed? According to the general consensus of the Shafi'i and the Hanafi madhahib, there were no more independent mujtahidun like the four eponym Imams. According to al-Tahtawi, al-Qaffal al-Shashi (d. 947) had issued a fatwa stating that his era was devoid of mujtahidun and that the practice of ijtihad had ceased (hence his nickname, al-Qaffal, one who closes). Al-Ghazali (d. 1111) also stated that there were no more mujtahidun during his lifetime.[41] Some scholars had suggested that one's conclusion on this matter depended on one's definition of a mujtahid, that perhaps there were no more mujtahidun al-qada', mujtahidun who ruled on legal matters of private practice. Al-Tahtawi argued that even by the more stringent definitions, *no* era was devoid of mujtahidun. He cited a number of opinions to support his argument: The Shafi'i scholars al-Qaffal, Shaykh Abu 'Ali al-Za'farani (d. 874), al-Qadi al-Husayn (Abu 'Ali al-Husayn al-Qarabisi, d. 859 or 862), and al-Ustadh Abu Ishaq al-Shirazi (d. 1083) all claimed some rank of ijtihad, implicit in their insistence that they were not following al-Shafiʿi but just happened to agree with his opinions.[42] Al-Shubrawi (Shaykh al-Azhar ʿAbdullah al-Shubrawi, d. 1757) stated that the mujtahid al-madhhab existed in his time but was rare. And al-Suyuti (d. 1505) went so far as to address his book to "those who were ignorant that ijtihad is an obligation in every era," and said further that only al-ijtihad al-mutlaq (unrestricted ijtihad) fulfilled this obligation, and so the gate of ijtihad could never close.[43] In support of this conclusion, al-Suyuti cited a hadith promising Muslims that God would send in every century someone to renew their religion. According to al-Suyuti, the person would undertake renewal of religion through reexamination of the sources of law, that is, through ijtihad. Although al-Suyuti himself made it very clear that he claimed only unrestricted ijtihad within the bounds of Shafiʿi hermeneutics, al-Tahtawi prevaricated, speculating that the kind of renewal of which al-Suyuti spoke was actually independent ijtihad.[44]

Despite al-Tahtawi's cautiousness, his underlying argument was clear: There was no real consensus that the gate of ijtihad was closed; in fact, some scholars had argued that ijtihad was necessary to ensure that the people would continue to reexamine their laws and their beliefs, to ensure that the community would not languish, prevented by received knowledge from opening itself to new ideas, to change, and to progress. Thus al-Tahtawi challenged his contemporaries' assumptions about the cessation of ijtihad, and, while his argument may appear superficially similar to traditional categorical definitions of ijtihad, he had contextualized ijtihad in a subtly different way. In effect, al-Tahtawi opened the accepted juridical definition of ijtihad to a social interpretation. According to al-Tahtawi, ijtihad was more than a methodology for approaching novel legal questions. It was a mechanism by which scholars could legitimize new fields of inquiry, and, like the scientific knowledge that could result from such inquiries, it was a necessary step away from stagnation toward progress.

Sayyid Jamal al-Din al-Afghani: ". . . they must disdain contentedness with taqlid . . ."

In the 1870s, al-Tahtawi's ideas about progress and ijtihad would gain support from another state-supported ʿalim. Sayyid Jamal al-Din al-Afghani was born in Qajar-ruled Persia and traveled widely in the Ottoman Empire and in British colonial India, everywhere teaching that Muslim communal weakness had led to domination by foreigners.[45] He was aware of religious reformers and reform movements in British India whose main ideas were similar to those of al-Tahtawi: Shah Wali Allah (1702–1762), who rejected taqlid and advocated ijtihad in the form of talfiq (juristic license to choose among the rulings of the madhahib), and the Ahl-i Hadith movement, which rejected taqlid and the authority of communal consensus entirely in favor of precedents embodied in hadith. The intellectual tradition of religious reform in India, as well as Shi'i legal traditions in Persia, likely contributed to the development of his own reformist thought, which, though similar to, was independent of al-Tahtawi's.[46]

In 1869 al-Afghani arrived in Egypt for a brief visit and met a few Azhari students. In 1871, Prime Minister Riyad Pasha invited al-Afghani back to do "a bit of teaching at al-Azhar" and persuaded the khedive to support him with a monthly allowance of £E 10 (three to ten times the amount of an Azhari 'alim's allowance). After a misunderstanding with Azhari shaykhs, al-Afghani removed his lectures to his home in Cairo's Khan al-Khalili.[47] Al-Afghani was enormously charismatic and attracted a significant following among the brightest minds in Egypt. Azhari students came regularly to his house for extracurricular nighttime readings in science and political philosophy.[48] In addition, al-Afghani encouraged his students to take up journalism and use his ideas to call people to cultural revival. The 'ulama could not do this, for they were like a "very narrow wick on top of which is a very small flame that neither lights its surroundings nor gives light to others."[49]

A Spirit of Inquiry

Al-Afghani taught that cultural revival required scientific and political revival. The first step would be for Muslims to understand their religion correctly and live according to its teachings. The Qur'an commanded Muslims to seek evidence for their beliefs, and to avoid accepting others' beliefs uncritically. This required a spirit of inquiry. Once they became curious, they would naturally want to explore deeper spiritual matters, which would revitalize them morally. They would then progress to curiosity about scientific matters, knowledge of which could be applied in commercial and military arts. Thus their inquiry would strengthen the community morally, materially, and militarily. They would be better able, therefore, to throw off foreign domination.

Al-Afghani taught that the Protestant Reformation held the secrets of successful revitalization. According to al-Afghani's interpretation of Martin

Luther, Christian European society had declined and lost its vigor because of submission to Church authority. So Luther began a revival based on application of human reason to religious sources.[50] Citing François Guizot, al-Afghani wrote:

> [O]ne of the most significant causes influencing Europe in its path to civilization was the appearance of a sect in this country that said: we have the right to investigate the sources of our beliefs, and demand proof for them. . . . And when this sect gained power and its ideas spread, the minds of the Europeans were freed from the malady of ignorance and stupidity, and they were stimulated into an intellectual circuit and returned to [the study of] scientific subjects and worked hard to acquire the elements of civilization.[51]

Al-Afghani commented often that Islam needed a Martin Luther; some of his associates believed he wanted to serve in that role.[52] He said the Protestant model of advancement was natural for Islam, which was

> almost unique among religions in censuring belief without proof, rebuking those who follow suppositions, reproaching those who act randomly in the darkness of ignorance, and chiding them for their conduct. This religion demands that the pious seek proof [for their beliefs] in the sources of their religion. . . . Its lessons articulate that happiness results from reason and insight, and that wretchedness and error accompany ignorance, neglect of reason, and the snuffing of insight's light.[53]

The true spirit of Islam was "progress and evolution," the assimilation of new ideas, the advancement of culture and civilization.[54] Thus it was a travesty that scholars considered the gate of ijtihad closed—it was antithetical to the true spirit of Islam. Al-Afghani made the following comment during an informal gathering:

> What does it mean that the gate of ijtihad is closed? By what textual authority was it closed? Which Imam said that no Muslim should do ijtihad for the purposes of jurisprudence, or derive guidance from the Qur'an and the sound hadith and struggle to renew and widen his understanding of them, or infer by means of analogy things that accord with the contemporary sciences?[55]

Had the founders of the four madhahib been alive, he claimed, they would still have been performing ijtihad. And because they would have access to new ways of understanding the world, their new interpretations of the sacred texts might be "closer to the truth" than ancient ones.[56] This was precisely the argument that al-Tahtawi made.

Expanding the Franchise of Ijtihad: A New Theory of Juristic Expertise

Al-Afghani went one critical step further. Ijtihad did not have to be restricted to high-ranking jurists. The Qur'an, he said, had been sent down to be understood and interpreted by humans using their own powers of reasoning. Al-Afghani cited the following verses: "'We sent not a messenger except [to teach] in the language of his [own] people, in order to make [things] clear to him' (14:4); 'We have sent it down as an Arabic Qur'an, in order that ye may learn wisdom' (12:2); 'A Book, whereof the verses are explained in detail; a Qur'an in Arabic, for people who understand' (41:3)."[57] Medieval jurists had interpreted these verses as requiring muftis to make legal advice clear to petitioners. But al-Afghani argued that anyone with a reasonable degree of religious learning could interpret the Qur'an, as long as one was sane, had mastered the Arabic language, and was familiar with the sound hadiths, the stories of the Companions, the rulings approved by consensus, and the rulings derived from unambiguous verses of the Qur'an or from analogy. This kind of knowledge was more widely available than it had been in the past, so the franchise of ijtihad could be expanded. This would result in a more informed, more committed, and therefore stronger Muslim community. Al-Afghani's interpretation was a radical departure from the existing theory of juristic expertise, which required memorization of the Qur'an as well as lengthy study of grammar, the sources of law, theology, jurisprudence, and the relevant books of precedents, all received from the lips of someone whose own orally delivered training connected him through the chain of transmitters to the original authors.

The conventional theory of expertise ensured that the franchise of ijtihad belonged to jurists and judges alone. And its focus was not rational inquiry to inspire progress, but exertion of the intellect to ascertain God's will on legal matters. As with al-'Attar and al-Tahtawi, al-Afghani taught that the 'ulama held in abeyance the progress of Islamic countries. Instead of keeping the practice of ijtihad alive, the 'ulama, as conservators of the religious/legal tradition, preferred to accept their forebears' judgments. Out of fear that ijtihad would produce new errors, they preferred to perpetuate old ones.

Al-Afghani, like al-Tahtawi, was subtly redefining taqlid and ijtihad. Whereas taqlid could be defined strictly as a method of adjudication, in which someone who did not have the knowledge and training to interpret religious sources followed the opinion of an authority on legal matters, al-Afghani described it as a violation of Qur'anic commands against blindly following one's forefathers, addressed to ignorant or stubborn pagans who refused to abandon their corrupt ways for the religion of the prophets.[58] This taqlid meant simply "blind imitation" of others' beliefs, and it cast a shadow over juristic taqlid. Furthermore, al-Afghani, like al-Tahtawi, gave the term a social meaning as cause of social stagnation:

> [T]he beliefs of the religion should be the first thing engraven on peo-
> ple's souls, built on solid evidence and sound proofs, so that their
> beliefs do not rest upon the opinions of others. They must disdain
> contentedness with following [taqlid] their forefathers on these mat-
> ters. If a tenet of faith is held in a person's imagination without proof
> and without evidence, he may not be convinced, and will not be a
> believer. Also, the mind of one who accepts beliefs on the basis of sup-
> position becomes accustomed to following suppositions, and he who
> is content to believe as did his forefathers suffers from the same harm
> [as did his forefathers] from foolish notions and divergences of opin-
> ion. The minds of those who follow supposition and are content with
> taqlid are prevented from moving beyond that to which their percep-
> tion is accustomed; they do not follow the schools of thought and
> they do not walk along the paths of thoughtful speculation. If they
> continue like this, ignorance will gradually deceive them. Stupidity
> ties their arms behind their backs so that their minds are prevented
> from performing any rational function at all. They become incapable
> of distinguishing between good and evil, and they are surrounded by
> wretchedness.[59]

Al-Afghani preached the following course of action. First the jurists had to be convinced that the revival of ijtihad would be beneficial for the Islam-ic community. Then the franchise of ijtihad had to be expanded, and ordi-nary Muslims had to be taught to read and understand the sources of their religion themselves, to develop critical acumen, and to form their own opinions. Then ijtihad would be used to reevaluate the sources of religion and reinterpret them in light of contemporary conditions, which would result in gradual adaptation of the legal tradition to the needs and concerns of contemporary Muslims. Moreover, ideally the principle of ijtihad should be applied to all kinds of knowledge, not just to religious sources. Ijtihad came to intimate an attitude toward knowledge itself, an attitude of critical curiosity and individual inquiry. Therefore the term *ijtihad* could be applied to any Muslim's exercise of his critical faculty and scholarship to arrive at an answer to a question, even a scientific question.

The Halqa as Perpetuator of Social Stagnation

Of course, this vision of reform would require alteration of the madrasa's methods of transmitting knowledge. According to al-Afghani and al-Tahtawi, al-Azhar epitomized a system imbued with taqlid. The institution of the halqa encouraged excessive deference to the opinions of instructors, as if the instructors were the ultimate arbiters of truth. Furthermore, some Azharis had fallen into the practice of teaching commentaries (shuruh) upon texts rather than the original texts themselves, or the super-commentaries (hawashi), or the marginal glosses (taqarir) upon the super-commentaries. Al-Afghani considered this indicative of stagnation, although it was in part a legitimate consequence of the need for continuous chains of transmission: One had to read the commentaries as well as the originals to avoid perverting the original author's meaning. Furthermore, these were not necessarily entirely derivative works. Some commentaries explained archaic linguistic terminology—crucial for students to know—used by authors from distant times or places; some were abridgments, or explications of undeveloped ideas in original texts, which in passing through the ideological screening of the commentator often became original works; some were refutations or defenses of doctrines; and some were syntheses of doctrines of different schools or divergent doctrines within a school.[60] For al-Afghani, the social functions served by these types of writings were irrelevant. The knowledge students needed resided in the original texts. Chains of transmitted interpretation led students away from the meanings contained within the written originals, and the interpretations became the object of knowledge to be memorized and reproduced. Students did not learn to apprehend on their own the meaning of the originals. Thus was the practice of taqlid entrenched in the minds of students, and thus were their critical faculties weakened.[61]

Al-Afghani attracted a large number of followers from among Azhari and civil school students. Many of his followers took his advice and became politicians or journalists. Some, like al-Afghani himself, became pan-Islamists who sought to strengthen and unify the worldwide Muslim community in order to enable Muslims to throw off Europe's yoke. Some were Christians, Jews, and secular nationalists who were less interested in Muslim unity than in strengthening the Arab or Egyptian nations. Some accepted European influences.[62] However, most were inspired by al-Afghani's activism and his belief that a critical approach to knowledge and acquisition of contemporary sciences were the keys to progress.

Shaykh Muhammad 'Abduh: "They are actually among the most destructive of fools."

The 1870s were the boom years of Arabic journalism, and along with progress-minded Christians from Syria, al-Afghani's students soon dominated the Egyptian presses.[63] Al-Afghani's followers aimed to convince the people that educational reform and science were beneficial and ignorance was dangerous. Almost universally, they blamed ignorance for social stagnation and portrayed science as the chief cause of European progress and an absolute requirement for Egyptian and Muslim advancement.

For example, al-Afghani's student Muhammad 'Abduh argued against taqlid while he was still a student at al-Azhar.[64] He wrote a journal article describing some Azhari students who discovered to their shock that one of their friends was studying dialectical theology (kalam). "What a scandal! They say: How can you study the incorrect sciences, such that you come under suspicion? Refrain, and be satisfied, and be as your father and grandfather were."[65]

His father hurried to the scene, rushed by rumors of his son's danger. 'Abduh asked: "[W]hat was this grave and horrid matter, this offensive, abominable event? . . . [H]is son was learning logic and theology, and ridding himself of the chains of ignorance." The student finally succumbed to pressure from the others and gave up the offending subjects: "[A]nd he closes up the record of his knowledge and spreads his ignorance."[66]

This piece did not represent 'Abduh's mature thought, but rather expressed his personal frustrations with education at al-Azhar. According to 'Abduh, the spiritual danger associated with dialectical theology was such that 'ulama actively discouraged students from pursuing it, suspecting those who did of unbelief. He believed this to be a fault inherent in the Azhari system. When 'Abduh was studying with al-Afghani at his house, someone threw stones through the windows. Al-Afghani's students reported later that they were "denigrated as heretics" and shunned.[67] A related problem,

according to 'Abduh, was that the 'ulama there refused to allow the teaching of logic and contemporary fields of learning, even sciences covered in
texts that Muslims had studied in previous centuries, or which were being
taught in Istanbul. He cited al-Ghazali (d. 1111) and Fakhr al-Din al-Razi
(d. 1209), who had said that these subjects were "duties incumbent on all
individuals" or at the very least incumbent on those who were capable.
'Abduh thought that contemporary learning was especially critical at this
time of "intermingling faiths." If Muslims were unable to secure their
beliefs via proofs, they would be "affected by the sayings of heretics, and
refuted by the infidels." Their faith would be shaken, the religion
destroyed.[68]

Furthermore, the new fields of learning were essential to the material
defense of the nation against the aggression of the militarized nations of
Europe, whom 'Abduh colorfully described as "voracious lions" inhabiting
a barren desert in which Egypt, their next meal, was stranded. If the 'ulama
would only look to the example of their more powerful neighbors, they
would see that the new fields of study were the source of that power. Egyptians would have to acquire them as fast as possible, lest the Europeans over-
whelm them. The time had come, 'Abduh declared, when slingshots and
arrows no longer sufficed for national defense: They needed bayonets, guns,
and armored ships. And these things could not be exchanged for handicrafts
such as Egypt was then producing; Egyptians would have to learn to build
them themselves.

Yet military strength alone was not sufficient. 'Abduh recognized that
real power lay in "abundance of ideas and knowledge," in the power of
intellectual hegemony. A nation with that power "overrides other nations.
Have they not seen that great strength means nothing these days? Do they
not know by what means our neighbors have reached the highest level of
greatness?. . . If they are aware of all this, should they not recognize that
unless they support the army of knowledge, they will be in danger? . . . They
do not know."[69]

Thus, by refusing to teach what even the greatest Islamic thinkers had
legitimized, al-Azhar's 'ulama were endangering the Islamic community.
The pivotal point of 'Abduh's argument in this article, and in most of his
writings on education thereafter, echoed al-Afghani and al-Tahtawi: The
'ulama must be in the vanguard of the acquisition of sciences. They had
moral influence over the masses, they could "crowd the mosques with their
preachers and their sermons and encourage and incite the people to learn
what they need to protect their religion." It was their responsibility "to

delineate for [the people] good and evil" and make clear that "knowledge is good and ignorance harmful to the soul and the body."[70]

But 'Abduh despaired of ever convincing the other 'ulama:

> We would rather put our fingers in our ears when [the new sciences] are mentioned and run for our lives as if the skies were falling! . . . [T]he matter among us is widespread and famous, especially among the noble factions [the muqallidun of al-Azhar] who are considered the very spirit of this nation. Indeed, even to this day they do not look at us with a merciful eye, nor do they see that these useful subjects will reflect on them and on the sons of their community with advantage, but rather they work with what might have been suitable for an age whose stars have fallen and whose pages have turned and whose horse has fled, not noticing that we have become a new creation.[71]

'Abduh soon turned to al-Afghani's lay ijtihad as the solution: "Anyone who can read can learn the principles of the discursive fields of knowledge from books."[72] For 'Abduh too, the meaning of a text was inherently present in its written form. Thus his campaign soon came to have an element within it that challenged, more explicitly than al-Afghani or al-Tahtawi had, the authority of the 'ulama.

From 1880 to 1882, 'Abduh served as editor in chief of the government journal *al-Waqa'i' al-Misriyya*. As such, he was also head of the government department of publications, had the power to censure or even close down any journal published in Egypt, and could exercise considerable influence over the quality and content of existing papers.[73] He used his power, demanding a high standard of clarity and style at *al-Waqa'i' al-Misriyya*, in keeping with the understanding of language promoted by al-Tahtawi, and he tried to impose that standard on all other periodicals. 'Abduh himself volunteered to serve as an instructor in a night school for journalists whose writing did not meet his standards. At one point he warned an errant journal that it "must provide a more competent editorial staff or be suppressed." 'Abduh became a major reformer of Arabic writing.[74]

Under his leadership, educational reform became one of the journal's chief concerns. 'Abduh had begun to develop a comprehensive agenda of educational reform, based on a concept of societal progress (tamaddun) that was in many ways the equivalent of the nineteenth-century European concept of civilization. 'Abduh first outlined tamaddun in 1881: "It is the sum of all kinds of perfection, without exception, whether literary, material, sensual, or metaphysical. Excelling in the industries is part of it; competing in the sciences is part of it; avoiding areas of deficiency is part of it; and adorning oneself with the most notable moral standards is its essence."[75] Individuals had to acquire these virtues in order that their society progress toward an ideal state.

This element of linear development indicated conceptual change. In Ibn Khaldun's classic study of society, the *Muqaddima*, the ideal social state was hadara, a condition of equilibrium in which proper moral guidance, taxation policies, and provision of justice and security encouraged economic prosperity and cultural florescence. Societies developed on a cyclical model; they rose into states of hadara, were weakened by the resulting luxury and complacence, and fell back out of them into a will-strengthening barbarism.

Because achieving tamaddun required individual moral development based on religious principles, 'Abduh criticized the type of education that the military and civil schools promoted. He was concerned that they might lead to the outright imitation of European customs. 'Abduh was no slave to the West, however. He had a special term for parents who were willing to send their children to foreign schools, where they were taught to disdain their own traditions: muqallidun al-gharb, those who practiced taqlid of the West. Taqlid to him was always unreflective, always damaging; it could not lead to valuable change. Rather, he advocated individual effort to acquire character and virtue, and advocated performance of civic duties. This would of course take a protracted effort, starting with the reform of education.[76]

What was required was a curriculum that supplied both the means of material success and a community identity that would stress the unity of Islam and pride in being Muslim. Like the educational systems of Europe, the purpose of education in Egypt should be production of moral individuals who had internalized civil norms. Individuals would progress from simplistic and false concepts to correct information, and in the process would become "capable of distinguishing between good and bad, harmful and useful," well-mannered, and accustomed to "the rules of human society." It would become second nature for them.[77] But the internalized norms would be those of Islamic morality.

The 'ulama of al-Azhar were still 'Abduh's foil: The public recognized that many of them were distinguished, capable scholars, but there were also "others who are habituated to the ancient methods and are accustomed to them, who are not able, even after a lengthy time, to depart from them."

Some could not apply their knowledge practically. Some were unable to teach effectively or use their knowledge, "and the students make fun of them and do not respect their professors."[78] Being habituated to ancient methods was to 'Abduh just another form of taqlid, which was causing a public loss of confidence in the 'ulama as trustworthy repositories of religious knowledge. But 'Abduh's own experience at al-Azhar also colored this assertion. 'Abduh's students would later report: "[G]enerally speaking, ['Abduh] hated the method of instruction at al-Azhar. He used to speak of its shortcomings and moan about the students' working with . . . explanation of expressions and useless things with which the students' hours were filled."[79]

If the 'ulama would not change on their own, the state—as the primary agent of progress—would have to circumvent them. In 1880, 'Abduh suggested that Khedive Isma'il include religious instruction in the civil schools, echoing al-Tahtawi's earlier inclusion of fiqh in the School of Languages and Accounting. The Ministry of Education would still have to supervise closely, "that they not be stuffed with the types of delusions that are contrary to the truth of religion, as is common among many teachers who appear to be 'ulama, whereas they are actually among the most destructive of fools."[80] Civil-school teachers, having been trained by 'ulama, might also perpetuate the taqlid mentality of the past. Ministry supervision of teachers would cull out teachers who were unprepared for the new methods of teaching or who were morally unfit to undertake the education of young children, perhaps by examinations.[81]

One area that needed attention, for example, was textbook writing. The writing style was not conducive to learning, and "[did] not agree with the method of instruction in the [civil] schools."[82] The students in the civil schools followed the European method of dividing class time into regular segments, such as an hour, so that several different subjects could be taught in a relatively short time. The textbooks, however, had been written with the intent that students study a single text for an extended period of time, perhaps a year or two, as was common in the halqa system. Appropriate texts would be clear, and not require explication.[83]

Furthermore, the ministry should see that Egyptians had to come to accept, as had the Europeans, that progress required openness to new ideas, and even more importantly, the ability to innovate, to invent. This openness was best learned in a European-model school system.[84]

Thus 'Abduh, in his influential position as chief editor of *al-Waqa'i' al-Misriyya*, helped to popularize the reformers' depictions of al-Azhar 'ulama

as traditionalists bound to taqlid and therefore to social stagnation. Furthermore, he went beyond them in advocating state intervention, by holding
the state out as an agent of positive change in lieu of action by the 'ulama
themselves.

In recognition of his concern for reform, in 1881 Minister Riyad Pasha
appointed 'Abduh as chair of a newly created executive council within the
Department of Education, charged to review government educational policy for the civil and foreign schools.[85] His work there, however, was cut
short by the British occupation and his temporary exile.

Al-Afghani's Nationalist Disciples: "O Azharis, it is not suitable for you to limit yourselves."

During the period between Isma'il's accession to the throne in 1863 and the
British occupation in 1882, thirty-three new Arabic periodicals opened in
Egypt. Only one of these was a "news" paper: *al-Ahram*. The rest were
mainly political journals. Followers of al-Afghani dominated the premier
periodicals of the period, including Adib Ishaq, who founded *Misr* [Egypt]
with Salim al-Naqqash in 1877; then *al-Tijara* [Commerce] in 1878 after
Misr was banned; then *Misr al-fatah* [Young Egypt], the organ of the eclec-
tic organization by the same name, in 1879; and then, from Parisian exile
until 1880, *Misr al-qahira* [Egypt the victorious]. Ya'qub Sanu' founded
Abu Naddara [The man with the spectacles] and its enormously popular
colloquial version, *Abu Naddara zarqa'* [The man with the blue spectacles]
in 1877; Mikha'il 'Abd al-Sayyid, a Coptic Christian, founded his sectarian
protest journal *al-Watan* [The homeland] in 1877; Ibrahim al-Laqqani
edited the Cairo semi-weekly *Mir'at al-sharq* [Mirror of the East] from
1879 on; and Ibrahim al-Muwailihi founded *Misbah al-sharq* [Lantern of
the East].[86]

These journalists were young Syrian and Egyptian men who protested
the excesses of the khedival government. Like their mentor, al-Afghani, they
were concerned about resisting the power of Europe and about Egypt's
financial situation. To their minds, Khedive Isma'il had not proven himself
to be fiscally responsible; only a year after he had come to the throne,
Egypt's foreign debt had doubled. In 1876, Isma'il accepted the Goschen-
Joubert arrangement, under which Egypt's total debt was estimated at
£E 89.3 million with an annual charge of £E 6 million. This included the
acceptance of two British and French controllers-general and a Commission
de la Dette Publique, whose purpose was to collect revenues and ensure that
Isma'il's creditors got their money. In February of 1879, there were demon-

strations, especially among the military.[87] Later that year, al-Hizb al-Watani [the Homeland or Nationalist Party] and other opposition groups declared their official existence.[88] Finally, on 25 June 1879, the Ottoman sultan, 'Abdulhamid II, acceded to foreign pressures to depose Isma'il and put Isma'il's son, Tawfiq, on the throne.

Tawfiq had not been the most popular candidate for the throne, and his legitimacy suffered from the outset because of his reliance on the British and French controllers who had helped to engineer his accession. Tawfiq moved to protect his authority against potential opposition leaders, and sent former allies Muhammad 'Abduh and Jamal al-Din al-Afghani into exile. 'Abduh was sent back to his home village for a few months, and al-Afghani left Egypt. But the debt remained—now estimated at 98.4 million pounds sterling—and in order to meet the annual charges, unpopular taxes were enforced.[89]

Opposition to Tawfiq now evolved into a constitutional revolution under the leadership of Ahmad 'Urabi, an Egyptian army colonel. The collaborationist minister, Nubar Pasha, was followed by Riyad Pasha as prime minister and Rifqi Pasha as war minister, whose policies of discrimination against native Egyptians in army promotions provoked native officers to rebel. Colonel Ahmad 'Urabi led a cadre of native officers against Riyad Pasha's restrictions on promotion of Arabic-speakers and succeeded in forcing Tawfiq to appoint a new ministry. The 'Urabi Revolt, as this revolution came to be called, resulted in a brief period of constitutional rule in 1881 and 1882, with Mahmud Sami as prime minister and Ahmad 'Urabi as war minister. However, 'Abdulhamid II, the Ottoman sultan, feared that the 'Urabists would mount a separatist movement, and, having lost Ottoman territories in Europe in 1878, the sultan was not willing to risk the loss of Egypt as well. European journalists frothed with speculation that the 'Urabist government might repudiate the debt, and Sultan 'Abdulhamid feared that this might provoke a British or French invasion.[90]

Throughout 1881 and 1882, as the sultan struggled to preserve Ottoman sovereignty over Egypt and prevent European intervention, journalists of al-Afghani's circle put forth several short-lived polemical periodicals.[91] Some were openly anti-European and opposed to the meddling of Europeans in Egypt's affairs; others opposed autocratic government. Whenever they wrote of educational reform, it was always with an eye to nationalist or communitarian propaganda. Education had to include modern subjects, and the purpose of education was to make the community stronger. Thus those who served the cause of reform served the nation. This new turn in the history of educational reform, in which criticism of the madaris became tinged with the imagery of nationalism, was another aspect of conceptual hybridization.

The first Egyptian nationalist party, al-Hizb al-Watani, may not have been nationalist in the twentieth-century liberal nationalist sense. The nationalists of the pre-British period were rarely secularists, and many did not conceive of their nation in specifically territorial or ethnic terms. Thus there are difficulties in translating the Arabic term *watani* as either "nationalist" or "patriot." These journalists nevertheless saw themselves as part of a coherent community defined by a common bond and shared interests. For most, the "nation" that had to be defended from imperial encroachment was either the community of Muslims (umma, milla, or millet) or the homeland (watan), which could mean anything from the local region to a broadly defined non-European community. In most cases, nationalist rhetoric was an expression of anti-khedive or anti-European sentiment, but not a desire to separate from Ottoman sovereignty. To some extent this was submerged in Egyptian-Arab communal memory, underneath Salim al-Naqqash's slogan "Egypt for the Egyptians!"[92] Although the rhetoric of nationalism was new, one can see in it threads of continuity with al-Tahtawi's and al-Afghani's arguments for madrasa reform, in particular the need to strengthen the community, however defined. And there is another similarity: Implicit in journalistic critiques of the madaris from the period between 1879 and 1882 was the argument against taqlid.

In August 1881, the nationalist journal *al-Tankit wa al-tabkit* published an article by one of its editors, Ahmad Effendi Samir. Ahmad Samir related how he had graduated from al-Azhar but found that the subjects offered there had not satisfied his curiosity. He had supplemented his studies by reading about history, geography, and politics, and came to believe that, if other Azharis did so as well, "their nations would obtain a universal advantage. . . . When I graduated from al-Azhar, I was not prepared (with the subjects I had learned there) [to do anything more than] understand what I saw inscribed on the pages of the books.[93]

According to Ahmad Samir, the deficiencies of 'ulama training were due to the belief that "man qallada 'alim^{an} laqa Allah salim^{an}"—that whoever follows the opinion of an 'alim (practices taqlid) would not make grievous errors in interpreting religion and would thus "meet God safely." Implicit in Ahmad Samir's argument is the idea that overcoming the taqlid mentality was necessary for advancement. This is implicit also in his plea to Azhari 'ulama:

[The number of students] attending Azhar in 1295 [1878 AD] (the year I graduated) reached over twelve thousand. If it were assumed that for every ten of them, one complied with my request, we would see more than a thousand people serving their nation, [a nation] that will not arise from this decline to the height of progress except through them. There is no nation without men, no men without learning, and no learning without assistance. And thus, O Azharis, it is not suitable for you, you being the spirit of the country, to limit yourselves to the subjects in which you specialize.[94]

The 'ulama were blocking the production of citizens, denizens of the modern nation. No longer was the expansion of knowledge into new realms imposed on the 'ulama simply by the precepts of their religion, as it was for al-Tahtawi and al-Afghani. Religious obligations and national needs were now one and the same.

'Abdullah Nadim, another Azhar-trained associate of al-Afghani, owned and co-edited the journal in which Ahmad Samir wrote.[95] He had been a writer for several of the pioneering journals owned by the Syrians Adib Ishaq and Salim al-Naqqash, and an editor of *Misr al-fatat* [Young Egypt] in the 1870s, and he had gone on to establish his own journals. In 1881 'Abdullah Nadim and Ahmad Samir established *al-Tankit wa al-tabkit* [Banter and blame], which became known for its abrasive nationalist polemics, along with Nadim's more strident nationalist paper, *al-Ta'if* [The wanderer].[96] In the months before the British occupation, Nadim had even been hailed as "the orator of al-Hizb al-Watani." On the eve of the 'Urabi Revolt, 'Abdullah Nadim entered al-Azhar and lectured the 'ulama on the necessity of supporting al-Hizb al-Watani's cause. One might think, given the reformers' depiction of the 'ulama, that they would have eschewed involvement in politics and remained reading their texts, dustily unaware, at their columns. In fact, all but two of the 'ulama did support al-Hizb al-Watani.[97]

'Abdullah Nadim was concerned about the condition and administration of the madaris. In one article, he condemned the conditions at the Ahma-di Madrasa in Tanta. 'Ulama remunerations at the mosque were too low, which forced the 'ulama to spend part of their time earning a living. Hence they could not devote themselves full time to learning and teaching, and the educations of their students suffered.[98]

Still, 'Abdullah Nadim, like Ahmad Samir, argued that the 'ulama also had to change. Like al-Tahtawi and 'Abduh, 'Abdullah Nadim suggested that the ranks of the 'ulama had been polluted by poseurs whose claims to be educated gave credence to the ignorance and disinformation they spread among the people. In *al-Tankit wa al-tabkit,* Nadim told the story of Shaykh Zifti, a shaykh who tormented him with a letter-writing campaign opposing the spread of civil education in Egypt. (Shaykh Zifti may have been a fictional rhetorical foil. The name that Nadim gave the shaykh, Zifti, is from the word *zift,* or "pitch," and connotes something unpleasant. In colloquial Egyptian, a person who is a zift is a zero, a deadbeat.) Nadim related that he had been traveling through the countryside, talking to people about the importance of sending their sons to school. Upon returning from his travels, he found that Shaykh Zifti had sent him several letters. The shaykh stated that "the schools are a recent development and every recent development is an innovation [bid'a] and every innovation is an error and every error is of Hell." Nadim argued that these attitudes frightened people away from the schools and encouraged them to think that the schools "cause[d] deviation from doctrine and corruption of the morals." [99]

Nadim then wrote back to Shaykh Zifti and asked him where he had been educated, and Zifti replied that he had attended some lectures at al-Azhar but read only the Qur'an. Men such as Zifti were more than merely ignorant; they were selfish too, concerned only with their prestige. A few lectures at al-Azhar did not confer learning, yet Zifti represented himself as an educated man. Nadim asserted that "this idiot" was "ignorant of his own capabilities and human meaning and limited to self-love." Shaykh Zifti's selfishness injured not only those boys whose education he prevented, but also the nation (al-watan). The nation needed educated men; thus it was important that the people send their sons to school. The influence of ignorant shaykhs, and by implication, the lack of formal registration at al-Azhar to winnow out dilettantes like Zifti, therefore constituted an obstacle to national advancement. [100]

Conclusion

The modernist 'ulama, bureaucratic reformers, and journalists, despite their diverse backgrounds and political orientations, shared a common thread of critique that hybridized European concepts of progress with Sunni Muslim legal terminology and communal identity. Al-Tahtawi and al-Afghani redefined the juridical practice of taqlid as a cause of social stagnation and broadened juridical ijtihad to mean an individualistic spirit of inquiry into all fields of knowledge. They then linked taqlid to the pedagogical methods of the madaris, and those methods and the 'ulama defending them to Egypt's weakness relative to Europe. Their students (most notably Muhammad ʿAbduh), who dominated the emerging periodical presses, then folded these ideas into a discourse on the relationship between education and the community as nation, in which European nations were the primary models.

The key to understanding why so many journalists blamed the ʿulama for the plight of the Islamic world was a similarity among these journalists' conceptions of progress. Many journalists wrote that the rapid progress that characterized Europe in modern times had occurred in Europe because of two factors: First, European "ʿulama," unlike Muslim ʿulama, had not considered themselves educated [ʿalim] if they had mastered only one subject. Unlike Muslim ʿulama who tended to specialize in a particular field of study, Europeans read as much as they could on as many subjects as possible. Furthermore, they wrote books and articles in periodicals in order to make the fruits of their labors available to other scholars and to the literate public. Second, European rulers supported their ʿulama and the spread of scientific learning by establishing and funding scientific societies, schools, and public libraries that everyone, "even peasant farmers," could use. Thus the learning of the European ʿulama was spread to the people, via printing, and the spread of learning to the people inflamed their curiosity about the world, and they began to investigate and invent, and to produce things like electricity, improved firearms, the telegraph, the telephone, and the railroad train.[101]

According to these journalists, progress such as occurred in Europe did not occur in Islamic countries because the two key factors, ʿulama willingness and rulers' support, were not present (of course, the journalists were ignoring the fact that al-Tahtawi, al-Afghani, and Muhammad ʿAbduh were also ʿulama). As the 1870s wore on, some journalists saw signs for cheer in the renewed support by rulers for science.[102] However, influential figures like al-Tahtawi, al-Afghani, Muhammad ʿAbduh, ʿAbdullah Nadim, and Ahmad Samir promoted the idea that, despite the best efforts of the journalists to encourage curiosity about scientific matters, the ʿulama still were dragging their feet, refusing to read newspapers, to study anything outside their own subjects, to become curious about science, to abandon the chains of taqlid that bound them to the past.[103] Thus these journalists made the ʿulama appear to be the cause of continued stagnation. Even worse, since the ʿulama were still responsible for most of higher education in Egypt, journalists feared that the ʿulama would pass their hermitic scholasticism on to their students, thus perpetuating ʿulama "ignorance" and Egypt's social stagnation.

The call to revive ijtihad itself was not new, having been used previously by al-Suyuti, al-Subki, and other reformers. However, ijtihad had previously been understood in the context of legal methodology, and it was not
viewed explicitly as a mechanism of legal or social change. From the late
nineteenth century on, due to efforts of reformers like al-Tahtawi and al-
Afghani, ijtihad was perceived and used explicitly as a mechanism of legal
and social change.[104] Moreover, these reformers chose to characterize ijtihad as having been a mechanism of social change in order to justify their
arguments as to what it should be. Thus their students selected out and perpetuated a specific tradition of ijtihad utilization and cessation, transmitting their "history" of 'ulama refusal to engage in ijtihad and the community's subsequent stagnation to journalistic audiences and Orientalists.
Furthermore, the students, convinced that their path to modernity was the
only one possible, could not perceive the problems inherent in social, educational, and legal systems based on the kind of ijtihad they embraced.

Egypt had indeed become a new creation. In the interstices between the
myths of empire that structured its past and resistance to an occupation that
had not yet happened, reformers were performing a new narrative of
nationhood—and in that performance, taqlid, the halqa, and the 'ulama of
al-Azhar were cast as the antagonists.

5

A CONSERVATIVE DEFENSE OF TAQLID

Most historians of al-Azhar and of the Islamic modernist movement assumed that the practitioners of taqlid made no attempt at defending it in written form. The fatwas of Shaykh Muhammad 'Ilish, chief Mufti of the Maliki legal school in Egypt from 1854 to 1882, disprove this.[1] 'Ilish, whose works historians have largely ignored, stridently opposed attempts to redefine and widen the scope of ijtihad. However, he cannot be simply categorized as an opponent of reform, because he became a colleague-in-arms with the reformers during the 'Urabi Revolt. This suggests that conservatives shared reformers' objections to foreign control.

Shaykh Muhammad 'Ilish spent the first nine years of his career in poverty despite his high office. His financial condition improved in 1863, when Khedive Isma'il increased his annual income from 800 to 1,500 piasters, and again in 1871, when the khedive gifted him with 100 feddans of land.[2] Between 1870 and 1882, Shaykh 'Ilish became one of the most powerful 'ulama in Egypt. The Shafi'i chief Mufti's position was vacant, so the Maliki Mufti became the sole voice balancing the state-supported Hanafi domination of al-Azhar. Furthermore, Shaykh 'Ilish earned public respect by his uncompromising reverence for the Imams, founders of the Sunni madhahib. 'Ali Mubarak, an outspoken critic of al-Azhar, remembered 'Ilish as a jurist whose ideas about personal piety and respect for the Islamic legal tradition had a profound effect on his generation; he even named 'Ilish "the mujaddid of this century," the paramount "renewer" of his age:[3]

> He has a majesty that terrifies the black-hearted one, and [his] lectures curdle the blood. . . . It is probable that he never, from his childhood to his old age, missed the Friday prayers. . . . Truly, he has overcome

those loathsome things with which Paradise is encircled. Out of his respect for God, upon entering a mosque, he puts his sandals into a bag, fearing that he might defile the mosque. . . . He never drinks coffee and will not bear even the scent of smoke; he never wears expensive clothing nor anything made of silk, and he avoids the tassel of the tarboush and stays away from kings, princes, and their ilk.[4]

Shaykh 'Ilish was also an extremely popular teacher; his lectures were regularly attended by audiences of over 200 students.[5] He could be rather cantankerous as well: His own writings reveal his intellectual arrogance and conviction that his madhhab's interpretations of the sources of law were better than those of the other madhahib. However, 'Ilish's arrogance was not especially unusual among leading Azhari 'ulama. 'Ilish's predecessor as Maliki Mufti, Mustafa al-Bulaqi, once denounced another 'alim because of an intellectual disagreement, and issued a fatwa calling the other shaykh an "idiot," who had "dishonored himself by demonstrating the intensity of his ignorance, his mis-memorization, and the superficiality of his intellect."[6] The reformist journalist Muhammad 'Abduh, who would later be elevated to high office himself, sometimes behaved just as arrogantly, accusing his opponents of ignorance and stubborn preference for the old ways.[7]

In July of 1854, Shaykh 'Ilish was appointed chief Mufti of the Maliki madhhab.[8] The 1850s had seen disturbances among the Maghribis, the largest and poorest student community at al-Azhar. Most Maghribis were adherents of the Maliki madhhab, as were the Sa'idis, the second largest community. It may have been hoped that Shaykh 'Ilish, as Maliki Mufti, would be able to put the fear of God into the rowdy Maliki students. By the 1880s, 'Ilish was one of the premier leaders of Egyptian scholarly society.

During the autumn of 1881, as opposition to Khedive Tawfiq's regime was approaching the boiling point, Azharis began to raise questions about the fitness for office of Hanafi Shaykh al-Azhar Muhammad al-'Abbasi al-Mahdi. Up to the time of Muhammad 'Ali, Azharis had elected their own leaders, subject to approval by those who held temporal power. According to the British observer Blunt, "[A]s a nominee of the khedive, [Shaykh al-'Abbasi] could not be relied on to give an honest *fetwa* . . . as to the legality of constitutional government." Azharis apparently believed that al-'Abbasi would rule against constitutional government—or had done so already—and permit Tawfiq to escape fulfilling promises he had made to reformers.[9]

On 5 December 1881, the students of al-Azhar voted to depose Shaykh al-'Abbasi and raise 'Ilish to the office of Shaykh al-Azhar. The khedive formed a commission to look into the matter. The commission found that Shaykh al-'Abbasi had done no wrong, so the khedive refused to recognize 'Ilish as Shaykh al-Azhar. Eventually they compromised: Al-'Abbasi was removed from his post at al-Azhar but remained Grand Mufti, and the khedive appointed a candidate from the Shafi'i madhhab, Shaykh Muhammad al-Inbabi, to head al-Azhar. Shaykh al-Inbabi, however, was weak and hampered by his lack of popular support among the Azharis. As Blunt's informer reported, "El Embabeh [al-Inbabi] had not been the most popular candidate, for the majority of the students had been for the Malekite el Aleysh ['Ilish], a man of high courage and religious authority. . . . Embabeh, a man altogether his inferior, obtained the vote only as the result of a compromise, the khedive having refused el Aleysh. Four thousand students voted at this election and there were only 25 dissentients."[10] Other British observers believed that al-Inbabi had been chosen because he was a Shafi'i, "like most Egyptians,"[11] but his appointment was probably also to mollify the disgruntled Shafi'is and prevent 'Ilish from gaining too much power. To further cement the compromise, the khedive established an administrative council that included seats for the heads of each madhhab; he appointed 'Ilish to the seat for the Maliki madhhab.[12]

This was a tumultuous time in Egyptian history. The Egyptians were embroiled in the constitutionalist 'Urabi Revolt, which had significant support from Westernized and religious leaders, as well as the military. For the first time Egyptians had an elected legislature, and as the story of 'Ilish's election suggests, even the students of al-Azhar had adopted democratic practices. Khedive Tawfiq had been forced to appoint the nominal leader of this movement, Colonel Ahmad 'Urabi, to his cabinet. Yet the country's finances were still held hostage for repayment of Egypt's debt to French and British creditors. These creditors were worried that Egypt's constitutionalists might repudiate the debt. Therefore, on 25 May 1882, Anglo-French naval commanders in Alexandria bay issued an ultimatum demanding dismissal of the constitutionalist cabinet and 'Urabi's exile.[13]

Khedive Tawfiq wanted to submit, knowing that it would restore his authority over the constitutionalist 'Urabists. He called a meeting on 26 May to explain his position, inviting military officers and 'ulama. Shaykh 'Ilish was among those attending. At the meeting, Tawfiq said he would not replace the ministers (who had already resigned in protest). One of the officers present protested that the British and French had no right to intervene, and that the army supported 'Urabi and would not follow anyone else. He and the other 'Urabist officers then abruptly left the meeting. Shaykh 'Ilish took the khedive to task, accusing him of responsibility for the presence of the Anglo-French fleet. Tawfiq reinstated the 'Urabist cabinet the next day and fled to Alexandria. 'Ilish then sent a telegram to the Sultan denouncing the khedive's attitude.[14]

By early June, 'Ilish and other leading 'ulama composed a fatwa, the import of which became widely known:

> Now Sheykh Aleysh, the great holy man of the Azhar, has issued a *fetwa* in which the present khedive, having attempted to sell his country to the foreigners by following the advice of the European consuls, is no more worthy of ruling over the Moslems of Egypt. He must therefore be deposed. All the Sheykhs of the Azhar, who consider Sheykh Aleysh as their spiritual head, have accepted the *fetwa*. . . . Sheykh Mohammed Khodeyr of the Azhar went with twenty-two Notables to meet Darwish Pasha [the Ottoman negotiator sent by the Sultan to resolve the dispute with the 'Urabists], and presented him with a petition signed by 10,000 persons in which they requested him to reject the proposals of the Powers and depose the khedive. . . . Embabeh (Sheykh el Islam), being afraid of both the khedive and the National Party, keeps aloof, and avoids politics under plea of ill-health.

Alone among the 'ulama elders, only the Hanafi Mufti Muhammad al-'Abbasi refused to sign the fatwa.[15]

In July, Khedive Tawfiq sought refuge on the British ships blockading the port of Alexandria, making it manifestly clear that he had accepted foreign help in restoring his power. Religious and civilian leaders met on 17 July in Cairo in a people's assembly (majlis al-'urfi), to rule the country in the absence of the khedive. Their council included the Chief Qadi 'Abd al-Rahman Nafid, the Hanafi Grand Mufti Muhammad al-'Abbasi, the Shaykh al-Azhar al-Inbabi, four khedival princes, the Coptic patriarch, the chief rabbi, leading merchants, some provincial notables, the technocrat 'Ali Mubarak, the journalist Muhammad 'Abduh (who served as secretary), Shaykh Hasan al-'Idwi, and the other leading muftis, including Shaykh 'Ilish. An acrimonious discussion ensued, in which 'Abduh and al-'Idwi called for deposition of the khedive, and 'Ilish suggested proclaiming jihad against the invaders. At a subsequent council meeting on 29 July, they resolved that the khedive was no longer legally in command of Egypt, that he was a traitor to Islam, that his decrees were invalid as long as he remained in British hands, and that 'Urabi was responsible for the defense of the country.[16]

This council ran an efficient administration. They continued to collect taxes, ran a balanced budget, and had four months of army provisions in reserve when the British took over. Also, in keeping with fatwas issued by Azhari 'ulama in previous months against persecution of non-Muslims, there were no massacres of Christians during this period.[17] But Shaykh 'Ilish did make use of this period of council rule to wage a campaign against what he saw as symbols of European immorality in Cairo. In September, Shaykh 'Ilish led a group of 'Urabists in removing an equestrian statue of Ibrahim Pasha from the Ezbekiyya district and four statues of lions from the Qasr al-Nil bridge on the edge of the Isma'iliyya district. These two districts represented the worldly sins of the khedival regime: The garden district of Ezbekiyya housed foreign consulates and businesses, bars, and hotels; and Isma'iliyya had been constructed as part of Isma'il's efforts to remake Cairo in the architectural image of Paris. Isma'il had erected the statues despite some public disapproval in the early 1870s. In late August, 'Urabists showed their disapproval of the regime's pro-Western cultural policies. They requested fatwas from all four madhahib, including one from the khedive's supporter Muhammad al-'Abbasi. Shaykh al-'Abbasi ruled that the statues were "reprehensible representations of beings with souls," equated them with the idols cleansed from the Ka'ba by the early Muslims in 630 CE, and said that the people had an obligation to remove them if the ruler did not.[18]

Shaykh 'Ilish's leadership in the attack on the statues helps to explain why he supported the 'Urabi nationalists. We do not know whether 'Ilish supported constitutional government in principle, but it appears that he did oppose the khedive's dealings with the Europeans and the Westernized modernity the khedive imagined for Egypt.

That is the Shaykh 'Ilish depicted in most historical sources. However, Shaykh 'Ilish the nationalist hero cannot be found in sources by reformers of al-Afghani's party. To them, he was a fire-breathing puritanical reactionary who was "zealous in his protection of religion, sharp-tempered, and quick to anger," an untiring opponent of educational reform. Muhammad 'Abduh considered 'Ilish one of his chief opponents, even though both were leading participants in the 'Urabi Revolt. For example, in the incident recounted in this book's introduction, 'Ilish publicly shamed 'Abduh while 'Abduh was still a student at al-Azhar.[19] 'Abduh had begun to hold classes with other students in which they read and discussed books not taught at al-Azhar. These books were difficult, and the students sometimes stayed up all night arguing about a book's meaning. Word of these meetings reached Shaykh 'Ilish, who sent his son to attend one of the classes. His son reported back that someone was teaching the commentary of al-Taftazani (d. 1389), the *Sharh al-aqa'id al-nasafiyya,* on the doctrines of al-Nasafi (d. 1142). The teacher had in his lesson on the previous day preferred the Mu'tazili school of theology over the accepted Ash'ari school. According to Rashid Rida, 'Abduh's student and protégé:

> Shaykh 'Ilish (may God have mercy on him) used to believe every-thing he heard . . . and it was too much for him that a student would read [with students] a book like that, which not even the eldest shaykhs were permitted to read. So ['Ilish] sent to ['Abduh] and ['Abduh] came to him while he was teaching his lesson in the Husayni mosque. Shaykh 'Ilish said: It has reached me that you are giving lessons on the *Sharh al-aqa'id al-nasafiyya.* He said: Yes. Shaykh 'Ilish said: And it has reached me that you preferred the Mu'tazili school over the Ash'ari school! ['Abduh] said: If I were to abandon Ash'ari taqlid then why would I practice taqlid of the Mu'tazili? Rather I would abandon taqlid altogether and use only the evidence. Shaykh 'Ilish said: I was told that by a trustworthy source. He said: Bring your trustworthy source who testified to that and let him distinguish between the two sects, here in front of us, and let him inform us as to which of them I preferred. Shaykh 'Ilish said: And someone like you can understand the *Sharh al-aqa'id?* He said: The book is at your service, and I am at your service, so question me as you like.[20]

'Abduh's response, "I would abandon taqlid altogether," intimates that 'Abduh, like al-Tahtawi and al-Afghani, associated taqlid with uncritical acceptance of the views of any authority, in this case, both the convention-ally accepted doctrines of Ash'ari theology and the more suspect doctrines of the Mu'tazilis. If 'Abduh were to abandon taqlid of the Ash'ari school, he would do so out of conviction that his own ijtihad was more trustworthy. If he had indeed valued an argument of the Mu'tazilis over the Ash'aris (which he did not admit), it would not have been done uncritically. He would have performed what he considered to be a duty enjoined upon him in the Qur'an, and sought evidence for the Mu'tazilis' arguments in the sources of religion. Like al-Tahtawi and al-Afghani, 'Abduh considered taqlid to be embedded in the pedagogical traditions of al-Azhar.

'Abduh's claim to be able to abandon taqlid altogether was rash. The greatest scholars known to the students were those who had not been bound to taqlid: the Sunni Imams and others who had elucidated the methods of jurisprudence. And 'Abduh, a mere student, claimed to match their training and wisdom? Rashid Rida reported that 'Ilish's students found 'Abduh's impertinence in front of the venerable shaykh 'Ilish intolerable; they snatched 'Abduh's turban from his head while others laughed, and 'Abduh departed bareheaded and shamed. Some claimed Shaykh 'Ilish had beaten him with a staff, or that 'Ilish had forbidden him from teaching. This event provoked a tide of rumors about 'Abduh, and about his mentor Jamal al-Din al-Afghani, who encouraged the students to read books not studied at al-Azhar. 'Abduh told Rashid Rida that he had not been banned from teaching, but that because of that incident he had moved his class from the mosque of Muhammad Bey Abu al-Dhahab to his home, and that he kept a cane by his side to defend himself in case 'Ilish came after him with his staff.[21]

'Abduh also accused 'Ilish of trying to sabotage his 'alimiyya exam.[22] 'Abduh's followers reported that he had been given a second-rank pass rather than a first-degree pass as a result of 'Abduh's dispute with 'Ilish, and that he would not have been allowed to pass at all had the Shaykh al-Azhar al-'Abbasi not intervened:

> [T]he shaykhs bore down on him until his examination became a dispute rather than a test. Some of them had sworn to divorce their wives if he received a score sufficient to allow him to teach. But Shaykh al-'Abbasi said that no one had been examined in that manner since he had become Shaykh al-Azhar, and he asked that ['Abduh] be given a first-rank pass. Then one of the shaykhs arose and wrote out for him a second-rank pass, sealed it, and affixed the seals of the other shaykhs. Shaykh [al-'Abbasi] accepted this unwillingly.[23]

Twenty-six years later, al-Azhar awarded 'Abduh an honorary first-rank pass.[24]

From a certain perspective, 'Ilish was not out of line. 'Abduh received his training at al-Azhar as a Maliki jurist, and it was therefore putatively 'Ilish's responsibility to rein 'Abduh in, to ensure he was not teaching books that were beyond his ability to understand and that he would adhere to the underlying principles of the madhhab in which he was being trained. It was also his responsibility to teach 'Abduh the etiquette of academic life.[25] Ironically, one of 'Abduh's later complaints was that the Azhar 'ulama did not supervise their students well enough.

The incident also reflected Shaykh 'Ilish's defense of the juridical authority of hadith. The Sunnis' main objection to the Mu'tazilis was that they held human reason to be able to distinguish good and evil, against the traditionists' argument that humans were incapable of doing so without the aid of revelatory texts (Qur'an and hadith).[26] 'Ilish also had to uphold the tradition that no Maliki had ever adopted non-Ash'ari theology. 'Ilish cited a fatwa by Maliki Mufti Mustafa al-Bulaqi, who himself cited Maliki jurist al-Subki, who stated that only "riffraff" from the other three madhahib recognized the Mu'tazilis or the anthropomorphists, and that the Malikis did not: "God Most High acquitted the Malikis of that. . . . [T]here is not to be seen a Maliki who is not Ash'ari of doctrine."[27] 'Abduh's apparent acceptance of Mu'tazili arguments constituted a threat to this tradition of the Maliki madhhab's theological purity.

To historians of al-Azhar reform, Shaykh 'Ilish's opposition to 'Abduh's teaching group represented the beginning of a vicious intellectual battle pitting 'Abduh and al-Afghani against the conservative 'ulama, whom Rida referred to as al-jamidun, the "frozen" or "stagnant" ones. This battle supposedly led to the expulsion of al-Afghani from Egypt in 1879.[28] Al-Afghani did not have an easy relationship with the Azharis, but the khedive banished him for nationalist agitation; 'Ilish did not hold the authority to banish him.[29]

Furthermore, Shaykh 'Ilish did not oppose reform per se. In fact, in 1856, 'Ilish had worked with Shaykhs al-'Arusi and al-'Abbasi—both of whom favored organizational reforms at al-Azhar—on shari'a court reform.[30] Indeed, 'Ilish's fatwas suggest that he should be understood as one whose concern for the moral character of Muslims overrode all others.

'Ilish derived his concept of reform from his training and long experience as a jurisconsult responsible for providing religious guidance. Therefore his approach to reform diverged markedly from that of al-Tahtawi, al-Afghani, and the nationalist journalists who derived their models from the Utilitarian order of European military schools. To 'Ilish, reform meant the purification of people's understandings of religion from the corruptions of ignorant delusions and wishful thinking. Those corruptions could potentially undermine public confidence in the law and in madhhab jurisprudence; it was this that 'Ilish saw as the real threat to Islamic society, not the supposed stagnation posited by reformers. Such was the importance of continuity and stability within the law that 'Ilish believed only 'ulama who possessed a degree of divine guidance could perform ijtihad without damaging the purity of the religion.

According to 'Ilish, the primary responsibility of the 'ulama was combating public lack of respect for Islam, for departures from its moral path led to social decay. To 'Ilish, even acts that others considered unrelated to religious belief were manifestations of one's respect or lack thereof for Islam. One of 'Ilish's more famous fatwas stated that sending students to foreign non-Muslim countries to learn their sciences was an insult to the Islamic tradition of learning.

> It is decreed in the shari'a of Islam that travel to the land of the enemy for commerce is a discredit to the Testament of Faith, and improper conduct, to say nothing of settling down in it or seeking knowledge in it. And it is decreed in the shari'a of the Muslims that the branches of knowledge that are to be sought are those having to do with shari'a and their tools, which are subjects related to Arabic language. More than that should not be sought, but rather should be avoided. It is known that the Christians learn nothing at all of the shari'a subjects or their tools, and that most of their sciences derive from weaving, weighing, and cupping, and these are among the lowest trades among the Muslims.

This fatwa was immortalized by Ahmad Hasan al-Zayyat and Pierre Cachia as an example of the obstructive attitude of conservatives toward the West.[31] However, we can complicate this by viewing the quotation in the context of 'Ilish's concerns. 'Ilish, a nationalist and purist at heart, associated Europe with "the land of the enemy." Nothing was to be gained from consorting with the enemy, and doing so could even devalue one's claim to be a Muslim. Furthermore, 'Ilish perceived a danger in delving into knowledge that did not derive from the Islamic traditions of religious inquiry: Such knowledge could lead believers astray, cause corruption of morals, and thus result in social decay.

There was a connection here to the issues discussed by al-Tahtawi, al-Afghani, and the journalists in relation to European sciences, whether 'Ilish intended it or not. The pedantic referral to "weaving, weighing, and cupping" was a clear dismissal of the applied sciences, which were not among those sciences he considered beneficial. This is supported by another of 'Ilish's fatwas. A petitioner asked him whether the earth was supported by something and what caused earthquakes. 'Ilish responded without any reference to geology or science, and gave an answer derived from hadith reports about what Muhammad saw during his visionary Night Journey.[32] Of course, the petitioner was asking this question of a religious scholar, not a geologist, and would have wanted to know what answer religious sources could provide. But the answer's implication was that such questions could be answered with reference to religious sources alone.

The fatwa could also be taken as an oblique attack on ijtihad. If the state of Muslim sciences was not in fact inferior to Western sciences, and acquisition of Western sciences (as opposed to morality) was not the key to cultural revival, then there would be no need to revive the Muslims' supposedly dormant spirit of scientific inquiry. If there were no need to revive the spirit of inquiry, there would be no justification for reviving ijtihad as al-Tahtawi and al-Afghani defined it.

'Ilish's concern for Muslim morality applied especially to Azharis. He reproached them for attending night celebrations of weddings and funerals, because "inappropriate activities" happened at these festivities. The least of these was that guests would be inattentive in listening to Qur'an recitations, requiring the reader to raise his voice in an inappropriate manner. When 'Ilish's son 'Abdullah, an Azhari 'alim himself, died in 1877, Azhari 'ulama wanted to hold the customary visitations and rituals that usually accompanied the funeral of an Azhari 'alim. Shaykh 'Ilish said: "I do not know what my son would do in his tomb if we held a party for him like the parties for weddings. I will not be one of those who feel they must fabricate something good out of this [i.e., his death]."[33] No inappropriate activities would accompany his son to the grave; solemnity and respect for religion would prevail.

Shaykh 'Ilish's concern for moral purity was the foundation of his conception of reform. It did not require abandonment of taqlid nor acceptance of European useful knowledge within the madrasa. 'Ilish disagreed with the new characterization of ijtihad as a means of combating intellectual and social decay. To 'Ilish, reformers' arguments would have seemed suspiciously similar to the ideas of revivalists like the Sanusis in Libya and the Wahhabis in Arabia, who also accepted a wide scope for ijtihad.[34] And so he chose the debate over the relative social values of taqlid and ijtihad to be his intellectual battleground.

Taqlid as a Means of Maintaining Social Stability

The fatwas on taqlid that 'Ilish recorded in his *Fath al-'ali al-malik fi al-fatwa 'ala madhhab al-Imam Malik* were framed as responses to the arguments of the Muhammadiyya sect. There were several sects known as Muhammadiyya in the eighteenth and nineteenth centuries, including the Wahhabis, the Sanusis, and the Ahmadiyya, and because neither 'Ilish nor his petitioners mentioned names, it is not clear to which they refer. As described in the petition, this group's leader rejected taqlid of madhhab fiqh and promoted instead the use of ijtihad and hadith as interpretive tools.[35]

In constructing his response to the revival of ijtihad, 'Ilish reiterated rulings on similar questions authored by several medieval and contemporary Maliki jurists, including his predecessor, the late Maliki Mufti Mustafa al-Bulaqi, and the controversial fourteenth-century mufti Abu Ishaq al-Shatibi. As Wael Hallaq has pointed out, this mode of discourse was characteristic of author/jurists like 'Ilish, who sometimes used the opinions of recognized authorities to lend legitimacy to entirely novel and sometimes controversial conclusions.[36] 'Ilish's conclusions may not have been novel, but neither were they irrelevant musings with no political significance. His choice of which rulings to present, and the context in which he presented them, suggests that his own fatwas were constructed with contemporary trends of reform in mind, not only those explicitly referenced. In any case, a defense of taqlid from the mid- to late century would not have been directed against the modernist reformers, the muhaddithun or muslihun, by name, since they were not really collectively identified as such until after the 1880s.

'Ilish's defense of taqlid may therefore be viewed against this backdrop: The modernist reformers' redefinition of ijtihad extracted it from its legal context and restructured it as a means of fulfilling the Qur'anic injunction to seek knowledge, in this case within the Qur'an and Sunna themselves. Ijithad became a mechanism for creating social change. Likewise, taqlid was deprived of its historical meaning within the evolution of the Sunni madhahib and recast as a mind-set explicitly forbidden by the Qur'an, a stubborn preference for the traditions of one's forefathers over the revealed Truth and the spirit of rational inquiry embodied in that Truth. In this case, the forefathers were the recognized authorities whose rulings and methods formed the bodies of precedent upon which madhhab jurists relied. In contrast, Shaykh 'Ilish viewed taqlid of madhhab rulings as the mechanism by which the fabric of Sunni society was held together. The definition of

Sunni—ahl al-sunna wa al-jama'a [the people of the way of the Prophet and the community]—connoted adherence to the Sunna or example of the Prophet. As Hallaq has suggested, consensus on those principles of law that bound Sunnis together defined the community: "No person could reject any of these constants [theories of language used in determining the epistemological value of scriptural statements, consensus, principles of reasoning . . .] and still claim affiliation with Sunnism."[37] Anyone who did not recognize the overall validity of those principles risked placing himself outside the community and could be deemed a threat to its unity. Therefore 'Ilish's fatwa collection, published in 1882,[38] may be seen as a conscious but cautious refutation of reformers' redefinitions of ijtihad and taqlid and an attempt to defend taqlid as the legal basis for communal unity.

The unnamed leader of the Muhammadiyya sect in the petition believed there were errors in the collections of madhhab rulings used by judges in applying the law. Yet jurists had elevated those books, by consensus, to the status of scripture. This leader advocated abandoning most madhhab rulings and keeping only those based on unambiguous statements in the Qur'an and the sound hadith—in the interest of "purifying" Islam. He therefore claimed to be a mujtahid.[39]

'Ilish disagreed. "It is not permissible," he declared, "for a layman ['ammi] to abandon taqlid of the four Imams and adopt rulings from the Qur'an and the hadith." Citing Ibn Farhun (d. 1397) and al-Laqqani (d. 1667), he asserted that upon this belief all Sunnis, not just the Maliki madhhab, had achieved consensus: It was an article of faith. Here 'Ilish outlined the conventional theory of juristic expertise. To perform ijtihad, a person had to be a scholar, and had to have in addition certain qualifications. According to 'Ilish, those qualifications were present only in an extreme minority of the 'ulama.[40] The Qur'an contained many passages the literal meaning of which was misleading; some could even be blasphemous. Only God, the Prophet, his Companions from the early community, and the Imams could interpret the Qur'an without danger of falling into error. Even jurists who were "thoroughly versed in religion" could only produce contingent interpretations.[41]

'Ilish, who was a member of the Shadhili Sufi order, imbued his defense of taqlid with a defense of Sufism as well.[42] According to 'Ilish, in order to perform ijtihad without endangering the community, one had to have access to sources of absolutely unimpeachable epistemological certainty. The Imams of the four madhahib, of course, were held to have performed ijtihad. How then did they ensure the certainty of their rulings? 'Ilish cited accounts that the Imams had encountered the Prophet in mystical visions and had been able to verify the validity and interpretation of various verses of the Qur'an and hadith reports. 'Ilish concluded: "If the mujtahidun [Imams] were not saints, there never was a saint on the face of the earth, ever."[43]

'Ilish had however to reconcile the Imams' equal access to the epistemo-logically unimpeachable source, the Prophet, with their having reached different conclusions and founded different madhahib. In this, he alluded to the social reality of the times. The Imams, he said, "knew that the matter had stabilized into a number of distinct madhahib, not into a single madh-hab," and they did not want to disturb this social reality, for the sake of justice and ittiba'. So divisions in the community were permitted to persist and presumably were not considered harmful. However, no scholar since the Imams had matched their mastery of religious texts, paired with the necessary mystical contact with the Prophet, to legitimately perform unre-stricted ijtihad (al-ijtihad al-mutlaq).[44] 'Ilish, like other legal scholars who dealt with the issue of closure of the gate of ijtihad, distinguished between unrestricted ijtihad and ijtihad within the body of rules set forth by the Imams of the madhahib. According to 'Ilish,

[A]ll those who claim al-ijtihad al-mutlaq mean by that al-mutlaq al-madhhabi, that is, [ijtihad] that does not deviate from the rules of his Imam, like Ibn al-Qasim and al-Asbagh with Malik, and Muhammad and Abu Yusuf with Abu Hanifa, and like al-Mazani and al-Rabi' with al-Shafi'i. It is not in the power of anyone after the four Imams to originate [hermeneutical] rules and derive them from the Book and the Sunna.[45]

According to the Shadhili Sufi Sidi 'Ali al-Khawwas, all those "whose hearts were enlightened by God" followed the madhahib. There were still mujtahidun, but they practiced ijtihad within the confines of their mad-hahib's established rules.[46] For 'Ilish, al-ijtihad al-mutlaq (unrestricted ijti-had), the rank claimed by al-Suyuti and defended by al-Tahtawi, was the same as al-ijtihad al-mustaqill (independent ijtihad). Their definitions dif-fered, and that mattered. 'Ilish could rhetorically dispense with a scholar's claims to unrestricted ijtihad by suggesting that the scholar claimed what only the Imams could do. Moreover, 'Ilish's ruling was not really about scholars, but about laymen. He therefore rejected the lay ijtihad proposed by al-Afghani and 'Abduh.

The next claim to be dispensed with was that there were errors in the books of Maliki jurisprudence, such as the *Mukhtasar Khalil*. The claim that these supposed errors invalidated centuries of legal scholarship and mandated a return to unrestricted ijtihad was, to 'Ilish, simply absurd. 'Ilish pointed out that Malik had been a scrupulous scholar. Like the other Imams, he had insisted that all reports of the Prophet or his Companions be carefully scrutinized and compared with one another. Any uncorroborated or suspicious reports were abandoned, and Malik did not record them in his compendium of hadith, *al-Muwatta'*.[47] As for the accusations by some that the rules of the Maliki madhhab sometimes contradicted reasonable or sound hadith, 'Ilish reminded his readers that Malik had preferred the actual practice ('amal) of the Muslim community of Medina, as he found it, over reports of that practice, which as secondhand knowledge were less trustworthy.[48] 'Ilish claimed that Medinan practices contradicting sound hadiths constituted evidence that the Prophet had abrogated those hadiths, and practices that contradicted the literal meaning of the Qur'an were evidence that the literal meaning "was not that intended and that rather what was intended was what they practiced. . . . 'If you see the Companions washing up to their elbows before prayer, then you wash like them.'"[49]

Moreover, the texts of Maliki jurisprudence (mukhtasarat) contained rulings upon which the community of Maliki 'ulama had achieved consensus. In accordance with numerous hadith reports that the Prophet had said his community could not agree unanimously in error, juridical consensus on behalf of the community rendered these rulings as epistemologically certain as an unambiguous statement in the Qur'an. The Muhammadiya revivalist's challenge to Maliki jurisprudence therefore negated the validity of consensus-sanctioned rulings. This effectively rendered him a heretic, someone who did not accept the fundamental assumptions that defined one as Sunni.[50]

Moreover, untrained laymen who took up independent ijtihad threatened the integrity of the law, for their rulings would conform to no standard and contradict the rules of the established madhahib. 'Ilish cited 'Abd al-Wahhab al-Sha'rani (d. 1565), who said, "You asked if it is incumbent upon someone who is incapable of studying the sources to be restricted to a specific madhhab. The answer is 'Yes', that is incumbent upon him so he does not lead himself and others into error." Sometimes the practices of the independent mujtahidun agreed with those of the sound madhahib, but sometimes they agreed with the deviant madhahib or violated the consensus of the community.[51]

'Ilish's concern for public adherence to the rulings of the madhhab is evident in another fatwa addressing whether muftis must, when faced with two equally suitable rulings on petition, choose one to present to the petitioner or provide both so that the petitioner may choose. His answer explicitly defended taqlid. According to Muhammad Fadel, taqlid had developed within the Maliki madhhab as a means of ensuring the rule of law and the consensus of the community over the contradictory rulings of independent mujtahidun.[52] According to Hallaq, by the end of the fourteenth century, taqlid functioned in all four main Sunni madhahib as a mechanism of self-regulation by which jurists ensured that no fatwas were issued that contravened the normative rulings of the madhahib, guaranteeing consistent application of the law within acceptable bounds. Muftis had to adhere to the established hermeneutic of legal theory, for an alternative hermeneutic—one that challenged the authority of consensus, for example—would invalidate much of the corpus of accepted rulings.[53]

From 'Ilish's point of view in the nineteenth century, when taqlid was threatened by redefinition, a clear distinction had to be drawn between the kind of taqlid described in the Qur'an and that used by Maliki jurists. For example, 'Ilish reported an opinion by the fourteenth-century Maliki jurist Abu Ishaq al-Shatibi that clearly defined the Qur'anic taqlid as different from the taqlid of legal methodology: "Abu Ishaq said that insistence upon following customs [ittiba'] has corrupted or contradicted the Truth. Following what one's forefathers and shaykhs and so forth did, that is objectionable taqlid."[54] In contrast, the legal mechanism of taqlid, far from being an instrument of social stagnation, prevented jurists from following "whims" and "worldly objectives" in judging cases and issuing fatwas. 'Ilish cited a lengthy debate as to whether it was permissible for a mufti to switch madhahib, to base his fatwa upon a ruling established in a madhhab other than his own, or even to base his fatwa upon an opinion that contradicts the opinions accepted by his madhhab. The arguments he cited described a lack of juristic consensus on these questions, because jurists' rulings differed according to historical circumstances, but the preponderance of Maliki opinion fell on the side of preserving the integrity of madhhab rulings. The madhhab, or each mufti in relation to his petitioners, had to endeavor to provide clear and consistent rulings on similar cases or questions. If not, the rule of law would break down. Two criminals charged with similar crimes could get different sentences, or two petitioners asking similar questions

could receive contradictory answers.[55] If the public perceived that the legal
system could not provide consistency in trying legal cases, it would begin to
question the legitimacy of the law itself, of the government providing legal
personnel, or of the educational system training the legal personnel.
According to prevailing notions of social order, public faith in the ruler and
in the law surrounding and protecting society was a necessary part of a circle of justice. If any one part of the circle was broken, society would dissolve
into injustice and disorder.[56] The challenge to taqlid threatened to break
that circle.

The rulings 'Ilish repeated and affirmed underscore the imperative to
preserve order through public adherence to clearly defined madhhab rulings. Again, his main source was al-Shatibi, who wanted to prevent rule by
whim in order to steer a middle course between two extremes of legal practice existing at his time. On the one hand, Sufis had upheld the mufti's obligation to provide all valid answers to petitions, so that the petitioner might
choose the most stringent ruling. On the other, jurists had upheld the same
obligation so that they might allow petitioners to choose the more lenient
ruling, in the interests of friendship or political influence. The former
entailed unnecessary hardship for the general public; the latter resulted in
corruption.[57] In one fatwa, al-Shatibi addressed the dilemma of a mufti
who finds more than one possible answer to a petitioner's question. Must
he tell the petitioner both answers? Must he present his answer unambiguously, by clearly valuing one over the other? Al-Shatibi replied: "When a
commoner presents his case to a mufti and says to him 'Extract me from my
whims and set me to following the Truth,' it is not possible at this time to
say to him 'There are two reports on your issue, so choose according to your
desire either of them you wish.' The meaning of that is legitimation of
whim without law."[58] The purpose of his office, the provision of clear legal
advice to laypeople, had to be upheld.

'Ilish cited a second case with a similar message. Shaykh al-Isfahani had
received a petition from a woman whose husband had no relations with her
but refused her a divorce. Isfahani's fatwa set out all the various rulings on
this matter. The woman did not understand and had to turn to another
mufti for a clear ruling. The mufti's primary duty was to provide the public with legal advice; logically then, it would have to make sense to the petitioner. 'Ilish's message was that muftis should represent the law to their petitioners as a unified body by practicing taqlid of the madhhab.[59]

Muftis could also be corrupted by their own desires for power or wealth.
Al-Shatibi reported that in his age, "Many of the muqallid jurists have

begun to give fatwas to this relative or that friend that he would not give to others . . . following his objective and desire, or the objective of this relative or that friend."[60] Shihab al-Din al-Qarafi (d. 1285) said further that muftis had to follow established madhhab rulings, or at least the Imams' preferred rulings. He forbade absolutely any "following [ittiba'] of whims." If muftis were allowed to exercise their own judgment in evaluating precedent, they would come under increased pressure to give favorable weight to bribes or political advantage, and they might value a decision they wanted over one that had stronger evidentiary support.[61] Thus adherence to the valid opinions set forth in the texts of the madhhab buffered the mufti from potential corruption, and enhanced public perception of the law's neutrality.

'Ilish's Maliki predecessors had also considered the specific question of switching madhahib, which had particular resonance for 'Ilish at that time. Government preference for Hanafi employees was leaching students away from the Maliki madhhab. Muhammad 'Abduh, for example, had received his training as a Maliki at al-Azhar, but showed inclination toward the principles of the Hanafi madhhab and was eventually appointed Grand Mufti, the highest-ranking Hanafi mufti in Egypt. 'Abdullah Nadim, the nationalist orator and journalist, had originally been Maliki but switched to the Hanafi madhhab.[62] Shaykh 'Ilish insisted that "[a mufti] should have only one madhhab that he thinks is correct and prefers above all others. He must be loyal according to his belief. If he is Shafi'i he cannot give fatwas as a Maliki or other, [nor can he give fatwas] in contradiction or opposition to his Imam." The issue was not which opinion was true—that of the Malikis or the Shafi'is or the other madhahib—but the maintenance of a coherent body of law and the restriction of deviations from consensus to mere madhhab disagreement.[63] Thus 'Ilish's Maliki predecessors required madhhab loyalty from laymen as well as muftis. 'Ilish cited Shafi'i scholar Ibn al-Salah to point out that if laymen were permitted to follow [ittiba'] any madhhab they wished, this would allow them to bring their petitions before muftis from several madhahib, so to have a better chance of receiving the answer desired. This would thus lead to "the following of amateurs and choosing between prohibition and permission."[64] Thus 'Ilish reminded his petitioner of the public's potential complicity in the decline of the rule of law, and the mufti's obligation to guide laypeople by accepted madhhab rules.

By upholding Maliki rulings on taqlid, 'Ilish defended the integrity of the Islamic legal tradition. Ijtihad of the type envisioned by reformers would challenge the rule of law by introducing legal indeterminacy. If used in jurists' official capacities as representatives of a coherent, neutral law to the public, it would damage the public perception of jurists' fairness and neutrality. Taqlid was essential to the Islamic legal tradition.[65]

Yet issues of authority also tied into 'Ilish's defense. The 'ulama played a critical role in Islamic societies as scholars, interpreters, and providers of legal advice. If lay ijtihad or ijtihad by state-trained legal personnel became the norm, the public would no longer need the conventionally trained 'ulama. If 'Ilish was as concerned about moral purity as records of his activities suggest, we may assume that he also would have been concerned about preserving his position of moral authority as mediator of texts, as spiritual guide. However, it is wise to be cautious here: His authoritarian attempts to instruct others in "correct" respectful behavior, his mobilization of students to force subordinate muftis to retract "incorrect" rulings, and his leadership to remove the reins of European control from the khedivate were not motivated solely by defense of power. To assume this was the case would be secular reductionism and ignores the possibility that someone could have genuine concerns about human morality and spiritual well-being. The motive "preservation of authority" fits all of his actions, but so does "concern for the relation of the legal system to public welfare." Indeed, the two cannot be separated: 'Ulama had to preserve their authority as mediators of textual knowledge in order to ensure their vision of morality was maintained, but they had first of all to defend the legal system underlying the very definition of the society they sought to guide. In an era when social stability was threatened by customs and laws imported from foreign and even non-Muslim countries, when government preference was encouraging Azhari students to abandon their own madhahib and become Hanafis, and when revivalists and reformers were spreading the dangerous notion that laymen could employ ijtihad on their own, taqlid became even more crucial as a mechanism for ensuring the continuity and internal consistency of the Islamic legal tradition. Laymen who practiced taqlid of a single established madhhab and received unequivocal direction from their muftis would not suffer from uncertainty about their religious duties, nor would they be led into error by phony mujtahidun who were unqualified to interpret the law. They would continue to have confidence in the religious law and belief in a coherent body of religious truths. And perhaps if the integrity of the law and confidence in the mufti's office were maintained, Muslims would be less inclined to accept the ways of the foreigners, whom 'Ilish defined explicitly as political enemies. Thus society's strength to resist its enemies lay in the coherence of the law and in the practice of taqlid.

Shaykh 'Ilish's Legacy

Shaykh 'Ilish's refusal to compromise on principles eventually brought him into conflict with the khedival authorities. Shortly before the 'Urabi Revolt, 'Ilish had disagreed with a fatwa issued by another leading Azhari shaykh, Hasan al-'Idwi. Shaykh al-'Idwi refused to rescind his fatwa, so 'Ilish and a council of other Azhari 'ulama met and had him banned from teaching at al-Azhar. Al-'Idwi ignored the ban and arrived as usual to meet his halqa. 'Ilish's students chased al-'Idwi out of the mosque and destroyed the palm-wood chair on which he sat, the symbol of his authority. Shaykh al-'Idwi refused to be subdued by this indignity and appealed to the khedive. The khedive held a council at the Citadel, after which al-'Idwi was restored to his position. His palm-wood chair was replaced, symbolically, with one of hardwood. The khedive reprimanded 'Ilish for overstepping his authority, declared him overworked, and reduced his official duties as Mufti.[66] A chastened Shaykh 'Ilish eventually stopped teaching at al-Azhar and sought refuge in the quieter mosque of al-Husayn. With the enlarging crowds at al-Azhar, 'Ilish's increasingly weakened voice could no longer be heard above the noise.[67]

Despite the reduction of his official role in Azhari politics, 'Ilish remained a figure of influence until the end of his life. His Arabic biographers agree that his outspokenness during the British trial of the 'Urabist constitutionalists led to his conviction for treason. This same trial resulted in the exile of 'Urabi, Muhammad 'Abduh, and others. 'Ilish's fate was harsher. In the first month of the British occupation of Egypt, Shaykh 'Ilish was arrested. He was eighty years old and was by then suffering from paralysis of the limbs; nevertheless he was carried from his home and incarcerated in a prison hospital, where he died in October of 1882 (9 Dhi al-Hijja 1299 H), apparently at the hands of the British or Tawfiq's henchmen.[68] Today he is remembered by some as an obstacle to progress, by some as a martyr of the struggle against European imperialism, and by others not at all.

Conclusion

Those whom history has forgotten are not always the powerless. 'Ilish—a powerful Mufti and revolutionary leader—suffered a century of anonymity, his views ignored by historians who allowed themselves to be persuaded by the polemics of modernist reformers. While 'Ilish may not have been the most likable character, he did participate in the same debate as the reformers over the relative social values of ijtihad and taqlid, and he sided at least

in his political activities with the nationalists. This carries several implications for understanding the legal conservatives' participation in the debate
over reforms at al-Azhar.

The essential point of contention between the reformers and 'Ilish was
whether an individual Muslim's religious practice must be grounded in personal knowledge of the Qur'an and hadith collections. The reformers suggested that the common people as well as the 'ulama must be able to perform ijtihad at some level. In the words of al-Afghani, "If a tenet of faith is
held in a person's imagination without proof and without evidence, he may
not be convinced, and will not be a believer." 'Abduh, following al-Afghani,
stated further that "it is clear that what is taken from our predecessors and
what our relatives told us, if not supported by proofs, will be affected by the
sayings of heretics and be refuted by the infidels." Although it was the duty
of the 'ulama to start the process of reviving ijtihad and teaching Muslims
the fundamental texts of their religion, the moral and material revival of the
people would have to proceed through individual effort, and the religious
education system would have to be changed to encourage this. These views
exemplified the modernists' faith in progress through advancement of
empirical knowledge: The people were capable of achieving this advancement, and through it the nation would become strong and be able to
defend itself against the encroachment of the European powers. An underlying premise of this argument was specific to the reformers' experiences as
journalists—that an increase in literacy and education was allowing more
Muslims to acquire and understand written materials and that this could
come to include the fundamental texts of the religious tradition. Thus their
program for national advancement required that Muslims undergo an epistemological paradigm shift—once the initial stages were passed, the 'ulama
would no longer serve as transmitters and interpreters of religious knowledge; such studies would no longer be something mysterious that required
a mediating interpreter. Of course, this paradigm shift would require
changes in the pedagogical practices of the religious schools as well as in
their curricula.

'Ilish's approach to the problem of contemporary Muslim society was
fundamentally different. Clearly, despite joining with the modernist
reformers in the 'Urabi Revolt, he did not subscribe to the same ideal of
national advancement as did the reformers and nationalist journalists. In
fact, his denial of any role for ijtihad in creating social strength undermined
the ideological structure of these reformers' concept of community. For
'Ilish, an individual's conviction in his religious belief had to be based on

his confidence in the law and the institution of madhhab jurisprudence. It was the rule of law, not the exercise of individual intellect, that reinforced the moral and political fabric of the society. Taqlid ensured unity and strength, whereas ijtihad would bring difference of opinion, political manipulation of the law, and vulnerability. Thus the status quo of Azhari education, with its heavy emphasis on lectures in linguistic interpretation, madhhab jurisprudence, and above all its insistence on an unbroken chain of transmitters communicating the "correct" authorial meaning of a religious text, supported the rule of law and social order. Moreover, since knowledge of applied sciences was not seen as relevant to communal strength, there was no need to include them in al-Azhar's curriculum. There was no need to change al-Azhar's pedagogical traditions.

6

EFFICIENCY, MISSION, AND THE MEANING OF 'ILM (1882–1899)

By the 1880s, al-Azhar was staggering under a student population ten times that of the previous century and still growing. Its informal administrative procedures were no longer able to serve the needs of the now-massive student body. Al-Azhar's quasi-contractual procedures for training students, well-suited to serve a few hundred at a time, were no longer sufficient either.[1] By this time, European models of educational order were so pervasive in the government, and among students and 'ulama, that they demanded efficiency in production of educated personnel and certification that stated students' qualifications for employment. These were alien demands for a system the ultimate goal of which was for a student to become a reliable part of a living chain of transmission, not an efficiently functioning cog in a bureaucratic or commercial machine. Pressures upon al-Azhar increased when bureaucrats began to establish vocational schools whose graduates competed with al-Azhar's. Consequently, al-Azhar students began clamoring for more training in practical subjects. At the same time, al-Azhar was physically crippled by environmental wear, and the crowding led to sanitary problems. Facing these conditions, 'ulama of al-Azhar accepted efficiency-based models of order and organization, and did not guard their territory from khedival encroachment. They tried instead to maneuver within the spaces still in contest, to reestablish the scholars' moral leadership within a community motivated to progress by Islamic ideals. One such contested space was the definition of subject material, of 'ilm, or knowledge.

The Reform Codes of 1885:
Al-Azhar's War Against Demography

In 1882, the British established a Veiled Protectorate under the leadership of Evelyn Baring, Earl of Cromer. The British restored Khedive Tawfiq to his throne and had leaders of the 'Urabi Revolt tried and exiled from Egypt, including Muhammad 'Abduh and 'Abdullah Nadim.[2] In November 1881, as a defensive measure during the 'Urabi Revolt, Tawfiq's newly formed Council of Notables had instituted a press law requiring all periodical publishers to acquire government licenses. Tawfiq had previously closed or suspended periodicals that were too vehement in their support of the 'Urabists' cause. But after the passage of the press law, the government simply shut down periodicals that persisted in criticizing the regime and imposed heavy fines on press operators who tried to avoid licensing. The British permitted Khedive Tawfiq to maintain this press law, which effectively quieted journalistic political agitation, until Lord Cromer ceased enforcing it in 1894.[3] Thus the campaign for reform of madrasa education in Egypt was temporarily deprived of its leading advocates and its main forum of expression.

However, an undercurrent of anti-taqlid, pro-science reformism was still evident in papers published by reformers in exile, such as *al-'Urwa al-wuthqa* (The Strongest Bond), issued by Jamal al-Din al-Afghani and Muhammad 'Abduh in Paris, and in Syrian journals primarily devoted to scientific subjects, such as Butrus al-Bustani's *al-Jinan* (The Gardens). *Al-'Urwa al-wuthqa* described the stagnation (jumud) of Muslims that had allowed European imperialists to dominate them. Causes of stagnation included the creed of fatalism ('aqidat al-jabr) and weakness of education, which was partially due to 'ulama negligence in spreading knowledge among the masses. The remedy for stagnation was to revive ijtihad in order to purify religious belief from corruptive accretions.[4] *Al-Jinan* was a Christian journal published in Beirut, and so it was not specifically concerned with the state of education at Muslim institutions. However, its audience was wide and its campaign for instruction in science was well-known. For example, as part of a series of articles entitled "al-Ta'lim" (Education), *al-Jinan* called for increased investment by the Ministry of Education in applied sciences, because it was by science alone that civilizations progressed.[5] *Al-Jinan's* authors also expressed concern over the apparent lack of progress in medicine and natural science, citing as its cause inherited attitudes toward philosophy and political repression of scientific study. *Al-Jinan* explicitly blamed 'ulama, claiming they avoided these studies out of desire for political favors. This criticism was directed at high-ranking

Ottoman 'ulama associated with Sultan 'Abdulhamid II, such as Shaykh Abu al-Huda al-Sayyadi and Yusuf al-Nabhani.[6] In contrast, *al-Jinan* held Muhammad 'Abduh's ideas up as a model to be emulated, praising his teaching at the Madrasa al-Sultaniyya in Syria, where 'Abduh had gone after leaving Paris. That school was open to all faiths; *al-Jinan* called it a "luminous star in the celestial sphere of learning."[7] Such descriptions of new civil schools contrasted sharply with reports of odious conditions at al-Azhar.

Most importantly, institutional and political developments of the post-revolt period continued to promote the modernist reformers' ideas. Khedive Tawfiq generally approved of the modernists' concepts of reform, despite his antagonism toward al-Afghani and his followers. Lord Cromer said of Tawfiq: "If he did not take any active part in initiating reforms, he was content that others should do so for him. If he could not lead the reformers, he had no objection to following their lead. If he did not afford very active assistance to the small band of Englishmen laying the foundations of a prosperous future for Egypt, neither did he interfere actively to place obstacles in their path; indeed, he often used his influence to remove obstacles."[8] In keeping with this sentiment, Tawfiq approved the reinstatement of the deposed Hanafi, Shaykh Muhammad al-'Abbasi al-Mahdi, to the office of Shaykh al-Azhar.

On 25 February 1881, the government had passed legislation establishing new rules for military conscription and forced labor, and, as in previous legislation of this kind, it provided that students of religion be exempted. Students' exemption caused problems not only for mosques, which had to absorb those fleeing from conscription, but also for local elites whose duty it was to come up with enough conscripts or laborers for public works projects. Azhari students reported that, as a result, village leaders had beaten members of their families and forced parents to serve in corvée labor in place of their absent sons. Since none of the religious schools had formal registration rolls, regional examination councils were now set up to verify claims of student status.[9]

On 24 March 1885, Shaykh al-'Abbasi issued a new regulation code for al-Azhar, under the inelegant title "The code for examination of those who want to teach at al-Azhar mosque." In the same year, the government's Council of Ministers issued a student registration code for all Egypt's major madrasas. Al-'Abbasi's code stipulated that exams must be held (they had lapsed from 1881 to 1886) and listed specific books to be taught in each subject for which examination was required.[10] One effect was to further constrict the curriculum, so that "the people of al-Azhar were devoted to that which was set forth in these required books as if it were a Royal Decree; thus it is no wonder that knowledge became [synonymous with] the book, and that reading of the book became the single object of instruction and education."[11] Another was a strengthening of existing rules that prevented ignorant imposters from teaching, since they would presumably be unable to teach the required texts.

However, the provision that specified texts for courses would also have prevented another Jamal al-Din al-Afghani or Muhammad 'Abduh from teaching controversial books in the required subject areas within al-Azhar, thus protecting the 'ulama's control of the knowledge to be transmitted to students. On the other hand, any student who received a second- or third-rank pass in the exams could take them again in order to achieve a higher rank, and the Shaykh al-Azhar could simply confer permission to teach upon those whose experience merited it. This al-'Abbasi had in fact done when 'Abduh's examiners gave him the second-rank pass; thus the new code gave students recourse to appeal an apparent sabotage of their exams. Perhaps Shaykh al-'Abbasi wanted to ensure that he retained some personal control over assignment of ranks in order to prevent problems similar to 'Abduh's. In practice, this opened the door to corruption. In later years, students who had left al-Azhar in despair of passing the exams returned and were simply granted permission to teach. In 1910, a review committee concluded that this provision undermined the purpose of the code "and thus opened the door that the examinations had been intended to close."[12]

According to the student registration code, all mosques were to establish formal registration procedures and to record the name and date of admission of each student and instructor. Any student who was not a registered lodger would not be permitted to receive daily bread rations (jarayat). Furthermore, even registered students would not be permitted to receive rations while on holiday, or if they were simultaneously pursuing a career in some foreign trade, or if they left al-Azhar for an extended period without permission. The student population had outstripped the capacity of the awqaf to feed them, and the registration code would prevent squatters and vagrants from receiving rations meant for legitimate students.[13]

One reason for this code was that the Council of Ministers was conducting a systematic review and reform of the shari'a court system and thus had considerable interest in ensuring that those who claimed to be students—upon graduation qualified for employment in the courts—were really students.[14] Since personalized certification of a graduate's qualification for professional life was now becoming unmanageable, bureaucratic procedures of registration, examination, and certification were devised. The code appears not to have been implemented before 1898, because student registration on so massive a scale required administrative structures that did not exist before 1895. Critics insisted the Azharis continued to absent themselves from classes at will, daily ration rolls continued to list names of students who had long since left al-Azhar as well as men of the trades and industries who could neither read nor write, and these illegitimate "students" still managed to collect their daily rations of bread.[15]

Thus by 1887, when Shaykh al-'Abbasi resigned, al-Azhar's academic offerings had continued to contract and its financial administration remained unaltered, despite the promulgation of reform codes. Al-'Abbasi's efforts in the service of administrative reform would be remembered by later generations as the first steps in the progression of al-Azhar education toward modernity.[16]

Market Competition and the (Re)Legitimation of Scientific Instruction

Shaykh Shams al-Din al-Inbabi replaced al-'Abbasi as Shaykh al-Azhar for a second term. He came to office at a time when graduates of newly established vocational schools were just starting to compete with Azharis for employment in teaching, courts, and the bureaucracy. This competition elicited considerable debate among the Azharis and government reformers concerning al-Azhar's role in supplying qualified personnel vis-à-vis that of the vocational schools. In this debate, Shaykh al-Inbabi took a controversial position in support of scientific studies.

In 1872, the technocrat 'Ali Pasha Mubarak and Shaykh al-Azhar al-'Abbasi had founded Dar al-'Ulum (House of Learning) for the explicit purpose of improving the training of Arabic and Turkish language teachers in Egypt. Dar al-'Ulum had begun as an informal public lecture series on a variety of religious and new scientific topics, but within two months it was organized into a formal school. Its teaching staff consisted initially of three al-Azhar 'ulama, who taught approximately thirty students drawn from the pool of Azharis. Because the market for language teachers was large and Dar al-'Ulum's first graduating classes were small, the first graduates did not threaten Azharis' employability. However, within five years Dar al-'Ulum expanded its curriculum to include training in arithmetic, geography, natural science, calligraphy, Hanafi law, and Qur'anic exegesis.[17] After 25 April 1887, Dar al-'Ulum students began taking an extra year of practicum studies as student teachers. Records of the graduates' jobs suggest that a certificate from Dar al-'Ulum was tantamount to guaranteed employment. As the khedive began to pursue reform of the shari'a courts, plans were made to modify Dar al-'Ulum's curriculum to ensure a supply of qualified employees to the court system. In 1888, 'Ali Pasha Mubarak asked Shaykh al-Inbabi and a committee of 'ulama to design a program for Dar al-'Ulum that would train Hanafi legal personnel for government employment in the shari'a courts. These court positions—qadis, muftis, and court deputies—were relatively few, and they made up the upper echelon of jobs traditionally filled by Azharis. The government had once before attempted, in 1837, to establish a separate School of Islamic Law and Jurisprudence for Hanafi personnel, under the leadership of al-Tahtawi. That school had been closed in 1851 following years of resentment. Azhari 'ulama may have been drafted for planning the new school in order to prevent the perception that the Dar al-'Ulum's shari'a program was just a renewed attack on al-Azhar's prerogatives.

In 1891, the Ministry of Justice instituted a recruitment exam for employment in the shari'a courts, and in 1893, Dar al-'Ulum developed a special certificate program in shari'a law. Al-Azhar did not yet offer certificates demonstrating qualifications in particular areas; students who did not take the 'alimiyya exams merely received ijazas showing the books they had mastered. Also in 1891, Dar al-'Ulum began a new program for training kuttab teachers, another traditional arena of Azhari employment. The competition between the two schools and Azhari resentment was temporarily resolved when, in 1895, a government study of the job market for legal personnel found there were not enough court jobs to absorb graduates from two schools. Dar al-'Ulum returned to its original objective, the training of Arabic-language teachers.[18] However, some 'ulama now believed that, if Azharis wished to compete with the graduates of the vocational and civil schools, al-Azhar would have to broaden its academic offerings.[19] An attempt at equivalence began with the offering of modern subjects at al-Azhar.

Fatwas on Science

In 1888, the khedive asked his qadi, Muhammad Bayram, to rule on the permissibility of introducing practical studies into Azhar's curriculum, including higher-level mathematics and natural sciences. Muhammad Bayram was in good standing with Lord Cromer, who described the shaykh as a "devout Moslem" whose "private life was irreproachable, whose religious faith was founded upon a rock, whose patriotism was enlightened, and whose public aims were noble," and who was possessed of faith "far more earnest than that of Mohammed Abdu." According to Cromer, "The subject which mainly interested him was how to bring Islam and its ways into harmony with modern society."[20] Qadi Bayram, however, referred the question to elder shaykhs, petitioning Shaykh al-Inbabi (a Shafi'i) and the Grand Mufti, Muhammad al-Banna' (a Hanafi), to issue fatwas. Bayram's petition suggested that he believed these sciences should be taught at all the old, great centers of Islamic education, including not only al-Azhar, but also the Zaytuna and Qarawiyin mosques in Tunisia.

> Is it permissible for the Muslims to learn the mathematical subjects such as geometry, arithmetic, astronomy, natural sciences, and . . . chemistry, and other than these among the remaining [topics of] learning, especially that upon which may be built increased power [quwa] in the Islamic community [al-umma], and considering the need to keep up with contemporary nations?

He argued that the Qur'an commanded Muslims to seek knowledge, especially in regard to religion, and also to prepare for defense. These sciences were required for defense. The quest for practical knowledge was considered a duty incumbent on the community, which could be fulfilled by scholars on its behalf—in legal parlance, a wajib kifayya. Muhammad Bayram thus suggested that the students must study these subjects as a religious duty.[21]

Bayram also asked if that duty applied to fields of knowledge not explicitly tied to religious studies. The instrumental fields, those that were tools to acquire others, were taught; might mathematics and natural sciences be permitted under the same rationale? Shaykh al-Inbabi replied unambiguously but with careful reference to well-known authorities:

> It is permissible to study the mathematical subjects such as arithmetic, geometry, and geography, because nothing in them contradicts religious matters. Indeed, that which they contribute to the benefit of religion or worldly affairs we are obliged to learn on behalf of the community [wujub^{an} kifa'i^{an}], just as we are obliged to learn the science of medicine, as al-Ghazali advised us in the passages of *The Revival* [*of the Religious Sciences*].[22]

In order to legitimate the study of natural sciences, Shaykh al-Inbabi had to make a distinction between them and the proscribed aspects of hikma, the fields of learning derived from Greek science and philosophy. He thus attempted to avoid the pitfalls into which Shaykh Hasan al-'Attar and Jamal al-Din al-Afghani's disciples had fallen. Shaykh al-Inbabi admitted that his conditional permission for the study of natural sciences contradicted some of the authorities, such as Ibn al-Salah and al-Nawawi, but he explained that they had forbidden the study of natural sciences because of their perspectives on the permissibility of using logic and analogy to interpret revelation, and their suspicion that natural sciences were irrevocably tied to the deviant beliefs of the philosophers. According to al-Inbabi, this suspicion of "naturist" or materialist sciences ('ulum al-taba'i'yin) need not apply to the study of nature ('ulum al-tabi'a). Nor did it apply to chemistry or algebra; the benefit of these sciences, like the benefit of natural sciences and mathematics, depended on how they were used. Thus al-Inbabi concluded that there was no harm in teaching these subjects as long as they were not used to contradict the shari'a—just as with logic or discursive theology. He went so far as to proclaim it a wajib kifayya, a religious duty, as it enabled 'ulama to better promote religious doctrines.[23]

Seventeen days after al-Inbabi issued his fatwa, the Hanafi Mufti Shaykh Muhammad al-Banna' issued his, agreeing with Inbabi's opinion.[24]

The Journalistic Debate

Despite the agreement of two of the most powerful 'ulama on this issue, their legitimation of scientific study in madaris was not to be accepted without debate. As in the past scholars had disputed such issues in public hearings,[25] now they disputed them in print. This particular issue elicited a wide range of opinions from the literate public. Azharis themselves were divided on the matter.

An al-Azhar shaykh named 'Ali Yusuf, who would later become a prominent writer and newspaper editor, provided the best sources for viewing the journalistic debate on this subject.[26] He stirred up controversy through an article in *al-Adab* [Polite letters], which made a prescient argument for interdisciplinary study. Different fields of knowledge needed to be studied in connection with one another in order to be truly understood. According to Shaykh 'Ali Yusuf, the Greeks had considered all branches of knowledge to be part of a unified whole. For example, the Greeks had treated as fundamental parts of science and theology subjects now considered supplementary, such as logic and grammar. According to 'Ali Yusuf, the 'ulama of recent times divided knowledge into artificial categories depending on subjects' relation to the study of religion. Religion and science were "estranged": "For the religious scholars claim an aversion to these [applied] sciences and discard them . . . and others believe religiosity to be a barrier between humanity and progress in this life."[27]

According to 'Ali Yusuf, the establishment of Dar al-'Ulum had been a first step in reconnecting the practical and religious branches of knowledge and returning Muslims to the path of progress. Because there was no legal distinction between the two branches, the next steps would be widening the scope of instruction in religious legal studies in the civil schools and introducing natural and mathematical sciences into al-Azhar. 'Ali Yusuf anticipated a negative response on the part of 'ulama, despite the fact that Azhari 'ulama had in the past taught science.[28] The claim that science had been taught at al-Azhar in the past was a bit of sophistry, much repeated by subsequent reformers. Azharis had taught general science, but not, for example, principles of earth science or evolutionary biology. Moreover, 'Ali Yusuf used the term '*ilm*, knowledge, to refer to Western principles of science, whereas the term originally had designated knowledge derived from orally transmitted texts, the model for which was religious sources.[29] This was a rhetorical ploy to accuse the Azharis of having abandoned a previous understanding of 'ilm that had encompassed sciences.

In eight successive issues, *al-Adab* printed readers' responses to Shaykh 'Ali Yusuf's claims, and his rebuttals. The rhetoric of this obscure shaykh seethed with subsurface challenges to 'ulama authority.

The headline to 'Ali Yusuf's articles read: "The Universalization of Education." By this he meant both unification of all forms of knowledge and spread of educational opportunity to all.

> The lack of connection between aspects of knowledge has cut the connections that knowledge demands and for which ijtihad-related wisdom [al-hikma al-ijtihadiyya] and national unity call. . . . If we searched now for the easiest way to spread education universally in this realm we would find that it would be widening the scope of al-Azhar so that it deals with mathematical subjects.[30]

'Ali Yusuf depicted graduates of a reformed al-Azhar curriculum spreading throughout the bureaucracy and countryside, promoting epistemological unity. Yet he acknowledged that such change would be hard to achieve. 'Ali Yusuf implied that Azhari 'ulama employed the separation of sacred knowledge from profane as a deliberate tactic for maintaining their authority. In service to that separation, the 'ulama willfully ignored arguments blurring distinctions between sacred and profane knowledge, and deliberately spoke, wrote, and taught in an Arabic style that 'Ali Yusuf termed "archaic," protecting their realm of knowledge from penetration by outsiders. Thus Azharis exemplified that which prevented the nation, here the Muslim umma, from progressing, and in so doing violated the traditional injunction to seek knowledge, which 'Ali Yusuf defined as *all* fields of knowledge. Azhari 'ulama were the most resistant barrier to strength and progress, and that barrier had to be removed in order to democratize education. The 'ulama had to jump on the bandwagon of their own obsolescence, because such a radical movement would require al-Azhar's stamp of approval.[31]

The debate over the introduction of sciences covered a range of objections and counterarguments, and many Azhari respondents supported Shaykh 'Ali Yusuf. 'Ali Yusuf singled out those who disapproved for refutation. Some 'ulama made a social argument: The study of applied sciences was unnecessary for a country like Egypt, in which most people were farmers. According to them, industry required applied sciences, but agriculture did not. The existing curriculum was adequate for a nation whose people did not need such specialized knowledge. 'Ali Yusuf declared this argument a cover for Azharis to hold on to power.[32] If the people were to improve themselves, to desire more than their current jobs, the established order of society would perish (yudi'u al-nizam). Those privileged by that order would also perish.[33]

One reader commented that al-Azhar students spent long years at the school, which wasted time and money. Addition of scientific subjects would only prolong the time students spent consuming the school's precious resources. 'Ali Yusuf replied that most al-Azhar students were transient learners; they attended only as many reading sessions as were necessary to enable them to obtain some sort of job. Most students were not even capable of ascending to the high levels for which lengthy study was required. Rather, the reform codes caused al-Azhar's financial problems; regulations gave shelter and rations to all students registered for their entire periods of study, without recognition of merit or need. 'Ali Yusuf concluded that the examination system required further refinement, and that students' results should be used in determining whether they qualified for financial support.[34]

'Ali Yusuf set up some respondents as straw men to suit his polemical aims. For example, one respondent declared: "Many natural sciences require proof, whereas law is derived from aural transmission [al-sam'] and reason has no part in it. The legal scholar looks for rational weaknesses after the judgment is rendered, not before." The writer probably did not mean that Muslim legal specialists used no reasoning, in the sense of rational argument, but rather that human reason was not an adequate or reliable tool for discerning truth, if it was used without reference to revelatory texts. If, as this respondent assumed, natural sciences were based on proofs derived exclusively from human reason, there would be little correlation between the traditions of inquiry in the religious sciences and those in natural sciences, and natural sciences would be superfluous to religious scholars' training. 'Ali Yusuf did not bother to cite the origins of this argument in legal traditions that preferred hadith over human reasoning, but merely stated that al-Azhar used to teach many subjects in the past, and it was not necessary that they be derived from the same methods.[35]

Another reader responded: "Natural [science] traces things to natural causes, and that is *shirk* [associating something with God's divinity or his powers and violation of the principle of God's essential unity]. . . . [W]e know that many who work with natural sciences ponder the Creator and His works and teach that these natural causes are merely the connection of God to causative factors." 'Ali Yusuf answered flatly that people do not become apostates from studying natural sciences. The publisher of *Jaridat al-Azhar,* Ibrahim Bey Mustafa, who was also a professor of chemistry at the School of Medicine, wrote to support 'Ali Yusuf, saying that God was the ultimate cause of natural events and therefore studying the natural sciences would not contradict shari'a.

All four critics presented valid points from a certain perspective. 'Ali Yusuf, however, did not address the deeper epistemological problems of the debate; he merely dismissed the respondents' concerns as cover-ups for maintaining 'ulama authority. Yet, like Shaykh Muhammad 'Ilish in his defense of taqlid, the respondents may have had genuine moral concerns. For example, another respondent proposed that the danger in offering sciences at al-Azhar was in their potential to divert students from religious studies:

It is the custom for students at al-Azhar to be interested in everything new—so if these subjects were introduced into al-Azhar, they would turn away from us [the scholars of religion], whether they were prepared for them or not. It would be as we witnessed in the days when Shaykh Khalil al-'Izazi used to teach a treatise on astronomy, when his halqa filled the spaces of the Mosque of al-Ashraf and students nearly abandoned shari'a studies. It may occur to you now, as they are

studying these subjects and yearning for them, no doubt they devote
themselves to them and do not even leave to the Azhari studies a sliv-
er of their attention. . . . If this is the case, the desired outcome, which
is training of people to be shari'a judges or muftis or imams of
mosques or professors, would be lost.[36]

In general, students approved of the introduction of new subjects; most
had no vested interest in maintaining 'ulama authority and were motivated
by curiosity and desire for employment. 'Ulama would have had at least
some professional anxiety about the maintenance of religious institutions
and the provision of adequately trained religious personnel. As the new
knowledge attracted more and more intelligent young men away from religious disciplines, religious institutions would suffer brain drain. 'Ali Yusuf
rejected this argument as well, asserting that, while Dar al-'Ulum taught
both sciences and religious subjects, science had not seduced its students
away from their original purposes.[37] His assertion was misleading. Dar al-
'Ulum students were not studying to become 'ulama or religious personnel;
their original purposes were different from those of al-Azhar students.[38]

Despite the objections raised in the journalistic debate, the campaign to
include sciences in al-Azhar's curriculum succeeded, thanks to the support
of Shaykh al-Azhar al-Inbabi, Khedive Tawfiq, and Qadi Muhammad
Bayram. However, as Azhari 'ulama had insisted, al-Azhar was a school for
the training of religious scholars, and its required courses continued to
reflect that fact. Scientific subjects were not required for the 'alimiyya examinations. Restriction of the requirements to religious subjects discouraged
students from diverting too much attention to electives in mathematics or
sciences.[39] And the sciences taught were not the modern sciences of Dar al-
'Ulum: The Azhar shaykhs offered readings of an astronomy text by Hasan
al-Jabarti (d. 1774) and a mathematics text by Ibn Haytham (d. 1039). Ibn
Khaldun's *Muqaddima*, a fourteenth-century text on social science and history, was not offered despite protests by Muhammad 'Abduh, who had
returned from his exile and immediately begun lobbying Shaykh al-Inbabi
to allow him to teach the *Muqaddima* at al-Azhar.[40]

Moreover, al-Azhar's 'ulama elders had to deal with more than curricular
reforms—the buildings needed physical renovation. Some repairs had been
made since its awqaf had been restored in 1858, but most renovations had
to wait until enough funds from the awqaf were collected to pay for them.
In 1892, al-Azhar's budget from its awqaf was pitiful, an annual total of
£E 4,378.[41] Teaching shaykhs were extremely underpaid: Those of the

highest rank received a monthly payment of £E 1.5, the second rank received £E 1, and the third 75 qurush—somewhat less than an artisan, and much less than a carpenter.[42] In comparison, at this time Dar al-ʿUlum ʿulama received monthly payments of £E 4, and Dar al-ʿUlum students received monthly stipends of £E 1.[43] New teachers at al-Azhar did not even receive stipends; they subsisted on bread rations and second jobs until the death of a senior teacher made a stipend available.[44]

The student population had leveled off but was still high—approximately 10,450 students[45]—despite underpayment of the teachers, the dilapidated physical structure, and the competition from other schools. As ʿAli Yusuf pointed out, the mosque's awqaf still offered shelter and bread to all registered Azhari students, and al-Azhar remained the most venerated Sunni religious educational institution in the Muslim Arab East. As al-Azhar's physical condition continued to deteriorate, the Azharis themselves constructed and debated models for adaptation of the great institution to the emerging needs of its massive student body.

"Al-ʿulama wa al-taʿlim" [Scholars and Instruction]: A Blueprint for al-Azhar's Renovation

ʿAbdullah Nadim, al-Azhar graduate and longtime associate, wrote in 1893 that the ʿulama had historically been either too closely tied to, or too isolated from, political influence, and that both trends had reduced al-Azhar's offerings in science and practical subjects.[46] The story of Shaykh ʿIlish's life demonstrates that this was simply rhetoric. The rest of ʿAbdullah Nadim's critique makes clear that he did not find al-Azhar's most pressing problems to be solely, or even primarily, the fault of the ʿulama. According to ʿAbdullah Nadim, al-Azhar's problems arose from underlying structural inefficiencies: Its physical and human infrastructure, equipped to deal with a few hundred students, could not be adapted to accommodate the massive influx of impoverished students (he claimed 10,000–20,000), and the budget from the awqaf was simply insufficient. These structural inefficiencies caused a series of collateral problems, which together were destroying al-Azhar's usefulness to its students and ultimately to society in general. Underlying his critique were Utilitarian notions of order, useful knowledge, certification, quality control, hygiene, and efficiency.

Overcrowding had caused two primary faults to appear. First, to ʿAbdullah Nadim's eye, the unsanitary conditions within the mosque and student residences had become unacceptable, and second, there were too few professors to manage the students and teach them the etiquette of academic life. Some were even "seen sleeping on their faces" during lessons. Further-more, their living spaces were overcrowded, and they had no servants to clean for them, so "their places of sleep stay filthy, rotten with leftover scraps of food and things that come off the bottoms of their shoes. . . . Their cloth-ing stays dirty and their bodies are rotten with the bodily secretions that have accumulated upon them and with the air pollution and the dust from the ground that sticks to them." Most were impoverished and had no changes of clothing. Conditions like this would inevitably lead to disease, and there were no doctors for the riwaqs.[47]

A secondary or collateral effect of overcrowding was that the older, more personal system of progression through elementary to advanced courses by permission of one's teacher was no longer feasible. Many students did not attend the same courses consistently, or would learn one third of one text, give it up as too hard, and then wind up sitting in an even more advanced halqa.[48] The personalized administrative procedures could not be adapted to deal with a high student-to-professor ratio (on average 44:1, or 56:1 including primary-level students), and chaos was the result.[49] There was no efficient administration of student progression, nor any way to ensure qual-ity control of the student as product.[50] Previously, students had been given certificates (ijazat) for each book completed under a certain shaykh's instruction, but according to Nadim, that certification process too had ceased to operate.[51] Thus 'Abdullah Nadim echoed concerns of the 'ulama that relatively ignorant students could claim to have al-Azhar educations—a claim that would win them a certain amount of respect and employabili-ty in rural villages, but would also inevitably contribute to the ruin of al-Azhar's reputation and public respect for the 'ulama.

Egypt's seven major festivals, during which al-Azhar was closed, caused some of this inefficiency. These held little importance for the large number of foreign students at al-Azhar and only delayed them from completing their studies. Also, students who disappeared for weeks at a time neverthe-less continued to receive daily rations.[52]

Previous reformers also had failed to recognize that al-Azhar's relatively minuscule budget imposed certain limits on its curriculum. Waqf contracts often specified the numbers of shaykhs to whom their funds could be dis-tributed. Hence, in 1893, 187 professors were responsible for teaching 10,451 students. There were twenty required subjects. The necessity of cov-ering those subjects—in addition to shaykhs' specialties—meant that pro-fessors sacrificed depth in preparation and presentation.[53] Also, because receipt of the 'alimiyya degree was tantamount to a teaching appointment, and because limits imposed on hiring by the availability of waqf funds made al-Azhar unable to support more than six new teachers annually, the administration had passed a new examination code in 1888, which limited the number of 'alimiyya degrees conferred to six per year, two from each of the three main madhahib.[54]

'Abdullah Nadim suggested a series of solutions to these multiple and interrelated problems; his article would later become a blueprint for reform. He did not, however, conform to his friends' modernist polemic, which reductively blamed al-Azhar teaching 'ulama for the ills of Egyptian society. Instead, Nadim criticized existing reform codes, which he said were more damaging than helpful in mitigating al-Azhar's troubles. Here Nadim, always identified as a nationalist reformer, echoed the concerns of al-Azhar shaykhs: "[T]he method of examination that was established recently is a method of handicapping the 'ulama and closing down al-Azhar. What I think is that it is an intrigue plotted against the 'ulama, and that they did not discern it." If, of 10,000 Azhari students, only six were permitted to graduate annually, it would take centuries for even the most capable to finish. Failing to gain certificates to teach, students would drop out. If foreign students had to leave without a degree, they would be "harmed" in a prohibited legal sense, having suffered greatly to reach Cairo. This led Nadim to suspect that foreigners had designed the code to be "a sword slicing at the 'ulama of al-Azhar." The limit on number of annual degrees would have to be dropped to remain consistent with principles of justice.[55]

Nadim envisioned a comprehensive redesign of al-Azhar's curriculum that would preserve its primary mission. The immediate problem, overcrowding, could be resolved by reducing enrollment to upper-level education only. If there was need for more upper-level instruction, the Shaykh al-Azhar should establish branch degree programs in every administrative capital. Also, all students requiring elementary instruction should be distributed among the lesser mosques. Many lesser mosques were empty, and because their waqf revenues were thus of no benefit to the public, their vacancy violated waqf stipulations.[56]

After dealing with overcrowding, the Shaykh al-Azhar should implement a strictly regimented system of progression: All students desiring entrance to the religious school system would have to apply, to submit to a physical exam ensuring they were disease-free and over twelve years of age, and to demonstrate that they had memorized the Qur'an and basic texts. All entrants would attend six years of elementary studies at mosques outside al-Azhar. Their progress would be measured by yearly examinations, for which they would receive certificates "like the certificates of the public schools, in order to motivate them and urge them to progress." Only those who had memorized the texts of the preparatory curriculum would be allowed to enter al-Azhar for further study.[57]

Third, the physical environment of al-Azhar would require attention. 'Abdullah Nadim suggested that no one but first-ranked professors be allowed to live within the mosque itself. Those who lived in riwaqs should be subject to regular inspection by an appointee of the Shaykh al-Azhar, someone who would monitor living conditions, supervise student behavior, and serve as tutor. To ensure that diseases were not passed among the students, they should have a clinic and physicians, which could be funded by awqaf that did not have restrictive specifications.[58]

Fourth, to further lighten the burden upon al-Azhar's awqaf, Azhari students would be held to a four-year degree program.[59] In Nadim's opinion, the existing system, in which upper-level students remained disciples of their teachers until they reached mastery, was unnecessary. As Nadim and the modernist reformers envisioned it, the purpose of education had changed: It was to produce proficiency in a specified subject, not mastery equivalent to that of the shaykhs.[60] If the total length of study was limited, each class would have to accomplish specific objectives. Shaykhs' lessons would be subjected to an unprecedented degree of micromanagement: They would use only preapproved texts, avoid use of super-commentaries or marginal glosses, and teach only in one or two specialties. For every required book, an appropriate fixed period of study would be designated, duties of students for that period would be stated, and students would be assigned specific lessons for each book, which shaykhs would be obligated to read "without adding to or subtracting from them." Because general contents of professors' courses would be fixed, students could then progress smoothly from elementary to more advanced classes according to a system of prerequisites. Students would not be permitted to move from one class to another without the instructor's permission, and professors would note attendance and report absences to the Shaykh al-Azhar, who would withhold students' daily rations for days on which they were absent. Students' grades would also suffer from prolonged absences, so legitimate holidays would have to be defined. Nadim suggested that students not miss more than 150 days of classes per year due to legitimate holidays.[61]

To further encourage efficient progression, anyone failing to complete the course of study within ten years would lose daily rations.[62] At the end of the four-year period, students would undergo an examination to ascertain what subjects they would be licensed to teach, and no one who lacked the full ten years of instruction would be permitted to teach.

Although creation of this bureaucratized system of examination administration would doubtless result in a greater number of applicants for the 'alimiyya degree, far more than six, Nadim suggested that students be allowed to proceed with exams anyway. A significant number of Azhari students were from outside Cairo; their only desire was to return to their own countries or provinces with degree in hand and obtain employment there. Those aiming to teach at al-Azhar would have to wait until a waqf-supported position was available, but, according to 'Abdullah Nadim, that was no reason to deny them graduation.[63]

Nadim then offered the next logical step: Only shaykhs who had themselves been examined and found competent in a particular field should be allowed to certify teachers. Nadim claimed that the current system allowed a man to sit with a shaykh for an hour and receive permission at the end to teach the shaykh's readings.[64] There is no sign that Nadim anticipated 'ulama opposition, although he was clearly suggesting that the current teaching staff undergo a kind of accreditation process.

There remained, of course, the issue of employability in fields other than religious education. Administrative reform by itself would not be sufficient to address the problem of al-Azhar graduates' inability to compete with graduates from specialized civil schools. Nadim noted, as his colleague Ahmad Samir had previously, that the denizens of al-Azhar suffered from intellectual isolation from contemporary developments. Everyone there, he said, was separated from the world, knowing nothing of geography, science, politics, industry, agriculture, commerce, or inventions. The students were essentially intellectual elitists, and this led them to insulate themselves from lesser fields of learning: "It is as if he is in a deserted den in terrible emptiness, his only companion someone just like himself."[65]

Nadim assumed that al-Azhar students were not interested in natural or applied sciences, religious studies having higher status. He recognized that al-Azhar was not training scientists, but thought that students should be aware of current events and that elementary students should leave qualified to study sciences in the civil schools. He suggested that perhaps the Waqf Administration should create a library of scientific and political journals for students to read in their free time, but also that al-Azhar should change its curriculum. Nadim also insisted that students know how to apply their knowledge to real-world problems. He claimed that most of the students could not spell and had bad handwriting, and that they could not write or edit anything "unless they stay up nights blackening and whitening their drafts," and even then they could achieve only the "required" and not the "desired" level of proficiency. It was as if they were poets who had read a great deal about writing, but could not do it, because they had never tried.[66]

Nadim suggested that professors adopt a new pedagogical style for instruction in these practical subjects. In the halqa, advanced students made annotated copies of the texts they studied, but shaykhs did not usually assign or grade written work. Shaykhs assumed that students had acquired the skills requiring graded homework at primary school. However, the influx of rural elementary students meant that handwriting, persuasion, elocution, and other elementary skills needed to be reintroduced to al-Azhar. Nadim envisioned that these skills would be taught with emphasis upon their usefulness for an 'alim. Students would learn different styles of oration, for example, so they would be able to adapt to different audiences and occasions.[67]

Both introduction of these subjects and examination of instructors would be controversial. As no 'ulama at al-Azhar at that time specialized in such subjects, those classes would have to be taught by non-Azharis. Nadim considered this inappropriate and stated that non-Azharis should teach at al-Azhar only until their own students could take over the classes.[68] Non-Azharis would not be familiar with the academic climate and traditions of Azhari 'ulama, he said. This was not due entirely to al-Azhar exclusivism. Because madaris tended to specialize in certain areas of knowledge, a graduate of Tanta or Qayrawan may not have had the same training as an Azhari and thus could not simply be given free license to teach at al-Azhar. That was doubly true of graduates of the civil school system. Again, the greater issue was that of the 'ulama's epistemological control, of their desire to maintain their own independence and freedom to ensure the continued integrity of religious knowledge.

Taken as a whole, 'Abdullah Nadim's administrative reform program was a comprehensive application of efficiency-based methods to madrasa education. The halqa system was to be replaced with assignment of students to classes, subjects to shaykhs, and books to subjects, with hierarchically ranked progression and surveillance by examination throughout. Gone would be the implicitly contractual, open reading sessions through which a few would rise to master orally meaningful readings and become living links in the transmission of knowledge. In their place would be an efficient transfer of knowledge, taking up a minimum of students' time and a minimum of financial resources, producing citizens armed with useful knowledge of science, communication skills, and religion that could be employed to serve the cause of national progress. It was a neat and orderly package, appealing to officials, technocrats, and like-minded 'ulama. It also admitted problems with previous reforms, appealing to those who had criticized them and contradicting our historiographical image of two discrete factions of modernist reformers and reactionary conservatives battling over al-Azhar.

Khedive 'Abbas, Muhammad 'Abduh, and the Azhar Administrative Council

Who was to accomplish this systematic remaking of the madrasa system? 'Abdullah Nadim addressed his appeal primarily to the new khedive, 'Abbas Hilmi II. By 1890, Khedive Tawfiq's government had relinquished most arenas of administration to British control, and a British official had commented that, for the first time, the British were in truth governing the entire country.[69] Unlike Tawfiq, 18-year-old prince 'Abbas was not content to perform as a front for British rule. Although 'Abbas had cordial relations with the British Consul Lord Cromer at his accession in 1892, Cromer suspected that the prince's French tutor and personal secretary, M. Rouiller, was fomenting an increasingly anti-British attitude in him. For perhaps two years, 'Abbas overtly sought a way to combat British power (and did so covertly for perhaps eight more). That meant exploiting those few fields of independent action available to him.[70] As one al-Azhar historian put it: "He found before him no means to that but the reform of al-Azhar."[71] 'Abdullah Nadim's plea justified khedival intervention in al-Azhar. It would "not be too expensive," he said, for the government to improve the teaching system at the mosque, provision the students better, and add to the Waqf Administration's stipends for the 'ulama. After all, the khedive already supplied non-waqf stipends for teachers of mathematics and foreign languages. Nadim also reminded the khedive that al-Azhar produced many of the government's own employees, as well as the judges, representatives of the country, muftis, and students of Dar al-'Ulum. "Thus al-Azhar is one of the schools upon which the government must spend money in order to benefit itself." It was different from the civil schools only in that it was independent of the Ministry of Education, but "this [did] not exempt it from the care and responsibility of the government." In fact, the impoverishment and overburdening of the poorer teachers, who had to hire themselves out at night as Qur'an readers, compelled government attention.[72] Thus the khedive, in intervening, would not only be serving his own interests and those of his government bureaucracy, but also those of the 'ulama and ultimately the nation.

Khedive 'Abbas probably read "al-'Ulama wa al-ta'lim" as it was originally printed in 'Ali Yusuf's new popular newspaper *al-Mu'ayyad*, which he had subsidized since 1892.[73] 'Ali Yusuf had befriended the khedive and became one of his most ardent and loyal supporters.[74] Furthermore, the khedive had already perceived that the British had left him little real authority except in the arena of religion. Early in his reign, he discovered that none of his cabinet or top military officers considered him the real head of government; they cleared everything with Cromer first.[75] Also, as titular ruler, 'Abbas relied on religious legitimacy that the 'ulama of al-Azhar helped to provide. All these factors predisposed 'Abbas to agree with Nadim.

Khedive 'Abbas appeared to be sincerely anxious about al-Azhar, as a pious Muslim and concerned ruler.[76] He became very interested in the modernist reformers' campaign; he was especially interested in the reformer Muhammad 'Abduh, who admired 'Abbas's attempts to limit British interference. According to the khedive's personal secretary, Ahmad Shafiq Pasha, 'Abbas sensed in 'Abduh "sincere patriotism [sidq al-wataniyya] and clarity of judgment." They met informally several times, discussing "what might be done in service of the nation [al-watan] and realization of its aspirations." 'Abduh suggested that the khedive act in arenas that the British would not touch because of their religious significance: al-Azhar, the awqaf, and the shari'a courts. He further suggested that 'Abbas begin with al-Azhar, and offered 'Abbas a memo on what needed attention. 'Abbas and some cabinet ministers read the memo and collectively designed a plan. Shortly thereafter, on 3 January 1895, the khedive decreed the creation of "a standing committee called the Azhar Administrative Council [Majlis Idarat al-Azhar], to which will be entrusted an investigation into reorganization of the rules of instruction, organization of the riwaqs and their funds, the ranks of the ulama and their regulation, the particulars of the attainment of kasawi al-tashrif [robes of honor], and in sum everything having to do with improvement of the mosque and continuation of its success."[77]

The creation of the Azhar Administrative Council was a major coup. The khedive was able to impose upon al-Azhar's independent administration a body empowered to change the mosque's educational programs. The state Council of Ministers was to enact its recommendations, not Azhari 'ulama. Likewise, the khedive and his advisors planned its composition. At first, the Shaykh al-Azhar did not even sit on this council; its chair was Shaykh al-Inbabi's deputy, a Hanafi mufti named Hasuna al-Nawawi.[78]

Al-Azhar's internal politics determined three seats on the council besides the chair's; these were held by 'ulama holding the highest positions at al-Azhar after that of the Shaykh al-Azhar himself: Shaykh Salim al-Bishri, Mufti and head of the Maliki madhhab; Shaykh Yusuf al-Hanbali, Mufti and head of the Hanbali madhhab; and Shaykh 'Abd al-Rahman al-Shirbini, a senior Shafi'i shaykh.[79] However, not all members of the council were al-Azhar 'ulama. Two were bureaucratic shaykhs: Muhammad 'Abduh, at the time a qadi in the People's Courts, and 'Abd al-Karim Salman, a deputy administrator of *al-Waqa'i' al-Misriyya*.

The newly formed Azhar Administrative Council immediately investigated 'ulama salaries and special financial awards known as robes of honor (kasawi al-tashrif), and by the end of the month it had already promulgated its first reform code.[80] The 1895 Code required all who undertook the examination to have spent at least twelve years in study, limited the examination period to ten days, allowed a Hanbali 'alim or two to be on exam committees for the rare Hanbali student, set standards for degrees of pass, provided for the awarding of kasawi al-tashrif to first-ranked students, permitted failing students to reenter the exams twice more at most, and created a new mark of distinction for students who passed optional examinations in additional subjects such as arithmetic, algebra, or history. This last point suggested to some that students who took these subjects would enjoy a degree of preference in employment at the mosque and bestowal of stipends.[81]

There was also considerable debate over the projects the council should undertake. The foremost concerns expressed in the press were about corruption of upper-level administration, intolerable crowding, and permissibility of new scientific instruction. Government intervention did not appear as a major point of contention at this time, although Shaykh al-Shirbini, the Shafi'i representative, left the council after serving for less than one month. He resigned on 31 January 1895, the day the first council decree was announced, pleading aversion to political matters.[82] Al-Shirbini's resignation accorded with a standard of 'ulama scholarship that held political activity as inherently corruptive, according to which the quest for pure knowledge demanded separation from the interests of those in power. Thus al-Shirbini's quiet removal of himself from the scene may be interpreted as a personal protest against both the intervention of the khedive in Azhari affairs and the involvement of Azharis in political matters. It suggests that some Azhari 'ulama passively resisted the khedive's actions, among that sector that is now mute due to their exclusion from surviving printed sources.

Muhammad 'Abduh was reportedly delighted by al-Shirbini's resignation. 'Abduh had originally nominated a reformist Dar al-'Ulum professor, Hasan al-Marsafi, who was now able to take the vacant council position. With Hasuna al-Nawawi and 'Abd al-Karim Salman, modernists now had a four-to-three advantage in voting.[83]

Many of the 'ulama did not resist the khedive's intervention but rather actively sought it. In July 1894, before the khedive's decree establishing the Azhar Administrative Council, a group of influential al-Azhar shaykhs had petitioned the khedive to take action against Shaykh al-Azhar al-Inbabi. They claimed that al-Inbabi gave too much financial preference to shaykhs of his own Shafi'i madhhab, and had proved himself incapable of dealing fairly with the other madhahib. Some 'ulama had unsuccessfully tried to convince him to resign.[84]

Khedive 'Abbas responded to the crisis on 26 December 1894 by appointing Hasuna al-Nawawi as Shaykh al-Inbabi's deputy. Shaykh Hasuna was a Hanafi, so the khedive may have intended that the Hanafi shaykh serve as a corrective for al-Inbabi's pro-Shafi'i abuses. Shaykh al-Inbabi was ill at the time, and some sources simply reported that Shaykh Hasuna was appointed to bear the responsibilities that the ailing Shaykh al-Azhar could no longer perform. The crucial point here is that influential Azhari 'ulama again petitioned the khedive for help in dealing with problems in their administration, rather than resorting to internal procedures for deposition and election. Such internal procedures may have been more disruptive than a khedivally imposed decision, either to inter-madhhab relations or to internal structures of influence. Whatever the motivation, the principle of separating al-Azhar from government influence was here not operative. And the khedive chose rule by committee, with a reformist Hanafi shaykh in the lead.[85]

Public Response:
"Let us be guided in the exchange of give and take."

The khedive's expressions of interest in al-Azhar spurred journalistic debates about madrasa education into more optimistic—and persuasive—language. The modernist critique had rapidly developed into a standard appeal. For example, an article by one 'Abd al-Rahman al-Sinnari, appearing in *al-Mu'ayyad* two days after the announcement of the council's formation, praised al-Azhar as "the greatest religious school in the Islamic world" and stated that its 'ulama had to update their interests. Islam could no longer be defended through treatises refuting the "philosophers and

Mu'tazilis, who no longer exist." Students needed to learn polite manners and basic tools like composition, such as could be found in the *Maqamat* of al-Hariri (1054–1122 CE), the *Kamil* of al-Mubarrad (826–898 CE), and *al-Bayan wa al-tabyin* of al-Jahiz (781–869 CE). Also, the professors had to be held to a schedule of lessons, for they did not spend equal time on each segment of their books, but tended to get drawn into certain parts, while the remaining parts received superficial treatment. Thus topics less intellectually stimulating tended to be left until last: "Morphology, in spite of its importance, is not cultivated at al-Azhar because the part of the book that contains the *Alfiyya* by Ibn Malik [a treatise on grammar in one thousand words] is read at the end of the year with extreme speed, such that the students cannot understand it. . . . In truth, all books are treated this way at al-Azhar." Al-Sinnari concluded with half a column filled with soulful praise of the khedive and expressions of surety that he would direct his attention to this mosque, "which is his and his *umma*'s most noble source of pride."[86]

There were, however, also some who expressed concerns about the types of reforms planned and directed the khedive's attention to al-Azhar's "real" problems. Hasan Husni al-Tuwayrani, editor of the literary journal *al-Nil*, provides an example. In his opinion, the issue of reform of al-Azhar had to be viewed from the perspective of spiritual service to the greater Ottoman Muslim community. The newspapers had been discussing the issue for some time, reform itself had become a long and ongoing process, and now he had heard that a special committee would be formed to guide reform. According to al-Tuwayrani, such a committee could best serve the interests of the community if, first of all, the community's views were made known: "Let them write to us their thoughts and if they oppose our idea we will publish it in its totality, though reserving for ourselves the right to respond. Through public opinion, let us be guided in the exchange of give and take to the best possible solution for the improvement of the state of al-Azhar Mosque."[87] Second, al-Azhar's mission had to be taken into consideration, especially when introducing subjects not taught at al-Azhar but rather in civil and foreign schools. Unlike those schools, al-Azhar was established specifically as a religious institution, and was not supported by public funds but by awqaf founded for it on the condition that it remain a religious school. That condition could not be changed just because it was inconvenient; all four madhahib agreed that provisions set by the waqf's founder were absolute. Therefore any curricular changes would first require an investigation of al-Azhar's awqaf.[88]

Many waqf charters supporting studies at al-Azhar did in fact stipulate the subjects to be taught.[89] Some were extremely specific in their stipulations for each and every expenditure of waqf revenues.[90] In addition, al-Tuwayrani continued, there were numerous riwaqs, each of which could have multiple supporting awqaf, all of which had been established under the assumption that they were supporting a religious cause. "Thus if these conditions [i.e., the religious character of the school] are changed, the stipulation is violated, and the proceeds of the awqaf will be spent in violation of the charter. It is necessary at all times to prevent the proceeds of the awqaf from being spent in ways other than those intended."

Al-Tuwayrani assumed, of course, that the new subjects to be introduced did not pertain to religion, and were in that sense fundamentally different from the subjects taught at al-Azhar in past centuries. He claimed that 'ulama would have to pervert or bypass the stipulations of the waqf charters in order to justify spending waqf revenues on the new subjects, and challenged them to provide fatwas from each of the madhahib that would allow them to do such a thing. Then he asked them:

> What is said in the ijma' of the 'ulama of Islam for almost ten centuries? They agreed on al-Azhar's remaining a solely religious madrasa, in which nothing would be taught other than specific subjects decided among the Azharis. Were they mistaken in that opinion? Stricken by what is proper for another people? Did they see that the times required this madrasa to change from a purely religious one, and rule thusly? Or did they see that there was no objection to the introduction of recent fields of knowledge, and so mixed the teaching of religions with worldly fields of knowledge and eliminated the special responsibility [al-Azhar] had carried out in the service of the umma and its religion all these years?

This statement is packed with challenge. First, al-Tuwayrani considered the right to choose which subjects would be taught at al-Azhar to belong to the 'ulama of al-Azhar. Thus he also opposed the domination of the Azhar Administrative Council by government bureaucrats and non-Azhari 'ulama. He appealed to the khedive to appoint to such a council ordinary 'ulama "whose offices are not limited to shaykh of so-and-so," and to let the chairmanship of the council be held by Chief Qadi Jamal al-Din Effendi, supreme judge of the Egyptian shari'a courts. The reform of al-Azhar was too important to allow it to be influenced by the interests of power, government pressures, and the petty bickering of officials. It should be undertaken with full acknowledgment of al-Azhar's religious mission "in the hands of God, the umma, and history, in front of millions." Second, al-Tuwayrani implied that the new subjects were intrinsically connected to their home environments in Europe and were out of place as subjects of study in Egypt (even in the civil schools). Such a suggestion challenged modernists' claims that the new sciences and modes of social thought and organization based on them were universally applicable. Third, he recognized the mission of the religious madrasa, and especially of al-Azhar, as being unique. In the past, the religious institutions had been the only loci of higher education, and the lack of specialization meant that nearly all knowledge fell within the purview of religious scholars. The situation in al-Tuwayrani's time was different. Because the government bureaucracy required employees to know subjects that were no longer within the purview of religious scholars, those employees should not be trained at religious schools. Religious schools were for the teaching of religion; those whose needs went beyond the knowledge provided by al-Azhar should be trained at schools that were not constrained by their sources of funding.

> Yes, perhaps we share recognition of the need for a religious and secular [dunyawiyya] madrasa-college, from which would graduate those who would be employed by or appointed to [government positions]. But this is not al-Azhar. [A secular college] could be founded with state monies and general, national cooperation. This would be a public blessing for which we could give thanks.

Furthermore, the importance of maintaining al-Azhar as a religious school went beyond purely national concerns: The need for teaching of religion and training of scholars was "perpetual, unceasing, and eternal[.] . . . Al-Azhar is a public recourse and refuge, not just for the Egyptians but also for the Muslim people in general, all the more so because all awqaf and benefits are fixed and established and may not be infringed."[91] In short, because waqf endowments were enforced indefinitely—in theory, "until God inherits the earth"—their stipulations that assumed al-Azhar's mission to be religious would confine it indefinitely to that role. This ensured that the Muslim community's need for guidance and education, which would also be eternal, would always be fulfilled.

Al-Tuwayrani's opposition to the introduction of new subjects did not answer the modernist reformers' claims that these subjects did pertain to

religion, in that the 'ulama needed to be aware of contemporary developments in order to better fulfill their functions as representatives of the religion to the people. And it ignored the fact that al-Azhar personnel who
taught these subjects were paid via government grants, not awqaf. Al-
Tuwayrani also implicitly accepted a Utilitarian differentiation between religious and secular fields of learning and upheld the separation of the two as
a means of preserving religion intact. He perceived the uses of different subjects of study to be fundamentally different, and he employed his concept
of that difference to defend a view of al-Azhar's education inspired by his
own spiritual consciousness. He was therefore operating within a conceptual dichotomy, secular versus religious, that he may have learned from the
European intellectual traditions he considered so inappropriate for al-
Azhar.

Al-Tuwayrani's article in *al-Nil* did produce at least one supportive
response, by an al-Azhar shaykh named Muhammad Sulayman al-Safti,
which was printed in the journal *al-Islam*. *Al-Islam's* editor, Ahmad al-
Shadhili al-Azhari, was also an Azhari-trained shaykh and a member of the
Shadhili Sufi order, like conservative mufti Muhammad 'Ilish. Shaykh
Ahmad wrote primarily about religious duties, but he also described contemporary scientific discoveries and clarified their relevance to believers'
religious lives. The articles published in *al-Islam* suggest that Ahmad al-
Shadhili did not oppose the new subjects in principle, including scientific
instruction, nor was he unwilling to see scientific subjects taught at the civil
schools.[92] Nevertheless, he printed al-Safti's article opposing their introduction into al-Azhar, agreeing with al-Tuwayrani but extending the argument
in a distinctly conservative direction. Al-Safti argued that al-Azhar did not
need new subjects: "The entire objective is to learn the shari'a, which is
based on the subjects currently taught there, not on other mathematical
subjects."[93] Shaykh al-Safti was a supervisor of the Ibtighawiyya riwaq and
knew well the students did not have time to take electives in new subjects. He sketched out the familiar slippery slope: Once students began to
be required to take new sciences, they would be gradually drawn away from
their religious studies. Al-Azhar would come to specialize in the subjects
that previously had only utilitarian value, and those subjects that religious
education upheld would vanish. The 'ulama would die out without any successors, leaving the community bereft of religious guidance. "Thus would
the shari'a of the Messenger of God, peace be upon him, be annihilated. All
of this for the sake of mathematical sciences and the fruits of progress,
which are said to cause the spread of skepticism."[94]

Here al-Safti engaged modernists' arguments that the new sciences were among the requirements for national advancement. The modernist reformers' definitions of progress required acquisition of empirical knowledge at the expense of religious expertise, and thus their definitions themselves must be faulty. Al-Safti pointed out that Egypt possessed a tradition of empirical science. Egypt boasted both 'ulama of the law and 'ulama of science, and though the two fields of knowledge were separated and their scholars might know little of the other field, it was not as if the country was scientifically barren. Nor was it bereft of civilization and cultural prosperity, which modernists argued resulted only from Western empirical traditions.[95]

Al-Safti also disagreed with the definition of reform used by proponents of the new fields of learning: "What is called the reform of al-Azhar is not really reform." Rather, according to al-Safti, it was an underhanded way to ensure that al-Azhar stayed as it was, since attention paid to the introduction of new subjects was attention not paid to al-Azhar's true problems.[96] True reform would leave al-Azhar's subject matter alone. But here al-Safti betrayed the extent to which he, too, had accepted Utilitarian methods of management. To this former riwaq shaykh, whose duties had included registration of the students and distribution of their benefits, reform was tartib, "organization." Reformers should address the matter of incoming students, their registration in the correct riwaqs, their progression from elementary to advanced subjects, and supervision of their morals and behavior. They should find a way to ensure that students understood their lessons well and learned how to teach before graduating. And they should address the problem of moral corruption.

Al-Safti complained that the Shaykh al-Azhar had violated al-Azhar's system of order by bypassing the system of examination in order to give degrees and teaching posts to his own favorites. According to al-Safti, it should have been the responsibility of the Shaykh al-Azhar to organize the 'ulama into groups to teach elementary, intermediate, or advanced subjects, to assign them books, and to allocate kasawi al-tashrif to those "whose houses are known among the people for religiosity and knowledge," and not for other reasons. In addition, the murattabat and other salaries should be allocated according to an 'alim's need; if he were poor or had a large family, he should naturally receive a larger allowance than a wealthy single man. Al-Safti warned that prejudice in such matters led to complaints.[97]

In short, al-Safti shared al-Tuwayrani's desire that reform be directed by concern for preservation of al-Azhar's original mission. That mission would be served not by the introduction of new sciences but by the creation of order within the mosque: "We beg those in power not to change what al-Azhar teaches of the religious subjects but rather to leave it as it is, with attention to its students, its teachers, its salaries, and its *kasawi al-tashrif,* so that the goal is order."

Al-Safti did not recognize as European the techniques of management he had accepted; he did not see them as colonization. They were merely useful. But he admitted that he opposed the planned reforms out of fear that the calls for new fields of learning were those of "Messieurs So-and-So who have no respect for mosques," who would introduce them into al-Azhar by force, and eventually change al-Azhar so that its jurisdiction was no longer that of a mosque, and its duty no longer the elucidation of the shari'a.[98] It is interesting that these critics of reform foreshadowed historian 'Abdullah 'Enan's comment that the reforms of the early twentieth century, which gave to al-Azhar its contemporary shape as a university with secular collegiate divisions, stripped al-Azhar of its unique religious character and made it into "a university like other universities" whose students were motivated by material desires.[99] But al-Safti, engaged in the construction of 'Enan's Azhar, did not idealize al-Azhar's pre-Utilitarian past.

A third Azhari 'alim, Muhammad al-Hifni al-Mahdi, wrote an article ostensibly addressing the etiquette and appropriate behavior for a learned man. But it also offered al-Mahdi's own views on the purpose and appropriate reach of scholarship. He commented that increasing specialization of knowledge obviated the 'ulama's need to hold universal knowledge, implying that the modernists' campaign to educate the 'ulama both in religious and "modern" fields was unnecessary. The salaf had stated that studying jurisprudence was a sufficiently rewarding task in and of itself. If the 'ulama and the students tried to study more than jurisprudence, if they aspired to more universal knowledge, they "would not work to achieve the degree of perfection that is the goal itself, and they will be limited to the minimal edges of each art."[100] The extent of human knowledge in these times was simply too vast to permit deep understanding of several fields; thus specialization was required. Furthermore, campaigns for the universalization or democratization of knowledge (such as that of Shaykh 'Ali Yusuf) were founded on faulty assumptions. First, they assumed that it would be beneficial for people to study all fields of knowledge. In the words of one 'alim cited in the article, the idea that it would be possible for a single person to know all subjects was a complete fantasy. Second, "it is not necessary for each person to learn all subjects of knowledge; rather it suffices that there be a group of 'ulama who preserve them."[101] The 'ulama's function, after all, had originally been to memorize and record oral reports about the religion and society of the early community, as a fard kifa'i, an obligatory duty that could be fulfilled by some on behalf of all. Most people were not mentally equipped for such an intellectually challenging task.[102] Thus the 'ulama had always served a specialized function. By implication then, al-Azhar's training should remain specialized. That is not to say that no reform at all was required, for if the 'ulama were to fulfill their functions as moral guides, they would have to be able to do so in an atmosphere that promoted orderly and cordial instruction in religious ethics.

Conclusion

During the 1880s and 1890s, the numbers of students at al-Azhar passed 10,000. The number of awqaf that provided funding for teaching and administrative support did not increase at the same pace; consequently the personalized administrative and pedagogical methods of the madrasa could not continue to function as they had in the past. This produced a cognitive break in the minds of those who observed conditions at the mosque: Even those who feared European encroachment began to value the regimentation, bureaucratic surveillance, and order of efficiency-based educational methods. Debates about the modernists' plans for reform continued, but the object of protest was never the need for tartib (organization). This betrays the extent to which literate Egyptians had naturalized Utilitarian-inspired administrative methods and had come to understand them as necessary adjuncts to recovery from a disorderly and stagnant past, essential elements of the hybrid nation they were articulating. This also explains why the lines between "modernist reformer" and "opponent of reform" appear sometimes to blur: No voices have survived that oppose the concept of reform as tartib.

None of the writers perceived Utilitarian models of order as a threat to the mission of the madrasa. They all ultimately aimed to protect the integrity of religious knowledge and preserve Islam's place within Egyptian society. They differed, instead, on the necessity and permissibility of teaching non-shari'a subjects in the madrasa. Journalist 'Abdullah Nadim and critic 'Abd al-Rahman al-Sinnari identified overcrowding and a subsequent moral decline among the 'ulama as primary obstacles to order. Former riwaq shaykh Muhammad Sulayman al-Safti said reform was tartib, an orderly system of registration and progression through courses. Muhammad Hifni al-Mahdi underlined the 'ulama's function in society as moral guides, which required a locus of learning in which they could actually teach ethical behavior. Hasan Husni al-Tuwayrani warned that al-Azhar's religious mission had to remain foremost in the reformer's mind; the legal and financial basis for al-Azhar's existence depended on it, and the addition of new subjects in accordance with someone else's definition of progress could threaten that mission. Nevertheless, al-Tuwayrani supported the idea of tartib, as long as it was directed by ordinary Azhari 'ulama. In sum, the merely slippery slopes of scientific endeavor were less threatening to al-Azhar than the abyss of its perceived disorder.

Moreover, the issue that historians have assumed to be most troublesome for reform opponents, the introduction of science, was debated on grounds that were central to the question of al-Azhar's place within Islamic society, while questions of the validity of scientific methods or positivist assumptions appeared as only embryonic concerns. Thus when the anonymous respondents to 'Ali Yusuf's debate used old arguments against natural causation and human infallibility to question the relevance of science to al-Azhar's curriculum, they may have indeed been concerned about rationalism and the quest for truth, but their overt argument was that al-Azhar existed to transmit specifically religious subjects, to train religious personnel according to a tradition that upheld the epistemological validity of textually transmitted knowledge and thus encouraged strength in the face of skepticism and doubt. The other respondents' pragmatic arguments, that addition of new subjects would lengthen the time of study or seduce students away from the religious subjects, similarly defended a particular vision of al-Azhar's mission. Ultimately, these critics were concerned about preserving the role of highly trained, madhhab-loyal religious specialists as moral and legal guides in society in the face of internal and external threats to communal unity.

Other themes of opposition challenged the philosophical implications of modernist reform, which purely administrative reforms could not ameliorate. One theme was the longstanding, although not universal, assumption that instruction in philosophical principles would engender doubts about the truths of revelation, undermining the institution of the 'ulama and bringing about indirectly the corruption and ruin of Islamic society. A second theme involved suspicions that 'ulama who worked for the state would be swayed by the needs of those in power and might not hold to the pursuit of truth. A third theme, implicit in the first two, was a defense of the authority of the 'ulama. 'Ali Yusuf's campaign for the universalization of education threatened the authority of the 'ulama as repositories and interpreters of sacred knowledge, as well as the integrity of the knowledge they preserved. This instinct for preservation was not merely manifested in conservation of social power, but also in control over transmission of knowledge, exegesis, and the scope of permitted interpretations of religious and academic texts.

At the heart of this debate was a contest over the meaning of '*ilm,* discursive knowledge. 'Ilm had previously been understood as textually derived knowledge, such as that acquired by reading or memorizing revelatory texts or hadith. Direct contact with an oral transmitter of the text was preferred, and in that sense 'ilm was empirical knowledge. Most 'ulama of this time also held affective knowledge (ma'rifa), of a world unknowable via sense perception, possible through mystical visions. 'Ilm was the province of the madaris; ma'rifa fell for the most part under the jurisdiction of Sufi orders. Because medieval physical sciences had also been termed 'ilm, reformers could maneuver this category to argue that madaris had always taught "science" and that therefore the new empirical sciences were proper subjects for the madrasa. This argument depended upon the questionable premise that modern and medieval sciences were univocally science. In the arguments of 'Ali Yusuf and the modernists, these new empirical sciences were implicitly (although rarely explicitly) higher in the hierarchy of subjects of knowledge, because they were those that led to progress. However, as some critics were aware, the definition of empirical knowledge, as held by contemporary European positivists, excluded revelation.[103] Thus Shaykh al-Safti could counter that the "mathematical sciences and the fruits of progress" sought by modernist reformers caused the spread of "skepticism" in society, and others could point to the danger that the new subjects would gradually edge religious subjects into obscurity. The meaning of 'ilm itself, and thus the mission of the madrasa, was now under question.

Several factors suggested that the struggle would end in the modernists' favor, despite their promotion of a positivistic epistemological hierarchy. First, the Azharis seemed to accept that the new khedive, 'Abbas Hilmi II, was competent to direct reforms, and 'Abbas Hilmi preferred for the time being to work through an appointed Azhar Administrative Council dominated by modernist reformers. Second, those who might oppose the modernists on ideological grounds were already halfway down the modernists' path.

7

THE SYRIAN RIWAQ
CHOLERA RIOT

In 1896, fears expressed both by Azharis and by government reformers about the sanitary and moral effects of overcrowding at al-Azhar were realized in spectacular fashion. The secretary of the Azhar Administrative Council, 'Abd al-Karim Salman, reported in 1896 that conditions within the Azhar compound were still poor. Impoverished students who could not afford private lodgings slept inside the mosque. Riwaqs founded to provide sleeping places for poor students were full, and students had taken to sleeping in the mosque loggias. Floors and courtyards were littered with bits of rotting food and infested with mice; puddles of water lay stagnant on the ground; chests, lockers, and dirty clothing cluttered the overcrowded sleeping areas; and the smell was overpoweringly bad. Many students appeared to suffer from skin diseases and other illnesses.[1] Of the six students who attempted the 'alimiyya examination that year, only one passed.[2] Al-Azhar graduate Shaykh Ahmad al-Shadhili furthermore reported that residents of the ethnic riwaqs had staked out seats in lessons. When a Sa'idi student sat in a "Syrian spot," fighting broke out. Police had to intervene, leading Shaykh Ahmad to beg God to reform al-Azhar.[3]

That summer, a cholera epidemic hit Egypt. In Cairo, deaths exceeded forty per day. Most of the cases were in Old Cairo, a southern quarter on the Nile inhabited mostly by native Christians and Jews. The government declared it placed utmost importance on preventing the spread of the disease.[4] On 1 June 1896, the cholera broke out in the Syrian riwaq at al-Azhar. Some riwaqs were buildings adjacent to the madrasa while others were porticoes of the madrasa itself. To a twenty-first-century reader, the idea of a cholera outbreak in a dormitory complex resonates with peril. But inhabitants of the Syrian riwaq preferred the risk of contracting cholera to handing their sick over to the state for hospital treatment. When state officials tried to take one ailing student to the hospital, his comrades resisted. A violent protest ensued which necessitated forceful intervention, and a student was killed.[5]

Recorded responses to the Cholera Riot all express a solidifying public belief that European efficiency-based techniques of order were necessary, indeed normal. The riot itself, however, reflects continuing suspicion of the state's overt exertion of power over religious institutions, in this case through use of violence to enforce a quarantine. The bodies of Azhari students became sites of contestation, with control of religious institutions as the prize. In this battle, the state—and the reformers—won. The disturbance led to the implementation of state-sponsored reforms debated over the previous two decades. Moreover, the Azhar Organization Code of 1896 imposed Utilitarian techniques of educational order not just at al-Azhar, but at smaller madaris as well. The plan followed almost exactly 'Abdullah Nadim's suggestions as laid out in "Al-'ulama wa al-ta'lim." Al-Azhar would embody Egyptian intellectuals' articulations of Egypt's hybridized modernity.

The Incident

Shaykh Ahmad published in *al-Islam* a lengthy account of what he called "the incident," as well as a summary of testimony submitted at a subsequent hearing and copies of official reports submitted to the Minister of the Interior.[6] His own account, culled from reports of eyewitnesses, was sympathetic to the Syrian students. In my reading of this incident, the public perception of fault is more important than actual fault, if such a thing could even be determined.

According to Shaykh Ahmad's sources, the student's illness was discovered at daybreak.[7] When asked, other students said they thought he had fallen ill from "a drink of water." The scientific journal *al-Muqtataf* had just printed a serialized article explaining how cholera was spread through polluted water sources;[8] the students' explanation suggests that Azharis were not as insulated from scientific findings as modernists assumed. The state required immediate notification and quarantine of epidemic disease,[9] so an Azhari guard went to the Darb al-Ahmar police station at 9:40 A.M. and returned with a doctor and the adjutant of the Darb al-Ahmar police station. They quarantined the Syrian riwaq and refused to let anyone accompany them to the top floor where the patient lay. Upon examination, the doctor determined that the patient had a contagious disease requiring hospitalization, and refused the victim's friends entry into the riwaq to see their "stricken brother." Two other students, a Syrian and a Maghribi, had already fallen ill and been taken by the doctor to the hospital, where they had died.[10] The students were thus anxious about handing over their friend to the doctor. The students asked to have the cholera victim delivered to one of their houses where he could be treated by a private doctor at their own expense. According to Shaykh Ahmad, the law permitted home care for those who could afford it. But in epidemic cases, the law clearly called for quarantine,[11] so the adjutant refused to let them do this and swore to have the student removed to the hospital. After some argument, one of the Syrian students stepped up to the adjutant and announced that they would not permit removal of the patient, even if they had to die to defend him. Soon other students were applauding and echoing his defiance. The adjutant feared the students were about to attack him, so he agreed when they asked him to stall until they could consult their riwaq shaykh. Exasperated and frightened, he then sent immediately for a military force of six soldiers, who took up positions around the riwaq.[12]

The riwaq shaykh, Shaykh Rafi', told the students to inform the Shaykh al-Azhar. Thus, at approximately 12:30 P.M., Shaykh al-Azhar Hasuna al-Nawawi first received word of the disturbance.[13] The students told him only that the patient had an injury and that they did not want to send him to the hospital because "all who go to the hospital die." Shaykh Hasuna therefore suggested that the patient be removed to a private home, but the student said the owner of the available house had forbidden it. Shaykh Hasuna then scolded the adjutant for bringing in soldiers, and demanded that Shaykh Rafi' be found and made to undertake his duty at the riwaq. Shaykh Hasuna then left to find the governor of Cairo, leaving the incident in the hands of the police and, he thought, Shaykh Rafi'. However, Shaykh Rafi' had by this time absconded; searchers reported that he could not be found.[14]

The situation had now attracted the notice of the city government. The deputy governor arrived, determined to remove the patient from the riwaq. He found the adjutant and his six soldiers standing outside the Syrian Gate. A mass of people surrounded the madrasa complex and the gate. The area of the Syrian riwaq itself was closed up and congested with students (not all Syrians) whose hands were filled with wood planks, canes, and bits of rock, and both the Shaykh al-Azhar and the riwaq shaykh were gone. Then a British inspector, one Mr. Rove, arrived and began conferring with the

deputy governor outside the gate. The students opened the gate from time
to time to hurl a stone at them, so the police shut and guarded all mosque
gates. Shortly afterward, Mr. Mansfield, British Deputy Chief of Police,
arrived, followed by the city governor, Mahir Pasha.[15]

Although the soldiers had been warned by the khedive's prime minister
to avoid force, Mansfield suggested they enter the mosque by shooting at
the gate until it opened. But the governor wanted to talk to the students
first. In his report, the governor noted that his first impulse was to meet
with the Shaykh al-Azhar, the riwaq shaykh, or "any one of the 'ulama," but
none of the 'ulama were present. He was told they had all left at the mere
rumor of a disturbance, and the riwaq shaykh had refused to speak to the
students, saying that he feared they would tear him apart. Thus the governor found it was left to him to attempt negotiation:

> When I found that it was necessary to offer advice to these zealots
> [muta'assibin], I resolved to enter myself into their midst and advise
> them, thinking that they might wait to see what an individual might
> say, because of course a single person could not take the patient
> away [by himself]. The deputy governor had let me know that they
> had struck him with rocks. . . . All of that did not prevent me from
> doing as I resolved, and I opened that gate and entered. At my mere
> entrance, rocks descended upon me at a rate I had not imagined.
> However, I was resigned to advance and embarrassed to withdraw.
> . . . I heard one of them say "the governor" and another say "Give it
> to 'im" [adiluh]. I was dismayed at this barbaric act and tried to dis-
> appear from sight a little to the side . . . but I saw nothing but the
> rocks like bolts of lightning descending. My left leg was struck
> about twice, and my forehead, and it was only by the grace of God
> that I did not lose my right eye. At once I retreated and exited by
> the gate, with the rocks striking my back. And they promptly shut
> the gate. Without exaggeration I say it is a wonder that I did not
> die.[16]

Other witnesses said that a sizable entourage actually accompanied him,
including the adjutant, the two British officials Mansfield and Rove, and
some police officers. This could hardly have been viewed as a nonthreaten-
ing party. The others were also struck by rocks and forced to withdraw.
Mansfield was hit in the head and body several times by rocks, but the
injuries left no marks. Mansfield said furthermore that the noise of the

crowd prevented him from hearing the governor, who was trying to regain control by yelling, "I am the governor, I am the governor!"[17]

The governor then quarantined the entire mosque and declared it an epidemic hospital. Nearby shops were closed, and the area was cordoned off and surrounded by police, thus marking it as dangerous territory, quarantining not just the disease but also the potential for violence. These actions signaled to passersby that events inside were abnormal and would be controlled.

Then police reinforcements arrived, led by the police chief, Mr. Claus. The police chief and governor conferred briefly and decided the cordon was insufficient: "Even with the large number of blockaders around the outside of the mosque, staying there would not be feasible as the rocks fell in large numbers from the windows." There was also danger of increasing tension between the students and soldiers, because the students had driven soldiers back from the gate with rocks and were now hooting at them, insulting them, and vowing to continue resistance. The governor decided that further "gentleness" would be taken as a sign of weakness, and tried to have the gate to the mosque opened a second time. The students had by then blocked it with an iron window screen. The opening was so small that a group of soldiers could not possibly enter without exposing themselves to the rocks. The students responded to knocking, but only by shouting from behind the gate that they were Muslim and subjects of the government, and that they preferred to keep the patient out of the hospital.[18]

At this point, the British police chief ordered the soldiers to break the gate down. The soldiers tore at one of its doors until a hole was opened in the corner large enough to allow soldiers to fire from it. As soon as the hole appeared, the students began throwing stones at the soldiers, although the closed gate protected their targets from harm. The police chief fired a blank shot into the air as a warning and then ordered his officers to open fire. They did so, at first firing one by one through the opening. When this had little effect, they fired at will from the street until the students scattered. The soldiers then entered the mosque "with shoes on and weapons unsheathed"[19] and saw that several students were injured and that one, struck five times, was obviously dead. They pursued one group of students to the roof, where more shots were heard. All captured within the mosque were arrested and jailed temporarily, including non-Syrians, visitors, and even 'ulama. The injured students were taken to the hospital. As for the cholera victim, he had died some time during the disturbance.[20]

Assigning Fault

There was plenty of blame to go around. Because non-Syrian students participated in the violence, the governor and the police considered it to have been a "general uprising against the orders of the government." At this, Shaykh Ahmad sarcastically commented, "How surprising" (ya lil-'ajab).[21] Law historian Khaled Fahmy has shown that nineteenth-century Cairenes felt state encroachment into their lives most deeply at times of death, when the state appropriated the bodies of their loved ones for autopsies and burial outside the city, away from the family.[22] This riot also expressed that deeply felt resistance. Its cause may have been less student fear of hospitals and more angst at separation from their comrade, the Syrian riwaq community having replaced their distant families, but the riot can be interpreted as rebellion against state encroachment.

This helps to explain why the governor blamed the shaykhs for the riot. "I hate to say this," he said; "the absence of the Shaykh of the mosque, the riwaq shaykhs, and the rest of the 'ulama during the incident is surprising." They were in loco parentis to the Syrian students. Whether approving or disapproving, they should have been the first to hear student complaints, but they abandoned their posts. He concluded that the office of Shaykh al-Azhar was nominal only and not deserving of respect.[23]

Shaykh al-Azhar Hasuna al-Nawawi, on the other hand, claimed that he would have been unable to quell the disturbance himself. Some of the Syrian students had come to his administration building and threatened him. Furthermore, he reminded his readers, in previous disturbances at al-Azhar state officials had suffered great "insults and disrespect" at the hands of students. He had feared he would be hurt, just as the riwaq shaykh had feared that students would "tear him apart." But Shaykh Hasuna's comment also reminds us that he implicitly regarded himself as a government official, as part of a hierarchy of authority the apex of which was not himself. Al-Azhar was not as independent administratively as it should have been ideally, but was subject to the rule of civil authorities. Therefore Shaykh Hasuna had left the mosque to seek a higher authority, the governor. Finding that the governor was already at al-Azhar, the shaykh had returned to find the cordon in place, preventing him from entering. Instead of making his presence known, the shaykh had gone back to the administration building and waited, secure in his belief that those responsible for dealing with the protesters would come looking for him if he was needed. He was still there when he heard the shots.[24]

For the disturbance itself, Shaykh Ahmad also blamed the 'ulama, tying the whole issue to the influence of foreigners on public perceptions of the 'ulama, the decline of the 'ulama as an institution, and the state's usurping of 'ulama rights to nominate their own leaders. According to Shaykh Ahmad, the students' original trepidation at sending their friend to the hospital, and their request to transfer him to a private home, did not justify the adjutant's dismissive treatment of them. The adjutant, he claimed, had absorbed a Westernizer's perspective on the 'ulama and students of religion, the foreigner's idea that the 'ulama had diminished until they were now "worth less than flies" and that there was no 'alim who cared for anything but a high position. Thus the adjutant was arrogant and ill-disposed to deal sympathetically with Azharis.[25]

The soldiers and government officials also shared to some extent in the blame, because the soldiers had been willing to violate the sanctuary of the mosque. Religio-cultural codes prohibit anyone from entering a mosque without symbolically leaving behind the concerns of worldly life; one must enter barefoot, cover one's head in humility, and sheathe—literally and metaphorically—one's weapons. The mosque is a place of peace and learning, a sanctuary from violence and persecution. In violating that principle, the soldiers had forsworn their own mission, because the duty of soldiers and justification for the military's existence was protection of religion and the national interest. The soldiers had met rocks with gunfire, had entered the mosque with their boots on, their weapons drawn, with violent intent, and had spilled blood and killed a student of religion. This was "the biggest calamity and worst catastrophe for al-Azhar Mosque, learning, the 'ulama, religion, and Muslims . . . the heart of the community [milla] was stricken with the killing of its fallen son, smeared with his pure blood." The British violation of the mosque was similar to that committed by Napoleon's troops during the French occupation, when French soldiers on horseback entered the mosque, smashed screens and furnishings, and defiled the sanctuary with blood and horse feces. That act had shown the Egyptians that the French did not respect Islam regardless of Napoleon's attempts to convince them otherwise, and this contributed to the Egyptian opposition movement. According to Shaykh Ahmad, the British had now done the same thing, very publicly. Furthermore, they had met rocks with gunfire. The state was exerting its control over the madrasa in the most striking way possible. To make matters worse, the governor, by acquiescing to this violent response, had demonstrated that he shared the discriminatory perspective of the police and the military.[26]

That foreign officers had participated in this violation was less of an issue for Shaykh Ahmad than its perpetration by agents of an interventionist and disrespectful state. The British police chief Claus had owned up to his sin at the hearing. He had admitted firing the first shots and ordering the soldiers to fire on the students. Shaykh Ahmad regarded this act of admission as indicating "marks of decency and self-respect in the police chief" that were lacking in Egyptian officials, who each tried to cover up their roles in the matter and point the finger at others.[27] However, the British were not blameless: Their own prejudices against the 'ulama and the religious institutions, which manifested themselves in their programs for reform, had affected others in the government and military. What Britons thought was edifying guidance was actually teaching Egyptians to undermine the madrasa and with it the "distinguishing marks" of Islam.[28]

In retrospect, then, Shaykh Ahmad concluded that the adjutant and the governor had been correct: The defiance of the students was indeed opposition to the government. However, this had not become true until after the adjutant and governor overreacted to a situation perceived as a crisis because of their prejudices against Azharis. The student who died from gunshot wounds had thus died a martyr, a victim of state encroachment and European-inspired prejudice.[29] The students themselves, in Shaykh Ahmad's opinion, were to blame only tangentially. They should have handed over the patient and should not have resorted to violence. Nevertheless, they acted out of genuine concern. Moreover, the students, *as students,* were ultimately not responsible for their ignorance and violence. Those who *were* responsible were those who had failed to instruct their pupils properly, especially the riwaq shaykh and the Shaykh al-Azhar.

Shaykh Ahmad agreed with the governor that the two ranking shaykhs had "abandoned the duties of their offices." According to Shaykh Ahmad, the Shaykh al-Azhar had effectively admitted, by saying he knew he could not subdue the students himself, that he was unable to perform his duties as administrator of al-Azhar, despite his protest that other shaykhs had failed to quell riwaq riots. Curiously, the journal *al-Mu'ayyad,* which almost always supported al-Azhar, suggested after the incident that a "higher authority" had forced the Shaykh al-Azhar to write that report as he did, and make those admissions. Shaykh Ahmad astutely observed that, if *al-Mu'ayyad* were correct, the shaykh would have then not only admitted his incapacity to manage the students, he would have also admitted falsifying evidence at the government's request. Thus he would have furthered state intervention and discredited himself as an independent legal authority. Because Shaykh Hasuna was at that time also serving as the Grand Mufti, the khedival government relied to some extent on his fatwas and had an interest in appointing someone whose views agreed with theirs. But if it became known that the Grand Mufti was in the government's pocket, many 'ulama would consider his fatwas invalid. Either way, Shaykh Ahmad declared, the Shaykh al-Azhar had disgraced himself and should not remain in office.[30]

The greater disgrace, however, fell on the mosque shaykhs in general. Even if the riwaq shaykh had arrived on time and had ordered the students to surrender their stricken comrade, "it would have been made an empty gesture." Shaykh Ahmad blamed the decline of the student body's character—they were just looking for an excuse to riot, so "the matter would still have flamed into a conflagration and the firing of bullets." The 'ulama had ceased to be moral guides for their students, and they had permitted the state to acquire power over them. This disgrace was manifested in the state's having preempted their right to appoint their own administrators. As Shaykh Ahmad pointed out, some of those administrators were "not even known to al-Azhar and its people." He thus connected the disturbance structurally to the perceived subordination of 'ulama leadership to the state, as embodied in the creation of the Azhar Administrative Council, the designation of the khedive's pet mufti as its chair, and the appointment of non-'ulama government bureaucrats to its membership.[31] Thus, although Shaykh Ahmad ended his article with a plea for reform, he disapproved of the khedive's extending state control over the madaris.

Perhaps, he suggested, the violence would not have occurred had the Azharis been permitted to elect their own Shaykh al-Azhar. Shaykh Ahmad had opposed Shaykh Hasuna's appointment from the outset.[32] In June 1895, he had printed a petition sent to the khedive by a group of al-Azhar 'ulama, asking him not to accept Shaykh al-Inbabi's resignation. Shaykh Ahmad commented that al-Inbabi had been a good Shaykh al-Azhar (contrary to the report of Azhar Administrative Council secretary, Salman), and that the greatest proof for that claim was that the petitioners had been senior 'ulama. Furthermore, by sending this petition of protest they had been fulfilling a duty. Shaykh Ahmad reminded his readers that "it is the custom upon the fall or resignation of the Shaykh al-Islam [i.e., the Shaykh al-Azhar] to elect a replacement by a gathering of 'ulama." According to him, this ensured that the new Shaykh would be chosen for his attributes as a scholar and a man of God: knowledge, piety, asceticism, humility, and willingness to serve as a weapon in the defense of Islam. A replacement chosen by the khedive for political reasons might not possess these characteristics and could thus be harmful to the community of Muslims.[33]

While Shaykh Ahmad did not mention the madhhab of those who protested al-Inbabi's resignation, Salman reported that the khedive received this petition in Alexandria and that it was signed by some thirty senior shaykhs of the Shafi'i "and other" madhahib. The khedive also received a telegram on the same subject, signed by ten 'ulama. The telegram stated that Shaykh Hasuna's character was too questionable for him to become Shaykh al-Azhar.[34] Considering this context, Shaykh Ahmad was implying that, if the Shaykh al-Azhar during the incident had been internally elected, he would not have had to fear student abuse as a state official. Perhaps the protesters would have recognized his authority. Perhaps the deaths could have been avoided.

Shaykh Ahmad's disapproval of state actions in the Cholera Riot and the Azhar Administrative Council was a minority opinion. According to a historian of Islamic presses, *al-Islam* offered "the single voice of opposition" to government intervention in al-Azhar Mosque at that time.[35] The only evidence we have of public reaction to the violation of the mosque also comes from *al-Islam,* and may have been exaggerated for dramatic effect. Shaykh Ahmad claimed that, when the soldiers and the English officials departed the scene with their cart carrying the dead and injured, they looked cheerful, "as if they had won an obvious victory." They were surrounded by witnesses of the event and onlookers, "over 60,000 inhabitants of the capital screaming and crying and bewailing the fate of those lost and the insult to religion."[36] In contrast, the popular scientific journal *al-Muqtataf,* run by Syrian Christian immigrants, asserted that the state's actions were justified by the need to prevent the spread of the epidemic, remarking: "Rational people have agreed that had the government not used determination in this incident the epidemic would have spread among the people in every place."[37] As it was, some 5,400 people had died from cholera in Egypt in the month of June, over 155 victims per day.[38]

After the incident, the khedive and his ministers also sanctioned the use of force, "expressing pleasure" at the actions of the police and awarding the governor, Mahir Pasha, with an Ottoman decoration of the second order "in satisfaction of his honorable service in the Azhar Incident and in recognition of his demonstration of tenacity and courage." Two days after the incident, the khedive convened the Council of Ministers, and decreed the deportation of sixty Syrian students, the trial of twelve of their leaders, and closure of the Syrian riwaq for a full year. Furthermore, the council "approved of the actions of the government men in suppressing the riot by force, and it was decreed also that His Grace the prime minister communicate to His Excellency Claus Pasha the chief of police of the capital and to Mr. Mansfield his deputy the satisfaction of the khedive's government with their course of action in the Azhar Incident and gratitude to them for their demonstrations of determination in suppressing the riot." The council laid the blame for the incident upon Shaykh Hasuna al-Nawawi and charged him with remedying conditions at the mosque so that they "would not be allowed to reach the point they reached [before]." The unsanitary conditions and rebellious behavior of the students were problems he had to solve; this was his duty as the Shaykh al-Azhar and as a government appointee.[39]

As for the participants, the police arrested eighty-two Syrians and twenty-three Egyptians, including some 'ulama.[40] Fourteen students were brought to trial on 11 June 1896. Twelve were convicted and sentenced, but only six were made to serve full two-year sentences.[41] Shaykh Ahmad thanked the defense lawyer, Isma'il Bey 'Asim, for his service "as a fellow lawyer." Curiously, he then complained that Egyptian lawyers were not allowed to serve in teams, unlike their counterparts in Europe, so that their jobs required long hours without rest: "To my sorrow, we are not like the Europeans except in that which may not be printed upon the pages of our newspaper. I ask the Most High to reform our condition, for there is no strength and no [power but in God]."[42] It appears, however, that Cairenes were more like Europeans than Shaykh Ahmad thought. The management of the Cholera Riot proceeded by panoptic technique: the use of quarantine and cordon to section off a disturbed space from that of normal citizens, to mark that area as dangerous, abnormal. By abandoning the mosque to search for someone who could manage the disorder, Shaykh Hasuna implicitly indicated acceptance of al-Azhar's subordination to the civil administration, of religious to temporal authority. The violence carried out within the mosque complex in the name of extracting a plague victim associated disorder, unsanitary conditions, disease, and riots with the denizens of the mosque, its "disorderly" educational system, and the apparent failure of that system to produce polite, productive, and qualified scholars of religion. And ultimately the riot furthered the extension of state control over religious institutions.

Consultative Negotiation:
The Azhar Organization Code of 1896

The shock of the cholera plague and the riot lent moral authority to the khedive's pro-reform position and seemed further to justify state intervention. The next three years were a fruitful period for al-Azhar reformers, because the period offered a unique conjunction of approval from all sources of relevant authority over the mosque's future: the Shaykh al-Azhar, the Azhar Administrative Council, the khedive, the majority of Azhari 'ulama, and public opinion. Within two weeks of the Cholera Riot, the Azhar Administrative Council had composed a sixth reform code whose reach far surpassed that of previous codes.[43] This incorporated or adapted many of the suggestions made by advocates of efficiency-based reforms, especially those of 'Abdullah Nadim in his article "Al-'ilm wa al-'ulama." But it also attempted to take into account criticisms of previous reform codes. The code passed without objection through the Council of Ministers on 27 June, fewer than ten days after having been submitted. Three days later, on 1 July, the khedive signed it into law. The quick passage of the 1896 Azhar Organization Code can be attributed in large part to the Cholera Riot, and to the 'ulama's increasing perception that Utilitarian techniques of educational order were necessary to manage the ten thousand students and hundreds of 'ulama.

The Azhar Organization Code of 1896 placed all aspects of al-Azhar's administration into the hands of the year-old Azhar Administrative Council and the Shaykh al-Azhar, including regulation of teaching, management of students, payment of employees, allocation of stipends to teachers and preachers, appointment and ranking of riwaq shaykhs, appointment of professors, expenditures for al-Azhar and its affiliated schools, creation of rules and standards for assigning and distributing daily rations, designation of holidays, organization of the riwaqs and the quarters where students resided, assignment of books, and hiring of non-Azhari teachers. Also subject to this code were the Ahmadi mosque in Tanta and two large madaris in Dassuq and Damietta. The madaris were to be remade on the model of the civil schools.[44]

The Shaykh al-Azhar was to be the chair of the Azhar Administrative Council, the executive head of al-Azhar and any schools affiliated with it, and would be held primarily responsible for implementing all laws and decrees pertaining to them. The council was now to be composed of five 'ulama appointed by the khedival administration (not necessarily Azharis), and it would convene every fifteen days. The code also stipulated that the council should be responsible for the election of all mosque shaykhs; this would legally preclude the khedive's unilaterally appointing his own nominees as Shaykh al-Azhar, as he had in Hasuna's case. Three of the five seats would always be held by the three madhhab Muftis. Thus the council's chairmanship would always be decided by a vote in which internally elected leaders would have a three-to-two advantage over non-Azharis.[45] This may have been a capitulation to al-Azhar leaders who already sat on the council, or it may have reflected a measure of consensus that al-Azhar's Shaykh should not be appointed by an outside authority or subject to governmental pressure.

The 1896 Azhar Organization Code also extended the Registration Code of 1885 by stipulating entrance requirements. Contained within the Azhar mosque complex were several primary-level Qur'an schools whose young pupils studied along with the elder shaykhs and advanced students in the mosque itself, although they were not considered Azharis. The new code established procedures for such primary students and those of other mosques to enter al-Azhar's program of instruction. Boys had to present a birth certificate or equivalent to prove they were at least fifteen years old, and had to demonstrate to an entrance committee of three shaykhs that they could read and write and had memorized half of the Qur'an (if blind, all of the Qur'an). If an applicant passed his entrance exam, he would then apply to the shaykh of the riwaq of his region for a room assignment. He was required to inform the riwaq shaykh of his name, title, homeland, and the shaykhs with whom he intended to study, and to present the shaykh with his birth certificate and a certificate of smallpox vaccination.[46] Students' bodies, as well as their minds, would be monitored.

Al-Azhar students would study subjects in two categories: maqasid and wasa'il. Wasa'il, the means of study, included grammar, morphology, three types of rhetoric, hadith terminology, logic, arithmetic, algebra, prosody, and rhyme. Arithmetic and algebra would be required for the 'alimiyya examination. Maqasid, or objects of study, included monotheistic theology, religious ethics, usul al-fiqh, Qur'anic exegesis, and hadith. Electives for those who sought government employment included Islamic history, composition, elocution, linguistic principles and texts, elementary geometry, and geography.[47]

The Administrative Council also regimented progression from elementary to advanced subjects. Students would not study the maqasid until they had mastered the wasa'il and had to complete the wasa'il within the first few years of their study. Furthermore, the Azhar Organization Code prohibited

use of super-commentaries and marginal glosses (hawashi and taqarir) during the first four years of study. To avoid confusion, beginners would study
original texts and simplified commentaries first. After four years of study,
students would be permitted to use the super-commentaries, but use of
marginal glosses would still require permission from the council.[48]

The council was also to set the beginning and end of each school year,
and holidays were limited to seven: 'Id al-Adha and 'Id al-Fitr; the birthdays
of Muhammad, al-Husayn, and the Egyptian saint al-Sayyid Ahmad al-
Badawi; the departure of the mahmal for Mecca; and the season of the Nile
flood.

To satisfy the need for certifying students who did not require a full
twelve years' training, but who wanted rather to become imams, preachers,
or primary-level Qur'an teachers, the council established a new oral exam
for the ahliyya degree, to be attempted after eight years and eight courses.
The Shaykh al-Azhar and three professors would officiate. The Organization Code retained the annual oral examinations for the 'alimiyya, to be
taken after a minimum of twelve years. Each examiner would ask questions
in his area of specialization only, thus acknowledging the need for formal
specialization. Examinees would have to demonstrate tahsil (substantive
memorization) and fahm (understanding). Detailed criteria delineated
three levels of pass. Because all teachers were now subject to appointment
by the council, no longer did a pass entail permission to teach, but only
qualification.[49]

Finally, the Organization Code set out rules and penalties to make discipline stricter among the elementary students, held the shaykhs responsible
for implementing them, and established by-laws to govern the relations
between al-Azhar and its affiliated schools. Salman commented, "Every part
of these eloquent rules was aimed at one objective, the attainment of the
essences of the religious sciences within a limited time by a method that is
easy to comprehend, and adornment with the fruits of these sciences—the
good qualities of morality and activity."[50]

Critically, the new code would only proceed if the 'ulama approved.
Salman reported:

It was in the Council's power to publish its decrees . . . and proceed
by merely announcing that they must be implemented as the code set
forth. However, it wanted the senior 'ulama to participate and give
them counsel on the matter, and [it wanted] to consider their opinions on every single issue, and for that reason there was decreed the

formation of a committee [lajna] of more than thirty of the well-known 'ulama of every madhhab, under the chairmanship of Shaykh Salim al-Bishri, who was at that time a member of the Council. Some of the other [Council] members were also attached to [the committee's] membership. The Shaykh al-Azhar wrote to the chair of this committee stating that and calling the 'ulama to meet in the Azhar Administration building, and they met.[51]

They would decide the best means to implement the directives of the Organization Code, to ensure that their own needs were met. One of the first acts of the council was to improve the financial condition of Azhari 'ulama, and in this effort they had the support of the khedive. On 29 June 1896, two days before the massive Organization Code was signed, the khedive issued a statement that the 'ulama's payment had been substantially the same since the days of Khedive Isma'il, and their budget had not changed significantly since Muhammad 'Ali had first introduced government financial control of religious institutions. By 'Abbas's order, the 'ulama were to receive increased pay according to their rank and seniority. Senior shaykhs of the ranks one through three were to receive a minimum stipend of £E 1, £E 2, or £E 3 per month. Newer shaykhs were to receive a minimum of £E 1,500 milliemes (£E 1.5) or £E 1,700 milliemes (£E 1.7). All shaykhs dependent on these monthly stipends (as opposed to the more prestigious kasawi al-tashrif or muthamman al-ghilal) could receive additional stipends of 15–60 piasters monthly. If a shaykh's sons also dedicated themselves to the study of the religious sciences, and could demonstrate having memorized the Qur'an, they would inherit their fathers' stipends.[52] This was a considerable improvement over the previous system, under which new teachers worked without pay until a senior shaykh died and a salary became available.

The khedive and the council also pursued the objective of promoting good moral behavior among the students. The khedive's budget included £E 600 for distribution among the shaykhs of the riwaqs and student quarters. Individual shaykhs would receive 60–200 piasters monthly, depending upon the importance of their positions and the number of students under their care, in addition to their income as 'ulama.[53] On 24 January 1897, the council implemented the code's strict rules for supervision of students by riwaq shaykhs. Riwaq shaykhs were to be drawn from the same riwaq as the students if possible. They would be accountable for entry of students into riwaq registers, recording their dates of arrival, departure, and absence during the academic year, and reporting to the Shaykh al-Azhar all who were exempt from military conscription. If shaykhs heard about or observed disruptive or immoral student behavior, they were to investigate the matter, settle minor incidents themselves, and report any major incidents to the Shaykh al-Azhar as soon as possible. They were to personally supervise the riwaq during the day when not actually teaching, and at night from a home within or nearby the riwaq, either personally or through a designated deputy. They were to distribute waqf benefits to those who deserved them, in accordance with a code promulgated by the Council of Ministers on 10 October 1885, and to perform the duties stipulated in riwaq waqf documents, such as recitation of the Qur'an and physical maintenance of the mosque. The riwaq shaykh was to provision the riwaq himself, tally the amount spent on supplies, and submit an annual report to the Shaykh al-Azhar, who would remit it to the Waqf Administration. If a riwaq shaykh or deputy shirked his duties, he would be subject to financial disciplinary actions entailed in the 1896 code.[54]

On 27 January 1897, the council implemented articles of the code that set out the days on which classes would be held and the penalties that would be enacted if shaykhs and students failed to show up on those days. Shaykhs had to inform the Shaykh al-Azhar of an anticipated absence, and students had to tell their riwaq shaykhs. Anyone who failed to show up for class consistently—student or 'alim—would first receive a warning from the Shaykh al-Azhar, and if the absences continued, his daily bread rations or stipends would be cut off. Truant students would no longer be exempt from military conscription. Benefits and exemptions would remain suspended for a period equal to the recipient's absence.

If a student was absent for more than thirty days during the academic year, the council would cut off his daily rations permanently, but he would still be permitted to return to classes. If his absence amounted to more than three months, he would have to repeat that year's classes. If a student had to repeat more than three years of classes, his name would be erased from al-Azhar's register of students and he would be forbidden from entering any examinations. Hence the maximum length of study for an 'alimiyya degree would be fifteen years.[55]

On 1 February 1897, the council defined the mutual responsibilities and duties of professors and students. Students would be required to attend at least three classes a day and could not have outside employment without approval of the Shaykh al-Azhar. Their personal conduct was to be "filled with the nobility of knowledge and religion." When sitting in class, they were not to speak in loud voices, work on material for other classes, or talk to anyone but the shaykh, whom they were to respect. They were not to pester the shaykh with questions that wasted time, and if they had to ask a professor about the same issue more than three times, they were to wait until after class. The decree also stated bluntly that students were not to harm classmates verbally or physically.

The 1 February decree also regulated progression from lower-level to higher-level classes. A student was required to finish an entire book with a single shaykh, and would not be permitted to advance until he received the shaykh's permission. Upon receipt of that permission, he would tell the shaykh which book he intended to study next. If the intended book was suitable for his level of comprehension, the shaykh would give him permission to move on.[56]

The shaykhs, for their part, were told they must serve as good examples (al-qudwa al-husna) in their morality and personal conduct. In addition, they were to take attendance either personally or by delegating that duty to someone else, to record student names and regional origins, and to ensure that students behaved well in class. When a student violated a rule of conduct, the shaykh was to take notice of the first offense, reprimand the student for the second offense, and on the third offense ban the student from class and remand him to the Shaykh al-Azhar for punishment. In no case were shaykhs to deliver punishment themselves, or to take any action that would reflect poorly on them as role models—no cursing students or their parents, no striking with canes or sandals. In accordance with their general commission to "direct the mind of the student to consider the issues and understand them and their meaning," the shaykhs were rather to try to make students understand what they had done wrong.[57] In terms of pedagogical regulations, shaykhs were to prepare their classes ahead of time; to conduct brief reviews following a holiday; to avoid digressions, speculative or disputed arguments, and confusing expressions in class; and to design their lessons to conform to a one- to two-hour period. All violators would be subject to financial penalties.[58]

Members of the Administrative Council had in mind specific abuses when they wrote this code. For example, in one incident, a senior Shafi'i shaykh had not prepared his lesson and had transposed a fa' for a ghayn while reading. When a student pointed out his error, the shaykh cursed him vociferously and swore that the letter was indeed a fa'. In another incident, a Maliki shaykh famous for his great age was lecturing to his class, which normally consisted of everyone present in the mosque. "It happened that his own marginal notes contradicted the commentary, so he undertook to bring the two into agreement by means of grammatical manipulations, with the objective of establishing his own view by correcting the language of the commentary. One of the students . . . said to him: 'Sir, this correction has involved a change in a principle of logic, for the universal has been reversed as though it were a particular . . . and its opposite (a particular) has been reversed to a universal, which logicians do not allow.' Replied the shaykh: 'No harm in that as long as the Arabic has been properly inflected.' "[59]

Given the debate that had ensued after Shaykh al-Azhar al-Inbabi's fatwa approved mathematical sciences, one might assume that the most difficult task the council faced would be the introduction of new sciences. This was not so. The council did study al-Azhar's budget from awqaf (as al-Tuwayrani had recommended), and it concluded it could not accomplish the desired reforms without help from the khedive. Accordingly, the council drew up a proposed budget and request for funding for the 1897 academic year and presented it to the khedive. Fortunately, the khedive recognized that many of al-Azhar's problems were caused or aggravated by the poverty of the mosque and many of its inhabitants. Thus he ultimately gave the council more than it had asked, and dedicated some waqf revenues to the teaching of arithmetic, geography, history, and handwriting, and to the creation of a centralized library.[60]

The khedive also funded a program for reforming the standard religious subjects through financial incentive programs. These programs encouraged professors to employ the methods of the new order and provided monetary rewards to students who performed well on an elective examination in any subject. The council chose twenty-four senior 'ulama of different madhahib as pilots to demonstrate the efficacy of the new methods: They were to select original texts and clearly written commentaries as readings, devote most of their teaching to the maqasid subjects, and drill their students in practical application of received knowledge. These 'ulama, called the 'ulama al-nizam (the scholars of order), were to be given £E 2 to £E 3.50 per month in addition to their regular salaries.[61]

The new subjects funded by the khedive (arithmetic, algebra, geography, composition, and calligraphy) were carefully integrated into the al-Azhar system. Because at that time no Azhari 'ulama taught those subjects, instructors from the civil schools were brought in. These teachers were referred to as mu'allimun (those who teach 'ilm) rather than being regarded as 'ulama, learned ones. However, the council tried to ensure some degree of familiarity between the Azhari 'ulama and the teachers of the new sciences by appointing only instructors who had studied religious sciences at al-Azhar. These former Azharis, it was hoped, would "take into consideration in their teaching the customs of the place and its people."[62] To protect the primacy of al-Azhar's religious curriculum, the khedive decreed that the new sciences were to be supplementary only. All students taking a new science had to take at least three courses in the religious sciences as well.[63] After integration of the new subjects and incentive grants, council secretary Salman reported that students were able to write well and that they were doing "better than expected" in arithmetic, geography, and history. The incentive grants for students were a success: Students took 5,629 optional exams in January 1898, and 2,909 passed. By the twentieth century, al-Azhar had fifteen shaykhs teaching arithmetic and two teaching geography, whose classes, according to Salman, were just as good as those in the civil schools. Many students were able to pass the civil schools' teaching certification exams in arithmetic and algebra and to gain employment in the civil, waqf, and private schools. A council investigation of the annual examinations found that students who took the new subjects in addition to their regular courses performed better than their counterparts who took only the standard courses. Salman claimed that this was readily apparent to anyone who read the lists of successful examinees sent to the khedive every year, and that none of the 'ulama objected to this until the end of December 1900.[64]

Throughout 1898 and 1899, the Azhar Administrative Council continued to implement provisions of the 1896 code. Successive council decrees fixed the school year according to the Islamic lunar calendar, with specified holidays and a fixed summer vacation, and named an admissions committee. In 1898, the council appointed a doctor to take charge of the students' health and established a clinic and dispensary in the 'Abbasiyya riwaq. New rules limited the number of students permitted to sleep in any one place, demanded greater cleanliness, and mandated removal of anyone with an infectious disease. The council also investigated abuses of funding and violations of the new laws. For example, one investigation of sons of deceased 'ulama revealed that some were not pursuing religious studies and so did not qualify to inherit their fathers' stipends. After a warning, the stipends were taken away and given to low-ranking shaykhs whose stipends had not yet been brought up to the 1896 standards.[65]

By emphasizing the primacy of religious studies over the new "instrumental" subjects, and by increasing payments to 'ulama, the council and the khedive demonstrated their concern for al-Azhar's religious mission as well as their desire to meet the demands of those who had earlier opposed reforms. Because their ultimate concern was preservation of al-Azhar's religious mission, the reform proponents and former opponents held common goals, and reforms imposed as a result of this process of consultative negotiation were successfully implemented.

Critiques?

Salman observed in 1905 that when the khedive approved the 1896 Azhar Organization Code mandating the teaching of nonreligious subjects at al-Azhar, "it did not occur to him at that time, nor to any of the leading 'ulama or the senior shaykhs of the Malikis or the non-Malikis, that this might lead to abandonment of the prevailing subjects at al-Azhar or that it would put an end to religion or cause the weakening of the Islamic doctrine, as everyone says these days."[66] Rather, when it became apparent that students who took electives in the new subjects tended to perform better on the yearly examinations, thus winning a greater share of the khedive's incentive grants, no 'ulama objected.[67] The journal *al-Islam,* which had so fervently opposed government intervention in the Syrian riwaq incident, indicated muted support for the 1896 code and subsequent council decrees,[68] and continued to point to the religious relevance of contemporary scientific discoveries. For example, Shaykh Taha al-Khalili wrote in *al-Islam* that science and religion provided two means of acquiring knowledge about the world. The forms and shapes of the physical world could be apprehended and described by human intelligence, or science, while religion told about that aspect of the world that could not be apprehended by the senses. All forms of human progress were derived from information gleaned from prophecy, and all forms of social decay (such as idolatry) resulted from abandoning the laws of the prophets. European laws and sciences were all ultimately inherited from Islamic sources, even their "discovery" of microbes, which he believed had been metaphorically described in the Qur'an (in this, Shaykh al-Khalili preceded 'Abduh and Rida, who also "discovered" microbes in the Qur'an). The chief danger of European culture and political domination was not from the principles of their sciences, but from their attempts to spread the concept of personal freedom (al-hurriyya al-shakhsiyya), which the author portrayed as an attempt to raise individual conscience above the very laws that guaranteed individual rights.[69]

Al-Islam also argued the need for more rigorous training of religious personnel. Muhammad 'Abd al-Halim Abu al-Fadl, a shaykh at the mosque of Sayyida Zaynab, warned that most rural preachers were unable to communicate adequately to the people the duty to "command the good and forbid the reprehensible." In order to undertake that duty, preachers had to be well-educated and morally upright. However, most rural preachers could do no more than read lines on a page without understanding their meaning. They could not read the newspapers that would help them acquire the information that people needed to have about the relevance of religion to their daily lives; hence, they preached only about asceticism and yearning for the afterlife. One can hear the echo of modernism in Abu al-Fadl's plea: "[F]or it is incumbent upon a community to lead the way for its people to awaken it from its sleep . . . and to direct the attention of the community to the fount of progress and civilization and clarify the means to luxury and happiness by training of the intellect."[70] Even the most conservative periodicals of this period are virtually devoid of the criticism of reform found in the papers of the early and mid-1880s and of the early twentieth century. Those that did criticize the reforms said only that they did not go far enough.[71]

Conclusion

The Cholera Riot generated widespread support for state-mandated reform in the mid-1890s. Within a period of three years, the khedive and the Azhar Administrative Council were able to substantially reorganize al-Azhar's madrasa in a manner that both followed the suggestions of earlier reform critics and satisfied demands of modernist reformers. As Hasan Husni al-Tuwayrani had hoped, the "exchange of give and take" in the journalistic debate came to be reflected in the regulation codes formulated by the Azhar Administrative Council. The opinions of ordinary 'ulama, as expressed in committees, formed the substance of those codes. Perhaps as a result, the new nonreligious sciences added to al-Azhar's curriculum included only those approved by Shaykh al-Inbabi, Muhammad al-Banna', and Muhammad Bayram in 1888. Natural sciences would not be taught, while other mathematical subjects whose study the Muftis officially approved became required studies. Moreover, the khedive circumvented the argument that al-Azhar's awqaf did not support instruction in nonreligious sciences by framing those new sciences as wasa'il, or supplementary means to an end that was unequivocally the acquisition of religious knowledge. In case there was any question regarding the legality of instruction in these sciences, the khedive funded them through nonspecific and newly endowed awqaf.

State intervention in the affairs of al-Azhar was, after the riot, a marginal issue. Reformers and critics alike tended to address the new khedive with hope that he would "direct his care" to the ailing religious institutions.

Notably, Shaykh Ahmad sanctioned the 1896 code despite his warnings that the leading 'ulama must be independent of political pressures and suspicions, and despite his disapproval of the khedivally appointed Administrative Council. Modernists considered the code a victory in a battle against stagnation and disorder. Salman stated that, through these reforms, al-Azhar went from chaos (fawda) into a "sort of order." Muhammad 'Abduh agreed: "Al-Azhar has moved, by this reform, from a state of general disorder to something of order, from a pitch-black gloom to a ray of light."[72]

But the Organization Code also attempted to restructure madrasa education completely, following the model set by the civil schools. The madrasa was now subjected to the paradoxes afflicting the modernist paradigm. Order was expected to efficiently produce qualified personnel whose up-to-date knowledge would help them teach religion to the nation in a manner its people could understand. Knowledge was no longer understood as the province of a class of specialists, something that shared in the sacrality of the textual sources of religion and law, but rather as something to be conveyed to everyone, although perhaps at a minimal level. The most important characteristic of the transmission of knowledge was no longer accurate reproduction of an author's meaning—modeled on the necessity of accurately reproducing meanings of sacred texts—but efficient communication of it to mass audiences. The paradox entailed here was that both the modernist reformers and those criticizing their efforts wanted to preserve the integrity of religious knowledge and the role of the 'ulama as moral guides, and to strengthen the community for its struggle against imperialism. But to accomplish these ends, they chose techniques that would subtly undermine their objectives. Consequent efforts to uphold the place of religion within the madrasa furthered state intervention and forced religious scholars into a defensive posture.

8

MUHAMMAD 'ABDUH AND
IJTIHAD

No history of the reform debates at al-Azhar can ignore Muhammad 'Abduh. He was the reform movement's most conspicuous and systematic advocate, an innovative jurist who had profound influence on twentieth-century Sunni thought. However, Muhammad 'Abduh played a less decisive role in crafting al-Azhar reforms than has been attributed to him. He did draft the program that the khedive implemented through the Azhar Administrative Council in 1896. But Azhari 'ulama modified those reforms and sometimes evaded them, necessitating negotiations not controlled by 'Abduh. This chapter tells how nationalist journalists, Khedive 'Abbas Hilmi II, and Azhari 'ulama joined forces to blunt his influence by depicting 'Abduh as a tool of imperialists and a vector of invasive European culture.

'Abduh had been one of several pupils of al-Afghani who adopted and promoted a linear, moral concept of societal development. As a journalist, he stridently advocated applying European models of education to al-Azhar. However, he was expelled from Egypt along with other leaders of the 'Urabi Revolt. He went to Paris, then to Syria, and returned to Egypt in 1889. 'Abduh worked tirelessly toward reform of religious education and the religious courts, and employed ijtihad in his work as a mufti, becoming extremely controversial. 'Abduh initially received the British stamp of approval for his "liberal sentiments." Khedive 'Abbas Hilmi II elevated 'Abduh by fiat to administrative power over al-Azhar in 1895, and to the position of Grand Mufti in 1899, where 'Abduh bore the standard of legal and educational reform until his death in 1905. 'Abduh disdained overt anglicization, and all his efforts were directed toward reviving public commitment to religion and unity in faith. He did internalize European ideals, but melded them creatively with Islamic concepts, creating a hybridized framework for an authentically Islamic revolution of thought. This held within it a potential for overturning British authority. In a classic "mimic man" scenario, Lord Cromer would later discredit him as not sufficiently earnest in his faith, too Westernized to be really useful.[1] Nonetheless, to his Egyptian critics, 'Abduh was a colonial agent. They tried to block his efforts through an ad hominem campaign that called public attention to positivist aspects of his campaigns and highlighted his connections to British occupiers. This campaign left him fatally weakened; he had to cede reform leadership to others whose political baggage could not as readily damage popular receptivity to reform.

In retrospect, 'Abduh hardly seems the right person to direct reforms at al-Azhar, considering his history of poor relations with its 'ulama. As a student, he had been a black sheep known for antagonizing his teachers and associating with political insurgents;[2] he had received only a second-rank 'alimiyya degree from al-Azhar. In Syria, he taught at a new Ottoman "secular" school, a school deemed by some Azharis to be of lesser prestige. And while 'Abduh had been a hero of the Azhari-supported 'Urabi Revolt, those erstwhile heroes had since become political pariahs—Sultan 'Abdulhamid even considered 'Abduh's nationalism suspect.[3] When 'Abduh returned to Egypt, having not yet received khedival pardon for his actions in the 'Urabi Revolt, former associates pretended ignorance of his return. Khedive Tawfiq forbade 'Abduh from teaching, saying he did not want 'Abduh to have "influence over the young." Much later, Khedive 'Abbas wrote in his memoirs that 'Abduh's association with the 'Urabist rebels "had left him with the indelible trace of a glorified blight."[4]

'Abduh's Plan for Egyptian Education

'Abduh's continuing efforts to point out perceived deficiencies in the Azhari system of education did nothing to endear him to his alma mater. According to 'Abduh's Syrian students, he often held al-Azhar up as providing an example of the kind of education that would ruin Islamic civilization and bring about its eclipse by European powers. Shakib Arslan, a student who later himself became a prominent reformer, wrote that, while 'Abduh praised a few al-Azhar shaykhs such as the Hanafi reformer Muhammad al-'Abbasi al-Mahdi, he "hated" Azhari pedagogy, which focused on 'ilm al-kuras, "study of marginal scribbles." The students' time was wasted with deciphering expressions and their potential interpretations. According to Shakib Arslan, Azhari 'ulama were so concerned with marginal commentaries on ancient texts, so isolated from contemporary events and fields of knowledge, that "they were not people of this age; indeed, they were not people of this world!"[5] Shakib Arslan and other students used 'Abduh's portrayal of al-Azhar as a foil for presenting 'Abduh's own methods in the best possible light. In contrast, 'Abduh presented his class material at a level easily comprehensible to his students and attempted to engage their intellects in interesting theological questions. One student even claimed that light issued forth from 'Abduh when he spoke, and another included 'Abduh in that class of signs (ayat) that are evidence of the existence of God.[6] Of course, we have only 'Abduh's own statements and his students' reiterations to suggest that other Azhari shaykhs were not likewise trying to engage their students on appropriate levels—or that intense grammatical study was not in fact necessary for accurate and knowledgeable transmission of the texts. To Azhari contemporaries, 'Abduh's comments were insults to the intelligence, prestige, and moral authority of the 'ulama. One Azhari shaykh censured *al-Manar,* a journal in which 'Abduh regularly published articles critical of the 'ulama: "*Al-Manar* is a harmful paper that treats the 'ulama with scorn and refuses to acknowledge the saints. I do not even like to see it, and thanks be to God, I have never read it at all."[7]

Azhari 'ulama were also not likely to approve of the comprehensive educational reform program that 'Abduh submitted to the khedive upon his return from exile in 1889. It included plans to renovate Dar al-'Ulum and al-Azhar, and contained language explicitly insulting to the 'ulama.[8] This program also bore the marks of 'Abduh's experience in exile, especially his discovery that European writings on education agreed with his own perspective.[9] To him, it seemed as if the principles of efficiency-based education were universal, and universally correct. One of the works he admired was Herbert Spencer's *On Education,* which 'Abduh had, as an exercise, read in French and translated into Arabic.[10] From this point on, 'Abduh's plans were peppered with such Spencerian ideas as the "utility" of certain subjects, the importance of active as opposed to rote learning, and the need to educate mothers. 'Abduh promoted Spencer's interest in moral education, and Spencer's argument that acquisition of science was a prerequisite for national strength.[11] 'Abduh's works also echoed Leo Tolstoy's emphasis on the importance of religious morality for individual happiness and correct functioning of society, as well as Auguste Comte's Law of the Three States. The ideal Islamic state, which embraced science, replaced Comte's final state of a positive, or scientifically based, society.[12] 'Abduh's reform program for Egypt, written shortly after he translated *On Education,* indicts the faults of the various types of schools, and suggests changing the schools to produce a population more orderly and respectful of legitimate authority. It is extraordinarily similar to Spencer's outline of practical and civil education, especially Spencer's "sciences related to indirect self-preservation" and "functions of the citizen."[13] The people, 'Abduh argues, are tools for a ruler to use to achieve his objectives for the country, and they will not be able to do the work that the ruler needs done unless they know the difference "between the beneficial and the harmful, between order and disorder." If the people do not learn these moral distinctions, the ruler will not be able "to establish stability for his authority, and all the reforms he imagined for them and for himself, which he put into the principles of his government, would be like straw on the water or drawings in the air."[14] Without a moral upbringing, people naturally tend toward disobedience and "disrespect for the matter of order."[15] Thus all Egyptian schools must be redirected toward moral and practical training that will make students able to discipline themselves and thus become useful and manageable tools for national construction.

The criticism 'Abduh offered most frequently was that students spent long periods of time in the schools without learning anything "of benefit." The katatib, for example, taught nothing but memorization of the Qur'an as "words without meaning." Students needed standardized curricula and short, easily understandable books. The civil schools needed to focus on vocational training and morality, not government service. The form of Arabic grammar taught "should be in keeping with ordinary correspondence and legal documents between commoners." Every subject should be commercially useful, practical, and aimed at producing docile, obedient citizens.[16] 'Abduh reserved special venom for al-Azhar's lack of an organized curriculum, regular registration and attendance policies, assessment of student learning, and moral supervision. "Then," he said, "there are those known as 'ulama." Casting doubt on their definition as learned ones, he noted that they were themselves trained at al-Azhar, and epitomized the product al-Azhar turned out. Although they were held up as moral models for the populace, the "evil and deviant" instruction they received made them more swayed by temptation, more prone to whim, and more gossipy than commoners. 'Abduh concluded that the 'ulama's condition was what kept the public from seeing the value of state guidance. The solution was to establish registration, attendance policies, examinations, courses on correct religious comportment, and rigorous moral supervision.[17]

Teachers of religion, furthermore, should be trained to explain to students the purpose of knowledge imparted, to give education a "real, meaningful basis." This would require changing the methods of teaching Qur'an commentary and hadith. Ideally this training would take place at a reformed Dar al-'Ulum, because its supervisors exercised much stricter control over student morality. 'Abduh even asserted that Dar al-'Ulum should replace al-Azhar. Only by this path of reform might the ruler rid the people of taqlid and the 'ulama, those "obstacles of ignorant fanaticism and guardians of idiocy disguised as guardians of religion." Finally, 'Abduh declared any who opposed this reform to be opposing the ruler's authority.[18]

The sentiments expressed in this plan endeared 'Abduh to Lord Cromer, who helped him gain appointments as a permanent member of the Shura Council for Legislation (a legislative advisory body of 'ulama), and as a civil court judge, first in the People's Courts and later in the Courts of Appeals. But his program for reform of education languished; the same sentiments that won him Lord Cromer's patronage might not gain him endorsement from the Azharis who were to be the main object of his reforms. So when in 1895 Khedive 'Abbas Hilmi elevated him to the Azhar Administrative Council, some 'ulama were livid.[19] From the point of view of 'Abduh's critics, he was an insulting upstart who lacked the moral fiber, political independence, and high degree of legal training necessary to undertake the tasks he claimed for himself: revival of ijtihad and renovation of religious education. Thus from 1897 to 1905, some of 'Abduh's critics engaged in a concerted ad hominem campaign to highlight his reform program's associations with the British and social Darwinism and thus to discredit his campaign for revival of ijtihad.

". . . denying the existence of God . . ."

The ad hominem campaign against Muhammad 'Abduh began in 1897, after 'Abduh published what was to become his most influential book, *Risalat al-tawhid* [Treatise on divine unity], initially a collection of lectures to his students at al-Madrasa al-Sultaniyya in Beirut. In this treatise, 'Abduh suggested that ideals and values commonly associated with European progress were in fact universal human ideals (wijdan al-sadiq), and that Islam embodied them best.[20] All religions had originally exhibited these ideals, but non-Muslims lost them over time. The revelation of Islam reintroduced them, and Europeans appropriated them during the Crusades. This appropriation then inspired the Reformation, which 'Abduh saw as the Christians' return to the essentials of their faith.[21] Thus 'Abduh believed he was reappropriating humanitarian values that were in origin and essence

Islamic. This reappropriation entailed—was indeed based upon—"cutting the chains of taqlid," which tied people to the unreasoned opinions and customs of their forefathers. Islam, said 'Abduh, "indicted as stupid and foolish those who accepted the legal dicta of previous scholars."[22] Freedom from taqlid liberated the authority of reason from all chains but submission to God, and allowed the individual to possess those things that religion intended: "free will and independence of opinion and thought, thus perfecting for him his humanity."[23]

By explicitly advocating acquisition of knowledge, Islam avoided the error that led European Christians to the mistake of secularism. European Christians had forbidden intellectual inquiry into their theological doctrines and separated the authority of individual rational inquiry from that of revelation. Thus believers in science came to think that science disproved religion and began to lose their faith.[24] This was not the case, 'Abduh asserted, with Islam: "[The Qur'an] orders us to investigate and employ reason . . . to achieve certainty about those things to which [the Qur'an] guides us. It forbids taqlid, and tells what happened to the communities who followed what their forefathers did . . . whose beliefs were totally destroyed and who disappeared as a people."[25] 'Abduh's treatise thus echoed the beliefs of his mentor, al-Afghani: It promoted scientific endeavor and attacked taqlid, which it defined as unreflective, instinctive slavery to existing ideas, contrasting it with intellect.

Some readers thought this text echoed a long-discredited rationalist school of thought, the Mu'tazili school, which held that truth could be attained via human reason and that, if reason and revelation seem contradictory, it is because the revelatory text has been incorrectly interpreted. For example, 'Abduh argued that the Qur'an "as read" was created—not eternal, as was conventionally believed. Some verses were therefore open to interpretation, and might possibly even include errors introduced by humans.[26] After the first edition was edited in 1898, rumors started to leak that *Risalat al-tawhid* contained serious heresies: "Mu'tazili incitements to evil," denials of the unity of God, and affirmations of atheism. Upon recommendation of the book's editor, the publisher (al-Manar) removed controversial material from all editions until 1925.[27]

To other readers, *Risalat al-tawhid* was a masterpiece. One enthusiast wrote to *al-Manar* saying that 'Abduh's treatise had "banished the clouds of fancy from the skies . . . in a manner no previous book or 'alim [had] ever done."[28] Nonetheless the ephemeral muckraking presses of Cairo and Alexandria swarmed to take advantage of the scandal, and soon stories of

ʿAbduh's "apostasy" were heard in every coffeehouse. The journal *al-Nahj al-qawim* [The right way] accused ʿAbduh of shortcomings of character and of "denying the existence of God and His unity, and ruling such in court."[29] ʿAbduh was never able to fully escape the taint of this scandal, which further alienated his Azhari colleagues.

". . . animated with liberal sentiments . . ."

Views expressed by ʿAbduh in the *Risalat al-tawhid* were not juristic ijtihad. ʿAbduh was not issuing fatwas calling for common folks to believe the Qurʾan was created. Nevertheless, they did represent ijtihad of the broadened definition that ʿAbduh and other reformers promoted. Those who rejected ʿAbduh's treatise and its abandonment of taqlid thus challenged the results of his ijtihad. According to his critics, if ʿAbduh's ijtihad resulted in dissemination of such unorthodox opinions, then he was unfit to serve in the courts and certainly could not be trusted to define the course of reform for the country's most prestigious religious institution.

Despite these doubts about ʿAbduh's fitness for religious office, events conspired the following year to promote ʿAbduh to the highest jurisprudential post in the land. On 18 April 1899, the British advisor to Egypt's judicial system, Malcolm McIlwraith, proposed that the composition of Egypt's high sharʿia court be reformed by including judges from the civil courts. Two qadis from the Courts of Appeals would attend sessions of the high court. Although McIlwraith claimed this was to combat corruption, it was widely perceived as blatant circumvention of Ottoman authority over Egypt. Both Ottoman-appointed chief qadi Jamal al-Din Effendi and Grand Mufti Shaykh Hasuna al-Nawawi rejected the plan, saying that appeals court judges did not have the same degree of training as shariʿa court judges, and that high shariʿa court judges could only be appointed by the caliph, i.e., the Ottoman Sultan. Shaykh Hasuna pointed out also that civil court judges pledged to uphold a different kind of law, a European-inspired code that in fact violated shariʿa provisions such as the prohibition against levying interest on loans. The shaykhs did not convince McIlwraith, and the matter was not dropped until Sultan ʿAbdulhamid himself intervened to convey his extreme displeasure.[30]

Immediately afterward, the British foreign minister directed Lord Cromer to replace the Ottoman-appointed chief qadi in Egypt and head of the high shariʿa court (Jamal al-Din Effendi) with a native Egyptian qadi drawn from Azhari ʿulama. Khedive ʿAbbas declared this another attempt to sever Egypt's legal ties to the Ottoman Empire, because the chief qadi was

appointed personally by Sultan 'Abdulhamid. "It is not in the public interest [maslaha] of Egypt," he said, "to cut that religious connection to the Sultan." It would allow the British to exert undue influence upon the appointment of the chief qadi and the entire judicial system. Muhammad 'Abduh,
the favored candidate for native qadi, refused to accept the position because
"conscience and religious sensibilities" required Egyptian allegiance to the
Sultan as caliph and head of the legal establishment.[31]

The British machinations did not succeed, but Cromer forced Shaykh
Hasuna to resign as Grand Mufti, claiming that Hasuna had "rendered
himself especially suspicious by the violence of his expressions and his dis-
courteous attitude toward the Ministers." At the time, Cromer was pressur-
ing Khedive 'Abbas to obey British directives; 'Abbas said he was manipu-
lated into replacing several officials who balked at British policy or who
appeared too independent.[32]

Khedive 'Abbas then elevated Muhammad 'Abduh from the Courts of
Appeals to the position of Grand Mufti, suggesting that 'Abduh's friendly
relationship with Lord Cromer might prevent further British incursions
into the religious establishment.[33] The khedive departed considerably from
accepted practice in doing this, because the Grand Mufti had to issue his
fatwas according to rules of the Hanafi madhhab, the official Ottoman legal
school. 'Abduh had been trained in the Maliki madhhab. Although it was
commonly held that "crossing madhhab boundaries" was one step down a
slippery slope toward legal chaos,[34] 'Abduh vowed to eschew Maliki law and
follow Hanafi rules instead.[35] Cromer approved 'Abduh's appointment as
effectively accomplishing reform, because it placed a civil court judge on
the high shari'a court, securing in a roundabout way what the more direct
approach had not. Cromer wrote: "The principal opponent to the proposed
change has been removed from his place" and his successor "is believed to
be animated with liberal sentiments and it is hoped that he will aid in the
course of reform."[36]

". . . what I think of this hell-spawned reform is that there will be chaos on the earth . . ."

From 1900 to 1902, 'Abduh's protégé Rashid Rida sponsored a series of discussions of ijtihad and taqlid intended to win converts to 'Abduh's position,
transcripts of which Rida published in his journal *al-Manar*. Rida presented these as verbatim records, reporting contributions by plausible visitors as
well as the two main participants, although the language may have been
recrafted to serve his rhetorical purpose. Chief participants in these discus-

sions were described as "a reformist youth" and "a muqallid," the latter a local jurist (faqih) and noted conservative preacher who believed at the outset that ijtihad was extinct and that all jurists were obligated to follow the rulings of the Imam of his madhhab (that is, to practice taqlid).[37] The muqallid's concerns highlighted the potential danger of 'Abduh's "liberal sentiments" to Egypt's socio-legal order.

Throughout the discussions, the anonymous reformer argued that the Islamic community suffered from the "malady" of disunity and corrupt beliefs. The germs of this malady, he said, were generated by disagreements over relatively minor issues of law and theology that occurred in the days of the Imams. These disagreements resulted in the formation of sects and madhahib in Islam. The 'ulama and jurists elevated the texts of their Imams over the original texts of the religion—the Qur'an and hadith collections—and demanded that all practice taqlid of the Imams. This contributed to divisions within the community and to intellectual laziness on the part of the believers, which undermined their faith. Both effects weakened Islamic society. To "cure" this weakness, taqlid of the Imams would have to be replaced by a kind of ijtihad based on the Qur'an and the practice of the salaf, which could be performed by anyone educated in Arabic; this would help strengthen beliefs and unify the Muslim community.[38] Naturally al-Azhar's curriculum and pedagogical traditions would have to be changed to incorporate the new emphasis on ijtihad.[39]

The debaters disagreed over definitions. For example, the reformer said Muslims should examine the biography, morals, and evidence of the person whose opinions they would adopt, and claimed that this was a kind of ijtihad. A Syrian qadi of the Hanafi madhhab sitting in on the conversation, possibly Shaykh Yusuf al-Nabhani,[40] pointed out that such activity would still be considered taqlid by many jurists: "We consider one who adopts the dictum of his Imam after learning his condition and becoming familiar with his evidence to be practicing taqlid." The reformer responded that when he was faced with a religious issue he could not resolve by himself,

I look at [the Imams'] evidence, and I use what I see to be the best of their opinions. So I am in one respect a performer of ijtihad, for I have insight into my religion and expend all effort in my power. In another respect I practice taqlid of the one whose guidance led me to investigate and set me on the path of proof. This is not the sinful, harmful taqlid.[41]

However, the reformer claimed juristic taqlid *was* the same taqlid banned by the Qur'an.[42] Here, the reformer and the two muqallidun agreed that people should hold religious beliefs out of personal conviction—of that, there was no question. But was examination of belief ijtihad or a type of taqlid? At one point in the discussions, the reformer acknowledged that most people were incapable of performing ijtihad on legal matters and social relationships, but insisted that this degree of ijtihad could be undertaken by those who had trained to be muftis, judges, and teachers.[43]

Furthermore, the reformer's ijtihad also implied critical examination of madhhab rulings, including those of the Imams. The conservative shaykh recoiled with horror from a suggestion that the Imams' works contained accretions to religion that had to be purged.[44] He admitted that the reformist vision was powerful, but warned that it ignored dangers inherent in criticizing the Imams and the madhhab works of fiqh. What they "imagined to be religious reform" would lead to "religious anarchy" by "destroying trust in the religious law."[45] The conservative appeared anguished at this prospect: "My heart constricts from hearing your argument for abandoning taqlid of the Imams . . . for I anticipate chaos in religion for the common Muslims."[46] Revival of unbridled ijtihad would only result in further divisions in the religious community: "What I think of this hell-spawned reform is that there will be chaos on the earth and a great corruption."[47] The muqallid did admit later that such limited ijtihad as the reformer described "would be easy" for the 'ulama, although it would still result in chaos for lay believers. The reformist replied that the lay believers were in chaos anyway, as they knew nothing of religion beyond the idea that God was One and which saints cured which diseases; they "practiced taqlid of one another" and were all equally ignorant.[48]

The concerns raised by the muqallid were similar to those raised by the Maliki Mufti Shaykh Muhammad 'Ilish in mid-century: Abandoning taqlid could undermine the prestige of conventionally accepted legal norms and threaten the stability of beliefs that imposed some unity on the Muslim community. These themes appeared repeatedly throughout critiques of reform, and especially in the criticisms leveled at Muhammad 'Abduh. Some detractors insinuated that his policies as Grand Mufti threatened the position of the Imams and thus posed a challenge to the common law that underlay the social order. His critics held furthermore that abandoning taqlid left mavericks like 'Abduh open to corruptive political influences. Thus 'Abduh's ijtihad as Grand Mufti was, to his critics, like applying badly mixed mortar to the legal foundations of Egyptian-Ottoman society.

". . . out of fear that evil touches me . . ."

Several of 'Abduh's actions as Grand Mufti were extremely controversial. On 25 June 1898, the khedive formed an Egyptian national bank to issue bank notes, loans, and seasonal advances to cultivators, and to carry out investment banking operations for the Egyptian government. In 1901, the government opened the Post Office Savings Bank, which paid interest on customers' deposits and attracted small-scale cultivators away from usurious moneylenders.[49] This became a matter of public debate because the Qur'an forbade riba' (interest on loans), and the permissibility of investment interest was unclear.[50] From 1898 to 1901, 'Abduh issued a series of fatwas on banking at the government's request. One allowed revenues from the waqf endowment funds, which ordinarily would remain in the treasury until they were used, to be placed in the national bank where they would be used in investment. Depositors would then receive a share of the profits. 'Abduh judged this investment scheme permissible because, he argued, the Qur'an prohibited only such interest as would increase the amount to be paid back on a loan. The proposed bank interest would benefit investors and thus the nation; it would not enrich creditors at the expense of impoverished individuals.[51] 'Abduh's opinion did not depart significantly from existing Ottoman investment practices, which included profit-sharing ventures and the sale of interest-yielding government bonds.[52] 'Abduh's private fatwas also permitted mudaraba, a profit-sharing investment agreement accepted since medieval times and common in Islamic lands.[53] In a mudaraba, an investor entrusts capital to an agent, who employs it in a business venture and then returns the principal and a previously agreed-upon share of the profits to the investor. The differences between this and an interest-bearing loan are important. First, the investor's potential gain is a proportion of actual profit earned, not a set amount or percentage of the principal loaned. There is no guaranteed return, and the investor retains the risk. If the venture fails, the investor suffers the loss. The agent loses only his time and cannot be impoverished as a consequence of the agreement. The Ottoman state had, however, been pushing the boundaries of the permitted in their sale of government bonds, which yielded a guaranteed return to investors and—if the state ever had to borrow more to pay the guaranteed return— endangered the financial health of the state.[54]

Thus 'Abduh's opinion did not even go as far as Ottoman state practice had gone, because he still insisted on the proportional profit-sharing arrangements of the traditional mudaraba.[55] Even so, he was ignoring the catch in applying private investment practices to public banking: In a bank, depositors are the investors. They lend money to the bank (which in a mudaraba would serve as the agent). The bank employs the funds in business ventures, and returns the principal and a proportion of the profit to depositors. If the bank failed, the depositors could lose not just potential profits but also their principal. So while 'Abduh's opinion appeared to satisfy the letter of the Qur'anic restriction, in that no usury was committed, it did not satisfy its intent to protect the poor from abuse. 'Abduh had given Cromer a draft of this fatwa. Khedive 'Abbas convened a council of 'ulama to consider the matter, and the council refused to condone the draft.[56] Subsequently, a vocal Egyptian press took up the issue. Muckraking journalists fastened themselves firmly to 'Abduh's trail for the next five years, determined to sniff out all evidence of British-inspired duplicity.

One of 'Abduh's most vehement critics was Muhammad Effendi Tawfiq, owner of one of the more prosperous colloquial presses in Egypt, *Humarat monyati* [She-donkey of my desire]. Issues bore the self-description "altaf jarida hizliyya jiddiyya jinaniyya bint kalbiyya"—"the funniest humorous, serious, paradisiacal son-of-a-bitch newspaper"—and appeared weekly from 1899 to 1904, except for brief periods when Tawfiq was on trial for libel. In January of 1901, *Humarat monyati* accused the Egyptian government of selling public rights to foreigners. In the lead article, a dervish vented his frustrations at the Egyptian papers to a hashish smoker. According to the dervish, readers could not trust the news because the papers never told them what was really going on in the country. The hashish smoker reminded him that "without them, dimwits like you might still not know that the English entered Egypt." But, said the dervish, the government had sold concessions for steamships, concessions for salt, and the budget to foreigners, and they had "raped the wealth of the people by taking their lands for an agricultural railroad and for public use—and who knows what that is . . . and it gave the streets of Cairo and Alexandria to the tramway to run over whomever it desires—and without compensation!" And on these matters the papers were silent.[57] Worst of all, a movement was afoot to take money from the awqaf, give it to the treasury, and then invest the money in a European bank, where the money would collect interest. The hashish smoker reminded the dervish: "Right, and who was it who wrote that fatwa, my brother? Yer uncle Shaykh Muhammad 'Abduh!" According to *Humarat monyati*, 'Abduh's legalization of interest on waqf monies contradicted stipulations of the awqaf's endowers that the money be used for religious purposes. It would put that money to forbidden use. "Our legal tradition says shame on you—you surrendered your money to someone who takes money in riba'!

And so you will be aiding something our Lord forbade!"[58] Tawfiq judged as sophistry the premise that earned interest would benefit the people, and he implied the mudaraba scheme would be dangerous for depositors.[59]

Humarat monyati also drew attention to the fact that all newspapers called Muhammad 'Abduh's actions, and the seizure of agricultural lands and streets, reform. What is reform then, it asked, but doing the will of foreigners at the expense of the people, whose waqf monies would be risked for interest, whose free use of the streets would be threatened by trolleys, and whose farms would be reduced for foreign companies' profits?[60]

'Abduh backed away from officially supporting the Post Office Savings Bank scheme. In 1903, he claimed that the bank's system of investment was unacceptable.[61] However, public mistrust of 'Abduh involved more than just financial matters. In July 1901, 'Abduh gave a speech at the Islamic Benevolent Schools in which he told an audience that qada wa qadr, or the idea that humans are endowed with certain qualities that predestine their actions, was one cause of Islamic decay. *Humarat monyati* could not resist: Tawfiq quoted the Qur'an to show belief in qada wa qadr was a duty of every Muslim, thereby "proving" that 'Abduh was a heretic influenced by European philosophies of free will.[62] Behind these blunt thrusts at 'Abduh's character lay the charge that ijtihad in 'Abduh's hands was a subversion of the shari'a to British imperial interests.

Such charges damaged 'Abduh's credibility at the highest levels and even threatened to destabilize the relationship between Khedive 'Abbas and Sultan 'Abdulhamid II. Later that month, 'Abduh traveled to Istanbul along with Shaykh 'Ali Yusuf, owner of the journal *al-Mu'ayyad*. Khedive 'Abbas was absent from the capital, escaping summer heat on the shores of the Bosporus, as was customary for the Ottoman elite. 'Abduh's reputation was by now so shaky that when the khedive's personal secretary heard he was in Istanbul, he wrote: "I had hoped that the two would not come to visit His Highness, as I had heard that the Mufti had been defamed. But they did come, and so I thought to meet them and escort them from the boat directly to Yildiz [Palace] to prohibit gossip."[63] When they had completed a courtesy visit with a representative of the Sultan, he directed them to a house on the Bosporus.

Trouble soon came from an unexpected quarter. 'Abduh accepted as guide and interpreter one Zaki Mughamiz, *al-Mu'ayyad's* aide in Istanbul. Mughamiz was a Christian poorly regarded by the government because he had converted to Islam and then reneged, involving himself with the Syrian Catholic Patriarch, who in turn had strong connections to *al-Muqattam*, an Anglophile newspaper in Egypt with anti-Ottoman sentiments. Thus 'Abduh became vulnerable to speculation that he was intriguing with the British and local Christians against the Sultan's authority while a guest of the khedive. 'Abduh moreover made politically sensitive visits without clearance. The khedive's secretary, Ahmad Shafiq Pasha, scrambled to do damage control. To protect good relations between the Sultan and khedive, he had to ensure that 'Abduh's visit was perceived only as an expression of loyalty to the Sultan: "I was certain that there was an evil scheme directed against His Excellency [the Mufti]. I was in a position to know that the smallest touch of it would destroy the calm relations between the khedive and the Sultan, if it were considered an insult to His Highness [the khedive] and the Egyptian government. Therefore I resolved to stop this campaign." Shafiq Pasha sent a memo to the Sultan assuring His Majesty of 'Abduh's loyalty and brought the Mufti to his own house "so that he would not be stricken with harm." 'Abduh was so alarmed that he considered taking refuge with the British ambassador in Istanbul, but Shafiq Pasha advised that such an action would be taken as a slight to the Sultan. Shafiq's efforts paid off: Sultan 'Abdulhamid accepted the guarantee of 'Abduh's loyalty but advised that 'Abduh not extend his stay in Istanbul.[64]

There was more behind this campaign than slighted sultanic pride. Shafiq Pasha's account notes that among 'Abduh's chief critics were Ibrahim al-Muwailihi and Shaykh Abu al-Huda. Ibrahim al-Muwailihi had a complex previous relationship with 'Abduh and the reform movement. He had been Khedive Isma'il's private secretary, and accompanied Isma'il into exile in 1879. Like 'Abduh, al-Muwailihi was an al-Afghani protégé, and had assisted in publishing *al-'Urwa al-wuthqa* while in Paris. In Europe and later in Egypt, he authored several pamphlets against Sultan 'Abdulhamid's regime. In 1898, al-Muwailihi supported 'Abduh's campaign to introduce contemporary subjects into al-Azhar; and he too argued that Muslims needed moral revitalization so they could combat imperialism.[65]

However, Ibrahim al-Muwailihi remained consistently pan-Islamist and by the 1890s had come to support Sultan 'Abdulhamid. A common theme of supporters' rhetoric was the need to preserve communal unity: "There is no tribalism (kavmiyyet) or nationalism (cinsiyyet) in Islam. Religion and nationality are as one. . . . Let there be no talk of tribalism and nationalism."[66] The Sultan's supporters tended to define any splinter group that might threaten communal integrity as deviant, whether that group was Shi'i, Wahhabi, Greek, or Young Turk. Some argued that unity was essential to combat "Christian powers" threatening the Ottoman state, and highlighted danger posed by "a small group of heretics who have fallen under the influence of skeptical European philosophy and positivism."[67] Many regarded European Christian missionaries as agents of imperial culture out to alienate Ottoman Christians from the state and as sources of anti-Ottoman sentiment in the Western press. 'Abdulhamid himself regarded them as "the most dangerous enemies of the social order."[68]

Al-Muwailihi's *Misbah al-sharq* is a classic example of a pro-'Abdulhamid newspaper in Egypt: At times it was scathingly anti-European, and it repeatedly criticized journals that abused the Sultan, especially the pro-British *al-Muqattam*.[69] According to some of *Misbah al-sharq*'s articles, "Christian influences" were the source of most social corruption and weakness in the Islamic world, and members of the Azhar Administrative Council were responsible for not combating them. In part because of European influence, journalism had decayed into mere materialism, and bribes bought journalistic silence on moral issues, weakening the community.[70] Al-Muwailihi's anti-*Muqattam,* anti-Christian stance provides the context for his attacks on 'Abduh in 1901. Al-Muwailihi found 'Abduh's rapprochement with the British, and his supposed conspiracy with Christian leaders through Mughamiz, too suspicious to let him continue serving in such an influential post as Grand Mufti.

Shaykh Abu al-Huda al-Sayyadi, another of 'Abduh's critics, was a Rifa'i Sufi and a friend of al-Muwailihi. Since 1873, Abu al-Huda had been naqib al-ashraf, head of the Prophet's descendants, in Aleppo. During 'Abdulhamid's reign, his fortunes advanced rapidly until he held one of the highest ranks in the Ottoman religious hierarchy (Rumeli qadi asker) and headed the Sufi orders in Istanbul. Shaykh Abu al-Huda wrote religious tracts as part of 'Abdulhamid's attempt to unify Muslims in the Ottoman Arab provinces under caliphal rule. Abu al-Huda published some 212 pamphlets on Muslim unity, making in them a graceful appeal for revival of Sufi spirituality. Abu al-Huda's religious revival ran counter to 'Abduh's; Abu al-Huda wrote that communal unity could only be accomplished through obedience to 'Abdulhamid's will as caliph. According to Abu al-Huda, those who criticized the Sultan or encouraged a distinctively Arabic cultural revival betrayed the Islamic community and aided its enemies.[71] This position offers an interesting parallel to that of muqallid jurists in Egypt, who held that communal unity could only be accomplished by juristic taqlid, i.e., obedience to the legal schools. 'Abduh, on the other hand, held that communal unity could only be accomplished by personal knowledge of, and commitment to, a reformed, "true" Islam. Although 'Abduh paid lip service to the Sultan, his entire intellectual enterprise was aimed against the spirit of submission—even to a benevolent caliph—that 'Abdulhamid's Sufi aides wished to inculcate in the population. Thus Abu al-Huda considered 'Abduh an enemy and a potential traitor to the Ottoman Empire.

Rumors continued to trail 'Abduh that summer of 1901. 'Abduh went to Geneva, a hotbed of Young Turk opposition to the Sultan. The Ottoman consul reported that 'Abduh was meeting with Egyptian students and "speaking against the Sultan," and the Ottoman ambassador to Great Britain warned that 'Abduh was distributing leaflets in Egypt against the Ottoman administration.[72] When 'Abduh told his British confidant, Wilfrid Blunt, about this incident, he said merely that the khedive was angry with him for performing a wedding for a prince of 'Abbas's family in Switzerland that summer. On other occasions 'Abduh admitted that he disliked the Sultan personally and considered him "the greatest scoundrel living."[73]

When this news came to light, the khedive's overworked secretary, Shafiq Pasha, found himself having to justify the personal guarantee he had offered the Sultan for 'Abduh's behavior. Shafiq Pasha insisted that rumors about 'Abduh's seditious activities were untrue and promised to investigate the matter of the leaflets, copies of which were included with the ambassador's missive. He said that "precautions were taken" but did not elaborate. When Khedive 'Abbas found out how Shafiq Pasha had aided the Mufti, he said Shafiq had "made the worst mistake of his life." A senior official of the Ottoman administration, 'Izzat Bey al-'Abid, reassured Shafiq Pasha that "what happened to Shaykh Muhammad 'Abduh was expected. But you put the matter to right wisely, thanks be to God, because the enemies of the Mufti had been stuffing the Sultan's head about him secretly for years."[74]

Thus 'Abduh's ijtihad as Grand Mufti of Egypt, his advocacy of controversial positions, and his political activities had reverberations in the greater political scene—seeming to threaten the Sultan's attempt to unify his Muslim subjects, raising the specter of Christian intrigue and Young Turk rebellion, and endangering the Sultan's relations with Khedive 'Abbas.

Even though 'Abduh showed no sign of stopping his intellectual campaign, he acknowledged that bad press had interfered with his ability to further religious reform. In a petition to Sultan 'Abdulhamid, 'Abduh said he had gone to Istanbul "to witness the greatness of Islam" and to see what could be done to strengthen it. He had hoped he might offer his service in exposing opposition to the Sultan among newspapers in Egypt. However, during his tour of the capital, many people had advised him not to put himself forth as the one to accomplish reform. This was, he said, "out of fear that evil touches me." Although he assured the Sultan of his personal loyalty, the public believed stories told by the press and were accordingly "terrified" of the damage he might do to the image of reform. "It had not occurred to me that suspicion accompanies my name," he lamented, "less so that it would cling to it."[75]

When 'Abduh returned home, *Humarat monyati* welcomed him with a classic colloquial diatribe. In dialogue with a fictional character, Siddiq ("honest one"), Tawfiq asks if the Mufti has ever performed the pilgrimage to Mecca in the Hijaz. Siddiq declares that the Mufti has "never in his life visited the Hijaz but there is no country of the Franks that he has not visited once or twice or three times!"

T: Go ask him why he goes to the countries of the Franks and does not go to the Hijaz!

S: You idiot! Don't say things like that—people will laugh at you.

T: So what if the people laugh at me. Is it me that does these things? How can he visit Europe, not visit the Hijaz, and still say "I am a Muslim"? Yes, he must have traveled to the Hijaz and not Europe this time because it is a religious obligation stipulated by Our Lord. When one of us has an easy life and is in a comfortable position, of course he cannot be a complete Muslim unless he performs the pilgrimage and visits the House of God, instead of what we do today, visiting the Pope.

S: Is it possible that it was his health that prevented him from going to the Hijaz?

T: You saw yourself that the Mufti of Islam went one year to look at the Paris Exhibition, and one year he went to bathe in who-knows-what baths. If you went to ask him about the Ka'ba, he would say he'd never seen it. Some shaykh "'Abdullah Quilliam," whose name is English, has done the pilgrimage twice and maybe more. Yes, shouldn't ['Abduh] have gone to the Hijaz this year instead of traveling to Europe, even just for the sake of knowing the place?[76]

Siddiq avers that the English consider 'Abduh an "enlightened man" from the "advanced classes"; to them, 'Abduh represents the height of civilization, and those who adhere to religious ritual are the trough. Tawfiq splutters:

> What's wrong with the pilgrimage? The pilgrimage is not a shame among the advanced! Or is it part of " civilization" that people must go to Europe yearly and not make the mistake of going to the Hijaz even one year to perform the duties to Our Lord . . . ?

> S: . . . maybe he goes for a change of air . . .

> T: There's no place here he can get new air? He has to go to Europe? Is it right for the Mufti of Islam to go from the house of the Caliphate of Islam to the house of the Christian caliphate, just like that, so fast that we cannot see whether he's coming or going?[77]

Medieval legal tradition had held that a mujtahid not only had to be extremely well-versed in legal sources and methodologies, but he had also to be a firm believer in Islam. Only he who met these conditions and was in addition a just person could serve as a mufti.[78] Tawfiq, by this time in a fit of moral righteousness, asserts that he himself, as a Muslim and one "zealous" for his religion, could not accept a mufti who had never visited the Ka'ba. This "reduced our worthiness in the eyes of the Europeans." It was the mufti's responsibility to defend religion against the challenge of European ideas, and "one who attaches so little importance to his religion will not be believed by anyone in his attempts to defend it." Thus 'Abduh had disqualified himself for the office of mufti, let alone Grand Mufti, and neither Muslims nor the English would accept his arguments.[79]

Such arguments often were linked to 'Abduh's campaign to reform education. According to *Humarat monyati*, 'Abduh had attracted English attention (from Douglas Dunlop, schools inspector) to the state of the katatib, so the English "improved" them and then raised prices to prohibit Egyptians from entering; he issued fatwas drawn from all four schools of law, not just the Hanafi school as he had been ordered to do; he gave speeches in which philosophy masqueraded as religion; he permitted riba'; and at al-Azhar he gave extra money to students who did well in geography and arithmetic, but not in Islamic subjects. This last practice encouraged students to leave religious studies for subjects that would bring them money—thus encouraging materialism and the slow death of shari'a. 'Abduh was not reforming religion, he was destroying it.[80]

Al-Muwailihi's newspaper *Misbah al-sharq* echoed these sentiments: Egyptians who spend their summers in Europe, al-Muwailihi said darkly, are "spooning out taqlid of the Westerners" to the masses and blindly imitating European customs and beliefs, even the idea that the heat of the summers would harm them.[81]

The Picture Scandal

This was only the beginning of a trend toward increasingly bold attacks on 'Abduh. In March 1902, *Humarat monyati* published a photograph of 'Abduh in Europe surrounded by a quartet of modestly dressed European ladies and their male chaperone. 'Abduh leans jauntily against a fence, grinning (Figure 8.1). This contrasts sharply with the official photograph of 'Abduh, in which he wears an appropriately dignified expression (Figure 8.2).[82] To understand Egyptians' reception of the European photograph,

Figure 8.1   Muhammad 'Abduh in Europe. *(Source: Humarat monyati* 4, no. 18 [1 March 1902]: 273.)*

Figure 8.2   Muhammad 'Abduh, official photograph. *(Source:* **Muhammad 'Abduh,** *Risalat al-tawhid,* **ed. Mahmud Abu Riyya [Cairo: Dar al Ma'arif bi Misr, 1315 H]: frontispiece.)**

consider that 'Abduh's own brother Hamuda Bey once left a party in hor-rified shame after colliding with two women in respectable European evening dress and seeing a British official dancing unconcernedly with the bare-shouldered wife of another man. Hamuda Bey referred to the women as "naked" and called the party an "abomination." Wilfrid Blunt told him, "My dear fellow, you do not understand that this is our work of civilizing the East, wait another twenty years and you will see all the Cadi's [sic] of Egypt with your brother the Mufti among them, dancing with ladies even more naked than these, and who knows, going with their own heads bare."[83]

Humarat monyati's photograph of 'Abduh with "naked" ladies was accompanied by an explanatory poem, which asserted that the shaykh in the photograph (strategically unnamed) was a dirty old man unfit to represent the law, who had abandoned the madhahib and become a khawaga (pejorative for "western gentleman"). In a following article, Tawfiq excoriated the shaykh for following Western customs, "shaming his turban" by behaving in ways that exhibited his arrogance, and using his cane to knock on mosque doors "as the tourists do." The foreigners, he said, had only contempt for Egyptians—all that could be gained from them was "a mouthful of bread unfit to be thrown to the dog."[84]

Tawfiq claimed that an anonymous source had been reporting 'Abduh's unorthodoxy to him for some time. However, 'Abduh's photograph came from a known source, an Azhari 'alim named Shaykh Hifni al-Mahdi. This may have been the same Shaykh Muhammad al-Hifni al-Mahdi who had in 1895 argued that the 'ulama must cultivate a public attitude of piety or risk alienating the people whom they were supposed to instruct.[85] Shaykh Hifni told Tawfiq that the picture was one of twelve such brought back from Europe by Prince Muhammad 'Ali, the khedive's brother and an outspoken critic of Cromer. The prince himself (or possibly Ibrahim al-Muwailhi) had given the picture to Shaykh Hifni with explicit instructions to deliver it to Tawfiq. This is plausible; 'Abduh had performed a wedding for one of the princes in Geneva that summer. Tawfiq was further given to understand that the khedive would "be thankful to him" if he made the picture public. Having found himself with this potentially explosive material, Tawfiq asked the 'ulama whether he should publish the picture. He claims to have received favorable fatwas, hearty encouragement, and praise for *Humarat monyati* from no less a personage than the new Shaykh al-Azhar, Salim al-Bishri.[86]

Tawfiq claimed it was a setup. As soon as the picture and its damning poem were published, Shaykh al-Azhar Salim al-Bishri went himself to the prosecutor and insisted that the government act to preserve the Mufti's reputation. Then he turned coat and supported Tawfiq throughout the resulting trial.[87] He thus virtually ensured that 'Abduh's perfidy would receive great public attention, because the trial broadcast the scandal. At the same time, he brought down a critic of the Sultan, because Tawfiq was now shunned.[88] His former informant Shaykh Hifni refused to acknowledge his greeting in the street. When Tawfiq showed up at his house, he told his servants to pretend he was not at home, saying, "That one is accused and it is not suitable for him to enter, lest it be thought he plays the role of the singer and I his composer."[89]

During his trial, Tawfiq protested that 'Abduh alone was responsible for his own embarrassment:

> I never in my life saw, nor have I heard, nor did there ever appear
> before me a shaykh depicted with that bearing, exposing himself to
> insinuation such as this. . . . I was terribly astonished, and my soul
> longed to depict this era in its wretched state. I found before me no
> path but to publish the picture of that shaykh, symbolizing the times.
> . . . If the picture was of the professor Shaykh Muhammad 'Abduh,
> then he is the slanderer, not I, for he does not dignify his position by
> presenting himself as such an example.

"What I said," he stated confidently to the prosecutor, "was for the edifica-
tion of the shaykh; it was not against him."[90] 'Abduh should not have con-
sented to have his photograph taken at all, especially not in that stance,
which let everyone see how he had taken on European customs. A man so
careless of religion could not be trusted with reform.[91] Thus Tawfiq echoed
the conservative critique: 'Abduh was a pawn of British interests and a vehicle through which foreigners subverted Islamic law, broke down indigenous
institutions, and took over the resulting weakened society.[92] In Tawfiq's
view, the principal cause of social weakness in the face of European domination was not taqlid, as reformers thought, but rather the influence of men
trying to conform shari'a to Western ideals, motivated by false conceptions
of reform and advancement.

The court sentenced Tawfiq to three months' imprisonment on the
grounds that the Grand Mufti's position had to be protected.[93] Just before
Humarat monyati was temporarily shut down, Tawfiq warned grimly that
journalists have a duty to be models of morality for their readers. He would
have betrayed his duty if he had remained silent; the closure of Humarat
monyati would not prevent the truth from getting out: "Shut down the
Humara [The she-donkey], and there will rise up al-Jahsh [The donkey
foal]. Shut down al-Jahsh, and there will rise up al-Arnab [The rabbit]. Shut
down al-Arnab, and there will rise up al-Katakit [The chicks]. . . . "[94]

It is of course possible that Tawfiq fabricated the entire story of the photograph's origins in an attempt to wrest profit from his notoriety. However,
his story brings together a plausible bunch of co-conspirators. Shaykh Salim
al-Bishri, Shaykh Hifni al-Mahdi, and now even the khedive all sought to
discredit 'Abduh publicly and to extract from his tainted stranglehold the
future of religious reform in Egypt. As for Tawfiq, his journal raged against
Sultan 'Abdulhamid, accusing him of regicide, paranoia, and treason to
Islam.[95] He was an outsider, rejected even by the Egyptian press association.[96] He made a convenient fall guy.

Ad Hominem 'Abduh

On 8 November 1902, shortly after aristocratic Egyptians returned from their summer travels, journalists Mustafa Kamil and 'Ali Yusuf informed the khedive of the rumors circulating about 'Abduh's unsuitability for office. Khedive 'Abbas was already frustrated with 'Abduh, because 'Abduh had repeatedly taken the British side on a series of issues, and 'Abbas had begun to call 'Abduh "the pawn of Qasr Dubara," a reference to the British Embassy in Cairo.[97] Confronted with the picture scandal, 'Abbas contrived a ruse to isolate the Mufti.

Since 1898, the British Commission of Health and Quarantines had repeatedly pressured the khedive to prohibit the Hajj because a cholera epidemic in the vicinity of Mecca could be spread by returning pilgrims and hence pose a threat to public health. But the khedive had always refused. Jurists told him that it was a matter of individual conscience and choice.[98] In 1902, however, the khedive seemed outwardly willing to accept the recommendation of the Commission of Health and Quarantines. He invited the Mufti, the Shaykh al-Azhar Salim al-Bishri, and Prime Minister Mustafa Fahmi Pasha to discuss the matter. According to Shafiq Pasha, before the meeting, Khedive 'Abbas secretly told Shaykh al-Azhar Salim al-Bishri that al-Bishri must insist on permitting the Hajj, no matter how strenuously 'Abbas himself argued for the opposite position. In this manner they could fool 'Abduh into believing the khedive had initially supported him. As 'Abbas predicted, when the four men met, 'Abduh advocated following the British advice. 'Abbas pretended at first to agree with 'Abduh, but eventually allowed Shaykh Salim to "persuade" him against it, and Mustafa Fahmi followed the khedive's lead, leaving only 'Abduh favoring prohibition.[99] Given that jurists had previously ruled there was no religious justification for banning the Hajj, 'Abduh was left with merely prophylactic arguments to protect himself from accusations of colluding with the occupying forces.

The following November 1903, 'Abduh returned from a trip to Britain, Switzerland, Algeria, and Tunis, reporting that Tunisians would regard exchanging French rule for British as a respite from hell. To the khedive, 'Abduh seemed to be campaigning for British rule. At the same time, 'Abduh was using his seat on the high council of the diwan al-awqaf to block khedival acquisition of waqf lands. 'Abduh's associates tried to convince him to let the khedive do as he wished with the awqaf, so that the khedive would let him do as he wished at al-Azhar. 'Abduh replied that no cause would make him consent to an illegal act. Afterward, 'Abduh told

Wilfrid Blunt that he believed the khedive had begun trying to remove him from the position of Grand Mufti. Blunt believed 'Abduh was "so firmly established" with the British that 'Abduh's influence would outweigh even that of the khedive, regardless of 'Abbas's machinations. 'Abduh himself brushed off the khedive's ire. When word reached 'Abduh that the khedive accused him of behaving as a pharaoh, 'Abduh merely said, "May God requite him. Is he the Pharaoh or am I? I'm only one of his subjects."[100]

'Abduh and Blunt both underestimated Khedive 'Abbas's ingenuity. In November 1903, 'Abbas began funding a *Humara*-like newspaper, *al-Zahir* [The obvious truth], designed to undermine reputations of British sympathizers.[101]

The Transvaal Fatwa

The campaign against 'Abduh was already in full swing when, in December of 1903, he issued his infamous Transvaal fatwa. 'Abduh had received a petition from a Muslim living in the Transvaal of South Africa, where Muslims were a minority in a largely Christian population. The petitioner wanted to know whether it was permissible (1) for Muslims to wear European-style hats if doing so eased commercial relationships with European clients, (2) for Muslims to eat meat slaughtered by Transvaal Christians, and (3) for a Muslim of the Shafi'i madhhab to perform communal prayers led by a Hanafi imam, even though the forms of prayer differed in some respects.[102] All three questions touched upon the issue of Muslim conformity to majority custom, which nineteenth-century muftis in North Africa had considered tashabbuh, imitative conformity verging on apostasy.

'Abduh's fatwa addressed each question with attention to the specific quandaries of Muslims as minorities. 'Abduh held that, because no specific regulations in the Qur'an or hadith prescribed male headgear, the fez or turban could not be considered specifically Islamic dress incumbent upon the believer. If the believer did not intend apostasy, wearing a hat was not tashabbuh. In regard to the prayers, Muslims had to recognize that although small differences in ritual might distinguish a Hanafi imam from a Shafi'i, both were still Muslims. A believer who denied the validity of prayers outside his own madhhab denied the unity of Islam, and the small community of Transvaal Muslims could ill afford sectarian divisions. The question of whether Muslims could eat meat slaughtered according to Transvaal custom, however, was more difficult. Muslims are only permitted to eat meat slaughtered by cutting the animal's throat in the name of God, and the Christians slaughtered their animals with an axe.[103] Recognizing that insistence upon this requirement might isolate Transvaal Muslims from their Christian neighbors, 'Abduh emphasized Qur'an verses that permitted Muslims to eat the same foods as People of the Book, i.e., Jews and Christians, such as Sura 5:5: "[T]he food of the People of the Book is lawful for you and your food is lawful for them." 'Abduh glossed over a specific restriction against eating animals killed "by violent blow." He stipulated, however, that the animals should be slaughtered according to Christian rites that permitted even the clergy to eat their meat. This judgment was based on an early ruling of the Maliki school by Abu Bakr ibn al-'Arabi. Throughout, 'Abduh elevated issues of intent, unity, and peaceful coexistence over potentially divisive technical details.[104]

A storm of criticism followed release of 'Abduh's Transvaal fatwa on 25 December 1903, mostly from people already seeking to unmake the Mufti: nationalist muckrakers, members of the 'ulama, and the khedive's partisans. On 29 December, the khedive's new pro-nationalist newspaper ran a front-page story decrying the fatwa as illegitimate.[105] On 31 December, the *Humarat monyati* incited newspaper editors to write about the fatwa: "Newspapers are . . . the summary of public opinion; they are the voice of the masses; they are the single mediator between the government and the people."[106]

In the midst of the controversy, on 5 January 1904, 'Abduh publicly signaled his final break with the khedive. The khedive was holding his annual 'id julus, a celebration of his succession to the throne, with a feast and ceremony to bestow 'ulama honors. The khedive had reportedly given the Azhar Administrative Council an oral directive to transfer a kiswa al-tashrif from a deceased 'alim to Shaykh Muhammad Rashid, mufti to the khedive's cabinet, but at the ceremony the council gave it to someone else. The khedive then demanded that Shaykh al-Azhar 'Ali al-Biblawi explain why his order had not been carried out. When Shaykh al-Biblawi hesitated apologetically, 'Abduh answered for him: "That which the Azhar Administrative Council does is the implementation of our Effendi's order—that is, the text of the law signed with the name of Your Highness. As for oral orders, the council does not rely on them." Before a hushed audience and red-faced khedive, 'Abduh declared that, if the khedive wished the council to allocate the kiswa according to his personal wishes, he would have to change the law governing council authority. Otherwise, transferral of these things was not the khedive's business.

Khedive 'Abbas left the celebration incensed and remained convinced from that day forth that 'Abduh was trying to wrest from his hands those few areas of influence that British dominion had left him. He began to encourage 'Abduh's enemies, with the intent of forcing 'Abduh's three council allies to resign (the Hanbali Mufti, Shaykh Abu al-Fadl al-Gizawi, and Shaykh Sulayman 'Abd). The khedive would replace them with shaykhs unambiguously loyal to himself, such as Shaykh Muhammad Rashid (intended recipient of the errant Kiswa), "so that the Administrative Council would be a powerful party to oppose ['Abduh's] influence."[107] The khedive also encouraged Shaykh al-Shirbitli of *al-Zahir* to collaborate with Muhammad Tawfiq al-Bakri, a pro-khedive member of the Azhar Administrative Council, and Mustafa Kamil, editor of *al-Liwa'*, in a press campaign against 'Abduh.[108] Because the khedive had financial connections to *al-Zahir* and supported Mustafa Kamil's informally constituted Nationalist Party until 1905,[109] the subsequent press outcry against the Transvaal fatwa can be understood as a function of power negotiations between the khedive and the Mufti.

Al-Babaghallo al-Misri was a handwritten leaflet of four pages, entirely devoted to scandalmongering and inflammatory sketches.[110] Its second issue included a drawing of 'Abduh holding the waist of a "naked" European woman, while a dog pawing his leg rendered him ritually impure (Figure 8.3). *Al-Babaghallo al-Misri's* litany of protests was typical of complaints against 'Abduh's ijtihad. Its author, 'Abd al-Majid Kamil, stated that 'Abduh was permitting things "forbidden by God." The Transvaal fatwa demonstrated that he was not of the Maliki madhhab but rather of "Maltese" madhhab—that is, European inclination—and that he ultimately served the interests of imperialism. Kamil reiterated familiar complaints about 'Abduh's "pilgrimages" to Europe, his consorting with "ladies," his permitting of riba', and his Mu'tazilism. There were also obvious slanders: 'Abduh had abandoned tenets of the faith, banned the pilgrimage, eaten the things the Transvaal fatwa permitted, and let himself be licked by dogs. His fatwas would Westernize the country, serving as weapons to "cut off the tongues that criticize his Europeanization." The leaflet concluded: "I wonder why the English government has not honored His Excellency the Professor with the title of 'Sir,' or 'Mister' at the very least?? . . . It occurred to me that he prefers the title 'Mister' to 'Sayyid.'. . . If you asked him to perform a marriage he would write the contract according to the madhhab of 'Darwin.'"[111]

'Abd al-Majid Kamil's argument was hardly sophisticated. But the reference to Darwin was not just a jab at 'Abduh's political alliances; it highlighted 'Abduh's very real ties to the Darwinist positivist Herbert Spencer. Dur-

Figure 8.3   Sketch of Muhammad 'Abduh. *(Source:* 'Abd al-Majid Kamil, "Al-Mister Muhammad 'Abduh, Mufti al-diyar al-Misriyya," *al-Babaghallo al-Misri* 1, no. 2 [12 January 1904]: 4.)

ing 'Abduh's visit to England in August 1903, he had requested specifically to meet Spencer because of his ideas on education. Wilfrid Blunt arranged the visit and translated for them.[112] Spencer's ideas had recently been profiled in the scientific journal *al-Muqtataf,* itself an occasional victim of nationalist venom.[113] Thus the reference to 'Abduh's alleged Darwinism probably caught the attention of the nationalistically inclined.[114]

Al-Zahir's arguments were more sophisticated. Its editor, Muhammad Abu Shadi Bey, and one of its writers, al-Shirbitli ('Abduh's former nemesis from *al-Nahj al-qawim*), dedicated long pages to the Mufti's errors, which, they claimed, were legion. They took aim first at the specific ruling that declared the food of Transvaal Christians lawful for Muslims, and then at

'Abduh's claims to be able to perform ijtihad. First, *al-Zahir* claimed that Transvaal Christians slaughtered their animals with an axe and extracted the meat while the animals were still living, extending their torture. This was forbidden by an unambiguous statement in the Qur'an (Sura 5:5).[115] Muslims are not permitted to eat animals that are mawqudha (fatally ill). An animal killed by a blow is in the last moments of its life mawqudha and thus its meat is forbidden. Furthermore, Christians did not have to recite the name of God before slaughtering an animal, an omission that also could render meat unlawful for Muslims.[116] The issue of whether Christian priests could eat the meat was irrelevant, because fundamental standards for edible meat simply weren't met under conditions 'Abduh permitted.[117]

According to the 'ulama consulted by *al-Zahir,* this verse about animal slaughter was revealed following a dispute between Muslims and mushrikun (idolaters) over God's agency in an animal's death. The idolaters had asked Muhammad, "If something has died, who killed it?" Muhammad replied "God killed it." The idolaters then said, "So then you claim that what you and your friends killed is *hallal,* and what God killed is *haram.*" God then sent to Muhammad the verse instructing him not to eat previously killed animals. The Qur'an also identified as mushrik (idolater) "someone who makes lawful something that God has made unlawful, or who made unlawful that which God has designated lawful" and consequently causes dissension in the community. The context of this verse allowed *al-Zahir* to insinuate that 'Abduh was by this definition a mushrik and that anyone who followed his fatwa and ate of dead meat was also a mushrik. "We infer from this that the situation is critical and that the position of ifta' [issuing fatwas] is surrounded by dangerous slippery slopes that necessitate absolute caution in every dictum issued." On this critical issue, 'Abduh should not have cited only the Qur'anic verse but also should have consulted the legal texts explaining the serious consequences of incorrect interpretation. A mufti's own opinion being fallible, he should have recourse to as much previous scholarship as possible to avoid leading laymen into error.[118]

In fact, *al-Zahir* continued, 'Abduh's decision agreed with no known madhhab but was based on his own opinion, which he indicated by using the terms "I think" and "my opinion is." 'Abduh had been appointed to deliver fatwas according to rulings of the Hanafi school, so his failure to do so required his dismissal.[119] The role of a mufti in an official position is taqlid, and those who believed 'Abduh had "the right to ijtihad" were simply wrong.[120] Moreover, 'Abduh's apparent error, the public outcry, and his unwillingness to defend himself had shaken the public's trust in him and in ifta'. As one anonymous writer put it, "It is incumbent upon His Excellency to announce that he is not a mujtahid mufti as long as he serves at the command of His Highness the Amir of Egypt, that his duties are defined by the restriction of ifta' to those things that have already been used as evidence in the madhhab of Abu Hanifa and no other."[121] 'Abduh's fatwa was, in short, "impermissible to adopt in any aspect."[122]

Yet al-Zahir implicitly accepted ijtihad. It said the Qur'anic verses pertaining to forbidden methods of slaughtering were unambiguous and in "eloquent Arabic, not Persian in need of interpretation and preferential weighing." There was no need for a mufti to tell people how to interpret the verses, for their meaning was plain and plainly contradicted 'Abduh's fatwa. Furthermore, it was not 'Abduh's place to offer his personal opinion on the matter as religious advice, for "no Muslim is obliged to follow another's opinion."[123] This was interesting because al-Zahir was implicitly doing what al-Tahtawi, al-Afghani, 'Abduh, and al-Manar had recommended in their campaigns for a new ijtihad: examining primary texts and using them to come to a firmer personal understanding of religion. Al-Zahir rejected only 'Abduh's claim to perform ijtihad for others.

Instead, al-Zahir proposed itself as provider of religious advice. It was engaged in "a jihad in the service of establishing the truth," and would serve not as mufti but as "a preacher, explaining to [the public] the judgment of God as it is recorded in your Qur'an." This would help to preserve "the dignity of ifta'."[124] This journalistic duty was especially important at that time, because circumstances made it difficult to consult another high-ranking mufti. For unexplained reasons, the paper charged that advice of the Ottoman sheyhulislam, the highest-ranking jurisconsult of the Ottoman Empire, would not result in a definite answer. And an alternate opinion could not be sought from the Shaykh al-Azhar, 'Ali al-Biblawi. "We know that the Mufti and the Shaykh al-Azhar are necessarily in agreement with one another; one of them never says what would contradict the dicta of the other. And we are not ignorant of the influence that the Mufti has over al-Azhar and those weak, oppressed ones there who are afraid of the Shaykh and are convinced of his violent power over them." They had lost confidence in themselves and could not resist.[125] It was this lack of religious leadership that the journal could address.

Al-Zahir asked a number of 'ulama to send in opinions of the fatwa and the issues it addressed. The 'ulama said at first that they didn't think 'Abduh intended harm but was rather trying to deal with the particular problems of a minority living under a "dictatorship." Nevertheless, they also quoted

'Abduh's fatwas to show that he was "not like Abu Hanifa": His rulings were not just slightly different from those of other madhahib—they contradicted all other madhahib.[126]

Some readers did come to 'Abduh's defense, accusing al-Zahir of libeling the Mufti to attract more readers. But they nearly always did so anonymously, as if afraid to face public knowledge of their sympathies. The fact that these defenses appeared in the Anglophile newspaper al-Muqattam and the Francophile al-Ahram only served to support his detractors' claim that 'Abduh represented Western interests. Al-Zahir countered that the English were trying to "change the ruling of God"; 'Abduh was helping them by applying principles derived from the civil courts in which he had served previously.[127]

In a notable exception to the timid anonymous support for 'Abduh, al-Manar insisted that 'Abduh honored his commitment to the Hanafi madhhab for official government fatwas, as was required. However, the Transvaal fatwa was for a private individual; 'Abduh was therefore free to rule according to his conscience, as he had done in other private endeavors, including his interpretation of the Qur'an for al-Manar. Rida reminded his audience that 'Abduh could hardly be expected to give personal advice based on taqlid, since in all other venues he had espoused the revival of ijtihad.[128]

On the day of the khedive's 'id julus, Mustafa Kamil, editor of the notoriously anti-British al-Liwa' [The standard], announced that he had earlier held back his words, hoping that 'Abduh would undertake some defense of his decisions, because a mufti had a responsibility to explain religious matters to the people. The Mufti's reticence in the face of public criticism contributed to his lack of credibility. Mustafa Kamil argued that 'Abduh could not simply expect the people to make obeisance to a mufti's views; they were free to have their own opinions. Al-Liwa' was taking the same stance as al-Zahir: The Nationalists had, in a turn of political tables, co-opted 'Abduh's campaign to encourage independent religious thinking among the people, but rejected his claim to be able to do the same in their name.[129] And the khedive approved, stating later that although Mustafa Kamil had been free to state his own views in al-Liwa', the khedive generally agreed with him: "He said, in my place, what had to be said and that which could not be said in my name."[130]

While this press campaign was in progress, Shafiq reported that a party of "'Abduh's enemies" had gone to Lord Cromer, taking with them a photograph of 'Abduh in what they considered to be a compromising position. Shafiq described the photograph as 'Abduh "with some foreign women . . .

a shameless picture that surprised the masses," which was responsible for its publishers being convicted "for drawing ['Abduh] and photographing him standing with a woman wearing the clothes of a dancer in a disgraceful condition." This was accompanied by the now-familiar "false accusation attributing to him unbelief and making forbidden things permissible," and denouncing him for "inducing the people of his nation to despise him." Shafiq wanted his readers to believe the photograph was a fake—he said 'Abduh's enemies "fabricated" a photograph. More likely it was the infamous *Humarat monyati* photograph or one of the other eleven taken of 'Abduh in Europe, accompanied by a drawing, because Shafiq added that the photo had appeared "in the newspaper *Humarat monyati,* and in *al-Babaghallo al-Misri,* and in *al-Arnab,*" and its publishers had been subjected to a criminal trial and sentenced to six and four months' imprisonment respectively.[131] Shafiq admitted to the damage done to the Mufti's reputation by causing the people "to despise" him. Because Shafiq explicitly named himself a partisan of the Mufti, his horrified reaction to the photograph and his testimony to public sentiment are doubly damning. Although Shafiq tried to paint 'Abduh's opponents in the worst possible light, those who presented the picture to Cromer were in all likelihood not exaggerating their case. They charged that the picture was evidence that popular sentiment among Muslims held 'Abduh in contempt because he had not respected his office, and that "he must resign to show concern for their feelings."

According to Shafiq, Cromer smiled sarcastically and said: "The Professor visits us here, and Lady Cromer and the wives of others attend his salons, so should we consider this an insult to him, or to us?"[132] Cromer was unwilling to accept an argument against 'Abduh that implied criticism of British women or superiority of Egyptian feminine dress. But more importantly, he could not sacrifice the one friend he had in power over religious matters. On 14 January, Lord Cromer refused Khedive 'Abbas's formal request to remove the Mufti, even though 'Abduh himself apparently had agreed to resign. Cromer said further that he would not let 'Abduh resign as long as he himself remained in Egypt.[133]

Conclusion

It is difficult not to feel sympathy for 'Abduh. He fell victim to historical forces. As literacy, education, and use of journalism grew, the public also grew in independent thought. By promoting wider use of ijtihad, 'Abduh provided an argument for the legitimacy of independent interpretation, at least for those who were qualified. Rashid Rida publicized 'Abduh's work in *al-Manar,* inspiring further discussion by journalists, some of whom were already predisposed to favor the idea through intellectual contact with al-Afghani. But 'Abduh's controversial ideas and, for some, his mimicry of foreign occupiers undermined his credibility after he was raised to the Azhar Administrative Council and the office of Grand Mufti. Furthermore, 'Abduh's condemnations of Azhari 'ulama produced ready allies for the khedive when 'Abduh's loyalties seemed to swing toward the British. Finally the nationalist presses, supplied with evidence by shaykhs and khedival agents, were able to use 'Abduh's own arguments for lay ijtihad against him, weaving their ad hominem attacks into the nationalist discourse on resistance to imperialism.

Ironically, 'Abduh provided his opponents with the tools they needed to discredit him. And his former British supporters, recognizing both the potential danger to themselves in his ideas and his unpopularity among his own people, eventually abandoned him as well.

9

WHO REFORMED AL-AZHAR?

'Abduh's exclusion from the khedive's entourage blocked his access to the avenues of power over al-Azhar after 1904. Shafiq Pasha castigated 'Abduh for antagonizing the khedive, saying he had "forfeited everything we had worked for and had lost the first step toward reforming al-Azhar."[1] However, the reform movement had not died; rather, it devolved upon those whose political associations and personal behavior were less controversial than 'Abduh's. Those who named and worked on committees that fleshed out provisions of the 1896 Azhar Organization Code, who created the plans really implemented, were not members of the Azhar Administrative Council but rather members of al-Azhar faculty, among them infamous "obstructionists." Collaborative efforts of these committees resulted in 1908 in a comprehensive reform package known as the Internal Reorganization Code, or simply "the New Order," that completely reorganized the madrasa, implementing bureaucratic administrative procedures and efficiency-based pedagogies, although in ways 'Abduh never envisioned.

Reception of the 1908 reform code was complicated by changes in the national political climate in Egypt after 1906. The 1905 Japanese victory in the Russo-Japanese war had fueled nationalist unrest. Arabic newspapers exulted in this first victory of an Asian country over the West. Then, in June of 1906, the British administration in Egypt tried to reassert its authority, leading to a wave of grassroots anti-British fervor. Five British officers hunting pigeons near the Delta village of Dinshawai accidentally set fire to a barn. Villagers whose livelihood depended on raising pigeons tried to disarm the officers with wooden staves. In the resulting fracas, the officers fired at least two shots, injuring a woman and three men. The villagers attacked and seriously wounded three officers, one of whom died from concussion and sunstroke after running five miles back to his camp in blistering summer heat. The officers claimed they had been lured into a trap, that the villagers had set the fire and committed premeditated murder. Lord Cromer decided to try the villagers under an 1895 law requiring a special tribunal for those who attacked military personnel and allowing a speedier trial and harsher penalties than the Egyptian criminal code permitted. Three British and two Egyptian officials sat on the tribunal. After about thirty minutes of questioning, the tribunal convicted twenty-one of the fifty-two villagers of premeditated murder and violent robbery. Four men were hanged, eight flogged, and the rest imprisoned. The hangings and floggings were carried out in public, with some 500 people from the village and surrounding area in forced attendance.[2] This incident inspired poets and folk balladeers to spread tales of British injustice throughout the countryside, and awakened popular sentiment against the occupation.[3]

Students now became the nucleus of popular demonstrations. In January of 1906, Douglas Dunlop, British advisor to the Ministry of Education, had issued new rules for the civil law school, which mandated that any student failing end-of-year examinations be expelled. Law students promptly abandoned classes and took to the streets for a week until the government promised to investigate the matter. This began a period of urban disturbances that lasted for several years.[4] This period also witnessed the emergence of students as a socially distinct, politically active class, the vanguard of nationalist agitation, championed by nationalist newspapers.[5]

As nationalist demonstrations filled Cairo's streets, al-Azhar once again erupted in seething discontent. Historians have assumed that this discontent arose from violent opposition to the 1908 Internal Reorganization Code, but exhaustive research disproves this. This student disturbance began as an orderly and organized strike in favor of reform. When the Azhari strikers were drawn into the larger arena of the 1908–1909 political protests, their orderly demonstrations degenerated.

These strikes signified the extent to which a century of reforms linked to Egyptian state-construction had affected Azharis. Students had accepted and now promoted the Utilitarian techniques of educational order that had been first outlined by Hasan al-'Attar and Rifa'a al-Tahtawi. An alliance also arose between poorly paid 'ulama and employment-oriented students, whose demands propelled conservative Maliki Shaykh Salim al-Bishri to lead a gradualist negotiation of the reform process. In short, it was conservatives, supported by the strong nationalist movement among students, who legitimated and led reform at al-Azhar.

Shaykh Salim al-Bishri

When 'Abduh was made Grand Mufti in 1899, he was terribly disappointed that he did not also become Shaykh al-Azhar, because he considered
that post a better position from which to enact reform. Khedive 'Abbas
intentionally withheld this post from 'Abduh, so he could use al-Azhar
'ulama to offset British influence over appointed positions. To fill the post
of Shaykh al-Azhar, he courted the opposite extreme of the 'ulama ideological spectrum.[6]

The newspaper *Misbah al-sharq* reported on the process of selection. Al-
Azhar elders nominated Shaykh 'Abd al-Rahman al-Shirbini, a respected
scholar. A group of workers and Sufis petitioned for Shaykh Hasuna al-
Nawawi to be returned to office, but al-Nawawi declined. Shaykh Muhammad al-Bakhit, a conservative opponent of 'Abduh, was nominated by two
lawyers with whom he had worked previously. Shaykh Muhammad 'Abduh
was a candidate "by reason of his office and reputation." Shaykh Salim al-
Bishri, the Maliki mufti, nominated himself.[7]

The khedive chose Shaykh Salim al-Bishri. According to Muhammad
Tawfiq, editor of *al-Humara,* Shaykh Salim was the man who had brought
'Abduh's compromising photograph to public attention. He was the uncon-
tested leading figure of the conservative faction at that time. He had been a
student of Shaykhs Muhammad 'Ilish and Ibrahim al-Bajuri and had served
as head shaykh of the Sayyida Zaynab mosque for some years before his
promotion.[8] As Maliki Mufti, Shaykh Salim also held the loyalty, at least
nominally, of the second largest madhhab at al-Azhar and the most dense-
ly populated riwaqs. In 1902, al-Azhar had 77 Maliki faculty, 100 Shafi'i,
72 Hanafi, and 3 Hanbali. In 1903, there were 10,740 Egyptian students
of mixed Maliki and Shafi'i adherence, plus 165 Maghribis and 73 African
students, mainly Malikis. In comparison, there were 273 "Eastern Arabs,"
primarily of the Hanafi madhhab. The khedive described the Maliki riwaqs
as by far the most overcrowded.[9] Shaykh Salim therefore had a considerable
power base within al-Azhar as well as the khedive's backing.

According to the records of al-Azhar Administrative Council secretary
'Abd al-Karim Salman (a government appointee and 'Abduh's associate),
Shaykh Salim was the arch hypocrite of al-Azhar reform. Salman wrote that
as a council member, Shaykh Salim had always been critical of the government appointees' suggestions. To balance their influence, Shaykh Salim had
led an effort to involve the 'ulama in formulating new regulations by creating committees. Even Salman acknowledged that reforms introduced in the
1890s by these committees engendered no opposition, including those that

introduced mathematics into the curriculum.[10] Yet, after Shaykh Salim's appointment as Shaykh al-Azhar, Salman complained that Salim had deliberately neglected to present to the council a plan for new book selection painstakingly developed by one of his own committees.[11]

Salman suspected a secret agreement between Shaykh Salim and the khedive, which would have explained why the shaykh encountered no khedival ire for his obstructionism. Moreover, Rashid Rida claimed the khedive used Shaykh Salim intentionally to block British attempts to control the mosque.[12] But Shaykh Salim had an independent agenda; he was not a perfect tool, and sometimes bucked khedival orders. When the book selection committee drew up its plan for assigning new sciences and books to instructors, Shaykh Salim presented it directly to the khedive, saying: "We do not agree to any of this unless you promulgate it as a khedival decree—if it is ordered of us, then we must follow it."[13]

Shaykh Salim's behavior was guided by a general principle derived from a hadith. The hadith related an incident in which the Prophet asked his Companion 'Umar to bring him some paper, so that he could write some instructions. 'Umar refused. Shaykh Salim suggested that 'Umar was "afraid that the Prophet (S.A.) might write such commands as it would be beyond them to obey or comply with and they would, therefore, deserve punishment, because what he would write down would be imperative and final and would not leave any scope for examination and interpretation by others. . . . ['Umar] therefore remarked, 'the Book of Allah is sufficient for us.'" The principle entailed, Salim wrote, was that "[t]he execution of an order, as a principle, is incumbent on the person or persons ordered to do a thing."[14] Apparently Salim held the converse to be true as well, at least if employed in defense of religion: If no direct order was given, no action was required.

The khedive relied upon Shaykh Salim to ensure that every suggested reform received approval from Azhari 'ulama. In one case, the khedive appointed a formal committee to develop a curricular plan for al-Azhar. Unlike appointees to Salim's committees, these committee members had graduated from civil schools. After much deliberation, they had come up with a plan covering subjects to be taught in al-Azhar, what books should be used, and how much time students should spend learning the subjects. Salman reported: "His Highness wanted to be guided by the pleas of the people, so he ordered that the work of the committee be presented to Shaykh Salim in order to bring to light his opinion. [Salim] gathered representatives of the shaykhs[,] . . . told them [of the plan], and wrote down some of their comments on it, and then presented these to His Highness."

The committee then met with the faculty "and the two factions discussed together until they came to a consensus as to what was best for knowledge and the scholars, and thus it was that together they worked out a beneficial path to the objective."[15] Shaykh Salim thus ensured broad 'ulama participation in the process of reform development.

This does not mean that he worked willingly with the Azhar Administrative Council, or that he instantly mastered bureaucratic administrative procedures. Salman claimed that in May 1900, the khedive issued an order mandating implementation of the mutually agreed upon reforms. Shaykh Salim neglected to tell the council how to put the new program into action. Council members visited his house repeatedly to get from him lists of newly retired shaykhs, teaching appointments, new subjects to be taught, and the number of teachers required for each subject. According to Salman, "If not for this urgent solicitation, the academic year would have passed and nothing would have been decided on the matter of these subjects."[16]

Perhaps Shaykh Salim did stall intentionally. The consensus reform package mandated that students spend extensive time during their first four years studying mathematics and geography, and rumors spread that khedival incentive awards, a legacy of 'Abduh, were being given only to students who took the new subjects. Some 'ulama wrote to the papers complaining that the new subjects distracted students from their essential studies, threatening al-Azhar's mission to train religious scholars. This theme of complaint had made a brief appearance in the 1880s but was notably absent during the mid-1890s. Its re-emergence at this time was probably due in part to the ad hominem campaign against 'Abduh and thus reflected anti-British sentiment.[17] Rashid Rida, in reporting the reasons why Shaykh Salim "opposed" the new program, wrote: "The intent of this was simply to thwart the attempts of Muhammad 'Abduh and leave everything as it was."[18]

To cite another example, in November 1899, the Azhar Administrative Council proposed to a committee of Azhari elders that the curriculum should include Arabic literature. 'Abduh tried to convince the committee that the study of literature would help students better understand the Arabic language and hence the religious texts they were being trained to interpret. Although he convinced four committee members, the majority decided that teaching literature would usurp time needed for the fundamental studies "without which the religion cannot be understood," and that literary studies were "nonessential" and "commendable but unnecessary" (amr ghayr wajib wa mustahsan ghayr lazim). Literary studies were thus allowed only as extracurricular activities.[19]

The response in the press reveals how modernist arguments for reform had become accepted, even among those who opposed 'Abduh. Ibrahim al-Muwailihi, whose attacks would dog 'Abduh in Istanbul, argued stridently against this decision. He said that Ibn Khaldun, among others, had demonstrated that study of grammatical rules does not convey facility in the language. Only extensive reading in the Arabic classics did so, while also encouraging good manners and "refined thought." Al-Muwailihi said the Azharis were "worthless" (laisu 'ala shay') at the Arabic language, because they taught only rules and not facility of comprehension or composition. "Even to this day, if the eldest elder and most learned 'alim among them were to be entrusted with the composition of a treatise on any subject . . . [it would be] contorted, muddled, obscure, impossible to understand, and filled with incongruous phrases in which expressions are misplaced." Obviously, such people could not teach students how to interpret the difficult Islamic legal texts. Yet the 'ulama refused to budge, declaring the teaching of literature at al-Azhar to be bid'a (a proscribed innovation) and thus protecting their monopoly over rule-based linguistic studies. Al-Muwailihi bewailed what would surely be the death of Islam: If the 'ulama failed to inject new life into language studies, language reform would fall to the mutamaddinin, those non-Muslim Arabs who sought to replace the old language of rhetoric and elegance with the colloquial. This would lead to the death of Qur'anic Arabic, so that it would become like Latin, empty phrases in the mouths of worshipers who knew not what they said.[20]

The 'ulama elders on the committee did not object to the study of literature per se, but claimed, following decade-old arguments, that time was too short to require it. This genuine concern for mission probably masked the added suspicion caused by repeated British attempts to impose their own will upon institutions of religious law. Some elder 'ulama would resist any reforms 'Abduh suggested, because they thought he was a pawn of British interests. Shaykh Salim also remarked, in a different context, that "[p]eople of middle and advanced ages are by their disposition unwilling to be subordinate to a young man and are averse to carrying out his commands."[21]

In this context, Shaykh Salim's actions could be interpreted as consistent with a strategy of political opposition encouraged but not entirely managed by the khedive.[22] As noted previously, Shaykh Salim would not disobey a direct khedival order. For the same reason, he avoided giving direct orders to the 'ulama regarding implementation, in accordance with the general principle that a leader should not command people to do things that they cannot. Commanding 'ulama to implement reforms would create a paradox for anyone opposed to them, because not fulfilling a peremptory command is a sin. In another case, Salim allowed overworked shaykhs to forgo examining candidates for the 'alimiyya degree. On the one hand, this resulted in the examination's becoming optional; on the other, it provided space for conscientious objection.[23]

Needless to say, Shaykh Salim's actions did not go over well with modernist reformers, who characterized them as blackly as possible, calling them greedy, unfair to students, and prejudiced against the new subjects. Rida charged that Shaykh Salim desired solely to thwart 'Abduh and to preserve the status quo. Salman accused Salim of nepotism and asserted that the government remanded Maliki riwaq waqf monies to the treasury so that Salim would be "unable to usurp [them] or give [them] to his sons." And Muhammad 'Abduh authored a long condemnation of the various ways in which Salim had "violated" the new disciplinary regulations.[24]

Again, Shaykh Salim's actions can also be construed positively, as attempts to address other concerns of his constituents. He campaigned throughout his term to have student incentive grants abolished, but also to use the funds to supplement incomes of impoverished shaykhs. Al-Azhar's stipend for teaching at this time was still at best three Egyptian pounds a month, whereas teachers in the civil schools were earning on average seven pounds a month. In other words, al-Azhar 'ulama earned somewhat less than a government weigher in the marketplace, and about the same as a skilled artisan.[25] Eventually the incentive funds were added to certain shaykhs' stipends.[26] Regarding Salim's own income, al-Muwailihi reported that, following his appointment as Shaykh al-Azhar, Shaykh Salim asked that his old stipend as mufti (£E 12 a month) be added to his hefty new salary of £E 71 a month. Although it was reported without comment, this request made him appear greedy. Another account, however, called Salim a master of "judicious administration" and said he distributed much of his income to "friends in need."[27]

Shaykh Salim also shared some concerns of his conservative predecessor as Maliki Mufti, Shaykh Muhammad 'Ilish, and others who felt that modernist reformers' ideas introduced divisive elements into the religious community at a time when communal solidarity was critical to its survival. In 1911, Shaykh Salim initiated a lengthy correspondence with Iraqi Shi'i scholar 'Abd al-Husayn Sharaf al-Din al-Musawi in an attempt to discover the true differences between the Shi'i and Sunni madhahib. In his first letters, Shaykh Salim suggested that the Shi'a should follow the faith of the majority, that is, Sunni Ash'ari jurisprudence:

> Consider how necessary it is for us all to be united at the present time, when the enemies of Islam have arrayed their forces against us. . . . We . . . by our discord and disunity are indirectly helping our enemies. Under the circumstances, the best thing for us to do is to stand united and gather around one center. Such unity can only be achieved if we adopt the same faith.[28]

This concern for unity in faith was overriding: Even though Shaykh Salim eventually was convinced that Shi'i jurisprudence did not diverge any more greatly from the Sunnis' than the Sunni madhahib diverged from one another, he still worried that the prejudices of the majority would make it impossible for them to accept the Shi'a.[29] In addition, if the Shi'a sect were legitimized, this would entail also admitting the possibility that Muhammad had designated 'Ali his successor, thus challenging the legitimacy of the first three caliphs and their supporters. Throughout the correspondence, Shaykh Salim insisted that the prestige and honor of the first caliphs and those who supported their succession had to be upheld.[30] If it was not, their legitimacy as authoritative sources on practices of the early community and religious law would come into question, leading to a crisis of faith among ordinary Sunnis at a time when religious solidarity was their greatest weapon against colonial incursions.[31] In fact, Shaykh Salim's views on the need for authoritative sources of law, such as those represented by the Sunni madhahib and Shi'i Imams, were so strong that a contemporary author thought it necessary to prove that Shaykh Salim was not in fact Shi'i.[32] Shaykh Salim also defended taqlid for laymen, again citing concerns about unity.[33]

In 1904, Muhammad 'Abduh and the modernist pro-ijtihad reformers posed a more immediate threat of disunity than the Shi'a. Shaykh Salim appeared to agree with modernist reformers on some issues, such as relieving social injustices. For example, 'Abduh, acting as Grand Mufti of Egypt, proposed new standards for adjudicating divorce cases in Egypt. The new statutes made it easier for women to obtain divorces when their husbands abandoned them or went missing during warfare. In August 1900, Shaykh Salim sent 'Abduh a letter of commendation, stating, "Our opinion regarding the ideas presented in this material is the same as yours. We have therefore signed it as an indication of our approval. We would also like to thank you for your concern with this important matter."[34]

However, neither the modernists nor Lord Cromer were willing to tolerate Shaykh Salim's obstructionism, no matter what social good it might do. By 1903, they had maneuvered Salim out of office, and a new Shaykh al-Azhar had to be chosen. The 'ulama and khedive could not decide among the nominees, Shaykhs Muhammad Bakhit, Ahmad Rifa'i, and Amin al-Mahdi, and Cromer rejected Hasuna al-Nawawi. The candidate ultimately selected in March 1903, Shaykh 'Ali al-Biblawi, was the naqib al-ashraf (leader of the local descendants of the Prophet), an uncontroversial compromise choice.[35] Unfortunately, if modernists expected that removing Shaykh Salim would reestablish 'Abduh as leader of reform, they were badly mistaken.

". . . because the work of the reformer may twist back on itself . . ."

In 1904, while 'Abduh was still mired in the quagmire left by the intrigue against him, and Azharis were still negotiating the newest reforms, new voices arose from among a conservative faction of al-Azhar 'ulama and students. By this time, significant cultural changes had occurred at al-Azhar. Support for the 'ulama-mediated reform codes had become widespread among al-Azhar students. Even though the Shaykh al-Azhar no longer mandated yearly examinations and the student incentive awards were no longer being given, sixty-eight students took the exams in 1904. Thirty-four passed. The elementary-level government exams were so tough that year that students who failed protested against the Ministry of Education. One even committed suicide, thus implying that certification by examination had become increasingly important to students.[36] By this time, students themselves were insisting that the examinations and awards had inspired them to greater efforts, and some shaykhs petitioned Shaykh al-Azhar 'Ali al-Biblawi to reimpose yearly exams. One shaykh even volunteered 200 pounds sterling of his own money to award successful examinees.[37]

However, al-Azhar was still plagued by old problems: The majority of its students were overwhelmed by poverty and ill equipped to adopt the rigorous lifestyle of a serious scholar.[38] Partly because of this, al-Azhar suffered from sporadic outbreaks of violence set off by overcrowding and disorganized allotment of student stipends.[39] In 1904, someone shot the Shaykh of the Maghribi riwaq; the French consul intervened, expressing dismay at the

Maghribis' poverty. In March 1905, Maghribi students forcefully prevented non-Maghribis from being housed in their riwaq and then occupied
rooms in the newly built 'Abbasiya riwaq, again necessitating French con-
sular involvement.[40] Although his attempt to interfere in al-Azhar housing
arrangements sparked this incident, Khedive 'Abbas rejected the Azhar
Administrative Council's plan for its resolution.[41]

The student disturbances were such that 'Abduh needed armed guards to
protect him while in the mosque precincts at night.[42] 'Abduh had begun
giving weekly lectures in Qur'anic exegesis at al-Azhar, an extension of his
duties as Grand Mufti. Although he attracted hundreds of listeners, many
listened with skepticism, even fear. 'Abd al-Baqi al-Surur, a young student
at the time, reported: "Our professors, may God forgive them, used to constantly criticize the Shaykh ['Abduh] in our presence and represent him as
being dangerous for religion and for the religious—subtly dangerous. As a
consequence . . . I used to flee from encountering the professor, for the sake
of my religion, and to flee from listening to his lessons, even though he was
a friend of my father."[43]

In 1904, Shaykh Muhammad al-Ahmadi al-Zawahiri, a recent al-Azhar
graduate, published a stinging critique of every aspect of religious education
entitled *al-'Ilm wa al-'ulama wa al-nizam al-ta'lim* (Knowledge, scholars,
and the system of instruction). Al-Zawahiri came from a family renowned
for pious leadership; his grandfather had been honored as a saint, and his
father was head shaykh of the Ahmadi Sufi sect.[44] Al-Zawahiri offered a
coherent vision of the 'alim's function within Islamic society that embraced
conservative concerns for Azhar's mission, the status of the madhhab
Imams, and public respect for the 'ulama. Yet he also promoted 'Abduh's
broadened concept of ijtihad.[45]

According to al-Zawahiri, the "poor morality" exhibited by shaykhs and
students of religion had caused the public to lose respect for them, and
they thus had little influence. Someone like Muhammad 'Abduh was
praiseworthy because he had achieved high influence by virtue of his own
intellectual power. Influence was important for accomplishing reform, but
not sufficient: "One is not an 'alim in truth unless the effect of one's learning appears in one's people."[46] Modernist thinkers had lost touch with religious custom and tradition, and hence with the public. Those who
opposed modernist reform, on the other hand, tended to locate their ideals
in past historical periods, distrusting innovative practices and isolating
themselves from contemporary events.[47] A true 'alim would combine the
"courage, reason, thought, and good explanation of Professor Muhammad

'Abduh with the humility, modesty, mildness, and piety of Professor Shaykh al-Shirbini."[48]

The real impediment to ensuring that students of religion received the correct mix of training was that most were peasants and had received little or no education before arriving at al-Azhar. Upon arriving, they did not even know to apply for admission, and might remain unadmitted for several months. They attended the same halqas as others from their hometowns, without understanding a thing. No guide existed to introduce them to the etiquette of academic life, or to supervise their studies.[49] Knowing nothing of etiquette or morality, such students engaged in consumption of alcohol and fornication, so that the word *mujawwir,* "student of religion," became a pejorative term. Rashid Rida claimed that outsiders called al-Azhar "the Stable," "the Asylum," and "the Ruin."[50]

Al-Zawahiri's solution reiterated Utilitarian techniques for dealing with large populations embodied in previous codes: regularize admissions, make the shaykhs responsible for supervising student behavior, implement existing codes that divided studies into wasa'il (means) and maqasid (ends), and include "new" subjects. However, this was also a balancing act. Al-Zawahiri told the "stagnant ones" that, if they had lived in Muhammad's time, they would have been the first to oppose the Prophet. But he also confirmed that some reforms were just as harmful as none at all and that "religiosity did not contradict civilization." To avoid ceding control to a single supervisory authority, al-Zawahiri asserted that the tasks of defining and implementing "necessary reform" were too important for one individual, or even one group, to decide. A general conference of all levels of 'ulama should be convened to decide the issue.[51]

In an article in *al-Mu'ayyad,* al-Zawahiri declared that he wrote *al-'Ilm wa al-'ulama* to aid the khedive in his fight to improve the religious schools, because their current condition prevented them from serving their functions. He agreed that before "what they call the new reform" there had been a conspicuous shortcoming in religious education, "built on taqlid and narrowness of thought." Then a well-known group began to attempt reforms with the best intentions, but it became clear that their reforms were worse than the initial conditions. Al-Zawahiri claimed that modernist reformers lacked an essentially religious spirit, perhaps because they encouraged an attitude toward learning that focused on worldly success. Furthermore, he said, many 'ulama believed reformers were challenging the authority of prophecy and slandering the Imams. Al-Zawahiri considered both the controversy and modernist models of education "a great danger to the future of

Islam and to the religious schools, which have begun gradually to turn from religious schools protecting religion and its mightiness into philosophical schools from which people graduate philosophiles whose nominal relation to religion has destroyed many of its principles, and they stray from it as an arrow strays from its mark."[52]

Al-Mu'ayyad praised al-Zawahiri's program as "a compromise position" between the demands for al-Azhar reform and the claims that the new reforms only worsened matters. He added that the latter needed no proof and was the opinion of most Azharis.[53]

Shortly after this, the Ottoman-affiliated journal *al-Jawa'ib al-Misriyya* asked one of the most respected al-Azhar shaykhs, Shaykh 'Abd al-Rahman al-Shirbini, what he thought of al-Zawahiri's book. Shaykh Shirbini responded that modernist reform was destroying religious education and "turning the mosque into a school of philosophy and literature to put out Islam's light." He portrayed 'Abduh's movement to revive ijtihad as denigration of the madhhab Imams and denial of their ijtihad. Students duped by Spencer's philosophies, he said, had only sarcastic comments for the Imams. This had led not to rejuvenation of education, but rather to chaos within the mosque and a loss of trust between students and shaykhs. Reforms had to ensure that al-Azhar remained a fortress protecting religion, and thus should include "protection of student health, vigilance over their comfort, and provisioning them with good food, and not principles of philosophy or the new high sciences." The government had enough schools of its own to teach those subjects. *Al-Mu'ayyad* agreed that nothing good had resulted from 'Abduh's reform movement.[54] This was by now a standard argument, emphasizing 'Abduh's threat to the social order and the authority of the 'ulama.

Within days of this interview's publication, Shaykh al-Azhar 'Ali al-Biblawi resigned, and the khedive instructed Mustafa Pasha, president of the Council of Ministers, to appoint Shaykh al-Shirbini in his place.[55] Shaykh al-Shirbini's article had elicited much praise. *Al-Mu'ayyad* even named al-Shirbini "the Imam of his era in religious studies and legal matters."[56] Once he became Shaykh al-Azhar, nearly all the regularly published papers vested their hopes for reform in him, with no intimation that this stance posed a contradiction. On the contrary, al-Shirbini was seen as a better leader for reform than 'Abduh. *Al-Mu'ayyad* reported receiving reams of telegrams expressing reverential jubilation at al-Shirbini's appointment, and voiced a fervent hope that the "men of Azhari reform" would be in the forefront of those who celebrated his appointment. The article in *al-Mu'ayyad* also criticized modernist reformers, warning that "the work of the reformer may twist back on itself until it almost becomes mere corruption if it is not understood completely or if it is introduced by force before there is preparation or accommodation for it."[57]

Lord Cromer opposed al-Shirbini's appointment, and Ahmad Shafiq expressed sincere doubts about al-Shirbini's administrative abilities. Al-Shirbini and another senior shaykh, Sulayman 'Abd, met with Shafiq to discuss al-Azhar's financial requirements shortly after the appointment. Shafiq reported that al-Shirbini was unaware of his fiscal and administrative duties; Shafiq had to tell him he would need more than £E 1,000 to run the school (in fact more like £E 5,000), and that he would have to do more than assign books and students to teachers.

Muhammad 'Abduh was incensed. He wrote a letter to several newspapers, accusing al-Shirbini of previously refusing the office of Shaykh al-Azhar to further his reputation for piety, and of rejecting subjects like mathematics already accepted into al-Azhar. 'Abduh virtually frothed at the mouth at al-Shirbini's reference to Herbert Spencer: "Where did he get the name of Spencer? What student mentioned it to him? Which of Spencer's principles has entered al-Azhar? And what does the shaykh mean by it specifically?" Unfortunately for 'Abduh, the only paper to print his letter was the pro-British al-Muqattam. Other newspapers pointed out that al-Muqattam's support for reform had effectively condemned the reform movement to failure; al-Muqattam called its friends talibiy al-islah (seekers of reform), but if that was so, then seeking reform was equivalent to insulting the Ottoman government and inciting revolution.[58]

'Abduh signed his letter only as "one of the al-Azhar 'ulama" in an attempt at anonymity. This meant only that his usual allies did not know that 'Abduh had sent it. 'Ali Yusuf, 'Abduh's friend, declared bluntly in al-Mu'ayyad that the anonymous author was impermissibly rude, that he clearly knew nothing about the issue, and that the letter was not fit to print. 'Ali Yusuf then launched a diatribe about how the 'ulama should set a better example by avoiding slander—rather ironic advice, considering 'Abduh's own suffering at the hands of libelers.[59]

On 22 March 1905, the khedive formally accepted al-Biblawi's resignation and said he was ready to accept resignations from anyone else wanting to offer one. Azharis should stay out of politics, he said; they should avoid causing disturbances and concentrate on religious studies. His invitation and warning were generally understood to be directed at 'Abduh.[60] Rumors began to circulate in the dailies that 'Abduh was going to resign from the

Azhar Administrative Council. Stories circulated that al-Shirbini had refused to work with the council unless it was composed entirely of al-Azhar 'ulama.[61] On 25 March 1905, 'Abduh did resign, followed by Ahmad al-Hanbali and 'Abd al-Karim Salman, leaving the council bereft of its government appointees.[62] The modernist reformers' domination of the Azhar Administrative Council was over.

". . . his death is the death of humanity . . ."

It might be noted, by way of explaining 'Abduh's caustic reply to al-Shirbini, that the beastly heat wave that smothered Egypt in March[63] may have exacerbated painful symptoms of the liver cancer that would kill him within four months. Despite his illness, 'Abduh did not resign as Grand Mufti. He planned to travel to Europe for a cure, but the disease progressed too swiftly, and he died in Alexandria on the evening of 11 July 1905.[64]

'Abduh's death was met by an outpouring of grief and assertions that reform had died with him. Rida brooded that "the worldly 'ulama ['ulama al-dunya] have lost their strongest pillar, who defended them from fanatics and the accusations of the stagnant ones. . . . The people of the nations recognize that his death is the death of humanity and the greatest loss to science and civilization."[65] Even 'Abduh's critic, Mustafa Kamil, acknowledged that despite their political differences, still he felt that "contemporary knowledge" had died with 'Abduh.[66] He said later, however, that 'Abduh should have resigned as Mufti following his dispute with the khedive; he "cared too much for having official influence. He would have had more real influence if he had resigned; we should have all worshiped him as the champion of our liberties."[67]

The Egyptian government went to great expense to transfer 'Abduh's body by special train from Alexandria to Cairo and to provide him both with one of the largest funerals of his era, and with a tomb worthy of his office.[68] The editor of al-Islam, Shaykh Ahmad al-Shadhili, commented grudgingly that 'Abduh was due that honor as an "official mufti" as well as for his roles as member of the Shura Council and president of the Islamic Benevolent Society. Still, Shaykh Ahmad insinuated that 'Abduh's book, Risalat al-tawhid, had corrupted popular belief via various "contradictions and errors," a reference to the earlier debate over 'Abduh's Mu'tazilism. Although 'Abduh had apologized for those errors, which he had said were due to his not having copyedited the book himself, they still remained to lead readers astray.[69] Even 'Abduh's own followers worried about potential unintended influences of 'Abduh's legacy: In June, Rida had felt obliged to

explain to *al-Manar*'s readers that 'Abduh did not advocate total abandonment of taqlid. True, 'Abduh had said that believers should always look to
the Qur'an for answers rather than following the judgments of others, but
he only meant they should not value the rulings of a jurist over the words
of God and the Prophet. The madhhab Imams' rulings were valid, but they
should be used in comparison with one's own reading of the Qur'an and
Sunna; what agreed with the Qur'an and Sunna could be used; what disagreed could be ignored.[70] Rida may have been trying to span the gap
between the modernists' broadened concept of ijtihad and conservative
fears of legal indeterminacy, but his suggestion that the Imams might have
contradicted the Qur'an or Sunna likely confirmed those fears.

The eulogic hyperbole about cessation of reform at al-Azhar after
'Abduh's death should not be taken at face value. The ad hominem campaigns had insulated reform from 'Abduh's imperialist collusion, and reform
continued. Within days of 'Abduh's resignation from the Azhar Administrative Council, the Shaykh of the Azhar-affiliated Alexandria madrasa,
Muhammad Shakir, presented to Shaykh al-Shirbini a comprehensive plan
for restructuring its elementary curriculum, which was met with a flurry of
the usual negotiatory debate.[71] Meanwhile, the empty Azhar Administrative Council seats were filled by two al-Azhar shaykhs rather than civil servants, thus achieving full Azhari control over the council's initiatives.[72]

Creating the New Order: The 1908 Internal Reorganization Code

Egypt's nationalists had for some time been distancing themselves from the
khedive, whose motives in supporting them seemed increasingly selfish.[73]
As Khedive 'Abbas lost his former partisans' sympathy, he sought to
strengthen his influence over al-Azhar. The pious Shaykh al-Shirbini
resigned after only a few years in office. The khedive refused to recognize
his resignation and instead insisted that the elderly, ailing shaykh had merely taken a three-month vacation. The "vacation" provided a convenient
cover for al-Azhar to be administered in the interim by a khedival
appointee, Muhammad Shakir, the Hanafi shaykh known for leading
reform at the Alexandria mosque.[74] When Shaykh al-Shirbini died in January 1907, the khedive nominated Muhammad Shakir to be the new
Shaykh al-Azhar. That appointment required British approval, but Cromer
considered Shakir too much the khedive's man. Under duress, 'Abbas selected Hasuna al-Nawawi, the Hanafi reformer whose opposition to British
intervention in the court system had previously forced his resignation from

al-Azhar's top position.[75] Rida commented: "At no other time has the office of Shaykh al-Azhar been so exposed to change and replacement as we now see it."[76] Shortly after his appointment as Shaykh al-Azhar, Shaykh Hasuna met with Shaykh Sulayman 'Abd, a leading Azhari scholar and former friend of Muhammad 'Abduh, and Ahmad Shafiq Pasha, the khedive's private secretary, to seek official approval for his plans for reform. Shaykh Hasuna's teaching career had been in the civil schools, whose administrative system he admired, and he wanted permission to implement parts of this system at al-Azhar. Shafiq agreed to discuss the matter with Khedive 'Abbas.

Meanwhile, the Azhar Administrative Council began discussing the project. Shaykh Muhammad Hasanayn al-'Idwi, the council member charged with reviewing the codes, considered the civil system unsuited to al-Azhar's needs and wrote to the khedive advising that al-Azhar should be reformed according to previous plans, that its instruction should remain free of constraint, and that, while new subjects should be introduced, they should serve the improvement of "Azhari" subjects.

Despite evidence of concerns about the plan, Shafiq began meeting with Muhammad Shakir, by now remanded to his former position as Shaykh of the Alexandria mosque. They reviewed the old Azhari codes and came up with a program of reform modeled on the civil schools. When the khedive returned from his summer vacation in Europe, Shafiq presented him with the proposal, recommending formation of a new council to coordinate efforts of Egypt's three main bodies of 'ulama (the Azharis, the Alexandrians, and the Ahmadis in Tanta). They would meet at al-Azhar under chairmanship of its Shaykh, thus giving al-Azhar administrators unprecedented authority over higher religious education in Egypt. As for the old codes, they were sufficient; they merely required strict implementation and enforcement following the model of the civil schools.[77]

On 3 December 1907, Shafiq reported that the khedive had asked him to review the Azhar Administrative Council's proposed code revisions with some cabinet ministers. These ministers amended some articles, then presented the code to the Council of Ministers for approval. The Council of Ministers formed a committee for the approval process, which included the Shaykh al-Azhar and all head muftis. "[The committee] reviewed the law and after long discussions and . . . other amendments it agreed on the project. I feared that some of the 'ulama would grumble, especially the reactionaries among them [al-raja'iyin], so I requested that the committee decide that there was nothing in the code that contradicted the principles of the Islamic religion, and that was done."[78]

However, by January 1908, Shaykh al-Azhar Hasuna al-Nawawi reported that 'ulama who had not been consulted resented their exclusion from
the review process, and they had petitioned the khedive to have the code
sent to them for review. Shaykh Muhammad Radi, a Hanafi, led this
protest. Shaykh Hasuna strongly disapproved, insisting that he represented
the Hanafi view and that the members of the committee accepted his
advice. Others contested this, saying that the committee might listen to
him but always returned to their original ideas. The petition was sent,
angering Khedive 'Abbas, who now became convinced that Hasuna had
failed to truly secure 'ulama approval.[79]

Underlying the teaching shaykhs' unease was a rumor that their ranks
would be culled through examination. An Azhari shaykh wrote to al-
Mu'ayyad, worried because the code's text included the phrase intikhab al-
mudarrisin (selection of teachers): "[T]hey talk constantly of it and explain
that intikhab [selection] cannot occur without imtihan [examination]." [80]
The code did entail an examination procedure intended to minimize hiring of non-Azhari instructors for the new subjects: The 'ulama would be
questioned to determine their ability to teach subjects outside their areas
of specialty. Those who could teach a new subject, say hygiene or geography, in addition to standard lessons in fiqh, would receive an additional
allowance. Some shaykhs feared the new program was an attempt to edge
them out of their jobs: "We hear that they won't give the 'alim his stipend
until after the examination, as in the government schools. . . . [T]hey want
to change al-Azhar completely and make it into a government-regulated
school for tarboush- and hat-wearers, the concerns of which would not be
those of the turbaned ones." Others felt shamed by the need for examination itself: "Will they examine us although we already hold our degrees and
al-Azhar holds our students? . . . By God, I do not know any committee
that could examine us. There may be among its members some of our students whose own examinations we attended, whom we gave teaching
degrees. . . . How humiliating!" A few shaykhs insisted that al-Azhar's old,
personalized ijaza system still functioned; What had been good enough for
the ancients needed no reform.[81] The system of the civil schools was too
impersonal, too orderly, too bureaucratic. In processing greater numbers
through a system administered by bureaucrats, the spiritual connection
between teacher and student, the chain of personal transmission of sacred
knowledge back to the earliest authorities, would be lost.[82] Despite the
genuine basis for these concerns, al-Mu'ayyad's reporter dismissed them as
"a result of the ancient 'ulama having decided to close the gate of ijtihad in

the faces of the Muslims." As in earlier descriptions of resistance to ijtihad and reforms, journalists polemically subsumed valid concerns under assertions that the 'ulama opposed anything new.[83]

Shortly after these reports were published, the khedive formally announced that he was going to allocate £E 10,000 from public awqaf to religious institutions, on condition that the money go toward reform of al-Azhar.[84] An Azhari shaykh wrote: "When the Azharis saw that written on the pages of the newspapers, they talked about it incessantly, thanking the khedive for his interest, and the 'ulama and the students came in waves congratulating each other."[85]

By March, the end of the Azhar academic year, plans arranged by Shafiq and Muhammad Shakir were in place. On 5 March, the khedive created the Highest Council (al-majlis al-a'la) to oversee affairs of al-Azhar, Alexandria, and Ahmadi mosques, composed of the Shaykh al-Azhar as chair in the khedive's absence; the Hanafi, Shafi'i, and Maliki muftis; Ahmad Shafiq Pasha; and the general manager of the awqaf. By mid-March, this council had met for the first time under Hasuna al-Nawawi's chairmanship and issued Internal Organizational Plan No. 1, known as al-la'iha al-dakhiliyya. It elevated Muhammad Hasanayn al-'Idwi, the Azhari shaykh who had reviewed the earlier reform plans, to the position of al-Azhar inspector, and divided al-Azhar's curriculum into three divisions (elementary, secondary, and higher) of four years each. Passage from one grade of study to the next was permitted by yearly written and oral examinations in three mandatory areas of study: religious subjects, Arabic language, and mathematical sciences. The new curriculum emphasized practical and vocational skills, such as composition, preaching, and the workings of Egypt's various court systems. The new system, including mandatory exams in all subjects, would be applied immediately to all grades of study. The council then created committees of 'ulama to examine all the students at al-Azhar and place them in grades appropriate to their knowledge.[86]

On 22 October, al-Mu'ayyad publicized the beginning of the new academic year. Starting on Wednesday, the 10th of Shawwal (5 November 1908), lessons would be held at al-Azhar according to the new system.[87] The "New Order" began smoothly. Ahmad Shafiq called it "a memorable day without precedent." The Shaykh al-Azhar supervised, with Inspector al-'Idwi, shaykhs, and civil servants assisting to direct students and instructors to classes. This led Ahmad Shafiq to explain why he had been able to effect such change at al-Azhar while the infamous 'Abduh had failed:

If the late Muhammad 'Abduh did not succeed previously in handling its reform, that may be attributed to, first, that the 'ulama elders grumbled at accepting the view of one of their students and would not submit themselves to the reforms he decided, to which they were not accustomed, especially in the matter of the new sciences, in some of which [were things] they considered contradictory to religion. Second, he used to look down on them and considered himself more amply provided with aptitude and knowledge than they were.

As for me, I would honor them by kissing their hands, respecting them, and treating them courteously. And I expended my utmost convincing them that I had no desire but to reform their condition materially and ethically. It was easy for them to accept my opinions, especially since they knew I obtained good favor by supporting the khedive and his government.[88]

Nonetheless, within a month problems appeared with the New Order. The first documented evidence of trouble appears in a letter from an Azhari teacher to Shaykh al-Azhar Hasuna al-Nawawi, printed in *al-Mu'ayyad* on 26 November. The teacher complained that the new system had flaws that made it more damaging than the old one. Those who taught elementary religious ethics to students in their first two years of study were assigned textbooks but not specific readings from those textbooks. The teachers thus chose the pages they wanted to assign. That in itself would not have been a problem, except that the administration, not the teachers, designed the examinations, and questions might not be addressed to the teachers' choices. The Azharis were facing the distinctly modern dilemma of assessment via standardized exams: the compulsion to teach to the test. Furthermore, the time allotted for each subject was relatively limited, precluding intensive study of the more complex texts. Preselected texts were not of the level previously attempted, and, because the students faced examinations on set texts every year, professors lost the flexibility they needed to make maximum use of their expertise. *Al-Mu'ayyad* reported receiving many letters in a similar vein.[89]

The code also mandated examinations for upper-level students in subjects they had never studied, which had never been taught at al-Azhar (such as probate courts), and for which there were no teachers. On 2 December, Azhari students wrote to point out that they were expected to take exams at the end of the year in subjects for which no teachers had been appointed.[90]

Furthermore, some 'ulama were not qualified to teach the classes assigned to them. On 7 December, first-year students complained that they were supposed to be studying eleven subjects, spread out over the week. However, during the first week their shaykhs had taught only grammar and fiqh, omitting the rest. The students protested that this contradicted the new system and would prevent the students from performing well on the yearly exams.[91]

The students knew they needed certification by examination to compete with graduates of civil and foreign schools. Although Azhari students had faced this problem since the 1872 founding of Dar al-'Ulum, by 1908 even more new schools were challenging the relevance of a degree from al-Azhar. A school for training shari'a judges and al-Azhar instructors, the Madrasat al-Qada', had opened in the fall; and the Egyptian national university had begun classes on 21 December.[92]

Letters and khedival speeches printed in *al-Mu'ayyad* during December and January reflect a consensus that, while the new system had improved matters somewhat, it was still in a trial phase and much work remained. *Al-Mu'ayyad* ran a special series of editorials on al-Azhar by Ibn al-Athir (a pen name), praising the whole reform process but highlighting student complaints. Notably, prospective students would undergo a "moral review" by an impersonal selection committee—rather than by village or neighborhood leaders who knew the student.[93] Also, some professors appointed to teach new subjects could merely explain the terminology. One octogenarian shaykh explained to his students that he had looked at their new textbook, *Taqwimat al-sihhiya* (Hygienic Regimes), and "in it are many things that are difficult for someone like me to understand" because they required knowledge of organic chemistry and medicine, such as muscles, infectious diseases, and microbes. Ibn al-Athir concluded that classes had to be taught by specialists, even if these had to be outsiders.[94]

Financial and political matters also fed the discontent. On 24 December, the Highest Council met to decide the budget. It decreed the 'ulama's current official stipends (£E 1–3/month for the rank-and-file professors) sufficient, but noted that some 'ulama were not actually receiving the full amount due them (some got as little as 100 piasters) while others received more. These discrepancies had to be corrected. Furthermore, the dreaded selection process for 'ulama was to begin at the end of the Islamic calendar year one month hence. No 'ulama would be assigned to teach the new subjects unless they had a certificate confirming their qualifications to do so or had previous experience in one of the madaris. The council acknowledged that some 'ulama would lose their teaching positions, and others might find stipends reduced. The reduction in faculty numbers would lead to increases in class sizes until "sufficient qualified teachers" could be found. However, any 'ulama judged unfit for teaching due to advanced age or for other reasons would keep their stipends.

To prevent opposition, the khedive and Shaykh Hasuna stripped the last vestiges of independent authority from the 'ulama, officially converting into government appointments the offices of Shaykh al-Azhar, his wakil or deputy, the madhhab muftis and their deputies, and the members of the Highest Council. Khedive 'Abbas thus completed the process of bureaucratizing al-Azhar's administration.[95]

At Khedive 'Abbas's yearly anniversary of his accession to the throne, new al-Azhar inspector Muhammad 'Ashur al-Sudfi gave a speech praising the New Order. He claimed that general administration of the madaris had improved and more students passed with distinction in mathematics, which the code had made a requirement for achieving the 'alimiyya. Although this was a period of experimentation, the madaris had been completely transformed. Al-Sudfi admitted, however, that some areas still "needed work."[96] This was a somewhat prophetic statement. During the following week, al-Azhar students began a series of quiet demonstrations, demanding adjustments to the reform code.

The 1909 Strikes:
" . . . we are partisans of Order . . . "

The political environment in which the Azhar demonstrations occurred was chaotic. Students at the civil schools of law, medicine, and engineering had begun to demonstrate publicly in support of the nationalist movement, and when demonstrations touched upon education, both the students and the journalists covering the events used the rhetoric of national benefit.[97] The students were inspired in part by writings in al-Liwa', now edited by the fiery 'Abd al-'Aziz Jawish. Jawish was a Maghribi from Alexandria who had begun his education at al-Azhar, gone on to Dar al-'Ulum, and thence had gone to London, where he received a degree in pedagogy and taught Arabic at Oxford University. There he acquired an appreciation for some aspects of British culture. Back in Egypt, he worked for the Ministry of Education and produced a textbook on pedagogical methods. He was nonetheless bitterly opposed to the British occupation of Egypt.[98] Under Jawish's tenure, al-Liwa' continued its anti-imperialist rhetoric but gradually became anti-khedive and pro–Young Turk.[99] It became the chief opponent of *al-Mu'ayyad*'s views, claiming that *al-Mu'ayyad* had betrayed the nationalist cause and rousing the students to demonstrate against the British and *al-Mu'ayyad*.

By early December, widespread demonstrations forced the government to consider implementing an article of the 1887 Madrasa Organization Code that prohibited madrasa students from planning demonstrations. Some madrasa students had joined the demonstrations and now adopted the strike—the new method of the nationalist movement—to demand revision of the new Azhar system. However, compared with the sometimes violent nationalist demonstrators, al-Azhar activists were models of respectable virtue. One news article said, "We praise the behavior of the students of al-Azhar, at which calm and tranquility now prevails."[100] Some Azhari students even disapproved of demonstrators from other madaris: On 30 December, a group of al-Azhar students telegraphed the Ministry of Public Education and newspapers complaining that the others were so rowdy that they reflected badly on student morality.[101]

On Thursday, 21 January, a group of about 100 Azhari students met in Gazira Gardens, where they made speeches and asked Shaykh Hasuna to satisfy their demands, all the while chanting "Long live the Shaykh of the Mosque!" Then they went to 'Abdin Square, where they cheered the khedive, and then to various newspaper headquarters, where they demanded copies of the papers to read. A larger group of demonstrators gathered on Saturday. *Al-Mu'ayyad* reported that the demonstrators' calmness was "something to be proud of," proving "their respectable and commendable morality."[102]

That Sunday a large Azhari demonstration took place in Qasr al-Nil Gardens, and 'ulama joined the students' protests. Two lists of student demands accompanied the next day's press reports. The first, dated the previous Thursday, explained the main grievances. Teachers were still not assigned for required courses in which students would be examined. Where there were teachers for new subjects, teachers at best could merely read the texts to students, "and if they are asked the meaning of a sentence or expression they say 'that is not my concern' or 'the situation does not permit me to explain.'" Furthermore, higher-level students were required to take examinations for the entire new curriculum, even though they had passed the years in which certain new subjects were taught. Finally, twelve years was simply too short a time in which to complete the ambitious curriculum. The demonstrators nonetheless wanted to keep the new subjects: "We ask that the time be lengthened so we can achieve the objective laid out for us. We do not ask that some subjects be removed, as that is not in our interest."

The second list, dated that Sunday, read: "We say to Your Excellencies before anything else that we are partisans of the Order who support it by every means possible. It is not our objective to stand in the path of order or delay it as the deluded ones claim." They demanded improvement of student living conditions, free books and writing utensils for the poor (as was common in civil schools), increased 'ulama wages, and 'ulama selection of al-Azhar administrators. They also wanted to know what positions various levels of examination would qualify them for; suggesting, for example, that an elementary degree should qualify one to become a village imam, preacher, or notary. They also protested exclusion of third-ranked 'alimiyya holders from positions as judges or muftis, arguing that all received the same training regardless of exam performance. They signed the petition "respectfully, the students of al-Azhar mosque."[103]

Although these student demands largely reflected the increasing need for certification in a bureaucratic job market, the plea for equitable 'ulama salaries suggested 'ulama collaboration. *Al-Liwā'* tried to distance the 'ulama and students from one another by claiming that most Azhari 'ulama thought that students deserved nothing, but other newspapers refuted that claim.[104] Alternative versions of the demands more clearly revealed 'ulama concerns, such as life pensions for the Shaykhs al-Azhar, free railway tickets for 'ulama traveling to work, and creation of a register listing all waqf documents pertaining to al-Azhar, as well extent of waqf properties and conditions imposed upon them.[105]

Some 'ulama publicly expressed solidarity with the students. An 'alim who signed himself "an old Azhari" acclaimed the Azhar demonstration as "a model of sobriety and reason never before seen in the history of demonstrations, which shows the people the difference between souls trained in religious manners and others." He assured the students that the factor most in their favor was that their demands were just and their behavior commendable.[106] Another shaykh noted that thousands of Azhari students had been on strike for six days without one incident of violence. He feared the administration of al-Azhar would attempt to "put out the light of this blessed movement" without giving its cause sufficient attention.[107]

Of course some wrote to chastise Azharis for involvement in what appeared to be political concerns, given the context of the period. An anonymous writer admired the Azharis' peaceful demeanor but criticized them for adopting the worldly and unsuitable methods of nationalist protest: "The people ask, of what the Azharis are complaining? What do they ask? Are they among those who strike and stop work? Have the strikers dared to venture even to the threshold of that ancient institution?"[108]

This criticism was met with a vehement defense of Azhari concerns. Salih Hamdi Hammad, a well-known modernist contributor to *al-Mu'ayyad,* asked, "Are the Azharis not of this umma? Do they not have the same right to strike? Indeed, the demands of the Azharis are just."[109] He argued that striking and other methods of democratic protest were now understood as intrinsic rights possessed by all members of the nation. This was especially so for those whose financial conditions were constrained by the structures of the old economy, such as waqf payments that could not be adjusted for inflation. Hammad's other writings suggest that national progress required individuals to exhibit a spirit of personal initiative,[110] which the Azharis were doing by standing up for their "rights." Hammad also projected a note of economic realism into the debate, pointing out that some Azhari 'ulama's stipends were less than those of teachers at the very smallest schools. "The smallest 'alim or teacher should not get less than £E 12 a year because the new economic conditions of the country do not permit living on less than this. The Azharis have gotten a poor lot—it is unfair not to listen to them when they complain." Yet he, like most shaykhs, pled for demonstrators to keep calm.[111]

By Tuesday, 26 January, the Azhar administration had formed a special tribunal to look into concerns of the 'ulama and student demonstrators. The tribunal met immediately and asked students in al-Azhar's courtyard to elect representatives who would present their demands. The following day, students elected ten, five of whom met with the tribunal and explained student complaints.

The tribunal compiled a list of seventeen student demands.[112] Job certification was a key issue: Students asked that the competing Madrasat al-Qada' be closed; its students should be transferred into al-Azhar's new program. Other demands confirm that the strikers sought fair transitional measures for current students: For example, upper-division students asked to be excused that year from taking exams in arithmetic and algebra for the 'alimiyya degree, so as not to delay their graduation. But they also wished to take the exams later "so that they may achieve the same [employment] as those who enter the New Order exams." They were not trying to revoke the new codes, but rather to have them implemented in a manner that did not put them into impossible situations: tests on subjects they had not studied, repetition of courses already finished, or denial of employment to which they previously would have had access. A government review board later concluded: "The mentioned demands . . . did not oppose the Order of al-Azhar Mosque."[113]

The special tribunal assured the students it would present their demands to the khedive, but warned that the tribunal would first have to meet several times to draft its own statement. There was no reason for them to continue their "useless demonstrations." *Al-Mu'ayyad* commented: "It is now the responsibility of the complainers to take their case to be judged, with calm, rationality, and proof, and to make public opinion a witness for them, not against them."[114]

A group of students nevertheless continued to demonstrate in the Gazira Gardens. Students from other schools joined them, and they vowed to continue the strike in the name of "solidarity, unity, and perseverance."[115] They did not remain calm. Some strikers tried to prevent shaykhs from delivering lessons. One professor, Amin Hamza, claimed that his students struck him when he sat down to begin his lecture and then forcibly removed him from the mosque.[116] Law students also agitated Azharis to maintain the strike. By this time, the strike was no longer just a protest against the code. By late January many Azhari strikers had joined the greater nationalist demonstrations going on among students of other schools. On 28 January, a large group of Azharis and Law School students marched in procession from Gazira Gardens. They filled the street from Qasr al-Nil to *al-Liwa'* headquarters and then made their way to 'Abdin Palace, chanting, "Long live the khedive." From there they continued to *al-Mu'ayyad's* headquarters, where the demonstration got out of hand. *Al-Liwa'* and *al-Mu'ayyad* had been engaged in an ideological battle, anti-occupation nationalists stridently challenging the more moderate position exemplified by Muhammad 'Abduh. *Al-Liwa'* had encouraged students to rebel against collaborators. The student marchers began screaming, "Down with *al-Mu'ayyad*" and "Long live *al-Liwa'*" and remained there for an hour, until the police came. *Al-Mu'ayyad* employees shut the doors and 'Ali Yusuf told them not to respond, but apparently some—or perhaps servants of nearby neighbors, as 'Ali Yusuf later insisted—climbed to the roof and threw mud and stones at the demonstrators. 'Ali Yusuf reminded readers that *al-Mu'ayyad* had up to this time advised students to return to their lessons and to await the committee's findings, and he washed his hands of further comment.[117]

Ahmad Shafiq and others also observed that the initially peaceful student demonstrations eventually came to violence only after al-Azhar students

were drawn into political movements. The larger demonstrations contained
agitators, perhaps sent by organized factions or even by the khedive, who
whipped up emotional responses from the crowds and used them to political effect. Al-Azhar professors warned against mixing Azhari affairs with
partisan concerns. There were "people who love to use these kinds of incidents for their own purposes and they do this by deception and intervention and appearing to look as if they are helping."[118]

On 28 January 1909, the special tribunal issued a formal request that al-
Azhar classes restart. On the morning of 30 January, most 'ulama appeared,
ready for their classes, but only a few dozen students showed up. Groups of
strikers tried to prevent anyone from entering the mosque gates, and police
had to interpose themselves between strikers and would-be returnees. A few
'ulama remained on strike as well. On 31 January, no classes were held.[119]

Al-Azhar's executives faced a quandary. The students had demonstrated
lack of confidence in the administration by continuing the strike after
good-faith efforts were made to address student concerns. Leniency might
encourage further disobedience. But public sentiment supported the demonstrators' cause, if not always their methods. In Tanta, the Shaykh of the
Ahmadi madrasa had just staunchly repressed a similar demonstration; now
the "people of Tanta" telegraphed al-Mu'ayyad asking that the Azhar students' demands be answered, to protect the "honor of the Muslims and the
heritage of the prophets."[120] A harsh response to disorder at al-Azhar might
be perceived as government disrespect for religion. Al-Azhar students did
their best to encourage positive views of their strike: A group calling itself
the "Committee of Azhari Unity" printed a newspaper asking that "God
and the people be witnesses for us that we did not start this movement. We
want to observe the Code, not to contradict the general system and not to
make a revolution. . . ." They complained that police menaced them even
at home, and that the administration had threatened to withdraw their
daily bread rations.[121]

The khedive warned on 31 January that student demands would not be
met as long as they remained "zealots," but that was the sole hint of dracon-
ian measures to come. At 5:00 P.M. on 1 February, al-Azhar's administration
decreed that, because strikers had failed to return to classes, all students
beyond the first and second years would be expelled. Strikers' stipends,
bread rations, and riwaq assignments would be transferred to remaining
elementary-division students. The administration charitably assumed these
younger students had been nonstrikers, because they attended classes mainly at affiliated mosques. Elementary-division classes would be moved from

the affiliated mosques to al-Azhar, and classes would restart on 6 February. Thus some 4,000 upper-division students found themselves barred from continuing their studies and stripped of housing and finances.[122]

There were no strikes on the following day. Student papers expressed disbelief in the mass expulsion. Hundreds of petitions flooded al-Azhar administration offering excuses for student truancy that had nothing to do with the strikes. On the morning of 4 February, 3,000 primary-division students lined up at the gate for reassignment. Some 1,000 upper-division students looked on: A few still called the "weak" to a renewed strike, but most appeared "pitiful, shaky, and trembling with worry." On 6 February, classes began again as planned; 'ulama held some 120 classes under supervision of Shaykh al-Azhar Hasuna al-Nawawi, and about 1,000 elementary-division students received bread rations previously allocated to their elders. Police stood outside the gates to prevent agitators from blocking the entrance. *Al-Liwa'* told the students that the government had sent police to start brawls with the students, and the tabloids claimed that so-called returnees were really disguised police instructed to shoot real students.[123]

On 7 February, penitent strikers returned in droves, begging their shaykhs to give them lessons. The leading demonstrators conferred with Shaykh al-Azhar Hasuna to clarify the strike's objective: to make administrators listen to student concerns. They claimed that, once the strike began in earnest, the presence of police at the mosque gates had discouraged even non-strikers from returning; many had just returned to their villages to wait out the crisis. They petitioned Khedive 'Abbas to forgive "the dreams of certain of our brethren" and to lift the punishment that had befallen even the innocent among them. They signed the petition "your sincere sons, the students of the Venerable Azhar."[124]

Shaykh Hasuna was unyielding. On 15 February, *al-Liwa'* accused him of frustrating hopes that the rift between al-Azhar leaders and students could be closed. By refusing to negotiate with them, the paper declared, the Shaykh taught students that cowardice and deceit were preferable to honorable protest; such an attitude would lead to al-Azhar's destruction. *Al-Liwa'* urged the students to continue their strikes. The unfortunate Shaykh al-Azhar Hasuna al-Nawawi had poor luck during his terms of office, having been al-Azhar leader during two student disturbances. Just as he had suffered abuse for failing to quell the 1896 Syrian Riwaq Cholera Riot, he also became the scapegoat for the 1909 demonstrations. He had never gotten along well with Khedive 'Abbas. The New Order's dissolution into chaos provided a convenient excuse to force Hasuna's resignation.

Shaykh Hasuna admitted publicly that he had failed to carry out the reforms with which the Highest Council had charged him, and he stepped down. *Al-Mu'ayyad* lamented his departure and blamed failure of the new code on insubordinate student nationalists: "[I]f they were able to make the country into a square of public revolution, they would do so without thinking of the consequences." [125]

At five in the afternoon on the day of Shaykh Hasuna's resignation, the Highest Council met under chairmanship of the khedive and issued an official pardon in the name of the Shaykh al-Azhar for 552 students who had submitted petitions for readmission and agreed not to participate in further demonstrations "against the New Order." All others wishing to apply for return were directed to the Mu'ayyad mosque to fill out request forms within fifteen days. Khedive 'Abbas pledged an additional £E 11,000 for al-Azhar's budget to meet needs of returnees. The decree was read publicly the following day and former strikers were once again given bread rations. According to *al-Mu'ayyad,* students crowded the streets, heading for the Mu'ayyad mosque, all the while shouting at the top of their lungs that they had not been among the strikers.[126]

On 17 February, some 200 chastened returnees bearing "re-entrance tickets" entered the mosque to talk with the awqaf's general manager about regaining their lost stipends. Although they behaved with proper deference in front of the authorities, when they entered the teaching areas they could not contain their resentment against the elementary students who had usurped their finances. Some seized the shaykhs' wooden chairs and broke them apart, using the pieces to drive younger students out of the mosque. Fighting became so fierce that even bystanders suffered visible wounds. The administration sent for the police, who entered the mosque (always a controversial matter) and used fire hoses to separate knots of brawlers. The police apprehended seventy-four students, most of whom turned out to be from the elementary division. Predictably, *al-Liwa'* characterized the police intervention as added evidence of government oppression.[127]

Following this violence, on the morning of 19 February, a large contingent of 'ulama went to meet the khedive at Qubba Palace. This group included the madhhab muftis, the Azhar Administrative Council, shaykhs of the riwaqs, and other elders of the 'ulama, and was led by former Shaykh al-Azhar Salim al-Bishri and the Mufti Bakr al-Sudfi. Like their students, they protested that there were problems with the 1908 code. This group was able to negotiate a full pardon for all al-Azhar students as well as temporary suspension of the New Order reform until such time as it could be reviewed. In the meantime, al-Azhar would proceed according to the 1895–1896 codes. Another outcome of this meeting was that Shaykh Salim was asked to become Shaykh al-Azhar for a second time. This is yet more evidence that Shaykh Salim was not the antireform, nepotist tyrant that modernist reformers made him out to be. If he were, it is doubtful that the khedive would have put him in charge of reactivating reforms that the khedive had mandated. Even the mildly reformist *al-Mu'ayyad* now remarked upon Shaykh Salim's independence and leadership.[128]

The students responded to the temporary suspension of the New Order with appeals for its reinstatement. They did not want it removed, they said, only that it be "gradually modified." Some called for a new strike, this time to ensure the code's return.[129] However, when classes resumed on 23 February, there were more urgent reasons to reinstate the new code. Elementary-division students who had received strikers' bread rations and stipends found that they lost these under the restored old codes. Furthermore, some 7,300 returnees were expected, and there was insufficient money to provide even legitimate upper-division students with their rations and stipends. In response to these problems, a student organization calling itself the Azhar Club Committee petitioned the khedive to reinstate the New Order code.[130] Ultimately, because of the funding shortage, lessons had to be abandoned for the remainder of the academic year.

On 15 October 1909, at the beginning of the next academic year, Shaykh al-Azhar Salim al-Bishri recommended that the revised New Order code be applied gradually, beginning only with the new students entering the first year of the elementary division. This gradualism accorded with implicit contracts with students; they would not be forced to meet requirements not in place when they agreed to attend the school. Thus Shaykh Salim worked to uphold the quasi-contractual element of madrasa education. According to one committee report, Shaykh Salim had in fact suggested this measure previously, but this time Khedive 'Abbas endorsed it.[131] The newly revised code included parts of the students' demands: Annual exams would be mandatory only for students in the first five grades, and the eight-year ahliyya certificate was temporarily revived and awarded by examination only in subjects the students had studied. The requirement of written and oral exams for the 'alimiyya degree was not rigidly applied. However, the revised code still fell short of satisfying student expectations.[132] Student disturbances persisted, and on 14 April 1910, the khedive constituted another government reform commission, the Lajnat Islah, which would study al-Azhar extensively, including the history of the reform movement and the problems with all previous reform codes. Although the reform commission's leaders were government ministers (Deputy Minister of Justice Ahmad Fathi Zaghlul, his assistant Deputy Minister of the Interior Isma'il Sidqi, and Deputy General 'Abd al-Khaliq Tharwat), they solicited suggestions from both the students and 'ulama, and used a gradualist plan of implementation.[133]

Negotiated Reform

On 27 September 1910, the khedive authorized transitional measures to be applied during the following academic year. In May, after the reform committee had completed its study, the administration issued the Azhar Reorganization Code of 13 May 1911 and the new Internal Organization Code of 26 June, known jointly as the 1911 Reform Program. The new code combined many suggestions of 'Abdullah Nadim, Muhammad 'Abduh, and Muhammad al-Zawahiri with transitional measures suggested by the students. At the same time, it expressed sensitivity for al-Azhar's unique position as a madrasa with pedagogical traditions of special historical relevance. Recognizing that certain revered al-Azhar elders had sincere misgivings about bureaucratizing the process of religious education, the code created a new institution outside bureaucratic regulation, the Corps of the Distinguished 'Ulama (Hay'at Kibar al-'Ulama). The Corps consisted of thirty senior professors who had served at least ten years as teachers, with at least four years in the upper divisions. In addition, they had to have published a scholarly treatise, passed an examination administered by other Corps members, and been voted in by simple majority. The Corps maintained an element of the traditional madrasa system in the midst of bureaucratic order: Each member held triweekly lectures on the traditional subject of his specialty. This was a deliberate strategy to keep students familiar with the old texts, and to preserve classic pedagogical techniques of close textual analysis and repartee with an audience. Later students reported that these lectures routinely attracted large audiences of both students and 'ulama. Because the lectures were open to the public, they also maintained the tradition of encouraging all members of society to pursue learning through informal means.[134] However, in all other parts of the madrasa, the informality and absence of surveillance that characterized older pedagogy were replaced by lists of criteria for professorial qualification and bureaucratically mandated lecture schedules.

Shortly after implementation of the 1911 Reform Program, al-Azhar graduates complained that the labor market could not absorb so many of them, and that even though the New Order graduates were preferred over traditionally trained 'ulama for government employment, they still could not compete with trained specialists from the Madrasat al-Qada'. The administration responded in 1923 by further increasing the period of study for the 'alimiyya to sixteen years, and by introducing yet another level of certification beyond the 'alimiyya, the shahadat al-takhassus or certificate of specialization, for which students would study an extra four years in the traditional manner in one of six traditional Azhari specialty areas. The 'ulama of the Corps taught all classes at this level. The certificate of specialization required a student to pass an examination and submit a written treatise on his chosen subject; this demonstrated the candidate's fitness to become an al-Azhar teacher according to the old standards. This preserved for the 'ulama the crucial element of personal transmission of knowledge at the highest levels, and assured that 'ulama who filled the top ranks of Egypt's informal hierarchy of religious guidance would have the same lengthy and rigorously textual education as their predecessors.[135] It thus addressed 'ulama fears that bureaucratic limitation of the length of study and demands for greater breadth would preclude true depth in any field.

Taqlid and Ijtihad

Critics claimed that the 1911 Reform Program preserved an element of taqlid in the system: reverence for the Sunni Imams and adherence to madhhab rules. Throughout the subsequent history of reform at al-Azhar, conservatives were identified with, and vilified for, continued resistance to a broadened role for the newly defined ijtihad in religious education. For example, the young conservative scholar Muhammad al-Zawahiri eventually became Shaykh al-Azhar. Although he had promoted reform in 1904, a historian wrote that "[h]e stopped reform at the line of revising the texts and methods of teaching, as set forth in his book *al-'Ilm wa al-'ulama wa al-nizam al-ta'lim,* and did not proceed to opening the gate of ijtihad in learning and religion, as had Shaykh Muhammad 'Abduh."[136] In other words, modernists continued to claim that students were not being taught to think independently about issues of belief. However, by 1911 even the shaykh most impugned by modernist reformers, Shaykh Salim al-Bishri, would admit at least rhetorically that the door of ijtihad "should remain open." This suggests that the reformers' campaign to redefine ijtihad more generally and to introduce it into the educational system had a degree of success, at least to the extent that a leading Maliki conservative would no longer perceive ijtihad as an inherent threat to social stability. Shaykh Salim took other steps in 1911 that previously would have been considerable intellectual risks. Following his correspondence with Shiʻi scholar ʻAbd al-Husayn Sharaf al-Din al-Musawi, Shaykh Salim agreed that Shiʻi hadith were sound, accepted that the Shiʻi Imams were objects of emulation equivalent to the Sunni Imams, and in the end agreed that the Shiʻa had not departed from the practice of the early community. These concessions and his permission for his letters on them to be made public paved the way for Shaykh al-Azhar Mahmud Shaltut in 1959 to recognize the Twelver Shiʻa Jaʻfari legal tradition as a fifth legitimate madhhab, alongside the Sunni madhahib.[137]

Conclusion

Who then reformed al-Azhar? Reform of religious education was not—was perhaps never—dependent upon leadership from historically recognized modernist reformers. The underlying motivations for the modernists' reform movement had been shared by most ʻulama, and thus after ʻAbduh was gone the work of reform continued.[138] Even Rida, ʻAbduh's most stalwart partisan, admitted that most ʻulama had not opposed reform. He tried to place the blame for rumors to that effect on an English paper, the *Globe,* whose assertions were picked up by *al-Liwaʼ*.[139] At least one English paper attributed ʻAbduh's failure to the ʻulama: "The ulama opposed his objective and thought, so he resigned . . . and perhaps his death was caused by his broken heart and disappointment of his hopes." But ordinary Egyptians were guilty as well. Qasim Amin attributed ʻAbduh's hardships to "an army of ignorant ones among the common people who had no education or reason that would qualify them to understand his objectives."[140] ʻAbduh's resignation, however, had been engineered not by conservative ʻulama but through the politically motivated ad hominem campaign. Shaykhs such as Salim al-Bishri, or newcomers like Muhammad al-Zawahiri and Muhammad Shakir, who did not share ʻAbduh's European connections, were better situated politically to lead the actual work of modifying the curricula in the religious institutions.

Yet ʻAbduh has passed into popular memory as "the founder of Islamic Modernism," the one who legitimated lay interpretation of the Qurʼan, who began the "Protestantization of Islam."[141] Just a few years after his death, his views of ijtihad and its historical cessation were being cited as literal truth in the press: When the ʻulama of al-Azhar raised concerns about reforms in 1908, it was assumed that the ʻulama were incapable of change, "a result of the ancient 'ulama having decided to close the gate of ijtihad in the faces of the Muslims."[142]

'Abduh once wrote: "The people of Egypt are an intelligent nation, governed by a manageable character and easily influenced, but they bear in mind a maxim, which is that a seed does not sprout in the earth unless the disposition of the seed is such that it will eat of the elements of the earth and breathe of its air. And if the seed dies, it is not the fault of the layer of earth where it was, or the seed and its health, but rather it is the fault of the sower."[143] Those who did eventually enact reforms were perhaps more appropriate sowers than 'Abduh, more attentive to "the disposition of the seed." The extreme gradualism and 'ulama participation advocated by these new sowers permitted reforms to acquire cultural assonance, an aura of rhetorical and political harmony with Egyptian intellectual and popular culture. 'Abduh was, in a Gramscian sense, a failed intellectual. An articulate and revolutionary thinker, he was politically inept where Azharis were concerned, and tried to bypass through state intervention the influential shaykhs whose cooperation was necessary to legitimate reform. Thus reform passed not into stagnation or total state surveillance, but into the hands of Azharis themselves.

And it flourished in their hands. The surviving lists of student demands from the 1909 strikes show that the strikers favored the Utilitarian models of order borrowed from the civil schools. Likewise, Shaykh Salim's leadership of the 'ulama group that negotiated the temporary suspension of the 1908 reform code cannot be taken as evidence that conservative scholars rejected reform. Shaykh Salim embraced itjihad and recommended crucial transitional measures for equitable implementation of the reform code. Furthermore, he and his conservative successors as Shaykh al-Azhar retained the chairmanship of the Azhar Administrative Council and the Highest Council, as well as supervisory authority over all levels of Islamic education. His administration implemented the renovated code of 1911. Shaykh Salim remained in office until 1917, and in 1915 a poll by the government journal *al-Waqa'i' al-Misriyya* named the Shaykh al-Azhar the most influential religious office in the country.[144]

The 1911 code did not end the story of 'ulama participation in reform. It was not the next-to-final act in the usurpation of reform by an increasingly bureaucratized and interventionist state. The concessions won by Shaykh Salim al-Bishri's gradualist faction ensured that the 'ulama's voice in negotiating reform lasted throughout the early twentieth century. The 1908 code, the student strikes, and the 1911 revisions did, however, illustrate the successful hybridization of madrasa education in Egypt. Neither 'ulama nor students perceived modernist reformers' Utilitarian concepts of order, efficiency, and bureaucratic administration as alien or invasive. The de-juridified concept of ijtihad was accepted in its new social meaning. But the pedagogical methods that devalued orally transmitted knowledge were relegated to elementary education only. At the highest level, madrasa education remained personal and contractual.

10

CONCLUSIONS

The debates over reform at al-Azhar played a critical role in the development of Sunni Islam in the twentieth century. Our understanding of the reform movement has been badly flawed, blinding us to the contributions of conservative scholars, the extent of state intrusion, and the long-term consequences of modernist ideas. This has occurred because historians of reform relied mostly on modernist sources, producing a skewed narrative that demonized conservative 'ulama.

Modernist sources were, and remain, the ones most readily available to us. Of the ten most popular Arabic journals in Egypt between 1870 and 1911, none opposed al-Azhar reform. Eight were either owned or controlled by Jamal al-Din al-Afghani or his disciples. All have gone through multiple reprints.[1] Moreover, the most influential Orientalists of the later nineteenth century in Egypt, such as Lord Cromer and Wilfrid Blunt, had friendships with "enlightened" reformers, especially Muhammad 'Abduh; they had no significant or sympathetic contacts among conservatives. Their own cultural ideals prejudiced them to favor the modernists in the first place; in addition, their Egyptian friends had to know European languages, which in itself would limit their circle of acquaintance. Conservative Azharis themselves did not usually seek out friends among the occupying forces.

Blunt's own writings show how his friendships with modernists led him to give precedence to their views. One of the few portrayals of conservative 'ulama found in Blunt's account of the 'Urabi Revolt comes from Blunt's memories of a conversation he had with Mahmud Sami, an 'Urabist minister and an associate of 'Abduh. Mahmud Sami, speaking casually after a dinner, explained that 'Urabi's nationalists had wanted to turn

Egypt first into a small republic, "like Switzerland," and then eventually into part of a pan-Islamic state, "but we found some of the ulema were not quite prepared for it and were behind our time."[2] Blunt reports a reformist's assessment of the 'ulama as "behind our time," not his own personal experience. Cromer reproduces similar assertions.[3]

Twentieth-century scholarship lionized Muhammad 'Abduh as leader of educational reform, citing modernist journals and early Orientalist accounts of his liberal sentiments and struggles against forces of 'ulama reactionism. These same accounts downplay the khedive's role in politicizing the debate. In general, the more derivative of modernist viewpoints a study was, the more likely it was to join the body of "authoritative scholarship" on the reform movement.[4] On the other hand, while modernist opinions were perpetuated by reprints of modernist journals, Orientalist repetitions, and uncritical scholarship, sources that expressed contrary views, especially of conservative Azharis, were allowed to lapse into obscurity. The depictions of conservatives in narratives of al-Azhar reform are mere caricatures. This suggests that the modernists did as much to represent "the Orient" to the West as did the Orientalists themselves, resulting in a kind of indigenous Orientalism.

The debate also generated an invented tradition of a stagnant Islamic law. Assertions of ijtihad's cessation had been used rhetorically throughout Islamic history, to bolster the authority of jurists. The modernists adopted this rhetoric, asserting throughout their campaign that contemporary scholars agreed the practice of ijtihad had ceased. Although scholars such as Rifa'a al-Tahtawi insisted that ijtihad was alive, the repeated assertions convinced most people that it had indeed died. Conservative scholar Muhammad 'Ilish countered by claiming that, indeed, the conditions under which unrestricted ijtihad could be practiced no longer existed. Instead of denying modernists the right to ijtihad, this argument reinforced their rhetorical position.

Furthermore, modernists' absolutist charge that taqlid permeated the intellectual culture of the 'ulama predisposed Orientalists to dismiss evidence they encountered of ijtihad utilization and to gloss over scholarly distinctions among degrees of ijtihad, leading later writers to generalize about stagnation within the Islamic legal tradition. Orientalists were thus able to cite the "evidence" of modernist campaigns to illustrate the dichotomy between Orient and Occident, in which only the West was active, and the Orient was passive, indolent, and unchanging.

For example, Dutch Orientalist Snouck Hurgronje misinterpreted writings by Shaykh al-Azhar Ibrahim al-Bajuri, leading later scholars, through selective quotations, to believe al-Bajuri agreed the "door of ijtihad" was closed. Hurgronje concluded: "[A]ll are in agreement that there are no independent practitioners of ijtihad, and that even lower levels of ijtihad are out of the reach of all."[5] On the contrary, al-Bajuri affirmed in his discussion of the types of ijtihad that judges had the choice of practicing taqlid or ijtihad within the bounds of madhhab rules.[6]

As a result of the invented, Orientalist-perpetuated thesis of taqlid stagnation, contemporary scholars of the Islamic legal tradition have spent many words combating avowals of the tradition's inflexibility. The misunderstanding has also led to pseudo-explanations for the rise of Islamic militancy in the twentieth century, including the assumption that "Islam's problem" is its being rigidly bound (i.e., by taqlid) to seventh-century codes of belief, and that modernity has torn Muslims from the comfort of tradition, leaving jagged and violence-encrusted edges.[7]

Twentieth-century scholarship also asserted that modernists revived ijtihad. Rather, modernists gave ijtihad a social definition and enlarged its franchise by encouraging laymen to proceed directly to the primary sacred texts of their religion for guidance. Modernists believed, in a positivistic sense, that Muslims would uncover in those texts the true, objective meaning of Islam, which to them had been covered up by centuries of juristic explanation and obfuscation. Muhammad 'Abduh never intended that ordinary people perform ijtihad for legal issues, only for matters of personal belief, but his arguments developed a life of their own in the popular press. Ijtihad is now understood by many Muslims as something anyone with a good understanding of Arabic and a copy of the Qur'an can do. That has led to a proliferation of interpretations, including politically motivated ones legitimating violence against authoritarian governments, against innocents, and against other Muslims.[8] To use the most obvious example, on 23 February 23 1998, Osama bin Laden, Ayman al-Zawahiri, and three other leaders of militant Islamic groups issued a fatwa calling upon all able Muslims to "kill the Americans and their allies—civilians and military." They cited in their argument six verses of the Qur'an, one prophetic hadith, and three political points on U.S. occupation of or aggression against Muslim peoples.[9] This fatwa preceded al-Qaida's attack on the U.S. embassies in Kenya and Tanzania and was intended to legitimate them; the Islamic legal tradition provides for legitimation of violence under certain conditions, if an acknowledged legal authority sanctions it in a fatwa. However, a fatwa is, or at least is supposed to be, a nonbinding legal opinion issued by a qualified specialist in law, that is, a mufti or a judge. As Rohan Gunaratna, author of *Inside al-Qaida,* has pointed out, "None of the recognised Islamic authorities (Sunni or Shia) regards Osama Bin Laden as a person capable of legitimately issuing one."[10] Ayman al-Zawahiri is not qualified either; he is a medical doctor. Although Bin Laden subsequently obtained similar fatwas from Afghani and Pakistani jurists, this was not widely known until after September 11, 2001. Those who acted on Bin Laden's behalf—and the Muslim public who approved those actions—accepted his lay ijtihad and his authority to issue a fatwa.

It can be argued that lay ijtihad mitigates the coercive power of the state. While a state may claim to promulgate the correct interpretation of religious sources, lay ijtihad puts the tools of alternative interpretation and resistance into the hands of every individual. Individuals could circumvent restrictions imposed by the frozen juristic past through lay ijtihad. Modernists Jamal al-Din al-Afghani and Muhammad 'Abduh believed in a "true" Islam and thought ijtihad would also normalize belief. Furthermore, they thought education based on ijtihad would produce a better-informed citizen and a more unified community. Taken to its logical conclusion, the modernists' vision of lay ijtihad constituted a democratization of religious knowledge that would motivate against arbitrary exercise of power.

In an apparently contradictory campaign, modernists sought to harness the power of the state to address institutional inefficiencies at al-Azhar, new marketplace demands for certification, and deficiencies in scientific and contemporary fields of knowledge. In the work of al-Afghani and in 'Abduh's early works, such interventions seem necessary to strengthen and unify the community to resist imperialism. However, their concomitant campaign for bureaucratically administered efficiency and centralized surveillance justified increased state control, as seen in the khedival intervention in al-Azhar during the Syrian Riwaq Cholera Riot, the crackdown on the 1909 student demonstrations, and the incorporation of madaris governance into the khedive's administration.

The conservatives had their own conflicting agendas: Shaykh Salim al-Bishri sought to permit self-regulating ethical groups, such as the 'ulama of al-Azhar, to rule themselves, an approach that co-opted utilitarian administrative techniques and used them to combat more-overt forms of British control. Ultimately, I believe, this approach allowed conservatives to achieve real reform. However, the conservatives relied heavily on the support of Khedive 'Abbas Hilmi II, and so remained subject to centralized power. The irony is clear: Modernists and conservatives struggled more than a century to enact or preserve methods of education each saw as best suited to prepare students to resist first government centralization and later imperialism. Nonetheless, in the process, both sides took steps that would ultimately weaken them. The modernists' promotion of lay ijtihad further splintered the Sunni community. And both modernists and conservatives ultimately acquiesced in state control over madrasa education, setting the stage for state manipulation of religious institutions in the twentieth century.

It seems unlikely that al-Azhar 'ulama could have avoided state intervention altogether. Muhammad 'Ali's centralization of certain awqaf and creation of a competing educational system set up conditions to which al-Azhar had to adapt. Muhammad 'Ali's successors' conscription policies led to steady increases in floating student populations, so that sheer demography wore away 'ulama resistance to efficiency-based administration and convinced them of the utility of a controlling gaze, especially when directed at student morality and allocation of waqf funds. However, Azharis still made use of available negotiative spaces. 'Ulama used the emerging media to reappropriate from the state the meaning of *'ilm*. Students protested state appropriation of their bodies in the 1896 Cholera Riot. The use of negotiative spaces worked in reverse as well: Khedive 'Abbas Hilmi II turned the entire religious establishment into a bulwark protecting Egyptian sovereignty from British encroachment, using nationalist presses and Azhari allies to discredit Muhammad 'Abduh. This ultimately allowed conservative 'ulama the space for their victory: the negotiated reform code of 1911, which blended administrative efficiency with personal, oral transmission of specialized religious knowledge.

Some will read modernist reform projects, and depictions of their opponents as reactionary obstacles to progress, as instances of conceptual colonization. However, to depict as colonization the victory of Utilitarian efficiency over madrasa education is to fetishize the precolonial past, as if it were an ideal state that would only be sullied by contact with the outside. If that were so, then history is a conglomeration of mutual cultural pollutions. Rather, the reformers sought to take up what they found useful in European culture and blend it with authentically Islamic concepts and practices. They were cultural hybrids who spoke multivocally through an emerging Arabic press. Their arguments with their opponents among the 'ulama were cultural negotiations, the outcome of which would be not only new forms of education, but a new nation. This nation would have a religious foundation in Islam, its citizens would be rooted to the foundation by their own independent readings of religious sources, communally unified and strengthened, and able to resist European encroachment on their values and independence. The conservatives' contributions ensured that the religious foundation stayed tethered to its legitimizing sources through lines of person-to-person transmission, through human connections.

NOTES

Chapter 1

1. Muhammad Rashid Rida, *Tarikh al-ustadh al-imam al-shaykh Muhammad 'Abduh*, vol. 1 (Cairo: Matba'at al-Manar, 1931).
2. Al-Azhar was preceded only by al-Qarawiyyin, in Fez, founded 859 CE. Although originally a Shi'i mosque, al-Azhar became Sunni when the Sunni Ayyubid dynasty took control of Egypt in 1171.
3. Dale F. Eickelman, *Knowledge and Power in Morocco* (Princeton, NJ: Princeton University Press, 1985), 168; Eickelman, "The Art of Memory: Islamic Education and Its Social Reproduction," in *Comparing Muslim Societies: Knowledge and the State in a World Civilization*, ed. Juan R. I. Cole (Ann Arbor: University of Michigan Press, 1992), 121–122, 125; Eickelman, "Who Speaks for Islam? Inside the Islamic Reformation," in *An Islamic Reformation?* eds. Michaelle Browers and Charles Kurzman (Lanham, MD: Lexington Books, 2004), 23.
4. Ian Almond, "'The Madness of Islam': Foucault's Occident and the Revolution in Iran," *Radical Philosophy* 128 (November/December 2004): 12–22; Almond, "Nietzsche's Peace with Islam: The Enemy of My Enemy Is My Friend," *German Life and Letters* 56, no. 1 (January 2003): 43–55.
5. See, for example, Roman Loimeier, "Is There Something Like 'Protestant Islam'?" *Die Welt des Islams* 45, no. 2 (2005): 245.
6. E. O. Wilson, "The Relevant Principles of Population Biology," in *Sociobiology* (Cambridge, MA: Belknap Press, 1975), 63–105.
7. Homi Bhabha, "Of Mimicry and Man" and "Dissemination," in *The Location of Culture* (London and New York: Routledge, 2004), 120–131, 199–244; Eric Hobsbawm and Terrence Ranger, *The Invention of Tradition* (Cambridge: Cambridge University Press, 1992).

Chapter 2

1. Albert Hourani, *History of the Arab Peoples* (New York: Warner Books, 1991), 143–145; A. Chris Eccel, *Egypt, Islam and Social Change: Al-Azhar in Conflict and Accommodation* (Berlin: Klaus Schwarz Verlag, 1984), 17.
2. Jane Hathaway, "Origin Myths," in *A Tale of Two Factions: Myth, Memory, and Identity in Ottoman Egypt and Yemen* (Albany: State University of New York Press, 2003).
3. Daniel Crecelius, "The Emergence of the Shaykh al-Azhar as the Pre-Eminent Religious Leader in Egypt," in *Colloque international sur l'histoire du Caire*

(Cairo: Ministry of Culture of the Arab Republic of Egypt, 1969), 109–123; Afaf Lutfi al-Sayyid Marsot, "The Role of the 'Ulama' in Egypt during the Early Nineteenth Century," in *Political and Social Change in Modern Egypt*, ed. P. M. Holt (Oxford: Oxford University Press, 1968), 267–270; and Afaf Lutfi al-Sayyid Marsot, "The Ulama of Cairo in the Eighteenth and Nineteenth Centuries," in *Scholars, Saints, and Sufis*, ed. Nikki R. Keddie (Berkeley: University of California Press, 1972), 149–166.

4.   'Abd al-Rahman al-Jabarti, *Tarikh aja'ib al-athar fi al-tarajim wa al-akhbar*, 4 parts in 3 vols. (Beirut: War ul-Jeel, n.d. [c. 1820]); also Thomas Philipp, ed., and Moshe Perlmann, trans., *'Abd al-Rahman al-Jabarti's History of Egypt*, 2 vols. (Stuttgart: Franz Steiner Verlag, 1994), 2:167, 187, 229, 247, 272, 329, 387, 413; 3:100, 110, 264, 455.

5.   Al-Jabarti, *Aja'ib*, 2:83, 4:97; Crecelius, "The Ulama and the State in Modern Egypt" (Ph.D. diss., Princeton University, 1967), 57–58, 60–70; Afaf Lutfi al-Sayyid Marsot, "A Socio-Economic Sketch of the 'Ulama' in the Eighteenth Century," in *Colloque international sur l'histoire du Caire* (Cairo: Ministry of Culture of the Arab Republic of Egypt, 1969), 315; Marsot, "Role of the 'Ulama'," 264–265; Marsot, "Ulama of Cairo," 156; Gabriel Baer, *A History of Land Ownership in Modern Egypt 1800–1950* (Oxford: Oxford University Press, 1962).

6.   Afaf Lutfi al-Sayyid Marsot, "Entrepreneurial Women," in *Feminism and Islam: Legal and Literary Perspectives*, ed. Mai Yamani (New York: New York University Press, 1996), 36–41.

7.   Al-Jabarti, *Aja'ib*, 2:177, 184–5, 192, 210, 221–3, 233, 265–6, 283, 317, 374, 415, 416; 3:22, 39, 263–264, 267, 351, 352, 396, 408, 465, 477; 4:169, 256. See also Crecelius, "The Ulama and the State," 55–57, and Daniel Crecelius, "Nonideological Responses of the Egyptian Ulama to Modernization," in *Scholars, Saints, and Sufis*, ed. Nikki Keddie (Berkeley: University of California Press, 1972), 172.

8.   Al-Jabarti, *Aja'ib*, 2:9, 157, 172–5, 263, 268, 275, 300–1.

9.   Timothy Mitchell, *Colonising Egypt*, chaps. 1 and 2 (Berkeley: University of California Press, 1991 [1988]).

10.   Roger Owen, *Middle East in the World Economy 1800–1914* (London: I.B. Tauris, 1993), 64.

11.   Owen, *World Economy*, 64–65; Eccel, *Social Change*, 73; Afaf Lutfi al-Sayyid Marsot, *Egypt in the Reign of Muhammad Ali* (Cambridge: Cambridge University Press, 1984), 67; Baer, *Land Ownership*, 3, 4; al-Jabarti, *Aja'ib*, 3:525, 4:214. On precedents, see al-Jabarti, *Aja'ib*, 3:443, 530. These lands may have been irsad, not true awqaf but rather agricultural lands held by the Ottoman treasury and "designated" by sultans for charitable uses. If so, Muhammad 'Ali's actions fit into a long tradition of Ottoman attempts to retake control of irsad. Al-Jabarti's claim that Muhammad 'Ali's actions were illegal is too biased to take at face value (Kenneth Cuno, "Ideology and Juridical Discourse in Ottoman Egypt: The Uses of the Concept of Irsad," *Islamic Law and Society* 6, no. 2 [1999]: 136–163). According to al-Jabarti, Muhammad 'Ali claimed ownership was not adequately documented, supervisors claimed more land

than stipulated in waqf documents, and some awqaf no longer served intended purposes because of mismanagement; he claimed government would administer the land in the best interests of the community (*Aja'ib*, 4:291–295).

12. This prohibition was revoked in 1851 ('Ali Mubarak, *al-Khitat al-tawfiqiyya al-jadida li-Misr al-qahira*, 20 vols. [Cairo: al-Hay'a al-Misriyya al-'Amma li al-Kitab, 1983 (1887)], 5:82–84).

13. Al-Jabarti, *Aja'ib*, 4:255. He did not assume state control over nonagricultural family awqaf in the Delta, although a large amount of the wealth of the 'ulama elders was held in that kind of waqf (Crecelius, "Nonideological Responses," 182 n.34). He also left untouched business facilities and horticultural lands endowed as awqaf and compensated those who could prove they had owned a waqf with a monthly pension and grants of land (Marsot, *Egypt in the Reign of Muhammad Ali*, 140–143). This, too, suggests he focused on irsad (Cuno, "Ideology and Juridical Discourse," 137–138).

14. Baer, *Land Ownership*, 4.

15. Al-Jabarti, *Aja'ib*, 4:366, compare with 4:295 n.3. By 1833, compensatory payments no longer appeared in reports on the Egyptian state budget (Baer, *Land Ownership*, 5).

16. Fred Haley Lawson, *Social Origins of Egyptian Expansionism during the Muhammad Ali Period* (New York: Columbia University Press, 1992); Marsot, *Egypt in the Reign of Muhammad Ali*, 60–74; Marsot, "Socio-Economic Sketch," 315, 318; Mansoor Moaddel, "The Egyptian and Iranian Ulama at the Threshold of Modern Social Change," *Arab Studies Quarterly* 15, no. 3 (Summer 1993): 29–31, 35–8; 'Abd al-'Aziz Muhammad al-Shinnawi, "Du role de l-Azhar dans la préservation du caractére arabe de l-Egypt sous le regne des Ottomans," in *Colloque international sur l'histoire du Caire* (Cairo: Ministry of Culture of the Arab Republic of Egypt, 1969), 247–289; Husayn Mu'nis, *al-Sharq al-islami fi al-'asr al-hadith*, 2nd ed. (Cairo: Matba'a Hijazi, 1938), 135–146; Crecelius, "Emergence," 112, 117; Crecelius, "The Ulama and the State," 111, 113–115; Baer, *Land Ownership*, 5–6; al-Jabarti, *Aja'ib*, 4:203–204, 207, 221, 226–229, 310–311, 320, 331.

17. Daniel Crecelius, *The Roots of Modern Egypt: A Study of the Regimes of 'Ali Bey al-Kabir and Muhammad Bey Abu al-Dhahab, 1760–1775* (Minneapolis, MN: Biblioteca Islamica, 1981).

18. Compliant 'ulama were of various classes. Early in Muhammad 'Ali's reign, peasants regarded him as liberator, freeing them from the grasp of greedy tax farmers (Kenneth Cuno, *The Pasha's Peasants: Land, Society, and Economy in Lower Egypt, 1740–1858*,[Cairo: American University in Cairo, Press], 5).

19. Al-Jabarti, *Aja'ib*, 3:517–8; Marsot, *Egypt in the Reign of Muhammad Ali*, 52.

20. Al-Jabarti, *Aja'ib*, 4:173–4.

21. Ibid., 4:198. These lands probably were irsad, and the 'ulama response echoes previous successful juridical defenses of irsad from state sequestration (Cuno, "Ideology and Juridical Discourse," 161).

22. Ibid., 4:256.

23. Al-Jabarti, *Aja'ib*, 4:308.

24. Gilbert-Joseph De Chabrol, "Essai sur les moeurs des habitants modernes de l'Égypte," *Description de l'Egypte,* cited in Michael J. Reimer, "Views of al-Azhar in the Nineteenth Century: Gabriel Charmes and 'Ali Pasha Mubarak," in *Travellers in Egypt,* ed. Paul and Janet Starkey (London: I.B.Tauris, 1998), 267.

25. James Heyworth-Dunne, *An Introduction to the History of Education in Modern Egypt* (London: Frank Cass & Co., Ltd, 1968 [1939]), 154, relying on Raimond Laorti-Hadji, *L'Egypt* (Paris: 1956), 245.

26. Edward Lane, *Manners and Customs of the Modern Egyptians* (London: J. M. Dent & Co.; New York: E. P. Dutton & Co.[1842]), 217.

27. Compare with Heyworth-Dunne, *History of Education,* 23, quoting Stanley Lane-Poole, *The Story of Cairo* (London: 1924), 298–302.

28. Mine Ener, *Managing the Poor and the Politics of Benevolence, 1800–1952* (Princeton, NJ: Princeton University Press, 2003), 11, 12, 150 n.4, 163 n.32. Some of al-Azhar's buildings were hundreds of years old, so deterioration alone cannot prove the government did not allocate al-Azhar adequate awqaf revenues. No one has yet located and compared waqf-income registers for al-Azhar before centralization with later government allocations (see reference to these registers in al-Jabarti, *Aja'ib,* 4:235).

29. J. A. St. John, *Egypt and Nubia* (London: Chapman and Hall, 1845), 246–247; Felix Mengin, *Histoire de l'Egypte sous le gouvernement de Mohammed-Aly ou, Récit des événemens politiques et militaires qui ont eu lieu depuis le départ des Français jusqu'en 1823,* 2 vols. (Paris: A. Bertrand, 1823), 2:327.

30. Florence Nightingale, *Letters from Egypt: A Journey on the Nile 1849–1850,* ed. Anthony Sattin (New York: Weidenfeld & Nicolson, 1987), 199.

31. Ehud Toledano, *State and Society in Mid-Nineteenth-Century Egypt* (Cambridge: Cambridge University Press, 1990).

32. Bayard Dodge, *Al-Azhar: A Millennium of Muslim Learning* (Washington, DC: Middle East Institute, 1961), 115. Crecelius claims recovery began in 1841 ("The Ulama and the State," 147–148). In 1835, Muhammad 'Ali created a government ministry to remove waqf disbursements entirely from private supervision, but it closed in 1838. 'Abbas reopened the waqf administration in 1851 for private awqaf (Baer, *Land Ownership,* 169.). Who administered private waqf revenues between 1838 and 1851 and public waqf revenues between 1838 and 1858 remains unclear.

33. Ener, *Managing the Poor,* 26; Dodge, *Al-Azhar,* 126; Crecelius, "Emergence," 117; Toledano, *State and Society,* 199; J. A. St. John, *Egypt and Nubia,* 245–247; Eccel, *Social Change,* 232; Lane, *Manners and Customs,* 84–85, 217.

34. Nightingale, *Letters from Egypt,* 196–197.

35. Mitchell, *Colonising Egypt,* 142–154. This process informed Max Weber's thesis of "transmission of charisma"–the power of revelatory texts, some of which was due to charisma of the revelatory figure, could be transmitted through correct reproduction of the words themselves. In that way the society could routinize or institutionally preserve the authority of the charismatic leader.

36. Mitchell, *Colonising Egypt,* 82–83.

37. Jonathan Berkey, *The Transmission of Knowledge in Medieval Cairo: A Social History of Islamic Education* (Princeton, NJ: Princeton University Press, 1992); Heyworth-Dunne, *History of Education*, 42, 66–75; George Makdisi, *The Rise of Colleges: Institutions of Learning in Islam and the West* (Edinburgh: Edinburgh University Press, 1981), 128–133; Mitchell, *Colonising Egypt*, 80–85.

38. See especially Eickelman, *Knowledge and Power*, 57, 64; see as example in Egyptian context, Muhammad 'Ilish, *Fath al-'ali al-malik fi al-fatwa 'ala madhhab al-imam Malik*, vol. 1 (Cairo: Sharikat Maktaba wa Matba'a Mustafa al-Babi al-Halabi wa Awladhihi, 1958 [1882]).

39. Al-Jabarti, cited in Heyworth-Dunne, *History of Education*, 72, 75.

40. Heyworth-Dunne, *History of Education*, 101–147.

41. Ibid., 110–111.

42. Ibid., 157–158; John W. Livingston, "Western Science and Educational Reform in the Thought of Shaykh Rifa'ah al-Tahtawi," *International Journal of Middle East Studies* 28, no. 4 (November 1996): 551.

43. Heyworth-Dunne, *History of Education*, 104–106.

44. Ibid., 106, 157–180, 221–223, 243–264, 301–307, 323–330, 393–395.

45. Ibid., 115–152.

46. Dodge, *Al-Azhar*, 197–198; Heyworth-Dunne, *History of Education*, 41 ff, 115–152.

47. Heyworth-Dunne, *History of Education*, 163–164, 177; Eccel, *Social Change*, 35; Afaf Lutfi al-Sayyid Marsot, "The Beginnings of Modernization among the Rectors of al-Azhar, 1798–1879," in *Beginnings of Modernization in the Middle East*, ed. William R. Polk and Richard L. Chambers (Chicago: University of Chicago, 1968), 272.

48. Heyworth-Dunne, *History of Education*, 210–215.

49. Livingston, "Western Science," 551; Eccel, *Social Change*, 158, 162, 165, 173, 205; Crecelius, "Nonideological Responses," 184–185, 197–198.

50. Mitchell, *Colonising Egypt*, 69–70.

51. Heyworth-Dunne noted al-Jabarti's lists of al-Azhar texts included more scientific topics than lists composed later in the century (*History of Education*, 45 n.3).

52. Al-Jabarti, *Aja'ib*, 3:51, 56–57, 64–65; 4:387; John W. Livingston, "Muhammad 'Abduh on Science," *Muslim World* 85, no. 3–4 (1995): 216–218; Marsot, "Modernization," 269–270; 'Abd al-Karim Salman, *A'mal majlis idarat al-Azhar, min ibtida' ta'sisihi sana 1312 ila ghayat sana 1322* (Cairo: Matba'at al-Manar, 1322 H [1905]), 87.

53. H. P. Grice, "Meaning," *Philosophical Review* 66 (1957): 377–388.

54. See Crecelius, "Nonideological Responses," 185; and Marsot, "Modernization," 272–273.

55. Peter Gran, *Islamic Roots of Capitalism, Egypt 1760–1840* (Austin: University of Texas Press, 1979), 76, 79; Livingston, "Muhammad 'Abduh on Science," 216, 217–219; Marsot, "Modernization," 273–276; al-Jabarti, *Aja'ib*, 3:69, 4:272, 325, 334; Mubarak, *Khitat*, 4:40–49; Ahmad Bey al-Husayni ibn Ahmad ibn Yusuf, *Muqaddimat murshid al-inam li birr umm al-Imam*

(manuscript, Dar al-Kutub, Qism al-Makhtutat al-Nadira, Fiqh al-Shafi'i 1522, microfilm no. 43166, reel 2), 597–609.

56. Al-Jabarti, *Aja'ib*, 3:322, 4:123–124; Gran, *Islamic Roots*, 84–88, 81,129, and appendix 1, 189–191; compare F. De Jong, review of *Islamic Roots of Capitalism*, in *International Journal of Middle Eastern Studies* 14 (1982): 381–399.

57. Gran, *Islamic Roots*, 102–109; Mubarak, *Khitat*, 4:38–39; 'Abd al-Mit'al al-Sa'idi, *Tarikh al-islah fi al-Azhar wa safahat min al-jihad fi al-islah* (Cairo: Matba'at al-I'timad, 1951), 19; Marsot, "Modernization," 273; De Jong, review of *Islamic Roots*, 389; al-Husayni, *Muqaddimat*, 2:600–601. Mubarak, *Khitat*, 4:39–40, has "students" rather than "elder 'ulama."

58. Hasan al-'Attar, *Hashiat al-'Attar 'ala sharh jam' al-jawami'*, vols. 1–2 (Cairo: al-Matba'a al-'Ilmiyya, n.d.), quoted in al-Sa'idi, *Tarikh al-islah*, 19–21. Also under title *Hashiat al-'Attar 'ala sharh Jalal al-Din 'ala jam' al-jawami' li 'Abd al-Wahhab al-Subki* by Mustafa al-Halabi Press, n.d. The probable date of publication of 1830 comes from F. De Jong, "The Itinerary of Hasan al-'Attar (1766–1835): A Reconsideration and Its Implications," *Journal of Semitic Studies* 28, no. 1 (Spring 1983): 115; Marsot, "Modernization," 273–274; Mubarak, *Khitat*, 4:40; al-Sa'idi, *Tarikh al-islah*, 21–24.

59. Al-'Attar, *Hashiat al-'Attar*, 1:225–226; quoted in al-Sa'idi, *Tarikh al-islah*, 20.

60. Al-'Attar, *Hashiat al-'Attar*, 2:461; quoted in al-Sa'idi, *Tarikh al-islah*, 21.

61. Al-'Attar, *Hashiat al-'Attar*, 1:225–226; quoted in al-Sa'idi, *Tarikh al-islah*, 19–20. See also Marsot, "Modernization," 274–275.

62. Gran, *Islamic Roots*, 123.

63. Hasan ibn Muhammad al-'Attar, *Al-Insha'*, rev. ed. (Cairo: Bulaq, 1835; repr. Cairo: Mahmud Tawfiq, 1936), 101–102; Gran, *Islamic Roots*, 156. Date of original composition was between 1825 and 1834.

64. Adrian Gully, "Epistles for Grammarians: Illustrations from the Insha' Literature," *British Journal of Middle Eastern Studies* 23, no. 2 (November 1996): 163.

65. Marsot, "Modernization," 274; Gran, *Islamic Roots*, 126; note discrepancy in dating term of office between Marsot and Eccel, *Social Change*, 136. On dates, see also Ahmad Badawi, *Rifa'ah Rafi' al-Tahtawi*, 2nd ed. (Cairo: Lajnat al-Bayan al-'Arabi, 1959), 67.

66. Sami 'Abd al-'Aziz al-Kumi, *al-Sihafa al-islamiyya fi Misr fi al-qarn al-tasi' 'ashar* (al-Mansura, Egypt: Dar al-Wafa' li al-Tiba'a wa al-Nashr wa al-Tawzi', 1992), 15–16.

67. Muhammad 'Abd al-Ghani Hasan, *Hasan al-'Attar* (Cairo: Dar al-Ma'arif, 1968), 40; excerpt in Gran, *Islamic Roots*, 127; Lane, *Manners and Customs*, 218, 221.

68. *Al-Waqa'i' al-Misriyya* 47 (29 August 1829) and *al-Waqa'i' al-Misriyya* 186 (April 1831); Gran, *Islamic Roots*, 127.

69. Heyworth-Dunne, *History of Education*, 128 n.3, 133; Gran, *Islamic Roots*, 130.

70. Heyworth-Dunne, *History of Education*, 125.

71. Hasan al-'Attar, manuscript entitled "Sharh al-'Attar al-musamma bi rahat al-abdan 'ala nuzhat al-adhhan" (Azhariyya, 3434 Riwaq al-Maghariba), folios 70–71, quoted in Gran, *Islamic Roots*, 104–105.

72. Antoine Clot, *Memoires de Clot Bey*, Appendix III, ed. Jacques Tager (Cairo: L'Institut français d'archéologie orientale, 1949), no. 88, 130–131, cited in Heyworth-Dunne, *History of Education*, 128; Gran, *Islamic Roots*, 130.

73. Al-Husayni, *Muqaddimat*, 2:607–608. See also Marsot, "Modernization," 274; Gran, *Islamic Roots*, 128.

74. A marginal note handwritten by al-'Attar on Muhammad ibn Ibrahim (Ibn al-Hanbali), "Durr al-hubb fi tarikh a'yan Halab," quoted in Gran, *Islamic Roots*, 129–130. I was unable to locate the original at the location Gran cites: Rifa'a al-Tahtawi's personal collection in the Maktaba Baladiyya in Sohag, Egypt, 60 Tarikh, vol. 2, folio 2.

75. Al-Husayni *Muqaddimat*, 2:608–609; Gran, *Islamic Roots*,128–129.

76. More work needs to be done to determine whether there were ideological reasons for opposing al-'Attar, perhaps by examining Shaykh al-Quwaysini, "Sanad al-Quwaysini" (Cairo: Dar al-Kutub, Makhtutat 23126B); Shaykh al-Quwaysini, "Mukhtasar sharh sullam" (Azhariyya, 34253 Halim 820); and a commentary on the *Sullam* responding to al-'Attar's work on logic by Mustafa al-Bulaqi (Dar al-Kutub, 120 Mantiq, Taymur).

77. See Marsot, "Modernization," 275; and Gran, *Islamic Roots*, 126, 158, 186, and 237 n.45.

78. Albert Hourani, *Arabic Thought in the Liberal Age 1798–1939* (Cambridge: Cambridge University Press, 1983 [1962]), 69; Gran, *Islamic Roots*, 97, 158, 162–163, 164; Badawi, *al-Tahtawi*, 15–17.

79. Heyworth-Dunne, *History of Education*, 265.

80. Badawi, *al-Tahtawi*, 17–19.

81. Rifa'a Rafi' al-Tahtawi, *Takhlis al-ibriz fi talkhis Bariz* (Cairo: al-Hay'a al-Misriyya al-'Amma li al-Kitab, 1993 [1834]), 302–303; Livingston, "Western Science," 544, 548; Mitchell, *Colonising Egypt*, 106–107; Hourani, *Arabic Thought in the Liberal Age*, 69. According to Badawi, al-Tahtawi, as imam, was not required to study at all. His studies reflect his own choice (Badawi, *al-Tahtawi*, 21).

82. Al-Tahtawi, *Takhlis*, 280–281.

83. Heyworth-Dunne, *History of Education*, 227; Eccel, *Social Change*, 156; Mubarak cited in Ahmad Amin, "'Ali Pasha Mubarak," *Zu'ama' al-islah fi al-'asr al-hadith* (Beirut: Dar al-Kitab al-'Arabiyya, 1979), 185.

84. Mitchell, *Colonising Egypt*, 148.

85. Muhammad Ibn Da'ud al-Sanhaji Ibn Ajrum, "The Parts of Speech," *Kitab al-Ajrumiyya* (n.p., c.720), n.p.

86. Muhammad 'Abduh, quoted in *al-Manar* 8 (19 July 1905), 381.

87. Berkey, *Transmission*, esp. 216–218.

88. Muhammad al-Ahmadi al-Zawahiri, *al-'Ilm wa al-'ulama wa al-nizam al-ta'lim*, 2nd ed., with introduction by Fakhr al-Din al-Zawahiri (n.p.: 1955 [1904]), 195.

89. Al-Tahtawi, *Takhlis*, 256.

90. Ibid., 349, 360.

91. Ibid., 255–257.

92. Ibid., 260–267.

93. Ibid., 373–375, 377, 379. Al-Tahtawi was quoting an Orientalist history of Egypt.
94. Ibid., 391–392.
95. I owe Kenneth Cuno for this insight.
96. Reproduced copy of al-'Attar's handwritten introduction to al-Tahtawi, *Takhlis*, 57.
97. The public received graduates of Muhammad 'Ali's schools, particularly doctors, veterinarians, and engineers, with aversion. The government was often the only place they could be employed (Heyworth-Dunne, *History of Education*, 229).
98. Heyworth-Dunne, *History of Education*, 168.
99. Ibid., 168–180.
100. Marsot, "Modernization," 272.
101. Shaykh al-Tahtawi, trans., *Qala'id al-mafakhir fi gharib awa'id al-awa'il wa al-awakhir* (Bulaq: Dar al-Tiba'a, 1833).
102. Heyworth-Dunne, *History of Education*, 266.
103. Edward Lane, ed./trans., *One Thousand and One Nights*, 2 vols. (London: Chatto and Windus, 1912), 2:64–65 n.4.
104. See quotations and interpretations of Lane in Gran, *Islamic Reform*, 163; and see also Badawi, *al-Tahtawi*, 140. Husayn Fawzi al-Najjar quoted Ahmad Badawi's quotation of Lane in *Rifa'a al-Tahtawi* (Cairo: Dar al-Misriyya li al-Ta'lif wa al-Tarbia, n.d.), 93; Livingston cited Gran, al-Najjar, and Badawi in "Western Science," 551. See also Louis Delatre, *Revue de l'Orient, de l'Algérie et des Colonies* 16 (September 1858): 135, quoted in Heyworth-Dunne, *History of Education*, 297. Delatre stated that al-Tahtawi's colleagues "detested him," but this reflected opinion of him twenty-four years after the publication of *Takhlis*, after al-Tahtawi had given some Azharis reason to dislike him by teaching Islamic law and theology in a military school in violation of al-Azhar's purview over religious education (Heyworth-Dunne, 297).
105. Lane, *One Thousand and One Nights*, 2:64–65 n.4.
106. Aida Ibrahim Nosseir, *al-Kutub allati nushirat fi Misr fi al-qarn al-tasi' 'ashar* (Cairo: American University in Cairo, 1990), entry no. 9/106–109.
107. Heyworth-Dunne, *History of Education*, 266.
108. See Marsot, *Egypt*, chap. 4, and al-Jabarti, *Aja'ib*, 4:48.
109. Crecelius, "Nonideological Responses."

Chapter 3

1. Al-Jabarti, *Aja'ib*, 3:439, 4:146–7, 153, 199–201.
2. Marsot, "Ulama of Cairo," 158.
3. Crecelius, "The Ulama and the State," 147–8.
4. Convention for the Pacification of the Levant, 15 July–17 September 1840, in *The Middle East and North Africa in World Politics: A Documentary Record*, ed. J. C. Hurewitz, vol. 1 (New Haven, CT: Yale University Press, 1975), 1:272–276; Toledano, *State and Society*, 181–182.
5. By the mid-1840s, the Egyptian military numbered approximately 80,000 (Toledano, *State and Society*, 73), but many military projects had been dropped or scaled back (ibid., 43); Marsot, *Egypt*, 239. For mixed effects of

Balta Liman treaty, see Donald Quataert, "Ottoman Manufacturing in the Nineteenth Century," in *Manufacturing in the Ottoman Empire and Turkey, 1500–1950* (Albany: State University of New York Press, 1994), 89, 97–98.

6. Toledano, *State and Society*, 20.
7. Heyworth-Dunne, *History of Education*, 223, 225–226, 287.
8. Rifaʻa al-Tahtawi, *Kanz al-mukhtar fi kashf al-aradi wa al-bihar* [A Selected Treasury on the Investigation of the Lands and the Seas] (Cairo: n.p., 1834); al-Tahtawi, *Qudamaʼ al-falasifa* [Ancient Philosophers] (Cairo: Bulaq, 1836); and al-Tahtawi, *Mabadiʼ al-handasa* [Principles of Geometry] (Cairo: Matbaʻa al-Amiriyya, 1842). *Mabadiʼ al-handasa* was reprinted four times, in 1843, 1853, 1863, and 1874 (Nosseir, *al-Kutub allati nushirat fi Misr*, 1/203; 5/122–126).
9. Al-Kumi, *al-Sihafa al-islamiyya*, 15–22.
10. Hourani, *Arabic Thought in the Liberal Age*, 71; Heyworth-Dunne, *History of Education*, 266, William Cleveland, *History of the Modern Middle East* (Boulder, CO: Westview Press, 1994), 90.
11. Heyworth-Dunne, *History of Education*, 268.
12. Ibid., 229–43, 288–309.
13. Toledano, *State and Society*, 41–42, 66; Heyworth-Dunne, *History of Education*, 288–291, 298, 303–307; Baer, *Land Ownership*, 169; Mubarak, *Khitat*, 5:82–84; Crecelius, "The Ulama and the State," 152.
14. Hourani, *Arabic Thought in the Liberal Age*, 72.
15. Heyworth-Dunne, *History of Education*, 317; Mubarak, *Khitat*, 9:43 ff. Al-Tahtawi's next book was *Qasida wataniyya Misriyya fi madh Saʻid* [A Patriotic Poem in Praise of Saʻid] (Cairo: n.p., 1955).
16. Toledano, *State and Society*, 181–2, 184; Heyworth-Dunne, *History of Education*, 293, 314.
17. Bayle St. John, *Village Life in Egypt* (London: n.p.,1852), 2:85–86; William Bromfield, *Letters from Egypt and Syria* (London: privately printed, 1856), 150–151; Maxime du Camp, "The Crew of the Cange," quoted in Gustave Flaubert, *Flaubert in Egypt, A Sensibility on Tour*, trans. Francis Steegmuller (Boston: Little, Brown & Co., 1972), 228; Mubarak, *Khitat*, 4:40; Heyworth-Dunne, *History of Education*, 397–8; Toledano, *State and Society*, 181–188; Ener, *Managing Egypt's Poor*, 35.
18. Reimer, "Views of al-Azhar," 267, 268; Eccel, *Social Change*, 232, 236; Dodge, *Al-Azhar*, 114; Juan R. I. Cole, *Colonialism and Revolution in the Middle East: Social and Cultural Origins of Egypt's ʻUrabi Movement* (Princeton, NJ: Princeton University Press, 1993), 38, citing Rifaʻa al-Tahtawi, *Rawdat al-madaris* 3, no. 2 (30 Muharram 1289), 11–13, for 1871–1872 (9,423 students, 312 ʻulama); and Heyworth-Dunne, *History of Education*, 28–29. Heyworth-Dunne gives the number of students in 1873 as 10,126.
19. Mitchell, *Colonising Egypt*, 85.
20. Toledano, *State and Society*, 197–199, 210, 217; Ener, *Managing Egypt's Poor*, 35, 150, n.4.
21. Mubarak, *Khitat*, 4:40–41; Toledano, *State and Society*, 183–184; Mitchell, *Colonising Egypt*, 41; Arthur Goldschmidt, *Biographical Dictionary of Modern Egypt* (Boulder, CO: Lynne Rienner, 2000), 33. See also Crecelius, "The

Ulama and the State," 155; and Heyworth-Dunne, *History of Education*, 316, 398.

22. Mubarak, *Khitat*, 4:40.
23. Dodge, *Al-Azhar*, 115. In 1856, Sa'id had endowed a waqf for the Citadel mosque (Mubarak, *Khitat*, 5:84–86; Crecelius, "The Ulama and the State," 155). The details of state waqf supervision during this period need more thorough exploration.
24. Marsot has the date as 1856, citing Mubarak, who gave no date but said the incident occurred while Sa'id was in the Hijaz on the lesser pilgrimage and the heir was still Ahmad Pasha. The regency council replaced al-Bajuri with a council of deputies shortly after the incident in August 1858 (Marsot, "Modernization," 276; Mubarak, *Khitat*, 4:40–41; Snouck Hurgronje, "E. Sachau, Muhammadanisches Recht Nach Schafiitischer Lehre," *Zeitschrift der Deutschen Morgenlandischen Gesellschaft* 53 (Leipzig, 1899): 125–167 (reprint [Gedagteekend: Kutaradja (Atjeh): 1898], 418).
25. Mubarak, *Khitat*, 4:40–41; see also Heyworth-Dunne, *History of Education*, 397.
26. Mubarak, *Khitat*, 4:40–41; see also Hurgronje, "E. Sachau," 417–418; Heyworth-Dunne, *History of Education*, 397.
27. Hurgronje, "E. Sachau," 418; Hourani, *Arabic Thought in the Liberal Age*, 67.
28. Amin, *Zu'ama' al-islah*, 195.
29. Afaf Lutfi al-Sayyid Marsot, *A Short History of Modern Egypt* (Cambridge: Cambridge University Press, 1985), 68; Cleveland, *Modern Middle East*, 92.
30. Mitchell, *Colonising Egypt*, 65–68, 178.
31. Michael J. Reimer, "Contradiction and Consciousness in 'Ali Mubarak's Description of al-Azhar," *International Journal of Middle East Studies* 29, no. 1 (February 1997): 63.
32. Amin, *Zu'ama' al-islah*, 184–190; Mitchell, *Colonising Egypt*, 71–74; Heyworth-Dunne, *History of Education*, 249–250. See Heyworth-Dunne for lists of schools still open (234, 292–3, 295, 297).
33. Mubarak, *Khitat*, 9:43. See also Heyworth-Dunne, *History of Education*, 143, 240, 248, 250, 253, 292, 294, 296–297, 298–299, 318.
34. Mubarak, *Khitat*, 9:43 ff; F. Robert Hunter, *Egypt under the Khedives 1805–1879: From Household Government to Modern Bureaucracy* (Pittsburgh: University of Pittsburgh Press, 1984), 129–130, 133.
35. Biography of 'Ali Mubarak in Heyworth-Dunne, *History of Education*, 253–4, 347–48; 'Ali Mubarak, *'Alam al-din* (Alexandria, Egypt: 1882), 816, quoted in Mitchell, *Colonising Egypt*, 63–64.
36. Mubarak, *Khitat*, 4:26–28.
37. Amin, *Zu'ama' al-islah*, 195.
38. Mubarak, *Khitat*, 4:26; Mitchell, *Colonising Egypt*, 80–82.
39. Mubarak, *Khitat*, 4:26, 31–32, 37, 40–41.
40. Mubarak, *Khitat*, 4:27, 29; Mitchell, *Colonising Egypt*, 67.
41. Heyworth-Dunne, *History of Education*, 271. Heyworth-Dunne lists students known to have participated in foreign missions, their employment records, and numbers of students who attended civil schools.
42. Walter J. Ong, *Orality and Literacy: The Technologizing of the Word* (London: Methuen, 1982), 74.

43. Wael B. Hallaq, *A History of Islamic Legal Theories: An Introduction to Sunni Usul al-fiqh* (Cambridge: Cambridge University Press, 1997), 146–148.

44. Heyworth-Dunne, *History of Education*, 398–399. He may have also wanted the air of legitimacy that concern for al-Azhar would bestow on his regime.

45. Alexander Scholch, *Egypt for the Egyptians! The Socio-political Crisis in Egypt 1878–1882* (London: Ithaca Press, 1981), 30–32; Marsot, "Socio-Economic Sketch," 318; Baer, *Land Ownership*, 159–160; Mubarak, *Khitat*, 1:88; Dodge, *Al-Azhar*, 116; Marsot, "Ulama of Cairo," 164.

46. Cleveland, *Modern Middle East*, 94.

47. Mubarak, *Khitat*, 4:41.

48. Marsot, "Modernization," 278–279.

49. Ibid., 280.

50. Ibid., 277.

51. Compare with Heyworth-Dunne, *History of Education*, 399 n.6; Marsot, "Modernization," 278 n.41; Scholch, *Egypt for the Egyptians!* 30–31.

52. Marsot, "Modernization," 277; Eccel, *Social Change*, 236, 300; Ta'limat al-Muhakimat of 1255 H, cited in J. N. D. Anderson, "Recent Developments in Shari'a Law II," *Muslim World* 41: 36 n.2.

53. Marsot, "Modernization," 277–279.

54. Rudolph Peters, "The Lions of Qasr al-Nil Bridge: The Islamic Prohibition of Images as an Issue in the 'Urabi Revolt," in *Islamic Legal Interpretation: Muftis and their Fatwas*, ed. Muhammad Khalid Masud, Brinkley Messick, and David S. Powers (Cambridge, MA: Harvard University Press, 1996), 214; Cuno, *Pasha's Peasants*, 8; Eccel, *Social Change*, 136–137.

55. Anderson, "Recent Developments," 36 n.2.

56. Eccel, *Social Change*, 123; Mubarak, *Khitat*, 4:27–28.

57. Eccel, *Social Change*, 123.

58. Mubarak, *Khitat*, 4:41; Salman, *A'mal majlis*, 8; Eccel, *Social Change*, 123.

59. Scholch, *Egypt for the Egyptians!* 31–32.

60. Law of 23 Dhu al-Qa'da, 1288 [3 February 1872], in the report of the Mashru' Lajnat Islah al-Azhar al-Ma'mur 1328/1910 (Cairo: al-Matba'a al-Amiriyya, 1910), 4. See also summaries of the 1872 law given in Mubarak, *Khitat*, 4:26–28, 40; and al-Sa'idi, *Tarikh al-islah*, 35–36.

61. Most who make this claim cite the French translation of the Lajnat Islah report (*Projet de réforme*), 'Ali Mubarak, or Muhammad Rashid Rida. Mubarak and Rashid Rida were never students at al-Azhar, and they did not witness first hand the reactions to the 1872 Code that they purport to describe. A committee of bureaucrats composed the Lajnat Islah report in 1910, through the lens of hindsight.

62. Mubarak, *Khitat*, 4:40; Lajnat Islah report, 4.

63. Lajnat Islah report, 4.

64. Mubarak, *Khitat*, 4:40.

65. Mubarak, *Khitat*, 4:27–28.

66. Michel Foucault, *Discipline and Punish: The Birth of the Prison*, trans. Alan Sheridan (New York: Vintage Books, 1979 [1975]), 218–228.

67. Mitchell, *Colonising Egypt*.

68. Lajnat Islah report, 4–5.

Chapter 4

1. Mitchell, *Colonising Egypt,* 150; Albert Hourani, "The Syrians in Egypt in the Eighteenth and Nineteenth Centuries," *Colloque international sur l'histoire du Caire* (Cairo: Ministry of Culture of the Arab Republic of Egypt, 1969), 229.

2. Ami Ayalon, *The Press in the Arab Middle East: A History* (New York: Oxford University Press, 1995), 19, 37; Hourani, "Syrians," 229; Beth Baron, *The Women's Awakening in Egypt: Culture, Society and the Press* (New Haven: Yale University Press, 1994); Amin Sami, *Taqwim al-nil,* 3 vols. (Cairo: Matba'at Dar al-Kutub al-Misriyya, 1915–1936), vol. 3, bk. 2: 579, 607; bk. 3: 1404, 1527).

3. Ayalon, *Press,* 18–19, 41; Muhammad Hasan and 'Abd al-'Aziz al-Dasuqi, *Rawdat al-madaris* (Cairo: al-Hay'a al-Misriyya al-'Amma li al-Kitab, 1975), 14.

4. *Rawdat al-madaris* 1, no. 1 (15 Muharram 1287 [1870]), 1, no. 5 (15 Rabi' I 1287 [1870]): 9, 12, supplement p. 5, supplement p. 13; 1, no. 10 (ghayat Jumada I, 1287 [1870]): 9; 1, no. 18 (ghayat Ramadan 1287 [1870]): 25, continued in 1, no. 19, p. 24.

5. Some Mu'tazili works remained standards for madrasa students from the Middle Ages until the eighteenth century, esp. the Qur'anic exegesis of al-Zamakhshari. Some 'ulama, such as Taj al-Din al-Subki (d. 771/1369), warned that only those secure in their adherence to orthodox opinions should read his work (Berkey, *Transmission,* 185 and 186 n.12; Heyworth-Dunne, *History of Education,* 45 n.4).

6. Ibn Khaldun, *The Muqaddima: An Introduction to History,* 3 vols., trans. Franz Rosenthal (New York: Pantheon Books, 1958), 3:299–300; Berkey, *Transmission,* 13; Heyworth-Dunne, *History of Education,* 61–62, 64–66, 82–83; Dodge, *Al-Azhar,* 50–52.

7. Waqfiyya of Fatimid caliph al-Hakim bi-Amr Allah for the mosques of al-Azhar, al-Hakimi, and al-Maquss and the Dar al-'Ilm (Cairo: 1010 AD), as described by al-Maqrizi. Reprinted in Mustafa Muhammad Ramadan, "Dawr al-awqaf fi da'm al-Azhar ka mu'assasa 'ilmiyya islamiyya," (The role of the awqaf in supporting al-Azhar as a religious teaching institution), a paper presented at the Nadwat al-tatawwur al-tarikh li-mu'assasat al-awqaf fi 'alam al-'arabi wa al-islam (conference on The Historical Development of the Institution of the Awqaf in the Arabic and Islamic World), Baghdad, April 1983 (Cairo: Dar al-Wafa' li al-Tiba', n.d.). Also see St. H. Stephan, trans., "An Endowment Deed of Khasseki Sultan, Dated the 24th of May 1552," *The Quarterly of Antiquities in Palestine* 10 (1944): 175–194.

8. Rifa'a al-Tahtawi, *Manahij al-albab,* chap. 1, part 1; and al-Tahtawi, *Murshid al-amin li al-banat wa al-banin,* 1:227. Both of the preceding are in Muhammad 'Imara, ed., *al-A'mal al-kamila li Rifa'a Rafi' al-Tahtawi,* 2 vols. (Beirut: al-Mu'assasa al-'Arabiyya li al-Dirasat wa al-Nashr, 1973). Juan Cole attributes al-Tahtawi's definition of useful knowledge to the influence of French positivist Saint-Simon (Claude-Henre de Rouvroy) (*Colonialism and Revolution,* 42–43).

9. This differed from British India, where Islamic reformers of al-Tahtawi's generation partially modeled concepts of useful education on those of Utilitarian colonial administrators (Muhammad Qasim Zaman, "Religious Education and the Rhetoric of Reform: The Madrasah in British India and Pakistan,"

Comparative Studies in Society and History [1999]: 299). In India, the authority of the British over education was more entrenched and of longer duration than in Egypt (Zaman, "Religious Education," 298–299).

10. Compare with Zaman, "The Madrasah in British India," esp. 295, 321, 322.

11. Al-Tahtawi, *Manahij,* 228.

12. Al-Tahtawi, *al-Murshid al-amin,* 229.

13. Al-Tahtawi's distinction between the two was similar to that of the Ahl-i Hadith in British India (Daniel Brown, *Re-thinking Tradition in Modern Islamic Thought* [Cambridge: Cambridge University Press, 1996], 31). Comparing al-Tahtawi's terminology with recent studies on ijtihad and taqlid suggests no consensus existed on distinctions between taqlid and ittiba' nor on the definition of ijtihad. See Lutz Wiederhold, "Legal Doctrines in Conflict: The Relevance of *Madhhab* Boundaries to Legal Reasoning in the Light of an Unpublished Treatise on *Taqlid* and *Ijtihad,"* *Islamic Law and Society* 3, no. 2 (June 1996): 260; and Wael Hallaq, "Was the Gate of Ijtihad Closed?" *International Journal of Middle East Studies* 16 (1984): 24–25, and 27 n.44. Compare with Baber Johansen, "Legal Literature and the Problem of Change: The Case of the Land Rent," in *Islam and Public Law,* ed. Chibli Mallat (London: Graham & Trotman, 1993), 36.

14. Muneer Goolam Fareed, *Legal Reform in the Muslim World: Anatomy of a Scholarly Dispute in the 19th and the Early 20th Centuries on the Usage of Ijtihad as a Legal Tool* (San Francisco: Austin & Winfield, 1996), 30–31.

15. Mohammad Fadel, "The Social Logic of *Taqlid* and the Rise of the *Mukhatasar,"* *Islamic Law and Society* 3, no. 2 (June 1996): 196; Fadel, "Adjudication in the Maliki *Madhhab:* A Study of Legal Process in Medieval Islamic Law" (Ph.D. diss, University of Chicago, 1995).

16. Fareed, *Legal Reform,* 33, 42–43.

17. Ibid., 44.

18. Omar A. Farrukh, "Zahirism," Islamic Philosophy Online, 2001–2004 http://www.muslimphilosophy.com/hmp/17.htm, accessed 21 July 2004.

19. Fadel, "Social Logic of Taqlid," 196; Fadel, "Adjudication," 261 n.165, 274, 283–84; Haifaa Khalafallah, "Understanding Islamic Law: A Historical and Structural Comparison between Islamic and English Common Law," paper delivered at the American Research Center in Egypt Seminar, 4 March 1998.

20. According to Hallaq, Ibn 'Aqil, a Hanbali (d. 513/1119), was the first to discuss this issue, and he concluded that there must be a mujtahid in every age ("Was the Gate of Ijtihad Closed?" 21–22). Al-Rafi'i (d. 623/1226), Ibn Abi al-Dam (d. 642/1244), and al-Baydawi (d. 685/1286), all Shafi'is, considered their time to be devoid of mujtahidun (Hallaq, "Was the Gate of Ijtihad Closed?" 23, 26; and Wiederhold, "Legal Doctrines in Conflict," 236 n.5). See also Wael B. Hallaq, "On the Origins of the Controversy about the Existence of *Mujtahids* and the Gate of *Ijtihad,"* *Studia Islamica* 63 (1986): 134–141.

21. Compare with Wiederhold, "Legal Doctrines in Conflict," which demonstrates that some jurists allowed crossing of madhhab boundaries.

22. Fadel, "Adjudication," chapter 3; Hallaq, *Islamic Legal Theories,* 153–156, 161.

23. Hallaq, *Islamic Legal Theories,* 154.

24. Aaron Spevack, "The Archetypal Sunni Scholar: Law, Theology, and Mysticism in the Synthesis of al-Bajuri" (Ph.D. diss., Boston University, 2008),

130–144; Hallaq, "Was the Gate of Ijtihad Closed?" and Wiederhold, "Legal Doctrines in Conflict," 235 n.2, 268.

25. Hallaq, "Was the Door of Ijtihad Closed?" 7–8; Leonard Binder, "Ideological Foundations of Egyptian-Arab Nationalism," in *Ideology and Discontent,* ed. David Apter (New York: Free Press, 1964), 143–144; Frank Vogel, "Closing of the Door of Ijtihad and the Application of the Law," *American Journal of Islamic Social Sciences* 10, no. 3 (Fall 1993): 399.

26. Fareed, *Legal Reform,* 73; Fadel, "Social Logic of Taqlid" and "Adjudication"; Wiederhold, "Legal Doctrines in Conflict," 260; Hallaq, "Was the Gate of Ijtihad Closed?" 24–25, 27; Spevak, "Archetypal Sunni Scholar,"133–136.

27. Hallaq, "Was the Gate of Ijtihad Closed?", 29–32; Hallaq, *Islamic Legal Theories,* 122, 154.

28. Rifa'a al-Tahtawi, "Baqa' hasan al-dhikr bi-istikhdam al-fikr," *Rawdat al-Madaris* 1, no. 3 (15 Safar 1287 AH): 13.

29. Ibid., 11, 12, 14.

30. Ibid., 14. Al-Tahtawi ignored the problem of conflicting hadith reports.

31. Ibid., 15.

32. Rifa'a al-Tahtawi, "Ta'rif al-taqlid wa tajazza al-ijtihad," in *al-Qawl al-sadid fi al-ijtihad wa al-tajdid* (Cairo: Matba'at Wadi al-Nil, 1870), 4 (also cited in 'Imara, *al-Tahtawi,* 227).

33. Al-Tahtawi, *al-Qawl al-sadid,* 6–8.

34. Spevack, "Archetypal Sunni Scholar," 133.

35. Ibid., 6–7.

36. Ibid., 7; Hallaq, "Was the Gate of Ijtihad Closed?" 25, 27.

37. Ibid., 8.

38. Al-Tahtawi, *al-Qawl al-sadid,* 8.

39. Al-Tahtawi, *al-Qawl al-sadid,* 8; compare the definition of *takhrij* used by Sherman Jackson ("extrapolation") in *Islamic Law and the State: The Constitutional Jurisprudence of Shihab al-Din al-Qarafi* (Leiden, Netherlands: E. J. Brill, 1996). Takhrij is conventionally used now to mean separation of strong from weak sources, such as hadith.

40. Al-Tahtawi, *al-Qawl al-sadid,* 8–9.

41. Al-Tahtawi, *al-Qawl al-sadid,* 9. Others also cite these: Hallaq, "Was the Gate of Ijtihad Closed?" 24, and "How the Door of Ijtihad was Closed," *Islamic Voice* 12–06, no. 0138 (June 1998).

42. Al-Tahtawi, *al-Qawl al-sadid,* 9.

43. Ibid., 10; Hallaq, "Was the Gate of Ijtihad Closed?" 27.

44. Al-Tahtawi, *al-Qawl al-sadid,* 10–11; Spevack, "Archetypal Sunni Scholar," 133.

45. For details of Jamal al-Din al-Afghani's biography and political activities outside Egypt, see Edward G. Browne's *Persian Revolution of 1905–1909* (New York: Barnes and Nobles, 1966); Nikki Keddie, *Religion and Rebellion in Iran: The Tobacco Protest of 1891–1892* (London: Frank Cass, 1966) and Keddie, *Sayyid Jamal ad-Din "al-Afghani": A Political Biography* (Los Angeles: University of California, 1972); and Elie Kedourie, *Afghani and 'Abduh: An Essay on Religious Unbelief and Political Activism in Modern Islam* (London: Frank Cass, 1997 [1966]).

46. Nikki Keddie, *An Islamic Response to Imperialism; Political and Religious Writings of Sayyid Jamal al-Din "al-Afghani"* (Berkeley: University of California Press, 1968), 8–9; Brown, *Re-Thinking Tradition*, 22–32, connects the Indian reform movements to Arab salafis.

47. Keddie, *Sayyid Jamal al-Din "al-Afghani,"* 81 n.1; Jurji Zaydan, *Tarajim mashahir al-sharq fi al-qarn al-tasi' 'ashar*, 2 vols. 2nd rev. ed. (Cairo: Matba'at al-Hilal, 1910), 2: 56; Sami Abdullah Kaloti, "Islamic Reformation and the Impact of Jamal al-Din al-Afghani and Muhammad Abduh on Islamic Education" (Ph.D. diss., Marquette University, Milwaukee, WI, 1974), 47; Ahmad Shafiq Pasha, *Mudhakkirati fi nisf qarn*, 3 vols. (Cairo: Sharikat Musahima Misriyya, 1934–1936, vol. 1–2; Dar al-Majallati li al-Tab' wa al-Nashr, n.d., vol. 3), 1:108–109.

48. John W. Livingston, "Muhammad 'Abduh on Science," *Muslim World* 85, no. 3–4 (1995): 222; compare Keddie, *Sayyid Jamal al-Din "al-Afghani,"* 90.

49. Livingston, "Muhammad 'Abduh on Science," 230.

50. Keddie, *Sayyid Jamal al-Din "al-Afghani"*, 392.

51. Jamal al-Din al-Afghani, *Radd-i-naichiriyya*, translated into Arabic by Muhammad 'Abduh as *al-Radd 'ala al-dahriyyin* [Refutation of the Materialists], reprinted in *al-A'mal al-kamila li-Jamal al-Din al-Afghani*, ed. Muhammad 'Imara (Cairo: al-Mu'assasa al-Misriyya al-'Ama li al-Ta'lif wa al-Nashr, n.d.), 1: 176–177. See Keddie, *Islamic Response to Imperialism*.

52. 'Abd al-Qadir al-Maghribi, *al-Bayyinat* 2, no. 4 (1925–6); quoted in Loimeier, "Is There Something Like 'Protestant Islam'?" 245.

53. Al-Afghani, *Radd*, 177.

54. Kaloti, "Islamic Reformation," 165.

55. Muhammad Basha al-Makhzumi, ed., *Khatirat al-Sayyid Jamal al-Din al-Afghani* (Beirut: al-Matba' al-'Ilmiyya li-Yusuf Sadir, 1931), 155; Kaloti, "Islamic Reformation," 61, n.28.

56. Al-Makhzumi, *Khatirat*, 178–179.

57. Ibid., 176–179.

58. Qur'an, 2:170–171, 5:104–105, 7:70–72.

59. Al-Afghani, *Radd*, 176.

60. Hallaq, *Islamic Legal Theories*, 147–148.

61. Kaloti, "Islamic Reformation," 82–92, citing al-Afghani's reply to Ernst Renan, and al-Afghani's articles in 'Abd al-Ghaffar, *Maqalat-i Jamaliya* (Calcutta: Ripon Press).

62. See Irene Gendzier, *Practical Visions of Ya'qub Sanu'* (Cambridge, MA: Harvard University Press, 1966).

63. Ayalon, *Press*, 19, 37, 44; Hourani, "Syrians"; al-Kumi, *al-Sihafa al-islamiyya;* see also Sami, *Taqwim al-nil* , vol. 3, bk. 2: 579, 607; bk. 3: 1404, 1527.

64. Muhammad 'Abduh, "al-'Ulum al-kalamiyya wa al-da'wa ila al-'ulum al-'asriyya," *al-Ahram* 36 (1877); reprinted with notes in *al-A'mal al-kamila li al-Imam al-Shaykh Muhammad 'Abduh*, ed. Muhammad 'Imara, 5 vols. (Beirut: Dar al-Shuruq, 1993), 3:15–22. (It is also reprinted in *al-A'mal al-kamila li al-Imam Muhammad 'Abduh*, ed. Muhammad 'Imara, 2nd ed., 3 vols. [Beirut: al-Mu'assasa al-'Arabiyya li al-Dirasat wa al-Nashr, 1980, 1st ed. 1972.)

'Abduh likely absorbed his empiricism and ideals of education from al-Afghani rather than Auguste Comte or Herbert Spencer. These early writings predate his knowledge of French (Rida, *Tarikh*, 1:1031, 1034).

65. 'Imara, *al-A'mal al-kamila* (1993 ed.), 3:15–16.
66. Ibid., 3:16.
67. 'Imara, *al-A'mal al-kamila*, 3:177–178; Scholch, *Egypt for the Egyptians!* 105–106, citing 'Abdullah Nadim in M. A. Khalaf Allah's edition of *'Abd Allah al-Nadim wa mudhakkiratuhu al-siyasiyya* (Cairo: 1956), 52. The story may be apocryphal, but it illustrates later writers' desire to characterize al-Afghani's students as a persecuted minority.
68. 'Imara, *al-A'mal al-kamila*, 3:17. 'Abduh refers to two types of duties Muslims must fulfill. A *fard al-'ayn* is a duty incumbent upon all individuals individually, such as prayer. A *fard kifaya* is a collective duty, performance of which by some members of society fulfills the requirement for all.
69. Muhammad 'Abduh, "al-Ma'arif," *al-Waqa'i' al-Misriyya* no. 990 (20 December 1880); reprinted in 'Imara, *al-A'mal al-kamila* (1980 ed.), 3:31.
70. Muhammad 'Abduh, "Al-'Ulum al-kalamiyya," in 'Imara, *al-A'mal al-kamila* (1980 ed.), 3:21–22.
71. 'Imara, *al-A'mal al-kamila* (1980 ed.), 3:17–20; see especially n.1, which reads, "Refers to the group of muqallidun who protected stagnation, specifically the men of al-Azhar in those days."
72. 'Abduh, "al-Ma'arif"; reprinted in 'Imara, *al-A'mal al-kamila* (1980 ed.), 3:32.
73. Charles C. Adams, *Islam and Modernism in Egypt: A Study of the Modern Reform Movement Inaugurated by Muhammad 'Abduh* (New York: Russell & Russell, 1968 [1933]), 47.
74. Ibid., 47–49, citing *al-Manar* 8, 406–409.
75. "Al-Tamaddun," *Al-Waqa'i' al-Misriyya* no. 1017 (20 January 1881), reprinted in 'Imara, *A'mal al-kamila* (1993 ed.), 2: 40.
76. Muhammad 'Abduh, "The Error of the Intellectuals," in Rida, *Tarikh*, 2:119–132, esp. 132.
77. Rida, *Tarikh* 2: 77–80; quoted in M. A. Zaki Badawi, *The Reformers of Egypt* (London: Croom Helm, 1976), 68.
78. Muhammad 'Abduh, "al-Ma'arif," *al-Waqa'i' al-Misriyya* no. 993 (23 December 1880); reprinted in'Imara, *al-A'mal al-kamila* (1980 ed.), 3:38.
79. Rida, *Tarikh*, 1:411.
80. Muhammad,'Abduh, "al-Tarbiyya fi al-madaris wa al-makatib al-miriyya," *al-Waqa'i' al-Misriyya* no. 957 (29 November 1880); reprinted in 'Imara, *al-A'mal al-kamila* (1980 ed.), 3:27.
81. 'Abduh, "al-Ma'arif" (20 December 1880), reprinted in 'Imara, *al-A'mal al-kamila* (1980 ed.), 3:35–36.
82. Ibid., 3:38.
83. Ibid.
84. 'Abduh, "al-Tarbiyya fi al-madaris wa al-makatib al-miriyya," reprinted in 'Imara, *al-A'mal al-kamila* (1980 ed.), 3:28.
85. Rida, *Tarikh* 2:166–167; Badawi, *Reformers*, 65–67.
86. See Ayalon, *Press*, 44–45; Gendzier, *Ya'qub Sanu'*, 55–61, 67; and Shafiq, *Mudhakkirati*, 1:109.

87. Gendzier, *Ya'qub Sanu'*, 54–55; Owen, *World Economy*, 132–133.
88. Gendzier, *Ya'qub Sanu'*, 50–73.
89. Owen, *World Economy*, 133; Keddie, *Sayyid Jamal al-Din "al-Afghani"*, 119–124; Shafiq, *Mudhakkirati*, vol. 1, 109–110; al-Sa'idi, *Tarikh al-islah*, 38–39.
90. Selim Deringil, "The Ottoman Response to the Egyptian Crisis of 1881–82," *Middle Eastern Studies* 24, no. 1 (January 1988), 3–24.
91. 'Abdullah Nadim's Alexandrian journals *al-Tankit wa al-tabkit* [Banter and Blame], a bi-weekly, and *al-Ta'if* [The Wanderer], a daily; *al-Burhan* [The Proof], founded in May by Hamza Fathallah; *al-Hijaz* [The Hijaz], founded by Ibrahim Siraj al-Madani in July; and Hasan al-Shamsi's two papers, *al-Mufid* [The Informer] and *al-Safir* [The Traveler] (Ayalon, *Press*, 45).
92. Scholch, *Egypt for the Egyptians!*
93. Ahmad Effendi Samir, "al-Azhar," *al-Tankit wa al-tabkit*, no. 9 (7 August 1881): 140–141.
94. Ibid., 141.
95. Amin, *Zu'ama' al-islah*, 202–204; and Ahmad Samir, cited in Zaydan, *Mashahir al-sharq*, 106–107.
96. Zaydan remarked that while *al-Tankit wa al-tabkit* appeared on the surface to be humorous, "its innards were serious" (Zaydan, *Mashahir al-sharq*, 109).
97. Zaydan, *Mashahir al-sharq*, 109.
98. 'Abdullah Nadim, "al-Masjid al-Ahmadi," *al-Tankit wa al-tabkit* no. 16 (16 October 1881): 254–255.
99. 'Abdullah Nadim, "Shaykh Zifti aw jahil," *al-Tankit wa al-tabkit*, no. 13 (11 September 1881): 208–209.
100. Nadim, "Shaykh Zifti," 209.
101. Al-Tahtawi, in Rida, *Takhlis*. For other uses of European concepts of progress, see Nofal Effendi Ni'mat Allah Nofal, "Fi haqiqat al-'ilm wa al-'ulama," *al-Jinan* (1 Ayar 1873): 298–299, and Nofal, "Fi haqiqat …" (continued) *al-Jinan* (15 Ayar 1873): 237–340; and "al-Ta'lim," *al-Jinan* (1 Nisan 1883): 202; and Samir, "al-Azhar," 140–141.
102. Nofal, "Fi haqiqat al-'ilm wa al-'ulama," 299, 341; "al-Madaris al-Misriyya," *al-Jinan* (1 Aylul 1880): 529.
103. Faris Shidyaq, "Fi taghyir ikhlaq man wala al-ri'asa," *al-Jawa'ib*, reprinted in *Kanz al-Ragha'ib fi muntakhabat al-jawa'ib* (Istanbul: Matba'at al-Jawa'ib, 1288 H [1872]), 2:164–168; Nofal, "Fi haqiqat al-'ilm wa al-'ulama," 299, 340; Samir, "al-Azhar," 141; al-Tahtawi, "Baqa' hasan al-dhikr"; al-Tahtawi, *al-Qawl al-sadid*.
104. See Johansen, "Case of the Land Rent"; Judith Tucker, *In the House of the Law* (Berkeley: University of California Press, 1998), 11–17. Compare Binder, "Ideological Foundations of Egyptian-Arab Nationalism," 143–145.

Chapter 5
1. 'Ilish noted in his commentary on the *Mosul al-tulab* that his name is spelled with a kasra on the 'ain and the lam (Khayr al-Din al-Zirikli, *al-A'lam*, 9 vols. [Beirut: Dar al-'Ilm li al-Malayin, 1984], 6:20, n.1).
2. Scholch, *Egypt for the Egyptians!* 31. At the time, 800 piasters was average; 1,500 was more in keeping with his elevated rank.

3. Mubarak, *Khitat,* 4:41–43.
4. Ibid., 4:43.
5. Yusuf Sarkis Alyan, *Mu'jam al-matbu'at al-'arabiyya wa al-mu'arraba* (Beirut: Dar al-Sader, 1990), 2:1373–1374.
6. Quoted in 'Ilish, *Fath al-'ali,* 48–51.
7. Muhammad 'Abduh, "al-Azhar al-sharif wa al-gharad fi islah turuq al-ta'lim fihi," *al-Muqattam* (18 March1905), 1; 'Abduh, "Shaykh al-Azhar yukhalifu qanunahu," reprinted in 'Imara, *al-A'mal al-kamila,* 180–184.
8. Heyworth-Dunne, *History of Education,* 39, 399.
9. Wilfrid Scawen Blunt, *Secret History of the English Occupation of Egypt: Being a Personal Narrative of Events* (New York: Howard Fertig, 1967 [London: T. F. Unwin, 1907]), 126; Scholch, *Egypt for the Egyptians!* 189; Gilbert Delanoue, *Moralistes et politiques musulmans dans l'Egypte du XIXè siècle (1798–1882),* 2 vols. (Cairo: Institut Français d'Archéologie Orientale du Caire, 1982), 136.
10. Telegram from Luis Sabunji to Blunt, in Blunt, *Secret History,* 127; Delanoue, *Moralistes,* 137.
11. Telegram from Malet to Granville in Cole, *Colonialism and Revolution,* 241.
12. Delanoue, *Moralistes,* 137.
13. Ephraim and Inari Karsh, *Empires of the Sand: The Struggle for Mastery in the Middle East, 1789–1923* (Cambridge: Harvard University Press, 1999), 55.
14. Scholch, *Egypt for the Egyptians!* 211; Delanoue, *Moralistes,* 138; Karsh, *Empires,* 56.
15. Telegram from Sabunji to Blunt (11 June 1882), in *Secret History,* 247–248; fatwa quoted in Peters, "Lions of Qasr al-Nil Bridge," 216–217.
16. Blunt, *Secret History,* 290; Shafiq, *Mudhakkirati,* 1:178; Delanoue, *Moralistes,* 139; Cole, *Colonialism and Revolution,* 240, 246–247.
17. Scholch, *Egypt for the Egyptians!* 260, 291; Cole, *Colonialism and Revolution,* 240.
18. 'Urabi's petition and Muhammad al-'Abbasi's fatwa quoted in Peters, "Lions of Qasr al-Nil Bridge, 217–220; Scholch, *Egypt for the Egyptians!* 282.
19. Muhammad Rashid Rida, *al-Manar* 8 (19 July 1905), 390–392; reprinted in Rida, *Tarikh,* 1:133–134; reprinted in 'Imara, *al-A'mal al-kamila* (1980 ed.), 3:192–193. The rendition in *al-A'mal* misleads; 'Imara used the title "Hiwar ma' Shaykh 'Ilish" [An Interview with Shaykh 'Ilish], suggesting Rida's story was an objective report.
20. Rida, *al-Manar* 8 (19 July 1905): 391.
21. Ibid., Rida, *Tarikh,* 1:134.
22. 'Abduh, quoted in Rida, *Tarikh,* 1:102–103.
23. Sulayman Rashad Hanafi al-Zayyati, *Kanz al-jawhar fi tarikh al-Azhar* (Cairo: 1904), 167; Eccel, *Social Change,* 219; Rida, *Tarikh,* 1:134. Following Rida's account: Adams, *Islam and Modernism,* 42–43; Mahmudul Haq, *Muhammad 'Abduh: A Study of a Modern Thinker of Egypt* (Aligarh: Institute of Islamic Studies, 1970), 3–5, see also 10–11.
24. Rida, *al-Manar* 8 (19 July 1905), 93.
25. Berkey, *Transmission,* 37.
26. D. Gimaret, "Mu'tazila," *Encyclopedia of Islam,* 2nd ed. (CD ROM edition), 9 vols. (Leiden, Netherlands: Brill, 2001), 7:791–792; Malcolm H. Kerr, *Islam-*

ic Reform: The Political and Legal Theories of Muhammad 'Abduh and Rashid Rida (Berkeley: University of California Press, 1966), 58–60.

27. 'Ilish, *Fath al-'ali*, 51. His assertion was incorrect.

28. Rida, *al-Manar* 8 (19 July 1905): 390–392; Adams, *Islam and Modernism,* 43.

29. Keddie, *Sayyid Jamal al-Din "al-Afghani",* 119–124; Shafiq, *Mudhakkirati,* 1:109–110; al-Sa'idi, *Tarikh al-islah,* 38–39.

30. Eccel, *Social Change,* 84–85, citing Filib ibn Yusuf Gallad, *Qamus al-idara wa al-qada',* 6 vols. (Alexandria, Egypt: Matba'at al-Qamus, 1890–95), 4:1650.

31. Ahmad Hasan al-Zayyat, "al-Wad' al-lughawi wa haqq al-muhdathin fihi," *Wahi al-risala,* 1st ed., 4 vols. (Cairo: Matba'at al-Salah, 1950), 3:171; Pierre Cachia, *Taha Husayn* (London: Luzac & Company Ltd., 1956), 86.

32. 'Ilish, *Fath al-'ali,* 35–36.

33. Mubarak, *Khitat,* 4:42–43.

34. For discussion of the relationship between the ideas of Muhammad al-Sanusi, Shah Wali Allah, Uthman dan Fodio, and the Wahhabis, see Ahmad Dallal, "Origins and Objectives of Islamic Revivalist Thought, 1750–1850," *Journal of the American Oriental Society* 113.3 (1993): 341–359.

35. Dallal, "Origins and Objectives," 357–358. This excludes the Wahhabis, who operated within the realms of Hanbali fiqh.

36. Wael B. Hallaq, "A Prelude to Ottoman Reform: Ibn 'Abidin on Custom and Legal Change," 37–61, in eds. Israel Gershoni, et. al., *Histories of the Modern Middle East: New Directions* (Boulder, CO: Lynne Rienner, 2002); Johansen, "Case of the Land Rent," 32, 36, 42, 43).

37. Hallaq, *Islamic Legal Theories,* 125–126.

38. The *Fath al-'ali* was printed three times within two years, suggesting wide circulation for a legal manual (Nosseir, *al-Kutub allati nushirat fi Misr,* 2/1331–1333).

39. 'Ilish, *Fath al-'ali,* 89.

40. Ibid., 89–90.

41. Ibid., 90–93.

42. 'Umar Rida Kahhala, *Mu'jam al-mu'allifin,* vols. 9–10 bound together (Beirut: Dar al-Ihya' al-Turath al-'Arabi, n.d.), 12; Mubarak, *Khitat,* 4:42–43.

43. 'Ilish, *Fath al-'ali,* 92, citing Sidi 'Ali al-Khawas, and 93, citing 'Abd al-Wahhab al-Sha'rani, *al-Mizan al-Kubra.*

44. Ibid., 90.

45. Ibid., 95–96.

46. Ibid., 96. It has proven difficult for twentieth century reformers to derive new and logically consistent principles of legal methodology, with the possible exception of Fazlur Rahman and Muhammad Shahrur, whose ideas have so far proved unacceptable to the general public (Hallaq, "Crises of Modernity: Toward a New Theory of Law?" chap. in *Islamic Legal Theories,* 207–254).

47. 'Ilish, *Fath al-'ali,* 92.

48. Ibid., 90–91. See Fadel, "Adjudication," 254–261, for a discussion of the use of 'amal in the Maliki madhhab.

49. 'Ilish, *Fath al-'ali,* 91.

50. Ibid., 92; Hallaq, *Islamic Legal Theories,* 207–209. 'Ilish did not acknowledge situations in which ijma' failed.

51. 'Ilish, *Fath al-'ali*, 104.
52. Muhammad Fadel, "The Social Logic of Taqlid" and "Adjudication."
53. Hallaq, *Islamic Legal Theories*, 207–209.
54. 'Ilish, *Fath al-'ali*, 66.
55. Fadel, "Adjudication," vol. 2, passim.
56. Hourani, *History of the Arab Peoples*, 145–146.
57. Hallaq, *Islamic Legal Theories*, 161, 174, 202–204.
58. 'Ilish, *Fath al-'ali*, 67.
59. Ibid., 70. See also Johansen, "Case of the Land Rent," 32–36, in which an Ottoman mufti's choice to follow a particular opinion constitutes an action that is legally binding on judges and thus is not merely relevant to the petitioners but also is a decisive element in the continual evolution of Hanafi doctrine. See also Hallaq, *Islamic Legal Theories*,181.
60. 'Ilish, *Fath al-'ali*, 77.
61. Ibid., 68.
62. 'Abdullah Nadim, *al-Ustadh* 3 (6 September 1892): 61–63.
63. The results of any ijtihad, being inherently fallible, could not be definitively proven. It was generally held that only one ruling could be true (i. e., expressing God's intent), but that in the absence of certain knowledge as to which was true, laymen could legitimately follow any acceptably derived ruling from any madhhab (Hallaq, *Islamic Legal Theories*, 27, 28, 124, 156).
64. 'Ilish, *Fath al-'ali*, 71.
65. Hallaq, Islamic Legal Theories, 207–209; Fadel, "Adjudication," 212, 234, 236, 266–267, 353–357.
66. Mubarak, *Khitat*, 4:43.
67. Ibid., 4:43–44. No dates are listed for 'Ilish's retirement to the Husseini Mosque.
68. Sarkis, *Mu'jam al-matbu'at*, 1371; Kahhala, *Mu'jam al-mu'allifin*, 12; al-Zirikli, *al-A'lam*, 19–20; Blunt, *Secret History*, 126; Alexander Meyrick Broadley, *How We Defended Arabi and His Friends: A Story of Egypt and the Egyptians* (Cairo: Research and Publishing Arab Centre, 1980 [reprint of London: Chapman and Hall, Ltd., 1884]), 35, 60, 67, 68, 71–72, 101, 102, 108–109, 110, 111–112, 365, 369–370.

Chapter 6

1. Berkey, *Transmission*, 33.
2. Blunt, *Secret History*, 323–363.
3. Ayalon, *Press*, 45, 46, 51–52.
4. Al-Kumi, *al-Sihafa al-islamiyya*, 72–77.
5. "Al-Ta'lim," in *al-Jinan* (1 Nisan 1883): 201–202.
6. "Al-Ta'lim" in *al-Jinan* (15 Ayar 1883): 296–297; *al-Jinan* (1 Ab 1883): 464–465; B. Abu-Manneh, "Sultan Abdulhamid II and Shaikh Abulhuda Al-Sayyadi," *Middle Eastern Studies* 15, no. 2 (May 1979): 131–153; Amal Nadim Ghazal, "Beyond Modernity: Islamic Conservatism in the Late Ottoman Period" (M.A. Thesis, University of Alberta, Edmonton, 1998); Rudolph Peters, "Religious Attitudes towards Modernization in the Ottoman

Empire: A 19th Century Text on Steamships, Factories, and the Telegraph," *Die Welt des Islams* 26 (1986): 76–105.

7.   "Al-Madrasa al-sultaniyya, " in *al-Jinan* (18 Kanun I 1885): 643–644; "al-Azhar," *al-Waqt* (1883).

8.   Lord Cromer (Evelyn Baring, First Earl Cromer), *Modern Egypt*, 1st ed., 2 vols. (New York: Macmillan Co., c. 1908), 2:330–331.

9.   Decree of 16 March 1882, cited in Eccel, *Social Change*, 161, 198.

10. Lajnat Islah report, 5; Mahmud Abu al-'Uyun, *al-Jami' al-Azhar: nubdha fi tarikhihi* (Cairo: Matba'at al-Azhar, 1949), 85–88; Eccel, *Social Change*, 235. Compare Dodge, *Al-Azhar*, 132; Eccel, *Social Change*, 160.

11. Lajnat Islah report, 5. Possibly exaggerated.

12. Ibid., 6.

13. Ibid., 6–7.

14. Eccel, *Social Change*, 100–101.

15. Lajnat Islah report, 7.

16. 'Abd al-Mu'izz Khatab, *Shuyukh al-Azhar* (Cairo: Matabi'a li al-Ahram al-Tijariyya, n.d.), 27; Zaydan, *Mashahir al-sharq*, 174–175; Ahmad al-Shadhili, "al-Islam fi al-Azhar," *al-Islam* 8, no. 4 (June 1905): 77–78; Shaykh al-'Abbasi also resigned from the office of Grand Hanafi Mufti at that time and was replaced by Shaykh Muhammad al-Banna'. He returned to that office after 1888 and continued to serve as Grand Mufti until his death in 1897 (Shafiq, *Mudhakkirati*, vol. 2, bk. 1, 32).

17. 'Abd al-Gawad, *Taqwim Dar al-'Ulum* (Cairo: Dar al-Ma'arif, 1950 [1947]), 6, 11; Eccel, *Social Change*, 163.

18. Eccel, *Social Change*, 162–165.

19. See similar trends in the United States in James Findlay, "The Era of Multi-purpose Colleges in American Higher Education, 1850–1890," and Roger L. Geiger, "The Rise and Fall of Useful Knowledge: higher education for sciences, agriculture, and the mechanic arts 1850–1875," both in Roger L. Geiger, et al., eds., *The American College in the Nineteenth Century* (Nashville, TN: Vanderbilt Press, 2000). On Britain, see T. W. Heyck, *The Transformation of Intellectual Life in Victorian England* (New York: St. Martin's Press, 1982).

20. Cromer, *Modern Egypt*, 2:182.

21. Muhammad Bayram, fatwa cited by his son, the reformer Mustafa Bayram, in "Tarikh al-Azhar," an Arabic offprint of a paper presented at the thirteenth convention for Scholars of Eastern Languages, Hamburg, September 1902 (American University in Cairo Library), 27; and also in al-Sa'idi, *Tarikh al-islah*, 40. See *wajib kifa'i* in the letters of Maliki mufti Salim al-Bishri, in 'Abd al-Husayn Sharaf al-Din al-Musawi, *al-Muraja'at* (Beirut: Mu'assasat al-A'lami li al-Matbu'at, 1983), p. 278, letter 95; equivalent of *fard kifaya* in Hallaq, *Islamic Legal Theories*, 117, 122, 144.

22. Shams al-Din al-Inbabi, fatwa dated 1 Dhu al-Hijja 1305 [1888], in Muhammad Bayram, "Tarikh al-Azhar," 27; parts of the fatwa also quoted in al-Sa'idi, *Tarikh al-islah*, 40–41.

23. Al-Inbabi, in Bayram, "Tarikh al-Azhar," 27–28; compare al-Sa'idi, *Tarikh al-islah*, 41–42.

24. Muhammad Muhammad al-Banna', Mufti al-Diyar al-Misriyya, fatwa no. 171 (17 Dhu al-Hijja 1305 [1888]); cited in Bayram, "Tarikh al-Azhar," 29; also quoted in al-Sa'idi, *Tarikh al-islah*, 42. Muhammad al-Banna' refused to issue fatwas until he had consulted with al-'Abbasi, whom he regarded as rightful Grand Mufti (Zaydan, *Mashahir al-sharq*, 2:174); this may simply be polite academic etiquette. See Ahmed Munir-ud-Din, *Muslim Education and the Scholar's Social Status up to the 5th Century Muslim Era (11th Century Christian Era) in the Light of Ta'rikh Baghdad* (Zurich: Verlag der Islam, 1968), 214; Berkey, *Transmission*, 38).
25. Ahmed, *Muslim Education*, 59–72.
26. Afaf Lutfi al-Sayyid Marsot, *Egypt and Cromer: A Study in Anglo-Egyptian Relations* (London: Murray, 1968),96.
27. 'Ali Yusuf, "Tafaru'at al-'ulum wa hajatuha ila al-rabita, " *al-Adab* 3, no. 90 (21 September 1889): 333–334.
28. Yusuf, "Tafaru'at," 334.
29. Hallaq, *Islamic Legal Theories*, 15.
30. 'Ali Yusuf, "Ta'mim al-ta'lim," pt. 2, *al-Adab* 3, no. 92 (5 October 1889): 449.
31. 'Ali Yusuf, "Ta'mim al-ta'lim," pt. 1, *al-Adab* 3, no. 91 (28 September 1889): 341–342.
32. Yusuf, "Ta'mim al-ta'lim," pt. 2, 449.
33. Ibid.
34. 'Ali Yusuf, "Ta'mim al-ta'lim," pt. 3, *al-Adab* 3, no. 93 (12 October 1889): 357–358.
35. Full texts of some responses were printed in issue no. 94 of *al-Adab* 3, no longer extant.
36. 'Ali Yusuf, "Ta'mim al-ta'lim," pt. 6, *al-Adab* 3, no. 96 (22 November 1889): 485–487.
37. Ibid.
38. 'Abd al-Gawad, *Taqwim Dar al-'Ulum*, 14–18.
39. Examination Law of 19 January 1888, in Lajnat Islah report, 7–8, appendix p. 13–15.
40. 'Abduh quoted in Rida, *Tarikh*, 1:425–426; Dodge, *Al-Azhar*, 133; Crecelius, "The Ulama and the State," 215.
41. This budget was separate from the awqaf funds for the riwaqs, the jarayat (murattab[an] jari[an], the daily "ongoing distribution" of bread to students and 'ulama), and the muthamman al-ghilal (individual stipends based on the cash equivalents of a fixed amount of grain). Payment in wheat or the value of wheat helped prevent inflation and currency devaluation from reducing the real value of fixed stipends from awqaf. However, those funds, too, ran short of demand. By 1910, incoming students had to wait one or two years before being eligible for a place in a riwaq or a bread allotment (Eccel, *Social Change*, 123–124).
42. Dodge, *Al-Azhar*, 133; John Chalcraft, interview by author, Cairo, Egypt, 29 April 1998.
43. Eccel, *Social Change*, 171; 'Abd al-Gawad, *Taqwim Dar al-'Ulum*, 11; Eccel, *Social Change*, 163.
44. Dodge, *Al-Azhar*, 133–134.

45. Eccel lists registration in 1893 at 8,259 upper-level "Azhar" students and 2,192 katatib students, 10,451 total, suggesting steady levels since 1876 (10,780). Students in al-Azhar's katatib did not receive jarayat rations (Eccel, *Social Change*, 232).
46. 'Abdullah Nadim, "Al-'ulama wa al-ta'lim," *al-Ustadh* 26 (14 February 1893): 602–606, 610.
47. Ibid., 607–608.
48. Ibid., 609.
49. There were 10,450 students enrolled in 1893, and 187 teaching shaykhs (Eccel, *Social Change*, 232, 237). In practice, the more popular shaykhs could attract audiences of several hundred students.
50. Nadim, "Al-'ulama wa al-ta'lim," 609.
51. Ibid., 615 [pages 613–615 misprinted as 713–715]. I found no other evidence to suggest ijazat were no longer being given.
52. Ibid., 608, 613, 614.
53. Ibid., 608–609.
54. Ibid., 610, referring to the Examination Code of 19 January 1888; Eccel, *Social Change*, 160–161.
55. Nadim, "Al-'ulama wa al-ta'lim," 610–611.
56. Ibid., 612.
57. Ibid., 613–614, 616.
58. Ibid., 613, 614, 616.
59. Ibid., 613.
60. Ibid., 609.
61. Ibid., 613, 614, 616.
62. Ibid., 614.
63. Ibid., 612.
64. Ibid., 615.
65. Ibid., 610.
66. Ibid., 607, 609, 615. This directly contradicted the letter written to *al-Adab*, whose author had fretted that Azhari students would be so interested in new subjects that they would abandon legal studies.
67. Ibid., 614–616.
68. Ibid., 615, item 19.
69. Alfred Milner, Undersecretary, Ministry of Finance, quoted in John Marlowe, *Cromer in Egypt* (New York: Praeger Publishers, 1970), 154. See also Shafiq, *Mudhakkirati*, vol. 2, bk. 1, 185; Rida, *Tarikh*, 1:427; Peter Mansfield, *The British in Egypt* (New York: Holt, Rinehart and Winston, 1972), 159.
70. Shafiq, *Mudhakkirati*, vol. 2, bk. 1, 52–56. See also Marlowe, *Cromer in Egypt*, 156–162; Marsot, *Egypt and Cromer*, 98–103; Mansfield, *British in Egypt*, 150–159). 'Abbas did not entirely give up hope of overthrowing the British until the Entente Cordiale of 1904 deprived him of French support (Marsot, *Egypt and Cromer*, 136).
71. Al-Sa'idi, *Tarikh al-islah*, 39; Rida, *Tarikh*, 1:427.
72. Nadim, "al-'Ulama wa al-ta'lim," 616 [second of two consecutive pages marked as 616].

73. *Al-Mu'ayyad* (18 January 1893). According to al-Kumi (*al-Sihafa al-islamiyya*, 152) the original printing offered the article a much wider circulation than its later reprint in Nadim's *al-Ustadh*.
74. Marsot, *Egypt and Cromer,* 97.
75. Cromer, letter to Khedive 'Abbas, n.d., and Rosebery, letter to Cromer, 16 February 1893, quoted in 'Abbas Hilmi II, *Last Khedive of Egypt: Memoirs of Abbas Hilmi II,* trans. and ed. Amira Sonbol (Reading, UK: Ithaca Press, 1998), 79–80; on oaths, see 81–82, 83.
76. 'Abbas Hilmi II, *Last Khedive.* Page 181, n. 19, says that his archives at the University of Durham, UK, contain hundreds of reports on doings at al-Azhar.
77. Shafiq, *Mudhakkirati,* vol. 2, bk. 1, 185.
78. Ibid.
79. Shafiq, *Mudhakkirati,* vol. 2, bk. 1, 186.
80. Ibid.
81. Lajnat Islah report, 8–9, appendix pp. 16–19.
82. Shafiq, *Mudhakkirati,* vol. 2, bk. 1, 186 and footnote.
83. Ibid.
84. Salman, *A'mal majlis,* 1; Rida, *Tarikh,* 1:427; Shafiq, *Mudhakkirati,* vol. 2, bk. 1, 216; Ahmad al-Shadhili, *al-Islam* 2, no. 5 (24 June 1895): 120; and al-Shadhili, *al-Islam* 3, no. 3 (13 April 1896): 72. See also Eccel, *Social Change,* 169; Lajnat Islah report, 8.
85. Salman, *A'mal majlis,* 1–2; Eccel, *Social Change,* 169.
86. Madwi 'Abd al-Rahman al-Sinnari, "Al-Azhar al-ma'mur wa amani islahihi al-munawwi," *al-Mu'ayyad* 1471 (5 January 1895): 1.
87. Hasan Husni al-Tuwayrani, "Al-Azhar fi Misr," *al-Nil* 4, no. 430 (31 January 1895): 4.
88. Ibid., 4.
89. Ramadan, "Dawr al-awqaf."
90. For example, one of al-Azhar's waqf documents stipulated everything down to how many candles, ropes, and buckets could be purchased per year (see al-Maqrizi's summary of al-Hakim bi-Amr Allah's waqf charter, 1010 AD, in Ramadan, "Dawr al-awqaf," 37–38).
91. Al-Tuwayrani, "Al-Azhar fi Misr," 5, page 51.
92. For example, Ahmad Muhammad al-Alfi, *al-Islam* 1, no. 9 (11 October 1894): 176–181; and "Tatbiq al-zalazil 'ala muqtadi al-zaman," *al-Islam* 1, 158.
93. Muhammad Sulayman al-Safti, "al-Azhar," *al-Islam* 1, no. 12 (27 January 1895): 267–271.
94. Ibid., 268.
95. Ibid.
96. Ibid., 269.
97. Ibid., 269–270.
98. Ibid., 270.
99. Mohamed Abdulla 'Enan, *Tarikh al-Azhar* (Cairo: Lajnet al-Taalif Press, 1958).
100. Muhammad Hifni al-Mahdi, "Adab al-'ilm wa al-'ulama," *al-Islam* 2, no. 9 (20 October 1895): 206–207.
101. Ibid., 207.

102. Ibid., 208.
103. Christopher Bryant, *Positivism in Social Theory and Research* (New York: St. Martin's Press, 1985), 1–6.

Chapter 7

1.   Ramadan, "Dawr al-awqaf," 45; Salman, *A'mal majlis,* 106–107; Dodge, *Al-Azhar,* 127; Mubarak, *al-Khitat,* 4:27, 29.
2.   Salman, *A'mal majlis,* 16.
3.   Ahmad al-Shadhili al-Azhari, "Hadithat al-Azhar," *al-Islam* 2, no. 7 (22 August 1895): 166–167.
4.   "Al-Kulayra," *al-Muqtataf* 20, no. 6 (1 June 1896): 479.
5.   Shafiq, *Mudhakkirati,* vol. 2, bk. 1, 227–228. This account is brief and missing key details.
6.   Ahmad al-Shadhili, "Hadithat al-Azhar al-Sharif—in the name of God the Protector," *al-Islam* 3, no. 5 (12 June 1896): 101–121. This article claims its reported testimonies of participants and transcripts of hearings are verbatim.
7.   Al-Shadhili, "Hadithat al-Azhar al-Sharif," 101.
8.   *Al-Muqtataf* 20, no. 5 (1 May 1896): 329–336; *al-Muqtataf* 20, no. 6 (1 June 1896): 409–414.
9.   Khaled Fahmy, "Law, Medicine, and Society in Nineteenth-Century Egypt," *Égypte/Monde arabe* 1, no. 34 (1998): 15.
10. Al-Shadhili, "Hadithat al-Azhar al-Sharif," 101, 102, 118.
11. Fahmy, "Law, Medicine, and Society," 15.
12. Al-Shadhili, "Hadithat al-Azhar al-Sharif," 102, 108–110, 114–116, 119.
13. Ibid., 102, 110, 118–119.
14. Ibid., 117–119.
15. Ibid., 103, 110, 115–116. Shaykh Ahmad's eye-witnesses claimed that only one student had thrown "dirt and pebbles" at the deputy governor (103).
16. Ibid., 103, 116.
17. Ibid., 110–111.
18. Ibid., 104, 111, 116–117, 119.
19. Ibid., 104, 111, 112.
20. Ibid., 104–105, 111–112, 117; "Hadithat al-Azhar," *al-Muqtataf* 20, no. 7 (1 July 1896): 558.
21. Al-Shadhili, "Hadithat al-Azhar al-Sharif," 109, 117.
22. Fahmy, "Law, Medicine, and Society," 43–45.
23. Al-Shadhili, "Hadithat al-Azhar al-Sharif," 117.
24. Ibid., 119–120.
25. Ibid., 102–103.
26. Ibid., 103, 105, 107, 112, 113.
27. Shaykh Ahmad carefully noted the discrepancies between the stories the adjutant told to the deputy governor and Shaykh al-Azhar on the scene and the stories that he told at the hearing (ibid., 114–115, 119; compare 109–110). Witnesses thought the governor, not the British police chief, had given the orders to break down the mosque's gate and start firing (112), and that the chief prosecutor had made a note to the effect that the police chief could not "make a frank statement" about the incident (112).

28. Ibid., 106.
29. Ibid., 104.
30. Ibid., 120.
31. Ibid., 120–121.
32. Opposition to reformist Shaykh al-Azhars went beyond madhhab rivalries. See al-Shadhili, "al-Islam," 77–78.
33. Ahmad al-Shadhili, "al-Jami' al-Azhar," al-Islam 2, no. 5 (24 June 1895): 116–117. Petition: Sukarta no. 5134, dated 29 Dhi al-Hijja 1312 [23 June1895].
34. Compare Salman, A'mal majlis, 3–5.
35. Al-Kumi, al-Sihafa al-islamiyya, 85.
36. Al-Shadhili, "Hadithat al-Azhar al-Sharif," 105.
37. "Hadithat al-Azhar," 558.
38. "Al-Kulayra," al-Muqtataf 20, no. 7 (1 July 1896): 558.
39. "Hadithat al-Azhar," 558–559.
40. Al-Shadhili, "Hadithat al-Azhar al-Sharif," 108; Eccel, Social Change, 173, citing al-Zayyati, Kanz, 194–196.
41. Ahmad al-Shadhili, "Mahakimat [sic] talabat al-shawwam," al-Islam 3, no. 5 (12 June 1896): 124. The defense argued lack of evidence.
42. Ahmad al-Shadhili, "Qadiat talaba al-shawwam," al-Islam 3, no. 7 (10 August 1896): 171.
43. Examination Codes of 1872, 1885, 1888, 1895; Registration Code of 1885.
44. Codes of 16 Shawwal 1312 and 6 Muharram 1313, in Salman, A'mal majlis, 10–11. These schools had been subordinated to al-Azhar administration in 1894.
45. Lajnat Islah report, 13–14; Salman, A'mal majlis, 15.
46. "Qanun al-Jami' al-Azhar," al-Islam 3, no. 7 (10 August 1896): 171–172.
47. Salman, A'mal majlis, 14; Lajnat Islah report, 14.
48. Ibid.
49. Lajnat Islah report, 14; Eccel, Social Change, 174–175. Roughly equivalent to riwaya and diraya (Berkey, Transmission, 30).
50. Lajnat Islah report, 15; Salman, A'mal majlis, 13.
51. Salman, A'mal majlis, 41. This committee met for the first time on 13 Rajab 1316/27 November 1898, but other members of the council also reported that the council's intent had been to work with the 'ulama ('Abduh, in Rida, Tarikh, 1:427, 428–429). Rida spoke of this committee in regard to the selection of texts, but it is clear that the text selection committee was a subcommittee of the larger body of 'ulama. This is an important distinction because 'Abduh and Salman complained later that Shaykh Salim al-Bishri had allowed the text selection subcommittee to lapse—which does not necessarily mean that he allowed the committee of 'ulama to lapse. There were no new reform "codes" (qawanin) relating to al-Azhar between 1896 and 1907. Reform proceeded by council decrees (iqrar) that implemented provisions of the 1896 Code.
52. "Qanun sarf al-murattabat bi al-jami' al-Azhar" (29 June 1896), in Lajnat Islah report, 9–12. Tradesmen and artisans had a similar tradition.

53. Salman, *A'mal majlis,* 20, 23. It is unclear whether this was to be a one-time or annual gift.
54. Azhar Administrative Council (AAC) decree (24 January 1897), articles 1–14, in "Nizamat al-Azhar al-jadidah," *al-Islam* 4, no. 3 (3 April 1897): 92–94; see brief summaries in Salman, *A'mal majlis,* 24; and Eccel, *Social Change,* 175, citing Gallad, *Qamus al-idara,* 82–88.
55. AAC decree (24 Sha'ban 1314), arts. 1–3, in "Nizamat al-Azhar al-jadida," 94–95. Article 4 stated that where the rules of murattab law and waqf stipulations forbade their being cut off, other punishments would be applied (95). The council issued a similar decree in March 1897: Students and professors who returned tardily from holidays would suffer suspension of their daily benefits for a number of days equivalent to their absence (Salman, *A'mal majlis,* 33).
56. AAC decree (1 February 1897), arts. 1–8, in "Nizamat al-Azhar al-jadida," 95–96.
57. This accords with medieval standards for student-teacher relationships (Berkey, *Transmission,* 34–39).
58. AAC decree (29 Sha'ban 1314), arts. 9–16, in "Nizamat al-Azhar al-jadida," 96–97; Salman, *A'mal majlis,* 33–35; Eccel, *Social Change,* 175, citing Gallad, *Qamus al-idara,* 82–88.
59. Salman, *A'mal majlis,* 35–36; Eccel, *Social Change,* 155.
60. Salman, *A'mal majlis,* 20, 27–32; Dodge, *Al-Azhar,* 128, 136, 168–169.
61. Salman, *A'mal majlis,* 18–23; Eccel, *Social Change,* 179–180.
62. Salman, *A'mal majlis,* 24–25.
63. Ibid., 27.
64. Ibid., 26–27.
65. See Salman, *A'mal majlis,* 17–18, 32–33; Eccel, *Social Change,* 175–176, citing Gallad, *Qamus al-idara,* 82–88.
66. Salman, *A'mal majlis,* 19.
67. Ibid., 26–27.
68. Ahmad al-Shadhili, "Qanun al-Jami' al-Azhar," serialized in *al-Islam* 3, no. 7 (10 August 1896): 171–172; no. 8 (9 September 1896): 195; no. 9 (17 October 1896): 219–220; and no. 6 (12 July 1896): 146; and "Nizamat al-Azhar al-jadida," 92–99.
69. Shaykh Taha al-Khalili, "Maziat al-din al-islami fi al-'alam al-tamaddun," *al-Islam* 4, no. 7 (2 August 1897): 216–222.
70. Muhammad 'Abd al-Halim Abu al-Fadl, "al-Khutaba' wa al-zaman," *al-Islam* 3, no. 12 (3 January 1897): 287–288.
71. Rashid Rida, *al-Manar* 1, no. 1 (1898) (vol. 1, 2nd ed.) (American University in Cairo Library Periodicals Collection), 9–14.
72. Salman, *A'mal majlis,* 15; Rida, *Tarikh,* 1:429.

Chapter 8

1. Bhabha, "Of Mimicry and Man," in *Location of Culture,* 126; Cromer, despatch no. 105 (6 June 1899), Foreign Office 78/5023; cited in Kedourie, *Afghani and 'Abduh,* 38; Cromer, *Modern Egypt,* 2:182.

2. *Al-Manar* 8 (1905): 402–404; Blunt, *Secret History,* 491; Kedourie, *Afghani and 'Abduh,* 20–23.

3. Sultan Abdulhamid had kept al-Afghani under house arrest until al-Afghani died in 1897. In 1883, the Sultan had even exiled 'Abduh temporarily from Syria for encouraging the Rev. Isaac Taylor in his attempt to unify the English reformed church and Islam (Wilfrid Scawen Blunt, *My Diaries: Being a Personal Narrative of Events 1888–1914.* 2 vols. [New York: Alfred A. Knopf, 1921], 2:94, entry for 3 April 1904).

4. Rida reported that someone saw Suleyman 'Abaza with 'Abduh and asked, "Who is this with whom you speak so courteously? Do you not know that our Effendi [Khedive Tawfiq] is angry with him?" Suleyman 'Abaza replied that 'Abduh was a friend revered for his knowledge and was not someone he would abandon out of political fears. Rida, *Tarikh,* 1:417, 418–419; 'Abbas Hilmi II, *Last Khedive,* 91.

5. Shakib Arslan's account of 'Abduh's life in Syria, quoted in Rida, *Tarikh,* 1:411.

6. Rida, *Tarikh,* 1:393–411; Mahmud Abu Riyya, introduction to Muhammad 'Abduh, *Risalat al-tawhid,* ed. Mahmud Abu Riyya (Cairo: Dar al-Ma'arif, n.d. [reprint of 1315 H edition]), 11–14.

7. Quoted in *al-Manar* 4 (7 March 1901): 54.

8. Muhammad 'Abduh, "Mashru' islah al-tarbia fi Misr" [Project for the Reform of Education in Egypt], reprinted in 'Imara, *al-A'mal al-kamila,* 3:106–122.

9. Adams, *Islam and Modernism,* 34; Marshall G. S. Hodgson, *Venture of Islam,* 3 vols. (Chicago: University of Chicago Press, 1974), 3:275; Kerr, *Islamic Reform,* 143.

10. Rida, *Tarikh,* 1: 1031, 1034. Some claim 'Abduh did not learn French until age 40, citing one sentence in Rida's *Tarikh,* which says only that 'Abduh learned French in sinn al-kuhula, middle age. But 'Abduh translated *On Education* before he turned forty in 1889, in order to improve his command of French.

11. Herbert Spencer, *On Education* (Cambridge: Cambridge University Press, 1932 [1854–1859]), 23, 28.

12. Rida, *Tarikh,* 2:513, 3:182; Hodgson, *Venture of Islam,* 3:275; 'Abduh, letter to Leo Tolstoy, in Haq, *Muhammad 'Abduh,* 13; Nadav Safran, *Egypt in Search of Political Community* (Cambridge, MA: Harvard University Press, 1961), 73–74.

13. Spencer, *On Education,* first essay; 'Abduh, "Mashru' islah al-tarbia fi misr," in 'Imara, *al-A'mal al-kamila* (1993 edition), 106–138).

14. 'Abduh, in 'Imara, *al-A'mal al-kamila* (1993 edition), , 3:110.

15. Ibid., 3:112.

16. Ibid., 3:118–120.

17. Ibid., 3:116–117.

18. Ibid., 3:123–125.

19. Eccel, *Social Change,* 163, 169–170, 177.

20. Kerr, *Islamic Reform,* 109.

21. 'Abduh, *Risalat al-tawhid,* 183–184. A footnote says that the Protestant faction that approximated Islam was "the sect of the Unitarians, most of whom are among the English and the Americans" (184 n.1).

22. 'Abduh, *Risalat al-tawhid*, 154.

23. Ibid., 155.

24. "Taraqa al-adyan bi taraqa al-insan" [Advancement of Religions with the Advancement of Humanity], chap. in 'Abduh, *Risalat al-tawhid*, 160–172.

25. 'Abduh, *Risalat al-tawhid*, 36–37.

26. Ibid., 56–57; D. Gimaret, "Mu'tazila," in *Encyclopedia of Islam*, 7:783a; compare Kedourie, *Afghani and 'Abduh*, 13–14. See also Baber Johansen, "Introduction," in *Contingency in a Sacred Law: Legal and Ethical Norms in the Muslim Fiqh* (Leiden, Netherlands: E. J. Brill, 1999).

27. Muhammad Rashid Rida, "Sajaya al-'ulama," *al-Manar* 1, no. 25 (6 September 1898); 465.

28. "Iqtirah fi al-islah al-islami," *al-Manar* 3, no. 3 (22 March 1900), 67.

29. Muhammad Rashid Rida, "Halat al-jara'id al-misriyya * wa al-ghamiza bi al-shaykh Muhammad 'Abduh," *al-Manar* 1, no. 18 (n.d.[July 1898]): 339–341; Rida, *Tarikh*, 1:699. The owner of this press, one Shaykh Muhammad al-Shirbitli, claimed that he had been told this by Shaykh Sulayman 'Abd, a well-known al-Azhar shaykh and friend of 'Abduh. Shaykh Sulayman 'Abd denied this under oath, but his relationship with 'Abduh became "tepid." Al-Shirbitli was tried and convicted of libel. *Al-Nahj al-qawim* is to the best of my knowledge no longer extant.

30. Shafiq, *Mudhakkirati*, 2:279–280; Kedourie, *Afghani and 'Abduh*, 37–38, citing Cromer's despatches no. 95 (18 May 1899) and no. 108 (13 June 1899), Foreign Office 78/5023.

31. Rida, *Tarikh*, 1:576–578; 'Abduh and Khedive 'Abbas Hilmi II, in 'Imara, *al-A'mal al-kamila* (1993 editon), 2:293.

32. 'Abbas Hilmi II, *Last Khedive*, 77–89; Shafiq, *Mudhakkirati*, 2:279–280; Rida, *Tarikh*, 1:578; Cromer, despatch no. 105 (6 June 1899, Foreign Office 78/5023; cited in Kedourie, *Afghani and 'Abduh*, 38.

33. 'Abbas Hilmi II, *Last Khedive*, 91.

34. Muhammad Rashid Rida, "Al-Muhawira al-tasi'a bayna al-muslih wa al-muqallid—al-taqlid wa al-talfiq wa al-ijma'," *al-Manar* 4, no. 10 (17 July 1901): esp. 363–367.

35. Sultan Abdulhamid II had since the 1880s been encouraging conversion to the Hanafi madhhab as a means of combating sectarian fragmentation of the Ottoman Muslim community (Selim Deringil, "Invention of Tradition as Public Image in the Late Ottoman Empire, 1808–1908," *Comparative Studies in Society and History* 35, no. 1 [January 1993]: 14–21).

36. Cromer, despatch no. 105 (6 June 1899), Foreign Office 78/5023; cited in Kedourie, *Afghani and 'Abduh*, 38.

37. Muhammad Rashid Rida, "al-Muhawirat bayna al-muslih wa al-muqallid: al-muhawira al-ula fi halat al-muslimin al-'ama" [Conversations between the Reformer and the Muqallid: the First Conversation on the General State of the Muslims], *al-Manar* 3, no. 28 (7 December 1900): 635–636.

38. Muhammad Rashid Rida, "al-Muhawirat bayna al-muslih wa al-muqallid: al-muhawira al-thaniyya," *al-Manar* 3, no. 29 (23 December 1900): 677; Rida, "al-Muhawirat bayna al-muslih wa al-muqallid: al-muhawira al-rabi'a," *al-Manar* 3, no. 32 (6 February 1901): 895, 897, 903; Rida, "al-Muhawira

al-khamisa . . . al-jafr wa al-zayirja," *al-Manar* 4, (7 March 1901): 53, 54; Rida, "al-Muhawira al-sadisa . . . al-ijtihad wa al-taqlid," *al-Manar* 4, no. 5 (5 May 1901): 165–169; Rida, "al-Muhawira al-sabi'a . . . al-ijtihad wa al-wihda al-islamiyya," *al-Manar,* 4 (19 May 1901): 206, 208, 215–216; Rida, "al-Muhawira al-tasi'a . . . al-taqlid wa al-talfiq wa al-ijma'," *al-Manar* 4, no. 10 (17 July 1901): 362.

39. Rida, "al-Muhawira al-sadisa," 166–167.
40. Amal Ghazal, "Sufism, Ijtihad, and Modernity: Yusuf al-Nabhani in the Age of Sultan Abd al-Hamid II," paper presented at the Middle East Studies Association, 5 December 1998. Al-Nabhani would have been serving at this time as a qadi in Beirut. He was known as a member of Sultan Abdulhamid's Sufi cadre and after 1905 as a vehement opponent of ijtihad and 'Abduh's *salafi* reform movement (David Dean Commins, *Islamic Reform: Politics and Social Change in Late Ottoman Syria* [London: Oxford University Press, 1990], 116–118).
41. Rida, "al-Muhawira al-tasi'a," 368–369.
42. See also Muhammad Rashid Rida, "al-Muhawira al-thamina . . . al-ijtihad wa al-wihda al-islamiyya," pt. 2, *al-Manar* 4, no. 8 (18 June 1901): 282–285.
43. Rida, "al-Muhawira al-tasi'a," 368.
44. Rida, "al-Muhawira al-sadisa," 169; on pp. 161–162 the reformer accused the Imams of "adding" to religion.
45. Ibid., 169, 212, 215.
46. Rida, "al-Muhawira al-tasi'a," 369–370.
47. Rida, "al-Muhawira al-sabi'a, 212–213.
48. Rida, "al-Muhawira al-tasi'a," 370.
49. *National Bank of Egypt, 1898–1948* (Cairo: privately circulated, 1948), 17–18 and foreword; Eric Davis, *Challenging Colonialism: Bank Misr and Egyptian Industrialization, 1920–1941* (Princeton, NJ: Princeton University Press, 1983), 72.
50. Qur'an 2:275–280, 3:130, 4:159–160, 30:39; Abdullah Saeed, *Islamic Banking and Interest: A Study of the Prohibition of Riba and Its Contemporary Interpretation* (Leiden, Netherlands: E. J. Brill, 1996), 1–2 and chapter two.
51. Muhammad 'Abduh, *al-Manar* 9 (1906): 332. Rida claimed 'Abduh was the first to exclude al-qard bi-fa'ida (deposit with interest) from the prohibition of riba' but "only in his private conversations" (Badawi, *Reformers of Egypt,* 223).
52. Murat Çizakça, *A Comparative Evolution of Business Partnerships: The Islamic World and Europe, with Specific Reference to the Ottoman Archives* (Leiden, Netherlands: E.J. Brill, 1996), 4–9, 66–85, 186–187.
53. Muhammad 'Abduh, fatwa no. 436, "Sharikat mudaraba," June 1901; in *al-Fatawa al-islamiyya min dar al-ifta' al-Misriyya,* vol. 3 (Cairo: Wizarat al-Awqaf, 1981), 879–885.
54. Çizakça, *Business Partnerships,* 4, 194; Saeed, *Islamic Banking,* 51–62.
55. Chibli Mallat, "The Debate on Riba and Interest in Twentieth Century Jurisprudence," in *Islamic Law and Finance* (London: Graham & Trotman, 1988), 74.
56. 'Abbas Hilmi II, *Last Khedive,* 252.

57. Muhammad Tawfiq, "Darwish wi abu hashish wi ghayr keda ma fish," *Humarat monyati* 3, no. 32 (8 January 1901): 497–502. Tawfiq styled himself "al-Azhari" in this issue.
58. Tawfiq, "Darwish wi abu hashish," 502–503.
59. Muhammad Tawfiq, "Fa-inna al-sultan Murad Khan," *Humarat monyati* 4, no. 10 (28 July 1901):145–152.
60. Tawfiq, "Darwish wi abu hashish," 504–505.
61. Mallat, "Debate on Riba," 72. Writing decades later and with benefit of hindsight, Khedive 'Abbas said he opposed 'Abduh's legitimation of interest from the beginning; it was Cromer's fault the bank scheme failed, for Cromer did not realize peasants would not want to exchange physical currency for a receipt promising them future gains on their investments ('Abbas Hilmi II, *Last Khedive*, 252–253).
62. Muhammad Tawfiq,"Wa hadha al-ustadh al-'allama al-shaykh Muhammad 'Abduh mufti al-diyar al-Misriyya," *Humarat monyati* 4, no. 10 (28 July 1901): 142–144.
63. Shafiq, *Mudhakkirati*, 2:378. The Yildiz palace was the usual guesthouse for visiting dignitaries from North Africa (Abu-Manneh, "Sultan Abdulhamid II," 139).
64. Shafiq, *Mudhakkirati*, 2:378–380.
65. Al-Kumi, *al-Sihafa al-islamiyya*, 62, 65–66; M. Sukru Hanioglu, *The Young Turks in Opposition* (London: Oxford University Press, 1995), 68; Ibrahim al-Muwailihi, *Ma hunalika min asrar balat al-sultan 'Abd al-Hamid* (Cairo: al-Markaz al-'Arabi li al-I'lam wa al-Nashr,1985), 84; al-Muwailihi, "Mustahsan ghayr lazim," *Misbah al-sharq* no. 79 (2 November 1899): 1–2; al-Muwailihi, "Jihad al-aqlam," *Misbah al-sharq* (29 April 1900); 'Abduh's *Radd 'ala Hanoteaux* was published at the same time.
66. Telegraph no. 22, from Abdulhamid to emissary in Egypt, 22 June 1882; quoted in Deringil, "Ottoman Response," 13; Blunt, *My Diaries*, 1:99. See also Engin D. Akarli, "Abdulhamid II's Attempts to Integrate Arabs into the Ottoman System," in *Palestine in the Late Ottoman Period*, ed. David Kushner (Leiden, Netherlands: E.J. Brill, 1986), 76–78.
67. Selim Deringil, "Legitimacy Structures in the Ottoman State: The Reign of Abdulhamid II (1876–1909)," *International Journal of Middle East Studies* 23 (1991): 346–349, citing documents in the Yildiz palace collection.
68. Deringil, "Invention of Tradition," 13.
69. Ibrahim al-Muwailihi, "al-Muqattam wa da'wa al-Nasraniya fi Misr," *al-Mu'ayyad* (7 April 1904).
70. Ibrahim l-Muwailihi, "Al-Sirdar wa al-Azhar," *Misbah al-sharq* 2, no. 57 (1 June 1899): 3; al-Kumi, *al-Sihafa al-islamiyya*, 148; compare al-Muwailihi, "al-'Ilm fi al-Islam," in *Misbah al-sharq* 4, no. 99 (6 April 1900): 1–3; al-Muwailihi, "Tada'ul al-fada'il," *Misbah al-sharq* 4, no. 163 (19 July 1901): 1 and "local news," 3; as well as sections in each issue on "dar al-khilafa"; idem, "Sirr al-taqaddum al-inglizi," *Misbah al-sharq* 2, no. 60 (22 June 1899): 3.
71. Abu al-Huda al-Sayyadi, *Da'i al-rashad li sabil al-ittihad wa al-inqiyad* [A Sensible Call to Unity and Obedience] (Istanbul: al-Matba'a al-Sultaniyya, c. 1880). See Abu-Manneh, "Sultan Abdulhamid II," 133–148; Commins,

Islamic Reform, 55, 105, 108; Hanioglu, *Young Turks in Opposition,* 50, 52, 55–56, 252–253 n.306.

72. Shafiq, *Mudhakkirati,* 2:382; Hanioglu, *Young Turks in Opposition,* 126–138, 145–155. It would be difficult to prove definitively that 'Abduh was involved with the Young Turks, since the pamphlets may not have been known to the central Young Turk organization, the Committee of Union and Progress (Hanioglu, *Young Turks in Opposition,* 4, 17).

73. Blunt, *My Diaries,* 2:12, entry for 24 October 1901; 2:36 and 94, entries for 19 December 1902 and 3 April 1904. 'Abduh tended to put on whatever face his audience would most appreciate, so it is hard to tell if 'Abduh leant towards Arab Young Turkism or Pan-Islamism. Blunt was religiously agnostic at best and sometimes wondered if Cromer was correct in judging 'Abduh agnostic (97, 105, 107, 111, 169, and esp. 217).

74. 'Izzat Bey was from Aleppo, like Shaykh Abu al-Huda, but worked to curb the latter's influence with the sultan. Shafiq, *Mudhakkirati,* 2:382; Akarli, "Abdulhamid II's Attempts to Integrate Arabs," 78; Akarli, "Ebul Huda," in *Unluler Ansiklopedisi* (Istanbul: Yurt, 1983).

75. Petition to Sultan 'Abdulhamid II for permission to leave the country, signed "Mufti al-diyar al-Misriyya, Muhammad 'Abduh, 31 July 1901—13 Rabi' II 1319," in Shafiq, *Mudhakkirati,* 2:379–381.

76. Muhammad Tawfiq, "Tawfiq wi Siddiq wi-ifrah wi-ta'liq wi rabbina yihanniku wi-yakfiku sharr id-diq," *Humarat monyati* 4, no. 13 (3 October 1901): 193–195.

77. Tawfiq, "Tawfiq wi Siddiq," 195.

78. Hallaq, *Islamic Legal Theories,* 118.

79. Tawfiq, "Tawfiq wi Siddiq," 197–198.

80. Ibid., 199–201.

81. Ibrahim al-Muwailihi, "al-Im'an fi al-tafarnuj," *Misbah al-sharq* 4, no. 174 (4 October 1901): 3. Note al-Afghani's influence on al-Muwailihi's Qur'anic definition of taqlid.

82. Muhammad Tawfiq, *Humarat monyati* 4, no. 18 (1 March 1902): 273.

83. Blunt, *My Diaries,* 2:40–41, entry for 8 February 1903.

84. Muhammad Tawfiq, "Fasl[un] fi tafsir kalam shaykhat al-hamir wa al-umdat fi al-bir wa al 'uhda 'a-ar-rawi," *Humarat monyati* 4, no. 18 (1 March 1902): 278–279.

85. Tawfiq, "Mas'alat al-Humara," 13; Tawfiq, "Ada mahdar tahqiq hukia 'an Tawfiq," *Humarat monyati* 5, no. 2 (14 April 1902), 20; Muhammad al-Hifni al-Mahdi, "Adab al-'ilm wa al-'ulama," 206–208.

86. Blunt, *My Diaries,* 2:12, 173; Tawfiq, "Mas'alat al-Humara,"15–16; Tawfiq, "Ada mahdar tahqiq," 28.

87. Muhammad Tawfiq, "Hakadha hal al-dunia," *Humarat monyati* 5, no. 9 (9 March 1903): 131.

88. Tawfiq, "Mas'alat al-Humara," 1–13.

89. Tawfiq, "Ada mahdar tahqiq," 20–22.

90. Ibid., 18.

91. Tawfiq, "Mas'alat al-Humara," 15.

92. Tawfiq, "Fasl[un] fi tafsir," 279.

93. Tawfiq, "Ada mahdar tahqiq," 17; Tawfiq, "Ihna mish fi keda," *Humarat monyati* 5, no. 3 (9 May 1902): 33–48. No new issues appeared until December.

94. Tawfiq, "Mas'alat al-Humara," 2–3, 8. The titles mentioned were like those used for gossip magazines, but no journals by these names existed at that time. A friend of Tawfiq actually did found a journal called *al-Arnab* in 1904, of which one issue is still extant: *Al-Arnab* 1, no. 8 (18 August 1904), Dar al-Kutub, zakiyya 4548.

95. Tawfiq, "Fa-inna al-sultan Murad Khan," 145–152; Tawfiq, "'Ul-li bi-llahi 'alayka ya amir al-mu'minin. . .," *Humarat monyati* 4, no. 9 (8 July 1901): 129–137, esp. 133.

96. Muhammad Tawfiq, "Sharikat al-jara'id al-Misriyya," *Humarat monyati* 4, no. 13 (3 October 1901): 208. Tawfiq shared some points with the Young Turks' Egyptian Islamist branch, which 'ulama dominated in its early phases. Tawfiq's hatred for Britain does not accord with Cromer's toleration of the Young Turks, but by 1901–1902, the Cairo branch was in turmoil and no cohesive point of view bound its members. Tawfiq later worked with anti-imperialist nationalist Mustafa Kamil, who in 1902 condemned the Young Turks as "agents of foreign powers" (Tawfiq, *al-Nusuh* [Cairo: 20 October–22 December 1892], Dar al-Kutub, dawriyyat no. 1000; and Hanioglu, *Young Turks in Opposition*, 36–37, 52, 81, 99, 101, 103–104, 119, 164, 199, 352 n.255).

97. Shafiq, *Mudhakkirati*, 2:411–413; Blunt, *My Diaries*, 2:15, 2:35; compare Marsot, *Egypt and Cromer*, 147; Lord Cromer (Evelyn Baring, First Earl Cromer), *Abbas II* (London: Macmillan Co., 1915), 77–79; 'Abbas Hilmi II, *Last Khedive*, 91.

98. Shafiq, *Mudhakkirati*, 2:279.

99. Ibid., 2:413–414.

100. Rida, *Tarikh*, 1:572–573; Blunt, *My Diaries*, 2:77, 78–79, entries for 12 November and 2 December 1903.

101. Rida, *Tarikh*, 1:563; Nasr al-Din Zaghlul and Darwish Mustafa, *al-Zahir* (Cairo: 1903–1942), Dar al-Kutub, dawriyyat 458.

102. Muhammad 'Abduh, fatwa no. 625, "Labs al-baranit wa dhabihat ahl al-kitab, wa salat al-shafi'i khalf al-hanafi," 25 December 1903, in *al-Fatawa al-islamiyya min dar al-ifta' al-Misriyya*, vol. 4 (Cairo: Wizarat al-Awqaf, 1981), 1298–1299.

103. "Forbidden to you are carrion, blood, the flesh of swine, and that on which has been invoked the name of other than God; that which has been killed by strangling, or by a violent blow, or by a fall, or by being gored to death, that which has been eaten by a wild animal, unless you are able to slaughter it in time, that which has been sacrificed to idols, and that which has been divided by raffling [i.e., used in gambling]" (Qur'an 5:3).

104. Charles Adams, "Muhammad 'Abduh and the Transvaal Fatwa," in *MacDonald Presentation Volume*, ed. W. G. Shellabear (NY: Books for Libraries, 1968 [Princeton, 1933]), 14–27.

105. Muhammad Abu Shadi, "Ra'i Mufti al-diyar al-misriyya fi labs al-quba'a wa akl al-lahm al-ghayr al-madhki wa salat al-shafi'iyya khalf al-hanafiyya," *al-Zahir* 9, no. 38 (29 December 1903): 1. Includes text of petition and fatwa.

106. Muhammad Tawfiq, "Ma hiyya al-jara'id wa ma hiyya wazifatiha fi 'alam al-'umran," *Humarat monyati* 5, no. 13 (31 December 1903): 195; see also Taw-fiq, "Aada taratish kalam (bi 'awdat al-ayyam) ya ummat al-Islam: ma tawah-hiduhu ya ustazna!" *Humarat monyati* (31 December 1903), 193–195.

107. Shafiq, *Mudhakkirati*, vol. 2, bk. 2, 34–41; *al-Mu'ayyad* no. 4155 (7 January 1904): 4.

108. Rida, *Tarikh*, 1:699.

109. 'Abbas Hilmi II, *Last Khedive*, 125–126; the khedive offered more tenuous support for the Nationalist Party after it was officially constituted in October 1907 and says that he preferred the more moderate views of 'Ali Yusuf (131–141).

110. 'Abd al-Majid Kamil, *al-Babaghallo al-Misri* 1, no. 1 (8 January 1904): 1. See also Indira Gesink, "Nationalist Imagery in Egypt's Tabloid Presses: A Draw-ing from the Egyptian Papagallo," *Modern Middle East Sourcebook*, eds. Cam-ron M. Amin, Benjamin C. Fortna, and Elizabeth B. Frierson (London: Oxford University Press, 2003).

111. 'Abd al-Majid Kamil, "Al-Mister Muhammad 'Abduh, Mufti al-diyar al-Misriyya," *al-Babaghallo al-Misri* 1, no. 2 (12 January 1904): 4–5.

112. Blunt, *My Diaries*, 2:66–67; eulogy by Harold Spender, *Daily Chronicle* (31 July 1905); Rida, *Tarikh*, 3:182.

113. Muhammad Tawfiq, *Humarat monyati* 4, no. 13 (3 October 1901): 203–208, referred to *al-Muqtataf* as "the Masonic Alexandrian paper" or "the infidel paper."

114. "Al-Faylasuf Herbert Spencer," *al-Muqtataf* 29, no. 1 (1 January 1904): 1–8, and subsequent issues, esp. "Ra'y Spencer fi ta'lim" [Spencer's Opinion on Education], no. 4 (1 April 1904): 289–295.

115. Muhammad Abu Shadi, "Ra'i Mufti," 1; Rida, *Tarikh*, 1:699.

116. Muhammad Abu Shadi, "Hukm Allah fi ra'i al-Mufti" *al-Zahir* 9, no. 41 (2 January 1904): 1; Abu Shadi, "Hukm Allah fi fatwa al-Mufti, part 3, rabbuna Allah la ghayruhu," *al-Zahir* 9, no. 45 (6 January 1904): 1.

117. Muhammad Abu Shadi, "Hukm Allah fi ra'i al-Mufti," part 2, *al-Zahir* 9, no. 42 (3 January 1904): 1; anonymous, "A-la yakhjalu al-muhawwasun," *al-Zahir* 9, no. 45 (6 January 1904): 3. See also Mustafa Kamil, "Mas'alat al-ifta'," *al-Liwa'* no. 1307 (14 January1904): 2; and Muhammad Rashid Rida, "Ta'yid al-fatwa wa haqiqatuha wa ma bihi al-ifta'," and Rida, "Qawl fi ijtihad al-mufti wa taqlidihi, " *al-Manar* (4 January 1904): 784, 785–786.

118. Abu Shadi, *al-Zahir* no. 41, 1; see also *al-Zahir* no. 42, 1.

119. Abu Shadi, *al-Zahir* no. 42, 1.

120. Abu Shadi, *al-Zahir* no. 45, 1; Abu Shadi, "Rabbuna Allah la ghayruhu. Mas'alat al-fatwa, part 4," *al-Zahir* 9, no. 46 (7 January 1904): 1.

121. "A-la yakhjalu al-muhawwasun," *al-Zahir* no. 45, 3.

122. Abu Shadi, *al-Zahir* no. 45, 1.

123. Abu Shadi, *al-Zahir* no. 38, 1; no. 45, 1.

124. Abu Shadi, *al-Zahir* no. 45, 1.

125. Abu Shadi, *al-Zahir* no. 46, 1.

126. Abu Shadi, *al-Zahir* no. 41, 1.

127. Mustafa Kamil, "Mas'alat al-ifta'," 2; *al-Mu'ayyad* no. 4153 (5 January 1904): 2; *al-Mu'ayyad* no. 4158 (11 January 1904): 1, 4; and "al-Din wa al-tarbia," *al-Mu'ayyad* no. 4159 (12 January 1904): 1, 2, 5; Abu Shadi, *al-Zahir* no. 41, 1; Abu Shadi, *al-Zahir* no. 42, 1; Abu Shadi, *al-Zahir* no. 45, 1; Abu Shadi, *al-Zahir* no. 46, 1.

128. Rida, "Qawl fi ijtihad al-mufti wa taqlidihi" and "Ta'yid al-fatwa wa haqiqatuha wa ma bihi al-ifta'," *al-Manar* 6, no. 20 (4 January 1904): 785–786, 784.

129. Mustafa Kamil, "Mas'alat al-ifta'," 2.

130. 'Abbas Hilmi II, *Last Khedive*, 136.

131. Shafiq got their names wrong and assigned them to ownership of one another's journals. I found no reprints of the *Humarat monyati* photograph, and the only scandalous pictures in the *Babaghallo* were the drawings already mentioned. *Humarat monyati* continued to harass 'Abduh, but only verbally ("Tahlil al-haram 'ala madhhab al-malik al-siyyam," *Humarat monyati* 5, no. 16 [12 March 1904]: 250–251). The relevant issues of *al-Arnab* are no longer extant. *Al-Arnab* did report a trial of the *Babaghallo*'s owner in "Qadiat al-Baba Ghallo," *al-Arnab* 1, no. 8 (18 August 1904): 101–108 (numbering inconsistent; details apparently in no. 7, no longer extant). *Al-Mu'ayyad* reported, "Today the 'Abdin court sentenced Muhammad Effendi Tawfiq, owner of the *Humara*, to six months' imprisonment and imposed fines on him for his slander of His Excellency the Mufti in issues of his newspaper" (*al-Mu'ayyad* no. 4213 [20 March 1904]: 5).

132. Shafiq, *Mudhakkirati*, vol. 2, bk. 2, 39.

133. Ibid., 39, 40.

Chapter 9

1. Shafiq, *Mudhakkirati*, vol. 2, bk. 2, 35.

2. Parliamentary Papers, Egypt no. 3, "Correspondence Respecting the Attack on the British Officers at Denshawai" (London: Harrison and Sons, 1906).

3. Jamal Mohammed Ahmad, *The Intellectual Origins of Egyptian Nationalism* (London: Oxford University Press, 1960), 63; Marsot, *Egypt and Cromer*, 173.

4. 'Abd al-Rahman al-Rafi'i, *Mustafa Kamil: ba'ith al-haraka al-wataniyya* (Cairo: Maktab al-Nahda al-Misriyya, 1939), 195; Marsot, *Egypt and Cromer*, 169–175.

5. Zachary Lockman, "Exploring the Field: Lost Voices and Emerging Practices in Egypt, 1882–1914," in eds. Israel Gershoni, et al., *Histories of the Modern Middle East: New Directions* (Boulder, CO: Lynne Rienner, 2002), 147–149.

6. Rida, *Tarikh*, 1:602. Shaykh Hasuna was originally succeeded by a relative, 'Abd al-Rahman al-Nawawi, who died within the month (Salman, *A'mal majlis*, 57).

7. Ibrahim al-Muwailihi, "Mat al-salaf * 'Ash al-khalaf," in *Misbah al-sharq* no. 61 (8 July 1899): 2–3; Shafiq, *Mudhakkirati*, 2:280.

8. Khatab, *Shuyukh al-Azhar*, 30.

9. Eccel, *Social Change*, 232, 236, 300; Khedive 'Abbas Hilmi II, "Khutbat al-Jinab al-'Ali," *al-Muqattam* no. 4862 (25 March 1905): 3.

272   Islamic Reform and Conservatism

10. Salman, *A'mal majlis*, 19.
11. Ibid., 60–61; compare Eccel, *Social Change*, 179–180.
12. Rida, *Tarikh*, 1:494–495.
13. Salman, *A'mal majlis*, 62.
14. Salim al-Bishri's correspondence with 'Abd al-Husayn Sharaf al-Din al-Musawi in *al-Muraja'at*, letter 87, pp. 262–264.
15. Salman, *A'mal majlis*, 62.
16. Salman gave the impression that the consensus package simply gathered dust. However, the khedive decreed its implementation in May 1900, which coincides with the beginning of the second academic year of Salim's tenure in office (Muharram 1318, or May 1900) (*A'mal majlis*, 71).
17. Salman, *A'mal majlis*, 19, 72.
18. Rida, *Tarikh*, 1:429.
19. Al-Muwailihi, "Mustahsan ghayr lazim," 1–2.
20. Ibid., 1–2.
21. Al-Bishri, *al-Muraja'at*, letter 91, pp. 272–273.
22. Salman, *A'mal majlis*, 122–123; *al-Muqattam* no. 4851 (13 March 1905): 3.
23. Al-Bishri, *al-Muraja'at*, letter 87, pp. 262–264.
24. Salman, *A'mal majlis*, 72–73; Rida, *Tarikh*, 1:428–429; Rida, "Mukafa'at imtihan al-talamidha fi al-Azhar," *al-Manar* (November 24, 1904): 716–717; Rida, *al-Manar* 8 (17 August 1905): 474; Salman, *A'mal majlis*, 112–113, see also 74–75; Eccel, *Social Change*,180–181; Muhammad 'Abduh, "Shaykh al-Azhar tukhallifu qanunahu," reprinted in 'Imara, *al-A'mal al-kamila*, 3:180–183.
25. Salary statistics from Eccel, *Social Change*, 254. Based on Dar al-Watha'iq documents, artisans could earn 7–10 piasters a day (£E 1.96–2.8/month) compared to an ordinary 'alim's wage of £E 1–3 a month. Skilled carpenters might make 25 p/day (£E 7/month). A government weigher earned £E 3.5 a month. John Chalcraft, interview by author, Cairo, Egypt, 29 April 1998.
26. Salman, *A'mal majlis*, 73–74, 120; Eccel, *Social Change*, 183; Rida "Mukafa'at imtihan al-talamidha," 717.
27. Ibrahim al-Muwailihi, *Misbah al-sharq* no. 67 (10 August 1899): 2; Khatab, *Shuyukh al-Azhar*, 30.
28. Salim al-Bishri, *al-Muraja'at*, letter 3, p. 31.
29. Ibid., letter 11, pp. 52–53.
30. Ibid., letters 17, 45, 57, 59, 61, 79, 83, 87, 99, passim.
31. Ibid., letters 4, pp. 32–35; 17, pp. 126–127; 39, pp. 161–162; 81, p. 250.
32. 'Ali Ahmad al-Salus, *'Aqidat al-imama 'and al-shi'a al-ithna-'ashariyya: Dirasa fi daw' al-kitab wa al-sunna . . . Hal kana Shaykh al-Azhar al-Bishri shi'ī^{an}?* (Cairo: Dar al-I'tisam, 1987), 170–181.
33. Al-Bishri, *al-Muraja'at*, al-Musawi's letter 4, pp. 32–35, and Salim's letter 5, p. 35, and letter 19, p. 129.
34. Salim al-Bishri, letter to Muhammad 'Abduh, quoted in Qasim Amin, *The New Woman*, trans. Samiha Sidhom Peterson (Cairo: American University in Cairo Press, 1995), 91.
35. Rida, *Tarikh*, 1:494–495; Salman, *A'mal majlis*, 60, 81–82. Some lamented Shaykh Salim's removal: see "Hakadha hal al-dunia," *Humarat monyati* 5, no. 9 (9 March 1903): 131.

36. Muhammad Rashid Rida, "Ijtima' al-talamidha wa intiharuhum," *al-Manar* 7, no. 9 (15 July 1904): 359–360.

37. Shaykh 'Abd al-Rahim al-Damurdash, petition to the Shaykh al-Azhar, printed in Rida, "Mukafa'at imtihan al-talamidha," 717–718.

38. Rida, "Mukafa'at imtihan al-talamidha," 716.

39. *Al-Mu'ayyad* no. 4215 (22 March 1904): 4.

40. Muhammad Rashid Rida, "Faransa wa al-Azhar," *al-Manar* 7 (8 December 1904): 738–744, esp. 738, 742; *al-Muqattam* no. 4851 (13 March 1905) 3; Salman, *A'mal majlis,* 122–123.

41. Salman, *A'mal majlis,* 116, 122–123; *al-Muqattam* no. 4857 (20 March 1905): 2; Eccel, *Social Change,* 183.

42. *Al-Muqattam* no. 4853 (15 March 1905): 2.

43. 'Abd al-Baqi al-Surur, Foreword to Jamal al-Din al-Afghani and Muhammad 'Abduh, eds., *al-'Urwa al-wuthqa* (Cairo: Dar al-'Arabi, 1957), 20; Eccel, *Social Change,* 177.

44. Eccel, *Social Change,* 156–157.

45. Al-Zawahiri, *al-'Ilm wa al-'ulama,* 233.

46. Ibid., 5.

47. Ibid., 17, 27, 32, 41.

48. Ibid., 43.

49. Ibid., 70–71.

50. Rida, *Tarikh,* 1:495.

51. Al-Zawahiri, *al-'Ilm wa al-'ulama,* 89, 92, 96–153, 154–end.

52. "Ra'y al-tawasut fi mas'alat islah al-azhar al-sharif: kitab maftuh ila samu mawlana al-khediw al-mu'azzam," *al-Mu'ayyad* 16, no. 4509 (11 March 1905): 5.

53. Ibid. Some readers thought al-Zawahiri's letter contradicted his book.

54. "Hadith ma' 'azim min 'ulama al-muslimin," *al-Jawa'ib al-Misriyya* (13 March 1905), in Rida, *Tarikh,* 1:502–504 (also reprinted as "Al-Azhar al-sharif wa al-gharad min islah turuq al-ta'lim fihi," *al-Mu'ayyad* no. 4513 [15 March 1905]: 1).

55. Salman, *A'mal majlis,* 116, 122–123; *al-Muqattam* no. 4857 (20 March 1905): 2; Eccel, *Social Change,* 183.

56. "Al-Azhar al-sharif wa al-gharad min islah turuq al-ta'lim fihi," 1.

57. "Ta'yin fadilat al-ustadh al-shaykh al-Shirbini shaykh[an] li al-Azhar," *al-Mu'ayyad* no. 4518 (21 March 1905): 5; *al-Mu'ayyad* no. 4523 (27 March 1905): 4; *al-Mu'ayyad* no. 4524 (28 March 1905): 4; *al-Muqattam* (20 March1905), 2.

58. *Al-Liwa'* no. 1766 (9 July 1905) 1; quoting an *al-Ahram* article.

59. Rida, *Tarikh,* 1:505–511; *al-Muqattam* no. 4856 (18 March 1905): 1; *al-Mu'ayyad* no. 4516 (19 March 1905): 5. See also "'Ulama al-Azhar wa al-siyasa aw al-siyasa wa al-Azhar," *al-Muqattam* no. 4858 (21 March 1905): 1; Rida, *Tarikh,* 1:511–512

60. *Al-Mu'ayyad* no. 4519 (22 March 1905): 4; Rida, *Tarikh,* 1:513–515; Amin, *Zu'ama al-islah,* 442; *al-Mu'ayyad* no. 4520 (23 March 1905): 4; *al-Islam* 8 no. 1 (March 1905): 6–10; *al-Muqattam* no. 4860 (23 March 1905): 2; *al-Muqattam* no. 4861 (24 March 1905): 2; "Khutbat al-jinab al-'ali,"

al-Muqattam no. 4862 (25 March 1905): 3; "al-Jinab al-'ali wa al-jami' al-Azhar," *al-Muqattam* no. 4861 (24 March 1905): 2–3.

61. *Al-Mu'ayyad* no. 4521 (25 March 1905), 4; *al-Mu'ayyad* no. 4518 (21 March 1905): 4.

62. *Al-Muqattam* no. 4862 (25 March 1905): 2; *al-Muqattam* no. 4863 (27 March 1905): 2; *al-Mu'ayyad* no. 4522 (26 March 1905): 4, 5. Ahmad al-Hanbali was Hanbali Mufti.

63. Temperatures ranged from 32–36 degrees Celsius in Cairo, two degrees lower on average in Alexandria. Combined with spring dust storms, this would have made for extreme discomfort (see weather reports in *al-Mu'ayyad* through end of March 1905).

64. Muhammad Rashid Rida, "Marad al-ustadh al-imam," *al-Manar* 8 (3 July 1905): 355–357; "I'tidhar li al-qurra' al-kuram," *al-Liwa'* no. 1768 (11 July 1905); Mustafa Kamil,"Khatb jalal: Anna Allah wa anna ilayhi raja'un," *al-Liwa'* no. 1769 (12 July 1905): 2; Rida, "Musab al-islam bi mawt al-ustadh al-imam," *al-Manar* 8 (19 July 1905): 375–379; "al-Shaykh Muhammad 'Abduh, mufti al-diyar al-Misriyya," *al-Muqtataf* 30, no. 8 (1 August 1905): 593–596.

65. Rida, "Musab al-islam," 376.

66. Kamil, "Khatb jalal," 2.

67. Blunt, *My Diaries,* 2:151.

68. Shaykh Ahmad al-Shadhili, "Ahamm al-akhbar: kullu man 'alayha faan," *al-Islam* 8, no. 5 (July 1905): 103; Muhammad Rashid Rida, "Ta'bin al-ustadh al-imam," *al-Manar* 8 (30 September 1905): 597–599.

69. Al-Shadhili, "Ahamm al-akhbar," 103.

70. Muhammad Rashid Rida, "Irad 'ala tark al-taqlid," *al-Manar* 8 (19 June 1905): 294–297.

71. *Al-Mu'ayyad,* no. 4524 (March 28) and *al-Mu'ayyad* no. 4525 (29 March 1905); *al-Islam* (March 1905): 17–23; *al-Muqattam* no. 4867 (31 March 1905): 1.

72. *Al-Muqattam* no. 4866 (30 March 1905): 2.

73. Marsot, *Egypt and Cromer,* 145–149.

74. Shafiq, *Mudhakkirati,* vol. 2, bk. 2, 106, 111; Abu al-'Uyun, *Al-Jami' al-Azhar,* 29; Eccel, *Social Change,* 195.

75. Shafiq, *Mudhakkirati,* vol. 2, bk. 2, 137.

76. *Al-Manar,* vol. 9, 679.

77. Shafiq, *Mudhakkirati,* vol. 2, bk. 2, 137–138.

78. Ibid., 138.

79. Ibid., 96–97, 139–140. Nor did 'Abbas coddle Shaykh Radi's faction. When 'Abbas met with 'ulama at the palace for celebration of 'Id al-Adha, Ahmad Zaki Pasha, master of ceremonies, called out to Shaykh Radi in a loud voice: "Hey Shaykh Radi, our Effendi is displeased with you ("ghayr radin 'anak," a pun) and doesn't want to meet you." Shaykh Radi was escorted from the palace.

80. *Al-Mu'ayyad* no. 5360 (6 January 1908): 5.

81. "Al-Qadim wa al-hadith," *al-Mu'ayyad* no. 5363 (9 January 1908): 2.

82. 'Enan, introduction to 'Enan, *Tarikh al-Azhar.*

83. "Al-Qadim wa al-hadith," 2.

84. Years later, Khedive 'Abbas would complain that he achieved only "inessential" reforms at al-Azhar and only after laborious negotiation and financial inducement: "I was not able to obtain anything from al-Azhar without . . . some pecuniary favour. For it seems that respect for tradition can sometimes evaporate, even at al-Azhar, before the demands of personal interest." At the time 'Abbas said only that stipulations of al-Azhar's existing awqaf could not be fulfilled due to administrative inefficiency, and while at some institutions it would be sufficient to reduce the number of students, this could not be done at al-Azhar—and no waqf stipulation prevented institution of order (nizam) within the mosque. "Islah al-Azhar al-sharif," *al-Mu'ayyad* no. 5366 (13 January 1908): 3; 'Abbas Hilmi II, *Last Khedive*, 181.

85. "Islah al-Azhar al-sharif," 3.

86. *Al-Mu'ayyad* no. 5420 (19 March 1908): 4; whole text in March issues of *al-Mu'ayyad;* see also Lajnat Islah report, "al-La'iha al-Dakhiliyyah"; al-Sa'idi, *Tarikh al-islah*, 73–78; Shafiq, *Mudhakkirati*, vol. 2, bk. 2, 140. Some sources refer to the high council as *al-Majlis al-'Ali* ("high" rather than "highest"), but the text of the reform code has *A'la.*

87. *Al-Mu'ayyad* no. 5603 (22 October 1908): 6.

88. Shafiq, *Mudhakkirati*, vol. 2, bk. 2, 140.

89. *Al-Mu'ayyad* no. 5628 (26 November 1908): 4.

90. *Al-Mu'ayyad* no. 5633 (2 December 1908): 5.

91. *Al-Mu'ayyad* no. 5637 (7 December 1908): 4.

92. Eccel, *Social Change*, 183–193; *al-Mu'ayyad* no. 4648 (21 December 1908): 3, 4; see also no. 5627 (25 November 1908): 2.

93. A series of articles begins with "al-Nizam fi al-Azhar: silsilat mulahazat wa iqtirahat," *al-Mu'ayyad* no. 5640 (12 December 1908): 2; Ibn al-Athir, "Tahqiq shakhsiyat al-talib," *al-Mu'ayyad* no. 5643 (15 December 1908): 6.

94. Ibn al-Athir, "Tawzi' al-durus 'ala asatidha," *al-Mu'ayyad* no. 5653 (27 December 1908): 1–2.

95. "Qararat al-majlis al-a'la li al-Azhar al-sharif," *al-Mu'ayyad* no. 5658 (7 January 1909). See also al-Azhar's budget figures in *al-Mu'ayyad* no. 5656 (30 December 1908): 5.

96. "Ihtifal al-Azhar al-sharif bi 'id al-julus al-khadiwi," *al-Mu'ayyad* no. 5661 (10 January 1909): 5; Muhammad 'Ashur al-Sudfi, "Khutba," *al-Mu'ayyad* no. 5662 (11 January 1909): 2.

97. *Al-Mu'ayyad* no. 5615 (10 November 1908): 4; "Mazahirat al-talaba," in *al-Mu'ayyad* no. 5625 (22 November 1908): 5.

98. Anwar al-Jindi, *'Abd al-'Aziz Jawish: Min ruwwad al-tarbiyya wa al-sahafa wa al-ijtima'* (Cairo: n.p., 1965), 6.

99. *Al-Mu'ayyad* no. 5559 (1 September 1908): 5; *al-Mu'ayyad* no. 5634 (15 December 1908): 5–6. Khedive 'Abbas scorned Jawish, whom he believed organized a 1914 assassination attempt ('Abbas Hilmi II, *Last Khedive*, 101, 137, 308, 313–314).

100. *Al-Mu'ayyad* no. 5639 (9 December 1908): 4.

101. *Al-Mu'ayyad* no. 5656 (30 December 1908): 4.

102. "Al-Azhariyun wa talabatuhum," *al-Mu'ayyad* no. 5672 (24 January 1909): 6.

276   ISLAMIC REFORM AND CONSERVATISM

103. Petitions, "al-Azhariyun wa mutalabatuhum," *al-Mu'ayyad* no. 5673 (25 January 1909): 5; see also "Ta'lim al-fuqara'," *al-Muqtataf* 34, no. 2 (1 February 1909): 203; Shafiq, *Mudhakkirati*, vol. 2, bk. 2, 106. Compare with al-Sa'idi, *Tarikh al-islah*, 79.
104. *Al-Mu'ayyad* no. 5680 (2 February 1909): 4.
105. Lajnat Islah report, 21–22.
106. "Kitab maftuh ila ikhwani al-Azhariyin," *al-Mu'ayyad* no. 5674 (26 January 1909): 5.
107. 'Abd al-Rahman Radi, "al-Muzahira al-Azhariyya: wa al-shakhsiyat," *al-Mu'ayyad* no. 5675 (27 January 1909): 4.
108. "Da'na min al-Azhar wa al-Azhariyin," article in unnamed paper, cited in *al-Mu'ayyad* (27 January): 1.
109. Salih Hamdi Hammad, "al-Azhariyun wa mutalabatuhum," *al-Mu'ayyad* (27 January): 1.
110. Lockman, "Exploring the Field," 143–144.
111. Hammad, "al-Azhariyun wa mutalabatuhum," 1.
112. Student demands, in Lajnat Islah report, 21–22.
113. Lajnat Islah report, 21.
114. On tribunal, *al-Mu'ayyad* (26 January): 4; *al-Mu'ayyad* (27 January): 4; "A'lan min mashyakhat al-Azhar," no. 5676 (28 January 1909): 5.
115. *Al-Mu'ayyad* (28 January): 5.
116. *Al-Mu'ayyad* (26 January): 4.
117. "Al-Azhariyun wa matalibuhum," *al-Mu'ayyad* no. 5677 (30 January 1909): 4; Arthur Goldschmidt, "The Egyptian Nationalist Party, 1892–1919" in *Political and Social Change in Modern Egypt: Historical Studies from the Ottoman Conquest to the United Arab Republic*, ed. P. M. Holt (London: Oxford University Press, 1968).
118. "Kitab maftuh ila ikhwani al-Azhariyin," *al-Mu'ayyad* no. 5674 (26 January 1909): 5; Shaykh Amr Sayyid al-Malt, cited in "Bayan haqiqa," *al-Mu'ayyad* (2 February 1909): 4; Shafiq, *Mudhakkirati*, vol. 2, bk. 2, 140. See also "Hizb al-islah al-dusturi: khutba 'umumiyyah: al-Azhar al-sharif," *al-Mu'ayyad* (20 February 1909): 4.
119. "Al-Azhariyun wa matalibuhum," *al-Mu'ayyad* no. 5677 (30 January 1909): 4; "Fi al-Azhar al-sharif" and "Nasharat al-Azhar," *al-Mu'ayyad* no. 5678 (31 January 1909): 4, 5.
120. "Mas'alat al-Azhar al-sharif" *al-Mu'ayyad* no. 5679 (1 February 1909): 4, 5; "Talabat al-jami' al-Ahmadi," *al-Mu'ayyad* (27 January): 4; al-Sa'idi, *Tarikh al-islah*, 80.
121. Al-Azhar student newspaper cited in *al-Mu'ayyad* (1 February): 5. Withdrawal of bread rations accorded with al-Azhar's penal code.
122. "Mas'alat al-Azhar: Sirat qarar," *al-Mu'ayyad* (24 February): 4.
123. "Mas'alat al-Azhar al-sharif," *al-Mu'ayyad* no. 5681 (3 February 1909): 4. *Al-Liwa'* cited in "al-Azhar al-sharif wa tulabuhu," *al-Mu'ayyad* no. 5682 (4 February 1909): 4.
124. *Al-Mu'ayyad* (4 February): 4; "Mi'at wa 'ashrun dars[an] fi al-Azhar al-sharif," *al-Mu'ayyad* no. 5683 (6 February 1909): 4; and "al-Azhar al-sharif wa 'awdat jami' al-talaba ilayhi," *al-Mu'ayyad* no. 5684 (7 February 1909): 4.

125. "Mas'alat al-Azhar al-sharif" (text of *al-Liwa'* included), *al-Mu'ayyad* no. 5692 (16 February 1909): 4.
126. "Mas'alat al-Azhar al-sharif," *al-Mu'ayyad* (16 February): 5; "al-Azhar...wa 'awdat jami' al-talaba. .." *al-Mu'ayyad* (7 February): 4.
127. "Mas'alat al-Azhar al-sharif," *al-Mu'ayyad* no. 5693 (17 February 1909); *al-Mu'ayyad* no. 5694 (18 February 1909): 4.
128. *Al-Mu'ayyad* no. 5695 (20 February 1909): 4. The khedival decree was issued 20 February 1909. Also see "Shaykh al-Azhar al-jadid," *al-Mu'ayyad* no. 5695 (20 February 1909): 4. He was not officially appointed until April 13 (*al-Mu'ayyad* no. 5738 [13 April 1909]). Compare al-Sa'idi, *Tarikh al-islah,* 88–89; Crecelius, "The Ulama and the State," 120; Eccel, *Social Change,* 195.
129. "Mas'alat al-Azhar al-sharif," *al-Mu'ayyad* no. 5696 (21 February 1909): 6.
130. *Al-Mu'ayyad* no. 5697 (22 February 1909): 4; no. 5698 (23 February 1909): 4; no. 5699 (24 February 1909): 4; and "Nadi al-Azhar," no. 5702 (28 February 1909): 5.
131. Khedival agreement decreed 19 October 1909, Lajnat Islah report, 20.
132. See Lajnat Islah report, 22–23; al-Sa'idi, *Tarikh al-islah,* 81–82.
133. This committee's studies and drafts make up the Lajnat Islah report; for the draft curriculum, see "al-Namadhij murfaqa bi al-taqrir al-muqaddam li-sahib al-'atufa Muhammad Sa'id Pasha, Qa'imqam al-hadra al-khidiwiyya wa ra'is Majlis al-Nuzzar," 1–39; for the draft administrative structure, see "Mashru' qanun al-jami' al-Azhar," 1–54; draft of the La'iha al-Dakhiliyya, 1–45; for texts of previous laws see last section, 1–48.
134. See Lajnat Islah report, "Mashru' qanun al-Azhar," pt. 7, articles 101–116, pp. 36–39. The subjects were fiqh and its texts and methods; hadith and its terminology; Qur'anic exegesis; Arabic studies; monotheistic theology, logic, and history; prophetic biography; and religious ethics. Al-Sa'idi witnessed some of these lectures in the 1920s (*Tarikh al-islah,* 84–85, 90, 94).
135. Al-Sa'idi, *Tarikh al-islah,* 88–89; Eccel, *Social Change,* 202.
136. Al-Sa'idi, *Tarikh al-islah,* 121; see also Muhammad Rashid Rida, *al-Manar wa al-Azhar,*1st ed. (Cairo: Matba'at al-Manar, 1353 AH).
137. See Salim, *al-Muraja'at,* 35, 126–127, 129, 315; publisher's Foreword to *The Right Path,* ed. Muhammad Amir Haider Khan (Blanco, TX: Zahra Publications, 1986), xxii.
138. *Al-Islam* 8, no. 3 (May 1905); "al-Islam fi al-Azhar," *al-Islam* 8, no. 4 (June 1905): 1–14.
139. Rida, *Tarikh,* 1:549; "Sada al-haditha fi Urubba, aw muqawamat al-nufudhiyin al-faransi wa al-Inklizi li al-ustadh al-imam fi al-islah" and "Mulahidhat *al-Manar* aw intiqaduhu 'ala dhalik," *al-Manar* 8, no. 6 (21 May 1905): 238–239, 239–240.
140. Spender, *Daily Chronicle*; Qasim Amin, eulogy in Rida, *Tarikh,* 3: 267.
141. "Muhammad 'Abduh," Wikipedia, http://en.wikipedia.org/wiki/Muhammad_Abduh (accessed 4 August 2006); Arthur E. Falk, email to author, 4 August 2006.
142. "Al-Qadim wa al-hadith," *al-Mu'ayyad* no. 5363 (9 January 1908): 2.
143. 'Abduh, *al-A'mal al-kamila* (1993 edition), 3: 113.

144. *Al-Waqa'i' al-Misriyya* no. 105 (11 November 1915), cited in Crecelius, "The Ulama and the State," 121.

Chapter 10

1. Al-Kumi, *al-Sihafa al-islamiyya,* 100.
2. Blunt, *Secret History,* 260–261.
3. Cromer, *Modern Egypt,* 161, 175, 185.
4. See Adams, *Islam and Modernism,* 78 n.3; W. H. T. Gairdner, "Some Notes on Present Day Movements in the Moslem World," *Moslem World* 1 (1904): 190; A. B. De Guerville, *New Egypt,* rev. ed. (London: William Heinemann, 1906 [c. 1905]), 157–158, 163; Zaydan, *Mashahir al-Sharq,* 300–308; Russell Galt, *The Effects of Centralization on Education in Modern Egypt* (Cairo: American University in Cairo, 1936); 'Uthman Amin, *Muhammad 'Abduh* (Cairo: Dar Ihya' al-Kutub al-'Arabiyyah, 1944); Dodge, *Al-Azhar,* 139; Suhail ibn Salim Hanna," Biographical Scholarship and Muhammad 'Abduh," *Muslim World* 59, no. 3–4 (1969): 300–307; Heyworth-Dunne, *History of Education,* 402; Eccel, *Social Change,* 178–183. Only Daniel Crecelius noted "incredible overemphasis" on modernists ("Nonideological Responses," 167).
5. Hurgronje, "E. Sachau," 385.
6. Hurgronje, "E. Sachau," 387; Spevack, "Archetypal Sunni Scholar," 130, 141–142.
7. "Islam has bloody borders" (Samuel Huntington, "The Clash of Civilizations?" *Foreign Affairs* [Summer 1993]: 35). See also Bernard Lewis, "The Roots of Muslim Rage," *Atlantic Monthly* 266, no. 3 (September 1990): 47–60.
8. Indira Falk Gesink, "'Chaos on the Earth': Subjective Truths vs. Communal Unity in Islamic Law and the Rise of Militant Islam," *American Historical Review* 108, no. 3 (June 2003), 710–733.
9. World Islamic front, fatwah on "Jihad Against Jews and Crusaders," *Al-Quds al-'arabi* (23 February 1998).
10. Rohan Gunaratna, *Inside al-Qaeda: Global Network of Terror* (New York: Columbia University Press, 2002), 7.

SELECTED BIBLIOGRAPHY

'Abbas Hilmi II. *The Last Khedive of Egypt: Memoirs of Abbas Hilmi II.* Translated and edited by Amira Sonbol. Reading, UK: Ithaca Press, 1998.

'Abd al-Gawad, Muhammad. *Taqwim Dar al-'Ulum.* Cairo: Dar al-Ma'arif, 1950 [1947].

'Abduh, Muhammad. *al-A'mal al-kamila li al-Imam Muhammad 'Abduh.* Edited by Muhammad 'Imara. 3 vols. 2nd ed. Beirut: Al-Mu'assasa al-'Arabiyya li al-Dirasat wa al-Nashr, 1980; 1st ed., 1972.

'Abduh, Muhammad. *al-A'mal al-kamila li al-Imam al-Shaykh Muhammad 'Abduh.* Edited by Muhammad 'Imara. 5 vols. 1st ed. Beirut and Cairo: Dar al-Shuruq, 1993.

'Abduh, Muhammad. *Risalat al-tawhid.* Edited by Mahmud Abu Riyya. 4th ed. of original version. Cairo: Dar al-Ma'arif, n.d. (reprint of 1315 H ed.).

Abu al-'Uyun, Mahmud. *Al-Jami' al-Azhar: nubdha fi tarikhihi.* Cairo: Matba'at al-Azhar, 1949.

al-Adab. [Weekly newspaper.] 1887–1889. Dar al-Kutub, dawriyat no. 801.

Adams, Charles C. *Islam and Modernism in Egypt: A Study of the Modern Reform Movement Inaugurated by Muhammad 'Abduh.* New York: Russell & Russell, 1968 [1933].

Adams, Charles C. "Muhammad 'Abduh and the Transvaal Fatwa." *MacDonald Presentation Volume.* New York: Books for Libraries, 1968; Princeton, NJ: Princeton University Press, 1933.

al-Afghani, Jamal al-Din. *al-A'mal al-kamila.* Edited by Muhammad 'Imara. Vol. 1. Cairo: al-Mu'assasa al-Misriyya al-'Amma li al-Ta'lif wa al-Nashr, n.d.; Vol. 2. Beirut: al-Mu'assasa al-'Arabiyya li al-Dirasat wa al-Nashr, n.d.

Ahmed, Jamal Mohammed. *The Intellectual Origins of Egyptian Nationalism.* London: Oxford University Press, 1960.

Ahmed, Munir-ud-Din. *Muslim Education and the Scholar's Social Status up to the 5th Century Muslim Era (11th Century Christian Era) in the Light of Ta'rikh Baghdad.* Zurich: Verlag der Islam, 1968.

al-Ahram. [Daily newspaper.] Edited by Salim and Bishara Taqla. Cairo: 1876–present. American University in Cairo microfilm.

Akarli, Engin D. "Abdulhamid II's Attempts to Integrate Arabs into the Ottoman System." In *Palestine in the Late Ottoman Period,* edited by David Kushner, 74–89. Leiden, Netherlands: E. J. Brill, 1986.

Akarli, Engin D. "Ebul Huda." In *Unluler Ansiklopedisi*. Istanbul: Yurt, 1983.

al-'Alwani, Taha J. "Taqlid and the Stagnation of the Muslim Mind." *American Journal of Islamic Social Sciences* 8, no. 3 (1991): 513–524.

Alyan, Yusuf Sarkis. *Mu'jam al-matbu'at al-'arabiyya wa al-mu'arraba*. Vol. 2. Beirut: Dar al-Sader, 1990.

Amin, Ahmad. *Zu'ama' al-islah fi al-'asr al-hadith*. Beirut: Dar al-Kitab al-'Arabiyya, 1979.

Amin, Qasim. *al-A'mal al-kamila*. Edited by Muhammad 'Imara. Cairo: Dar al-Shuruq, n.d.

Anderson, J. N. D. "Recent Developments in Shari'a Law II," *Muslim World* 41 (1951): 34–48.

al-Arnab. [Humor journal.] Edited by Husayn Tawfiq. Cairo: 1902–1904. Dar al-Kutub, zakiyya no. 4548.

al-'Attar, Hasan. *Hashiat al-'Attar 'ala sharh Jalal al-Din 'ala jam' al-jawami' li 'Abd al-Wahhab al-Subki*. N.p.: Mustafa al-Halabi Press [1830].

al-'Attar, Hasan ibn Muhammad. *al-Insha.'* Rev. ed. Cairo: Bulaq, 1835; reprinted Cairo: Mahmud Tawfiq, 1936.

al-'Attar, Hasan. "Sharh al-'Attar al-musamma bi rahat al-abdan 'ala nuzhat al-adhhan." Manuscript. Azhariyya, 3434 Riwaq al-Maghariba.

Ayalon, Ami. *The Press in the Arab Middle East: A History.* New York: Oxford University Press, 1995.

al-Azhar: Tarikhuhu wa tatawwuruhu. Introduction by Muhammad al-Bahi. Cairo: Dar wa Matabi' al-Sha'ab, n. d.

Badawi, Ahmad. *Rifa'a Rafi' al-Tahtawi*. 2nd ed. Cairo: Lajnat al-Bayan al-'Arabi, 1959.

Badawi, M. A. Zaki. *The Reformers of Egypt*. London: Croom Helm, 1976.

Baer, Gabriel. "'Ali Mubarak's Khitat as Source for the History of Modern Egypt" and "Social Change in Egypt: 1800–1914." In *Political and Social Change in Modern Egypt*, edited by P. M. Holt, 13–27, 135–161. London: Oxford University Press, 1968.

Baer, Gabriel. *A History of Landownership in Modern Egypt 1800–1950*. London: Oxford University Press, 1962.

al-Bajuri, Ibrahim. *Hashia al-mussamma bi tahqiq al-maqam 'ala kifayat al-'awwam fi 'ilm al-kalam li Shaykhihi al-Shaykh Muhammad al-Fadali*. Cairo: Matba'at al-Azhariyya al-Misriyya, 1317 H [1899].

Baron, Beth. *The Women's Awakening in Egypt: Culture, Society, and the Press*. New Haven, CT: Yale University Press, 1994.

Bayram, Mustafa. "Tarikh al-Azhar." Arabic offprint of a paper presented at the thirteenth convention for Scholars of Eastern Languages, Hamburg, September 1902. American University in Cairo library.

Bayumi, Zakaria Sulayman. *al-Tayarat al-siyasiyya wa al-ijtima'iyya bayna al-mujaddidin wa al-muhafizin: dirasat tarikhiyyah fi fikr al-Shaykh Muhammad 'Abduh*. Cairo: Al-Hay'a al-Misriyya al-'Amma li al-Kitab, 1973.

Berkey, Jonathan. *The Transmission of Knowledge in Medieval Cairo: A Social History of Islamic Education.* Princeton, NJ: Princeton University Press, 1992.

Bhabha, Homi. *The Location of Culture.* New York: Routledge, 2004.

Binder, Leonard. "Ideological Foundations of Egyptian-Arab Nationalism." In *Ideology and Discontent,* edited by David Apter. New York: Free Press, 1964.

Blunt, Wilfrid Scawen. *My Diaries: Being a Personal Narrative of Events 1888–1914.* 2 vols. New York: Alfred A. Knopf, 1921.

Blunt, Wilfrid Scawen. *Secret History of the English Occupation of Egypt: Being a Personal Narrative of Events.* New York: Howard Fertig, 1967 [London: T. F. Unwin, 1907].

Botiveau, Bernard. "Contemporary Reinterpretations of Islamic Law: The Case of Egypt." In *Islam and Public Law,* edited by Chibli Mallat, 261–277. London: Graham & Trotman, 1993.

Broadley, Alexander Meyrick. *How We Defended Arabi and His Friends: A Story of Egypt and the Egyptians.* Cairo: Research and Publishing Arab Centre, 1980; reprint of London: Chapman and Hall, Ltd., 1884.

Brockopp, Jonathan E. "Rereading the History of Early Maliki Jurisprudence." *Journal of the American Oriental Society* 118, no. 2 (1 April 1998): 233–238.

Brown, Daniel. *Re-thinking Tradition in Modern Islamic Thought.* Cambridge: Cambridge University Press, 1996.

Bryant, Christopher. *Positivism in Social Theory and Research.* New York: St. Martin's Press, 1985.

Census of Cairo 1868. Notes on numbers of mujawirin in Cairo. Sijjilat Muhafizat Misr, Ta'dad nufus muhafizat Misr 1285, Dar al-Watha'iq lam/1/84. 69 registers. Ijmali [totals] file new number 109; old number 270.

Çizakça, Murat. *A Comparative Evolution of Business Partnerships: The Islamic World and Europe, with specific reference to the Ottoman Archives.* Leiden, Netherlands: E. J. Brill, 1996.

Clot (Bey), Antoine. *Memoires de Clot Bey.* Edited by Jacques Tager. Cairo: L'Institut français d'archéologie orientale, 1949.

Cole, Juan, R. I. *Colonialism and Revolution in the Middle East: Social and Cultural Origins of Egypt's 'Urabi Movement.* Princeton, NJ: Princeton University Press, 1993.

Commins, David Dean. *Islamic Reform: Politics and Social Change in Late Ottoman Syria.* London: Oxford University Press, 1990.

Crecelius, Daniel. "The Emergence of the Shaykh al-Azhar as the Pre-Eminent Religious Leader in Egypt." In *Colloque international sur l'histoire du Caire,* 109–123. Cairo: Ministry of Culture of the Arab Republic of Egypt, 1969.

Crecelius, Daniel. "Nonideological Responses of the Egyptian Ulama to Modernization." In *Scholars, Saints and Sufis,* edited by Nikki Keddie, 167–209. Berkeley: University of California Press, 1972.

Crecelius, Daniel. *The Roots of Modern Egypt: A Study of the Regimes of 'Ali Bey al-Kabir and Muhammad Bey Abu al-Dhahab, 1760–1775.* Minneapolis, MN: Biblioteca Islamica, 1981.

Crecelius, Daniel. "The Ulama and the State in Modern Egypt." Ph.D. dissertation, Princeton University, 1967.

Cromer, Lord (Evelyn Baring, First Earl Cromer). *Abbas II.* London: Macmillan Co., 1915.

Cromer, Lord (Evelyn Baring, First Earl Cromer). *Modern Egypt.* 1st ed. 2 vols. New York, Macmillan Co., c.1908.

Cuno, Kenneth. "Ideology and Juridical Discourse in Ottoman Egypt: The Uses of the Concept of Irsad." *Islamic Law and Society* 6, no. 2 (1999): 136–163.

Cuno, Kenneth. *The Pasha's Peasants: Land, Society, and Economy in Lower Egypt, 1740–1858.* Cambridge: Cambridge University Press, 1992; Cairo: American University in Cairo Press, 1994.

Dallal, Ahmad. "The Origins and Objectives of Islamic Revivalist Thought, 1750–1850." *Journal of the American Oriental Society* 113.3 (1993): 341–359.

Davis, Eric. *Challenging Colonialism: Bank Misr and Egyptian Industrialization 1920–1941.* Princeton, NJ: Princeton University Press, 1983.

De Guerville, A. B. *New Egypt.* Rev. ed. London: William Heinemann, 1906 [c. 1905].

De Jong, F. "The Itinerary of Hasan al-'Attar (1766–1835): A Reconsideration and Its Implications," *Journal of Semitic Studies* 28, no. 1 (spring 1983).

De Jong, F. Review of *Islamic Roots of Capitalism. International Journal of Middle Eastern Studies* 14 (1982): 381–399.

Delanoue, Gilbert. *Moralistes et politiques musulmans dans l'Egypte du XIXe siècle (1798–1882).* 2 vols. Cairo: Institut Français d'Archéologie Orientale du Caire, 1982.

Deringil, Selim. "The Invention of Tradition as Public Image in the Late Ottoman Empire, 1808–1908." *Comparative Studies in Society and History* 35, no. 1 (January 1993): 3–29.

Deringil, Selim. "Legitimacy Structures in the Ottoman State: The Reign of Abdulhamid II (1876–1909)." *International Journal of Middle East Studies* 23 (1991): 345–359.

Deringil, Selim. "The Ottoman Response to the Egyptian Crisis of 1881–82." *Middle Eastern Studies* 24, no. 1 (January 1988): 3–24.

Dodge, Bayard. *Al-Azhar: A Millenium of Muslim Learning.* Washington, DC: Middle East Institute, 1961.

Dor (Bey), Victor Edouard. *L'Instruction publique en Egypte.* Paris: A. Lacroix, 1872.

Eccel, A. Chris. "'Alim and Mujahid in Egypt: Orthodoxy Versus Subculture or Division of Labor?" *Muslim World* 78, nos. 3–4 (1988): 189–208.

Eccel, A. Chris. *Egypt, Islam, and Social Change: Al-Azhar in Conflict and Accommodation.* Berlin: Klaus Schwarz Verlag, 1984.

Eickelman, Dale F. "The Art of Memory: Islamic Education and Its Social Reproduction." In *Comparing Muslim Societies: Knowledge and the State in a World Civilization,* edited by Juan R. I. Cole. Ann Arbor: University of Michigan Press, 1992.

Eickelman, Dale F. *Knowledge and Power in Morocco.* Princeton, NJ: Princeton University Press, 1985.

Eickelman, Dale F. "Who Speaks for Islam? Inside the Islamic Reformation." In *An Islamic Reformation?* edited by Michaelle Browers and Charles Kurzman. Lanham, MD: Lexington Books, 2004.

'Enan, Mohamed Abdulla. *Tarikh al-Azhar.* Cairo: Lajnet al-Taalif Press, 1958.

Ener, Mine. *Managing the Poor and the Politics of Benevolence, 1800–1952.* Princeton, NJ: Princeton University Press, 2003.

Fadel, Muhammad. "Adjudication in the Maliki *Madhhab:* A Study of Legal Process in Medieval Islamic Law." Ph.D. diss., University of Chicago, 1995.

Fadel, Muhammad. "The Social Logic of *Taqlid* and the Rise of the *Mukhatasar.*" *Islamic Law and Society* 3, no. 2 (June 1996): 193–233.

Fareed, Muneer Goolam. *Legal Reform in the Muslim World: Anatomy of a Scholarly Dispute in the 19th and the Early 20th Centuries on the Usage of Ijtihad as a Legal Tool.* San Francisco: Austin & Winfield, 1996.

al-Fatawa al-islamiyya min dar al-ifta' al-Misriyya. 20 vols. Cairo: Wizarat al-Awqaf, 1979–1992.

Findlay, James. "The Era of Multipurpose Colleges in American Higher Education, 1850–1890." In *The American College in the Nineteenth Century,* edited by Roger L. Geiger et al. Nashville, TN: Vanderbilt Press, 2000.

Foucault, Michel. *Discipline and Punish: The Birth of the Prison.* Translated by Alan Sheridan. New York: Vintage Books, 1979 [1975].

Geiger, Roger L. "The Rise and Fall of Useful Knowledge: Higher Education for Sciences, Agriculture, and the Mechanic Arts 1850–1875." In *The American College in the Nineteenth Century,* edited by Roger L. Geiger et al. Nashville, TN: Vanderbilt Press, 2000.

Gendzier, Irene. *Practical Visions of Ya'qub Sanu'.* Cambridge, MA: Harvard University Press, 1966.

Gershoni, Israel. "Arabization of Islam: The Egyptian Salafiyyah and the Rise of Arabism in Pre-revolutionary Egypt." *Asian and African Studies* 13, no. 1 (1979): 22–57.

Ghazal, Amal Nadim. "Beyond Modernity: Islamic Conservatism in the Late Ottoman Period." M.A. Thesis, University of Alberta, Edmonton, Canada, 1998.

Ghazal, Amal. "Sufism, Ijtihad, and Modernity: Yusuf al-Nabhani in the Age of Sultan Abd al-Hamid II." Paper presented at Middle East Studies Association, 5 December 1998.

Gran, Peter. *Islamic Roots of Capitalism, Egypt 1760–1840.* Austin: University of Texas Press, 1979.

Gully, Adrian. "Epistles for Grammarians: Illustrations from the Insha' Literature," *British Journal of Middle Eastern Studies* 23, no. 2 (November 1996): 147–166.

al-Hakim, Muhammad Bey Diri, ed. *Tarikh hayat al-maghfur lahu 'Ali Mubarak Pasha.* Privately printed. Harat al-Saqa'in, Egypt: al-Matba'a al-Tibbiyya al-Diriyya al-Ka'ina, 1894.

Hallaq, Wael B. *A History of Islamic Legal Theories: An Introduction to Sunni* Usul al-fiqh. Cambridge: Cambridge University Press, 1997.

Hallaq, Wael B. "On the Origins of the Controversy about the Existence of Mujtahids and the Gate of Ijtihad." *Studia Islamica* 63 (1986): 134–141.

Hallaq, Wael B. "A Prelude to Ottoman Reform: Ibn 'Abidin on Custom and Legal Change." In *Histories of the Modern Middle East: New Directions*, edited by Israel Gershoni, et al., 37-61. Boulder, CO: Lynne Rienner, 2002.

Hallaq, Wael B. "Was the Gate of Ijtihad Closed?" *International Journal of Middle East Studies* 16 (1984): 3–41.

al-Hami, Muhammad Kamal al-Sayyid Muhammad. *Al-Azhar jami'an wa jami'atan, aw, al-Azhar fi alf 'am.* Cairo: al-Hay'a [. . .] li-Shu'un [. . .], 1982.

Hanioğlu, M. Şükrü. *The Young Turks in Opposition.* London: Oxford University Press, 1995.

Haq, Mahmudul. *Muhammad 'Abduh: A Study of a Modern Thinker of Egypt.* Aligarh, India: Aligarh Muslim University, 1970.

Hathaway, Jane. "Origin Myths." In *A Tale of Two Factions: Myth, Memory, and Identity in Ottoman Egypt and Yemen.* Albany: State University of New York Press, 2003.

Hathaway, Jane. *The Politics of Households in Ottoman Egypt: The Rise of the Qazdaglis.* Cambridge: Cambridge University Press, 1997.

Heyworth-Dunne, James. *An Introduction to the History of Education in Modern Egypt.* London: Frank Cass & Co., Ltd., 1968 [1939].

Hobsbawm, Eric, and Terrence Ranger. *The Invention of Tradition.* Cambridge: Cambridge University Press, 1992.

Hoebink, Michel. "Thinking about Renewal in Islam: Towards a History of Islamic Ideas on Modernization and Secularization." *Arabica* 46, no. 1 (January 1999): 29–62.

Hourani, Albert. *Arabic Thought in the Liberal Age 1798–1939.* Cambridge: Cambridge University Press, 1983 [1962].

Hourani, Albert. *History of the Arab Peoples.* New York: Warner Books, 1991.

Hourani, Albert. "The Syrians in Egypt in the Eighteenth and Nineteenth Centuries." In *Colloque international sur l'histoire du Caire*, 221–233. Cairo: Ministry of Culture of the Arab Republic of Egypt, 1969.

Humarat monyati. [Weekly humor journal.] Edited by Muhammad Tawfiq "al-Azhari." Cairo: 1899–1904. Dar al-Kutub, dawriyyat no. 272.

Hunter, F. Robert. *Egypt under the Khedives 1805–1879: From Household Government to Modern Bureaucracy.* Pittsburgh: University of Pittsburgh Press, 1984.

Hurgronje, Snouck. "E. Sachau, Muhammadanisches Recht Nach Schafiitischer Lehre," *Zeitschrift der Deutschen Morgenlandischen Gesellschaft* 53 (Leipzig, 1899): 125–167; reprint Gedagteekend: Kutaradja (Atjeh): 1898.

Husain, Zohair. "Muhammad 'Abduh (1849–1905): The Pre-eminent Muslim Modernist of Egypt." *Hamdard Islamicus* 9, no. 3 (1986): 31–39.

al-Husayni, Ahmad Bey al-Husayni ibn Ahmad ibn Yusuf. "Muqaddimat murshid al-anam li birr umm al-imam." Manuscript. Dar al-Kutub, Qism al-Makhtutat al-Nadira, Fiqh al-Shafi'i 1522. Vol. 2, microfilm no. 43166.

Hussein, Taha. *The Days: Taha Hussein, His Autobiography in Three Parts.* Translated by E. H. Paxton, Hilary Wayment, and Kenneth Cragg. Cairo: American University in Cairo Press, 1997.

Ibn Khaldun, *The Muqaddima: An Introduction to History.* Translated by Franz Rosenthal. 3 vols. New York: Pantheon Books, 1958.

'Ilish, Muhammad. *Fath al-'ali al-malik fi al-fatwa 'ala madhhab al-imam Malik.* Vol. 1. Cairo: Sharikat Maktaba wa Matba'a Mustafa al-Babi al-Halabi wa Awladhihi, 1958 [1882].

'Ilish, Muhammad. *Hidayat al-murid li-'aqidat ahl tawhid wa sharhiha 'umdat ahl al-tawfiq wa al-tasdid li Muhammad ibn Yusuf al-Sanusi; wa bi hamishihi, Sharh al-musamma bi al-futuhat al-ilahiyya al-Wahhabiyya 'ala manzuma al-miqriyya al-musammat ida'at al-dujna fi i'tiqad ahl al-sunna.* Cairo: al-Matba'a al-Bahiya al-Misriyya, 1306 H [1888/89].

al-Islam. [Monthly religious journal.] Edited by Shaykh Ahmad 'Ali al-Shadhili al-Azhari. Cairo: 1894–1912. Dar al-Kutub, dawriyyat no. 213.

al-Jabarti, 'Abd al-Rahman. *Tarikh aja'ib al-athar fi al-tarajim wa al-akhbar,* 4 parts in 3 vols. Beirut: War ul-Jeel, n.d. [c. 1820].

Jackson, Sherman. *Islamic Law and the State: The Constitutional Jurisprudence of Shihab al-Din al-Qarafi.* Leiden, Netherlands: E. J. Brill, 1996.

al-Jinan. [Bimonthly journal.] Edited by Butrus al-Bustani, Salim Effendi, and Najib al-Bustani. Beirut: 1870–1885. American University in Cairo, Arabic periodicals.

al-Jindi, Anwar. *'Abd al-'Aziz Jawish: Min ruwwad al-tarbiyya wa al-sahafa wa al-intima'.* Cairo: n.p., 1965.

Johansen, Baber. *Contingency in a Sacred Law: Legal and Ethical Norms in the Muslim Fiqh.* Leiden, Netherlands: E. J. Brill, 1999.

Johansen, Baber. "Legal Literature and the Problem of Change: The Case of the Land Rent." In *Islam and Public Law,* edited by Chibli Mallat, 29–47. London: Graham & Trotman, 1993.

Kahhala, 'Umar Rida. *Mu'jam al-mu'allifin.* Vols. 9–10 bound together in 1 vol. in this edition. Beirut: Dar al-Ihya' al-Turath al-'Arabi, n.d.

Kaloti, Sami Abdullah. "Islamic Reformation and the Impact of Jamal al-Din al-Afghani and Muhammad Abduh on Islamic Education." Ph.D. diss., Marquette University, Milwaukee, WI, 1974.

Keddie, Nikki R. *An Islamic Response to Imperialism; Political and Religious Writings of Sayyid Jamal al-Din "al-Afghani."* Berkeley: University of California Press, 1968.

Keddie, Nikki R. *Sayyid Jamal ad-Din "al-Afghani": A Political Biography.* Los Angeles: University of California, 1972.

Kedourie, Elie. *Afghani and 'Abduh: An Essay on Religious Unbelief and Political Activism in Modern Islam*. London: Frank Cass, 1997 [1966].

Kedourie, Elie. "'The Elusive Jamal al-Din al-Afghani', a Comment." *Muslim World* 59, no. 3–4 (July/October 1969): 308–314.

Kerr, Malcolm H. *Islamic Reform: The Political and Legal Theories of Muhammad 'Abduh and Rashid Rida*. Berkeley: University of California Press, 1966.

al-Khafaji, Muhammad 'Abd al-Mun'im. *Al-Azhar fi alf 'am*. Parts 1–3. Beirut: 'Alam al-Kutub; Cairo: Maktabat al-Kuliyya al-Azhariyya, 1988.

Khalafallah, Haifaa. "Understanding Islamic Law: A Historical and Structural Comparison between Islamic and English Common Law." American Research Center in Egypt Seminar presentation, 4 March 1998.

Khatab, 'Abd al-Mu'izz. *Shuyukh al-Azhar*. Cairo: Matabi'a li al-Ahram al-Tijariyya, n.d.

al-Khoury, Nabeel Abdo, and Abdo J. Baaklini. "Muhammad 'Abduh: An Ideology of Development." *Muslim World* 69, no. 1 (January 1979): 42–52.

Kraemer, Jorg. "Tradition and Reform at al-Azhar." *Middle Eastern Affairs* 7 (March 1956): 89–94.

al-Kumi, Sami 'Abd al-'Aziz. *al-Sihafa al-islamiyya fi Misr fi al-qarn al-tasi' 'ashar*. al-Mansura, Egypt: Dar al-Wafa' li al-Tiba'a wa al-Nashr wa al-Tawzi', 1992.

Lane, Edward. *Manners and Customs of the Modern Egyptians*. 2 vols. in 1. London: J. M. Dent & Co.; New York: E. P. Dutton & Co., 1842.

Levtzion, Nehemiah, and John O. Voll. *Eighteenth-Century Renewal and Reform in Islam*. Syracuse, NY: Syracuse University Press, 1987.

Livingston, John W. "Muhammad 'Abduh on Science." *Muslim World* 85, no. 3–4 (1995): 215–234.

Livingston, John W. "Western Science and Educational Reform in the Thought of Shaykh Rifa'ah al-Tahtawi." *International Journal of Middle East Studies* 28, no. 4 (November 1996): 543–564.

al-Liwa'. [Monthly journal issued 1900–1904; daily newspaper issued 1900–1912.] Edited by Mustafa Kamil; also edited by 'Abd al-'Aziz Jawish. Cairo. Dar al-Kutub, dawriyyat no. 450; U.S. Library of Congress.

Makdisi, George. *The Rise of Colleges: Institutions of Learning in Islam and the West*. Edinburgh: Edinburgh University Press, 1981.

al-Makhzumi, Muhammad Basha. *Khatirat Sayyid Jamal al-Din al-Afghani al-Husayni*. 1st ed. Beirut: al-Matba' al-'Ilmiyya li-Yusuf Sadir, 1931; 2nd ed. Beirut: Dar al-Fikr al-Hadith, 1965.

Mallat, Chibli. "The Debate on Riba and Interest in Twentieth Century Jurisprudence." In *Islamic Law and Finance*, edited by Chibli Mallat. London: Graham & Trotman, 1988.

Mallat, Chibli, ed. *Islam and Public Law: Classic and Contemporary Studies*. London: Graham & Trotman, 1993.

al-Manar. [Weekly religious journal.] Edited by Muhammad Rashid Rida. Cairo: 1897–1935. American University in Cairo, Arabic periodicals collection.

Mansfield, Peter. *The British in Egypt.* New York: Holt, Rinehart, and Winston, 1972.

al-Maraghi, Muhammad. *Majmuʻat al-wathaʼiq al-khassa bi-islah al-Jamiʻ al-Azhar.* Cairo: n.p., 1929.

Marlowe, John. *Anglo-Egyptian Relations 1800–1956.* London: Cresset Press, 1954.

Marlowe, John. *Cromer in Egypt.* New York: Praeger Publishers, 1970.

Marsot, Afaf Lutfi al-Sayyid. "The Beginnings of Modernization among the Rectors of al-Azhar, 1798–1879." In *Beginnings of Modernization in the Middle East,* edited by William R. Polk and Richard L. Chambers, 267–280. Chicago: University of Chicago Press, 1968.

Marsot, Afaf Lutfi al-Sayyid. *Egypt and Cromer: A Study in Anglo-Egyptian Relations.* London: Murray, 1968.

Marsot, Afaf Lutfi al-Sayyid. *Egypt in the Reign of Muhammad Ali.* Cambridge: Cambridge University Press, 1988 [c.1984].

Marsot, Afaf Lutfi al-Sayyid. "Entrepreneurial Women." In *Feminism and Islam: Legal and Literary Perspectives,* edited by Mai Yamani. New York: New York University Press, 1996.

Marsot, Afaf Lutfi al-Sayyid. "The Role of the 'Ulama' in Egypt during the Early Nineteenth Century." In *Political and Social Change in Modern Egypt,* edited by P. M. Holt, 264–280. London: Oxford University Press, 1968.

Marsot, Afaf Lutfi al-Sayyid. *A Short History of Modern Egypt.* Cambridge: Cambridge University Press, 1985.

Marsot, Afaf Lutfi al-Sayyid. "A Socio-Economic Sketch of the 'Ulama' in the Eighteenth Century." In *Colloque international sur l'histoire du Caire,* 313–319. Cairo: Ministry of Culture of the Arab Republic of Egypt, 1969.

Marsot, Afaf Lutfi al-Sayyid. "The Ulama of Cairo in the Eighteenth and Nineteenth Centuries." In *Scholars, Saints, and Sufis,* edited by Nikki R. Keddie, 149–166. Berkeley: Univeristy of California Press, 1972.

Marsot, Afaf Lutfi al-Sayyid. "The Wealth of the Ulama in Late Eighteenth-Century Cairo." In *Studies in Eighteenth Century Islamic History,* edited by Thomas Naff and Roger Owen, 205–216. Carbondale: Southern Illinois University Press, 1977.

Marsot, Afaf Lutfi al-Sayyid. *Women and Men in Late Eighteenth-Century Egypt.* Austin: University of Texas Press, 1995.

Mashruʻ Lajnat Islah al-Azhar al-Maʻmur, 1328/1910. Cairo: al-Matbaʻa al-Amiriyya, 1910. Works of the government reform committee as presented by Muhammad Saʻid Pasha; texts of all reform codes between 1872 and 1910 included in appendixes. American University in Cairo library.

McCarthy, Justin A. "Nineteenth-Century Egyptian Population." *Middle Eastern Studies* 12, no. 3 (October 1976): 1–39.

Misbah, Mohamed. *Al-Azhar: A University between Two Ages.* N.p.: I. N. Thut World Education Center, 1983.

Misbah al-sharq. [Weekly newspaper.] Edited by Ibrahim al-Muwailihi and Muhammad al-Muwailihi. Cairo: 1898–1903. Dar al-Kutub, dawriyyat no. 1194.

Mitchell, Timothy. *Colonising Egypt.* Berkeley: University of California Press, 1991 [1988].

al-Mu'ayyad. [Daily newspaper.] Edited by 'Ali Yusif. Cairo: December 1889–December 1915. Dar al-Kutub, dawriyyat no. 60.

Mubarak, 'Ali. *al-A'mal al-kamila li 'Ali Mubarak.* Edited by Muhammad 'Imara. Vol. 1. Beirut: al-Mu'assasa al-'Arabiyya li al-Dirasat wa al-Nashr, 1979.

Mubarak, 'Ali. *al-Khitat al-tawfiqiyya al-jadida li-Misr al-qahira.* 20 vols. Cairo: al-Hay'a al-Misriyya al-'Amma li al-Kitab, 1983 [1887].

Mu'nis, Husayn. *al-Sharq al-islami fi al-'asr al-hadith.* 2nd ed. Cairo: Matba'a Hijazi, 1938.

al-Muqattam. [Daily newspaper.] Edited by Ya'qub Sarruf, et. al. Cairo: 1889–1952. Dar al-Kutub, dawriyyat no. 65.

al-Muqtataf. [Monthly scientific journal.] Edited by Faris Nimr and Ya'qub Sarruf. Beirut, Alexandria: 1876–1952. American University of Cairo, Arabic periodicals.

al-Musawi, 'Abd al-Husayn Sharaf al-Din. *al-Muraja'at.* Beirut: Mu'assasat al-A'lami li al-Matbu'at, 1983 [correspondence between author and Shaykh al-Azhar Salim al-Bishri, c. 1911].

National Bank of Egypt, 1898–1948. Cairo: privately circulated, 1948.

al-Nil. [Daily newspaper.] Edited by Hasan Husni al-Tuwayrani. Cairo: 1889–1915. Dar al-Kutub, dawriyyat no. 413.

Nosseir, Aida Ibrahim. *al-Kutub allati nushirat fi Misr fi al-qarn al-tasi' 'ashar.* Cairo: American University in Cairo Press, 1990.

Ong, Walter J. *Orality and Literacy: The Technologizing of the Word.* London: Methuen, 1982.

Owen, Roger. *Cotton and the Egyptian Economy 1820–1914.* Oxford: Clarendon Press, 1969.

Owen, Roger. *Middle East in the World Economy 1800–1914.* London: I.B. Tauris, 1993.

Peters, Rudolph. "*Idjtihad* and *Taqlid* in 18th and 19th Century Islam." *Die Welt des Islams* 20, nos. 3–4 (n.d.): 131–145.

Peters, Rudolph. "The Lions of Qasr al-Nil Bridge: The Islamic Prohibition of Images as an Issue in the 'Urabi Revolt." In *Islamic Legal Interpretation: Muftis and their Fatwas,* edited by Muhammad Khalid Masud, Brinkley Messick, and David S. Powers. Cambridge: Harvard University Press, 1996.

Peters, Rudolph. "Religious Attitudes towards Modernization in the Ottoman Empire: A 19th Century Text on Steamships, Factories and the Telegraph." *Die Welt des Islams* 26 (1986): 76–105.

Philipp, Thomas. "Introduction." In *The Autobiography of Jurji Zaidan.* Washington, D C: Three Continents Press, 1990.

Quataert, Donald. "The Age of Reforms, 1812–1914." In *An Economic and Social History of the Ottoman Empire,* edited by Halil Inalcik and D. Quataert. Vol. 2. Cambridge: Cambridge University Press, 1994.

Quataert, Donald. "Ottoman Manufacturing in the Nineteenth Century." In *Manufacturing in the Ottoman Empire and Turkey, 1500–1950*. Albany: State University of New York Press, 1994.

al-Quwaysini, Hasan. "Mukhtasar sharh sullam." Azhariyya, 34253 Halim 820.

al-Quwaysini, Hasan. "Sanad al-Quwaysini." Cairo: Dar al-Kutub, Makhtutat 23126B.

Rabi', Magirah 'Ali Salih. *al-Dawr al-siyasi li al-Azhar 1952–1981*. Cairo: Markaz al-Buhuth wa al-Dirasat al-Siyasiyya, 1992.

al-Rafi'i, 'Abd al-Rahman. *'Asr Isma'il*. Vol. 1. Cairo: 1932.

Ramadan, 'Abd al-'Azim. *Tarikh al-madaris fi Misr al-islamiyya*. Cairo: Al-Hay'a al-Misriyya al-'Amma li al-Kitab, 1993.

Ramadan, Mustafa Muhammad. "Dawr al-awqaf fi da'm al-Azhar ka mu'assasa 'ilmiyya islamiyya." Paper presented at the Nadwat al-tatawwur al-tarikhi li-mu'assasat al-awqaf fi al-'alam al-'arabi wa al-islam, April 1983, in Baghdad.

Ramadan, Mustafa Muhammad. *Dawr al-Azhar fi al-hayat al-Misriyya iban al-hamla al-faransiyya wa matla' al-qarn al-tasi' 'ashar*. Cairo: Matba'at al-Jabalawi, 1986.

Ramadan, Mustafa Muhammad. "Dawr al-Azhar al-thaqafi wa al-'ilmi fi Ifriqiya." *Majallat Kulliyat al-Lugha al-'Arabiyya* 15, no. 4 (1997): 303–420.

Ramadan, Mustafa Muhammad. *Tarikh al-islah fi al-Azhar fi al-'asr al-hadith, 1872–1961*. Cairo: Dar al-Wafa' li al-Tiba', 1984.

Rashwan, Malik Muhammad Ahmad. *'Ulama' al-Azhar bayna Bonaparte wa Muhmmad 'Ali (1798–1840)*. Cairo: Matba'at al-Amana, 1989.

Rawdat al-madaris al-Misriyya. [Monthly educational journal.] Board of directors included Rifa'ah al-Tahtawi and 'Ali Mubarak. Cairo: 17 April 1870–8 September 1877. Dar al-Kutub, dawriyyat nos. 506–509.

Reimer, Michael J. "Contradiction and Consciousness in Ali Mubarak's Description of al-Azhar." *International Journal of Middle East Studies* 29, no. 1 (February 1997): 53–69.

Reimer, Michael J. "Views of al-Azhar in the Nineteenth Century: Gabriel Charmes and 'Ali Pasha Mubarak." In *Travellers in Egypt*, edited by Paul Starkey and Janet Starkey. London: I.B. Tauris, 1998.

Rida, Muhammad Rashid. *Al-Manar wa al-Azhar*. 1st ed. Cairo: Matba'at al-Manar, 1353 H.

Rida, Muhammad Rashid. *Tarikh al-ustadh al-imam Muhammad Abduh*, 3 vols. Cairo: Matba'at al-Manar, 1908, 1910, 1931.

Rivlin, Helen Anne B. *The Agricultural Policy of Muhammad 'Ali in Egypt*. Cambridge, MA: Harvard University Press, 1961.

Roberson, B. A. "The Emergence of the Modern Judiciary in the Middle East: Negotiating the Mixed Courts of Egypt." In *Islam and Public Law*, edited by Chibli Mallat, 107–139. London: Graham & Trotman, 1993.

Saeed, Abdullah. *Islamic Banking and Interest: A Study of the Prohibition of Riba and Its Contemporary Interpretation*. Leiden, Netherlands: E. J. Brill, 1996.

Safran, Nadav. *Egypt in Search of Political Community.* Cambridge, MA: Harvard University Press, 1981.

Said, Edward. *Orientalism.* New York: Random House, 1978.

al-Sa'idi, 'Abd al-Mit'al. *Tarikh al-islah fi al-Azhar wa safahat min al-jihad fi al-islah.* Cairo: Matba'at al-I'timad, 1951.

Salamah, Jirjis. *Athar al-ihtilal al-Britani fi al-ta'lim al-qawmi fi Misr.* Cairo: Maktaba al-Anglo al-Misriyya, 1966.

Salman, 'Abd al-Karim. *A'mal majlis idarat al-Azhar, min ibtida' ta'sisihi sana 1312 ila ghayat sana 1322.* Cairo: Matba'at al-Manar, 1322 H [1905].

al-Salus, 'Ali Ahmad. *'Aqidat al-imama 'and al-shi'a al-ithna-'ashariyya: hal kana Shaykh al-Azhar al-Bishri shi'i^{an}?* Cairo: Dar al-I'tisam, 1987.

Sami, Amin. *Taqwim al-nil.* 3 vols. Cairo: Matba'at Dar al-Kutub al-Misriyya, 1915–1936.

al-Sayyadi, Abu al-Huda. *Da'i al-rashad li sabil al-ittihad wa al-inqiyad.* Istanbul: al-Matba'a al-Sultaniyya, c. 1880.

al-Sayyadi, Mukhlis. *al-Azhar wa mashari' tatwirihi 1872–1970.* Beirut: Dar al-Rashid, 1992.

Scholch, Alexander. *Egypt for the Egyptians! The Socio-Political Crisis in Egypt in 1878–1882.* Published for the Middle East Centre at St. Antony's College, Oxford; London: Ithaca Press, 1981.

Shafiq, Ahmad (Pasha). *Mudhakkirati fi nisf qarn.* Vols. 1–2. Cairo: Sharikat Musahima Misriyya, 1934–1936. Vol. 3. Cairo: Dar al-Majallati li al-Tab' wa al-Nashr, n.d.

Shahhat, 'Abdullah Mahmud. *Manhaj al-imam Muhammad 'Abduh fi tafsir al-Qur'an.* Cairo: al-Majlis al-'Ala li Rifa'iat al-Funun wa al-Adab wa al-'Ulum al-Ijtima'iyya, 1960.

Shaked, Haim. "The Biographies of 'Ulama' in Mubarak's *Khitat* as a Source for the History of the 'Ulama' of Nineteenth-Century Egypt." *Asian and African Studies* 7 (1971): 41–76.

Shalaby, Ahmed. *History of Muslim Education.* Karachi: Indus Publications, 1979.

al-Shannawi, Kamil. "Al-Azhar Discipline." *Middle Eastern Affairs* 7 (March 1956): 108–115.

Shidyaq, Faris. *Kanz al-ragha'ib fi muntakhabat al-Jawa'ib.* Vol. 1. Istanbul: Matba'at al-Jawa'ib, 1288 H.

al-Shinnawi, 'Abd al-'Aziz Muhammad. "Du rôle de 1-Azhar dans la préservation du caractère arabe de 1-Egypt sous le règne des Ottomans." In *Colloque international sur l'histoire du Caire,* 433–435. Cairo: Ministry of Culture of the Arab Republic of Egypt, 1969.

Spevack, Aaron. "The Archetypal Sunni Scholar: Law, Theology, and Mysticism in the Synthesis of al-Bajuri." Ph.D. dissertation, Boston University, 2008.

Starrett, Gregory. *Putting Islam to Work: Education, Politics, and Religious Transformation in Egypt.* Berkeley: University of California Press, 1998.

Suruf, Fu'ad and Linda Sidq, eds. *Fihris al-Muqtataf.* 3 vols. Beirut: American University in Beirut, 1967.

al-Tahtawi, Muhammad 'Izzat. *Min al-'ulama' al-ruwad fi rihab al-Azhar.* Cairo: Maktaba Wuhba, n.d.

al-Tahtawi, Rifa'a Rafi'. *al-A'mal al-kamila li Rifa'a Rafi' al-Tahtawi.* Edited by Muhammad 'Imara. 2 vols. 1st ed. Beirut: al-Mu'assasa al-'Arabiyya li al-Dirasat wa al-Nashr, 1973.

al-Tahtawi, Rifa'a Rafi'. *al-Qawl al-sadid fi al-ijtihad wa al-tajdid.* Cairo: Matba'at Wadi al-Nil, 1870.

al-Tahtawi, Rifa'a Rafi'. *Takhlis al-ibriz fi talkhis Bariz.* Cairo: al-Hay'a al-Misriyya al-'Amma li al-Kitab, 1993 [1834].

al-Tanahi, Tahir. *Mudhakkirat al-imam Muhammad 'Abduh.* Cairo: Dar al-Hilal, 1963.

al-Tankit wa al-tabkit. [Weekly journal.] Edited by 'Abdullah Nadim. Alexandria: 6 June 1881–22 October 1881. Dar al-Kutub, dawriyyat no. 2309.

Tawfiq, Muhammad Amin. "The Awqaf in Modern Egypt." *Islamic Quarterly* 42, no. 4 (1998): 257–265.

Toledano, Ehud R. *State and Society in Mid-Nineteenth Century Egypt.* Cambridge: Cambridge University Press, 1990.

Tucker, Judith. *In the House of the Law.* Berkeley: University of California Press, 1998.

al-Tu'imi, Muhyi al-Din. *al-Nur al-abhar fi tabaqat shuyukh al-Jami' al-Azhar.* Beirut: War ul-Jeel, 1992.

al-Ustadh. [Weekly educational journal.] Edited by 'Abdullah Nadim. Cairo: 1892–1893. AUC Arabic periodicals.

Vatikiotis, P. J. "Muhammad 'Abduh and the Quest for a Muslim Humanism." *Arabica* 4 (1957): 54–72.

Vogel, Frank. "The Closing of the Door of Ijtihad and the Application of the Law." *American Journal of Islamic Social Sciences* 10, no. 3 (Fall 1993): 396–401.

al-Waqa'i' al-Misriyya. [Official government biweekly journal.] Cairo: 1828–1942. Dar al-Kutub, dawriyyat nos. 71, 545.

al-Waqt. Cairo: 1887. University of Chicago microfilm.

Warner, Nicholas, ed. *An Egyptian Panorama: Reports from the 19th Century British Press.* Cairo: Boraie, Shaalan & Co., 1994.

Wiederhold, Lutz. "Legal Doctrines in Conflict: The Relevance of *Madhhab* Boundaries to Legal Reasoning in the Light of an Unpublished Treatise on *Taqlid* and *Ijtihad.*" *Islamic Law and Society* 3, no. 2 (June 1996): 234–289.

Wilson, E. O. "The Relevant Principles of Population Biology." In *Sociobiology,* 63–105. Cambridge, MA: Belknap Press, 1975.

Winter, Michael. *Egyptian Society under Ottoman Rule 1517–1798.* London: Routledge, 1992.

Yunus, 'Abd al-Hamid, and 'Uthman Tawfiq. *al-Azhar.* Cairo: Dar al-Fikr al-Arabi, 1946.

Yusif, 'Ali, ed. *Muntakhabat al-Mu'ayyad.* Vol. 1. Cairo: Matba'at al-Mu'ayyad, 1890.

al-Zahir. [Daily pan-Islamist newspaper.] Edited by Nasr al-Din Zaghlul, Darwish Mustafa. Cairo: 1903–1942. Dar al-Kutub, dawriyyat no. 458.

Zakhura, Ilyas. *Mir'at al-'asr fi tarikh wa rusum akabir al-rijal bi Misr.* Vols. 2–3. Private printing, Ilyas Zakhura, Qantarat al-Dikka, Egypt, 1916.

Zaman, Muhammad Qasim. "Commentaries, Print, and Patronage: Hadith and the Madrasahs in Modern South Asia." *Bulletin of the School of Oriental and African Studies* 62, no. 1 (1999): 60–81.

Zaman, Muhammad Qasim. "Religious Education and the Rhetoric of Reform: The Madrasah in British India and Pakistan." *Comparative Studies in Society and History* (1999): 294–323.

al-Zawahiri, Fakhr al-Din al-Ahmadi. *al-Siyasa wa al-Azhar min mudhakkirat Shaykh al-Islam al-Zawahiri.* Cairo: Al-Jami'a al-Azhariayya al-Haditha, 1945.

al-Zawahiri, Muhammad al-Ahmadi. *al-'Ilm wa al-'ulama wa al-nizam al-ta'lim.* 2nd ed., with introduction by Fakhr al-Din Zawahiri. N.p.: 1955 [1904].

Zaydan, Jurji. *The Autobiography of Jurji Zaidan.* Edited by Thomas Philipp. Washington, DC: Three Continents Press, 1990.

Zaydan, Jurji. *Tarajim mashahir al-sharq fi al-qarn al-tasi' 'ashar.* 2 vols. 2nd rev. ed. Cairo: Matba'at al-Hilal, 1910 [1st ed. serialized by Dar al-Hilal, 1902–03; 1st rev. ed. 1907].

al-Zayyat, Ahmad Hasan. "Risalat al-Azhar" and "al-Wad' al-lughawi wa haqq al-muhdathin fihi." In *Wahy al-risala.* Vol. 2, 37–40. Vol. 3, 170–182. Cairo: Mataba'at al-Risalah, 4 vols., 1949–1950.

al-Zayyati, Sulayman Rashad Hanafi. *Kanz al-jawhar fi tarikh al-Azhar.* Cairo: 1904.

Ziadeh, Nicola A. *Sanusiyyah: A Study of a Revivalist Movement in Islam.* Leiden: E. J. Brill, 1958.

al-Zirikli, Khayr al-Din. *al-A'lam.* 9 vols. Beirut: Dar al-'Ilm li al-Malayin, 1984.

INDEX

'Abbas Hilmi I, Viceroy of Egypt,
16, 40–41, 42, 45
'Abbas Hilmi II, Khedive of Egypt,
40, 129, 141, 157, 165, 169,
171, 176, 177, 180, 188, 199,
212, 213, 223, 235
'Abduh and, 130, 166, 172, 187,
189–190
accession of, 217
Administrative Council and,
129–132, 206
al-Azhar and, 211, 224
Cromer and, 195
Hasuna al-Nawawi and, 211
Nadim and, 130
al-'Abbasi al-Mahdi, Muhammad
(Shaykh al-Azhar), 51–52, 90,
92, 93, 95, 96, 113, 114, 166
candidacy of, 51
code by, 113
column reapportionment plan by,
52
Dar al-'Ulum and, 115
deposing, 91
resignation of, 115
rise of, 54
support for, 53
'Abd, Sulayman (Shaykh), 190, 209,
212

'Abd al-Rahman Sami Pasha, 25–26
'Abd al-Sayyid, Mikha'il, 82
'Abduh, Hamuda Bey, 184
'Abduh, Muhammad (Grand Mufti),
1, 5, 7, 13, 83, 85, 92, 93–94,
105, 112, 114, 117, 122, 162,
182, 206–207, 212, 226, 227
'Abbas and, 130, 166, 172, 187,
189–190
'Abd al-Rahman al-Shirbini and,
209
ad hominem, campaign against,
187–188
Administrative Council and,
129–132
al-Afghani and, 77, 78, 108, 165
'alimiyya exam of, 95, 114
apostasy of (alleged), 170–171
Arabic writing and, 79
arrogance of, 90, 95
campaign against, 169, 188–195,
221
criticism by, 80, 168
criticism of, 166, 169, 175,
177–179, 180, 183, 185–186,
197, 202, 203
Cromer and, 166, 169, 171–172,
176, 194–195, 268 n.73
death of, 210, 211

exile of, 107
failure of, 214–215
fatwas by, 175, 176, 188, 193, 194
Herbert Spencer and, 190–191
ijtihad and, 79, 102, 171, 174,
    177, 180, 192, 195–196, 206,
    208, 233
'Ilish and, 93–96
investment interest and,
    175–177, 182, 267 n.61
al-Jinan and, 113
journalism and, 77–82
Khedive 'Abbas Hilmi II and,
    130, 172, 185–186
legacy of, 201, 214–215
"liberal sentiments" of, 172
Maliki training of, 95, 105, 172
modernism and, 6, 228
mudaraba, 175
muqallidun al-gharb
    (Westernizers), 80
nationalism of, 166
photo of, 183 (fig.), 184, 194–195
pledge broken, 182, 192, 194
pledge to follow Hanafi
    madhhab, 172
on power, 78
reform and, 2, 79, 82, 165, 177,
    181, 204, 208, 229, 232
religious instruction and, 81
religious office and, 171
resignation of, 210, 228
Risalat al-tawhid, 169–171
Salim al-Bishri and, 204–205
sketch of, 191 (fig.)
sympathy for, 195–196
taqlid and, 77, 80, 81–82, 87,
    94–95, 108, 112, 167, 170,
    171, 174, 192, 194, 211, 232
true Islam and, 234

'ulama and, 79, 87, 93–95, 122,
    166, 193
'Urabist rebels and, 92–93, 107,
    112, 166
'Abdulhamid II, Sultan of Ottoman
    Empire, 171, 172, 179
'Abduh and, 166, 178, 180
Khedive 'Abbas Hilmi II and, 177
Tawfiq and, 186
'ulama and, 113
'Urabists and, 83
al-'Abid, 'Izzat Bey, 180
Abu al-Fadl, Muhammad 'Abd al-
    Halim, 162, 163
Abu Hanifa, 64, 70, 101, 193, 194
Abu Naddara zarqa', 82
Abu Shadi, Muhammad Bey, 191
Abu Yusuf, 101
al-Adab, 'Ali Yusuf in, 118, 119
al-Afghani, Jamal al-Din, 60, 79, 88,
    94, 95, 97, 112, 113, 114,
    118, 170, 178, 193, 196, 231
'Abduh and, 77, 78, 108, 165
Azharis and, 72, 76–77
cultural revival and, 72
education and, 59
expulsion of, 96
ijtihad and, 73–76, 79, 86, 88,
    98, 102
nationalist disciples of, 82–86
Protestant Reformation and, 72–73
scholarly attention for, 4
taqlid and, 71–72, 75, 76, 87
true Islam and, 234
'ulama and, 87
Ahl-i Hadith movement, 72
Ahmad Ibn Kamal Pasha, 70
Ahmadi Mosque, 30, 85
Ahmadiyya, 99
al-Ahram, 82, 194

Alfiyya (Ibn Malik), 133
'*alimiyya*, 217, 219
  degree, 53, 54, 122, 124–125,
    127, 156, 158, 166, 220
Amin, Qasim, 228
*Aperçu historique sur les moeurs et
  coutumes des nations* (Depping),
  33
al-'Arabi, Abu Bakr ibn, 189
al-Arnab, 186, 195, 269 n.94
Arslan, Shakib, 166, 167
al-'Arusi, Mustafa, Shaykh al-Azhar,
    27, 43, 50–51, 53, 96
  appointment of, 48
al-Asbagh, 101
al-'Attar, Hasan, 7, 43, 57, 74, 118,
    198
  Clot Bey and, 26
  critique of, 23–28, 30
  death of, 27–28, 54
  Muhammad 'Ali and, 25–26
  reform and, 36
  scorn for derivative works and, 25
  al-Tahtawi and, 28–35
  writings of, 24
awqaf. *See* waqf
al-Azhar
  budget for, 124–125, 160
  conditions at, 16, 37, 46, 113,
    126, 127, 160, 205–206, 207
  curriculum at, 28, 40, 57, 109,
    124–125, 140, 161, 163, 202,
    220
  described, 1, 3, 16
  disturbances at, 43, 47, 143–153,
    198, 205–206, 217–226, 234
  education at, 23–24, 56, 59, 136
  mission of, 133, 135, 137–138,
    140, 161–162, 201, 206
  mosque, 149, 219

pejoratives for, 207
reform at, 2–8, 28, 35–36, 53,
    81–82, 96, 108, 123–129,
    134–135, 137, 154, 165,
    167, 197, 198, 199–200,
    232
sciences at, 119, 121–122
state intervention at, 163–164
students at, 2–3, 14, 17, 21,
    41–42, 85, 111, 127
subjects at, 20, 39, 136, 137,
    155, 160–161, 200, 220
teaching at, 3, 53, 94, 124–125,
    128, 215
University, 2
al-Azhar, Shaykh (rector), 10, 13,
    26, 39, 42, 43, 46, 49, 50,
    51, 52, 53, 56, 57, 91, 95,
    113, 114, 130, 131, 151
  Azhar Administrative Council
    and, 154–155
  choosing, 151, 158, 205
  degree programs and, 125
  office criticized, 150, 152
  overcrowding and, 125–126
  punishment by, 159
  reform and, 154
  state authority and, 38
  'ulama and, 24, 27
al-Azhar Administrative Council,
    129–132, 134, 141, 143, 151,
    152, 155–156, 157, 161, 163,
    164, 165, 169, 179, 189, 190,
    196, 197, 199, 201, 206, 210,
    211, 224, 229
  code by, 159–160
  reform and, 154
  Shafiq and, 212
  Shaykh al-Azhar and, 154–155
al-Azhar Club Committee, 225

Azhar Incident. *See* Syrian Riwaq
    Cholera Riot
Azhar Organization Code (1896).
    See reform codes
Azhar Reorganization Code (13 May
    1911). *See* reform codes
Azharis
    court positions and, 116
    criticism of, 24, 27, 29, 37, 45,
        46, 76, 77, 80, 115, 120,
        123–125, 127, 132–133,
        136, 137, 143, 150,
        166–167, 168
    fears of, 143
    morality and, 98
    prejudices against, 150

al-Babaghallo al-Misri, 190, 195
al-Badawi, al-Sayyid Ahmad, 156
al-Bajuri, Ibrahim, 42, 43, 199, 233
al-Bakhit, Muhammad, 199, 205
al-Bakri, Muhammad Tawfiq, 190
al-Banna', Muhammad, 117, 118,
    163
al-Baydawi, 24
Bayram, Muhammad, 116, 117,
    122, 163
Bentham, Jeremy, 12, 55
al-Biblawi, 'Ali (Shaykh al-Azhar),
    189, 193, 205
    resignation of, 208, 209
bid'a (innovation), 48, 86, 202
bin Laden, Osama, 233, 234
al-Bishri, Salim (Shaykh al-Azhar),
    5, 131, 157, 185, 186, 187,
    199–205, 224, 227–228, 234
    'Abduh and, 203, 204
    ijtihad and, 229
    income for, 203
    independence of, 225

on jurisprudence, 204
madrasa education and, 225
obstructionism of, 205
reform development and, 198,
    201
reliance on, 200–201
taqlid and, 204
'ulama and, 201, 229
on Umar, 200
Blunt, Wilfrid, 184, 231
    on al-'Abbasi, 90
    'Abduh and, 180, 188, 191
    on al-Inbabi, 91
    on Muhammad 'Ilish, 92
al-Bulaqi, Mustafa, 90, 96, 99
al-Bustani, Butrus, 112

centralization, 10, 11–17, 35, 41,
    235
certificates of madrasa student status,
    54
certificates of graduation, 126
cholera, 145, 147, 152, 154
    outbreak of, 143–144
Cholera Riot (1896). *See* Syrian
    Riwaq Cholera Riot
Citadel, the (fortress of Muhammad
    'Ali), 27, 40, 107
civilization, 73, 79
civil schools, 80, 81, 116, 129, 160,
    168, 212, 213, 216, 217
Claus, Mr., 147, 150, 153
Clot, Antoine Bey, 26, 34
code (1872). *See* reform codes
code (1895–1896). *See* reform codes
code (1908). *See* reform codes
Comité de Conservation, 16
commentaries, 18, 25, 76, 156
    language of, 160
    teaching, 169

Commission de la Dette Publique, 82
Commission of Health and Quarantines, 187
Committee of Azhari Unity, 222
communications, 22, 129
community
-as-nation, 59
education and, 87
identity, 80
reformers' concept of, 108
Companions of the Prophet, 62, 74
Comte, Auguste, 167
conscription, 41–43, 54, 56, 113
conservatives, 5, 6
education and, 235
modernists and, 2
Considerations sur les causes de la grandeur des romains et de leur decadence (Montesquieu), 39
Corps of the Dinstinguished 'Ulama, 226
Council of Ministers, 113, 114, 130, 131, 153, 154, 158, 208, 212
Courts of Appeals, 169, 171, 172
Cromer, Evelyn Baring, Lord, 116, 117, 129, 130, 166, 171–172, 185, 198
'Abd al-Rahman al-Shirbini and, 209
Hasuna al-Nawawi and, 172
Khedive 'Abbas Hilmi II and, 195
Muhammad 'Abduh and, 169, 176, 194, 195, 231
patronage of, 169
Salim al-Bishri and, 205
on Tawfiq, 113
Veiled Protectorate and, 112
Cromer, Lady, 195

cultural revival, 72, 73, 98
curriculum, 28, 40, 57, 109, 116, 140, 161, 163, 168, 173, 202
revising, 5, 124–125, 126

Dar al-'Ulum, 123, 131, 216, 217
'Abduh and, 169
curriculum at, 116
establishment of, 115, 119
reform of, 167
sciences at, 122
shari'a program of, 116
students at, 129
Darwin, Charles, 190, 191
Department of Education, 45, 82
Department of Schools, 38
Depping, Georg Bernhard, 29, 33
Description de l'Egypte, 14
Dinshawai incident, 197–198
Dunlop, Douglas, 182, 198

education, 29, 32–33, 45, 59, 195, 217
'Abduh and, 87, 96, 166–169
administrative, 22
civil, 86, 168
community and, 87
debates about, 132
deficiencies in, 166
democratizing, 120
efficiency-based, 139, 144, 167
elementary, 21, 33
increase in, 3, 108
Islamic, 1, 17, 229
mass, 23
modernists/conservatives and, 207–208, 235
new forms of, 236
practical, 168
purpose of, 83–84

education *(cont.)*
   technical/vocational, 19
   textual, 227
   'ulama and, 116, 140
   universalization of, 33, 140
   utilitarian models of, 47, 55,
      144, 198
   See also Madrasa education;
      religious education
educational systems, 19, 21, 22,
      104, 207–208
   Egyptian, 39
   European, 13, 59, 80
   Utilitarian, 47, 55, 144, 198
Effendi, Jamal al-Din, 134, 171
Egyptian Islamic Jihad, 7
Egyptian Polytechnic, 44
Egyptian School, 44
'Enan, 'Abdullah: on reform, 138

Fahmi Pasha, Mustafa, 187
Fahmy, Khaled, 148
*Fath al-'ali al-malik fi al-fatwa 'ala
   madhhab al-Imam Malik*
   ('Ilish), 99
fatwas, 5, 7, 26, 70, 90, 92, 93, 97,
      98, 99, 100, 103, 104, 151,
      160, 171, 175, 176, 234
   issuing, 192
   on science, 116–118
   Transvaal, 188–195
fiqh (Islamic jurisprudence), 17, 20,
      40, 66, 81, 99, 174, 213, 216,
      277 n.134
Foucault, Michel, 4, 55

Gazira Gardens, 218, 221
al-Ghazali, 9, 12, 70, 78
al-Gizawi, Abu al-Fadl, 190

Globe, 228
Goschen-Joubert arrangement, 82
Grand Mufti, 52, 91, 105, 117, 151,
      165, 182, 204, 206
   'Abduh as, 172, 174, 175, 179,
      180, 188, 196, 199, 210
Grice, H. P., 22
Guizot, François, 73

hadith, 9, 18, 20, 29, 45, 53, 62,
      63, 67, 68, 72, 73, 98, 99,
      101, 102, 108, 155, 169, 173,
      188, 200, 233
   classification of, 64
   human reasoning and, 121
   judicial authority of, 96
   oral transmission of, 64
   Shi'i, 228
   Sunnis and, 2
halqa, 17–19, 22, 31, 35, 39, 40,
      49, 54, 57, 60, 81, 88, 107,
      124, 207
   illustration of, 49, 50
   pedagogical style in, 128
   social stagnation and, 76–77
   teaching in, 17
Hamas, 7
Hammad, Salih Hamdi, 220
Hamza, Amin, 221
Hanafi madhhab, 38, 39, 40, 50,
      51–52, 64, 68, 70, 89, 90, 92,
      105, 106, 113, 116, 117, 118,
      130, 132, 166, 172, 173, 182,
      199, 211, 213, 214
   Hanafi fiqh as subject, 115
   mujtahid rankings, 69–70
Hanafi Mufti, 51, 105, 214
Hanafis, 50, 51, 52, 68, 106
   ranks of, 69–70

Hanbal, Ahmad ibn (founder of
    Hanbali madhhab), 64
al-Hanbali, Ahmad (Hanbali Mufti),
    190, 210, 274 n.62
al-Hanbali, Yusuf (Hanbali Mufti),
    131
Hanbali madhhab, 39, 199, 255 n.35
    defined, 64, 131
    first to discuss closure of door of
        ijtihad, 249 n.20
    muftis as allies of 'Abduh, 190,
        210, 274 n.62
al-Hariri, 133
al-Haytami, Ibn Hajar, 69
Hifni al-Mahdi, Shaykh, 185–186
al-Hifni al-Mahdi, Shaykh
    Muhammad, 138, 139–140
Highest Council, 214, 216, 217,
    224, 229
Hijaz, 43, 181, 182
hikma ("wisdom," applied sciences),
    60–61, 119
Homeland Party, 83, 84, 85
Humarat monyati, 186, 188, 189,
    195, 199
    on 'Abduh, 176, 177, 180,
        181–182, 183, 184–185
Hurgronje, Snouck, 233
al-Husayn, Mosque of, 94, 107
hybrid/hybridization, 5, 54, 57, 67,
    84, 86, 139, 144, 165, 230,
    235–236
    conceptual colonization, 4, 5, 57,
        235

Ibn al-Athir, 216
Ibn al-Qasim, 101
Ibn al-Salah, 105, 118
Ibn Farhun, 100

Ibn Haytham, 122
Ibn Khaldun, 80, 122, 202
Ibn Malik, 133
Ibrahim Pasha, 12, 26, 40, 41
    on mosques/revenues, 13–14
    statue of, 93
'id julus (coronation anniversary),
    189, 194, 217
al-'Idwi, Hasan, 92, 107
al-'Idwi, Muhammad Hasanayn,
    212, 214
ifta' (issuing of fatwas), 192
ijma' (communal consensus), 63, 64,
    134, 255 n.50
ijtihad, 59, 62–66, 72, 89, 94, 97,
    99, 100, 109, 119, 165, 172,
    173, 190, 193, 213–214, 227,
    234
    'Abduh and, 79, 102, 171, 174,
        177, 180, 192, 195–196, 206,
        208, 233
    attack on, 98
    cessation of, 66, 70, 232, 249 n.20
    continuity of, 70, 249 n.20
    definition of, 6
    gate of, 65, 73, 213, 229, 233
    independent, 101, 102
    lay, 106
    performing, 65, 66, 74–75, 76,
        174, 233
    promotion of, 235
    revival of, 6–7, 75–76, 99, 108,
        169, 194, 208, 233
    social meaning of, 66–71, 98
    taqlid and, 227–228
    'ulama and, 66, 74, 88
'Ilish, Muhammad (Maliki Mufti), 1,
    89, 92, 94, 102, 104, 105, 106,
    123, 136, 174, 199, 203, 232

'Abduh and, 95–96
as "Aleysh," 91, 92
anonymity for, 107
death of son, 98
fatwas by, 5, 97, 98, 100
hadith and, 96
ijtihad and, 7, 97, 101
intellectual arrogance of, 90
leadership of, 93, 107
on madhhab divisions, 101
morality and, 98
Muslim society and, 108
popularity of, 90
reform and, 96, 108
switching madhahib, 103
taqlid and, 99, 121
'ulama and, 91
'Urabi Revolt and, 107
'ilm (discursive knowledge), 17,
61–62, 111, 119, 141, 160,
206
"Al-'ilm wa al-'ulama" (Nadim), 154
al-'Ilm wa al-'ulama wa al-nizam al-
ta'lim (al-Zawahiri), 206, 207,
227
imams (prayer leaders), 122, 156, 219
Imams (founders of Sunni madhahib),
63, 64, 70, 73, 89, 95, 99, 102,
105, 206, 207, 208, 211, 227,
228, 266 n.45
qualifications for independent
ijtihad, 100–101
taqlid of required, 173–174, 204
Imams, Shi'i, 204, 228
imperialism, 3, 107, 164, 196
al-Inbabi, Shams al-Din (Shaykh al-
Azhar), 91, 92, 116, 117,
118, 122, 163
fatwa by, 160
Hasuna and, 130, 132

resignation of, 151, 152
al-Insha' (al-'Attar), 25
Internal Organization Code. See
reform codes
Internal Organizational Plan No. 1.
See reform codes
Internal Reorganization Code
(1908). See reform codes
Iqbal, Muhammad, 66
al-Isfahani, Shaykh: fatwa of, 104
Ishaq, Adib, 82, 85
Islam
cultural forms of, 5
progress/evolution and, 73
respect for, 97
straight path of, 9
al-Islam, 136, 152, 210
Ahmad in, 144
on religious training, 162–163
Islamic Benevolent Schools, 177
Islamic Benevolent Society, 210
Isma'il, Khedive of Egypt, 40, 43,
50, 53, 60, 81, 89, 93, 157,
178
accession of, 82
'Ali Mubarak and, 45
deposing of, 83
foreign debt and, 82
government of, 52
reforms and, 44, 51
regard for, 47
'ulama and, 51
ittiba', 62–66, 68, 101, 103, 105
al-'Izazi, Khalil, 121

al-Jabarti, 'Abd al-Rahman, 10, 13,
14, 32, 35
al-Jabarti, Hasan, 122
al-Jahiz, 133
Jam' al-jawami' (al-'Attar), 24

jamidun ("frozen" or "stagnant" ones), 96. *See also* "stagnant ones"

jarayat (bread rations), 114, 258 n.41, 259 no. 45

Jaridat al-Azhar, 121

al-Jawa'ib al-Misriyya, 208

Jawish, 'Abd al-'Aziz, 217, 275 n.99

al-Jinan (al-Bustani), 112, 113

Jomard, Edme François, 32

journalistic debate, 118–123

al-Kafrawi, 30

al-Kamil (al-Mubarrad), 133

Kamil, 'Abd al-Majid, 190–191

Kamil, Mustafa, 187, 190, 194, 210

Kasawi. *See* Kiswa al-tashrif

Katatib. *See* Kuttab

al-Khalili, Taha, 162

al-Khawwas, 'Ali, 101

Khedive: title, meaning of, 40, 44

Kiswa al-tashrif ("robe of honor," financial award), 52, 53, 130, 131, 137, 138, 157, 189–190

Kitab al-Ajrumiyya, 30

knowledge, 111
    discursive, 141
    sacred/profane, 119–120
    transmission of, 60, 141, 164, 227, 230
    useful, 61–62
    Utilitarian concepts of, 61

Kuttab (elementary-level Qur'an schools), 14, 29, 116, 168, 182, 259 n.45

Land Law, 16, 43

Lane, Edward, 14–15, 16, 34
    misinterpreted, 34

al-Laqqani, Ibrahim, 82, 100

Law of the Three States, 167

law schools, 69, 221
    Madrasat al-Qada' (School of Jurisprudence), 216, 220, 227

legitimacy, 53–54

literacy, 3, 31, 60, 108, 195, 201

al-Liwa', 190, 194, 217, 219, 221, 223, 224, 228

Luther, Martin, 72–73

madaris (schools), 11, 17, 19, 23, 29, 38, 41, 42, 56, 57, 86, 98, 113, 129, 139, 141, 144, 149, 150, 164, 216, 217, 226
    colonization of, 6
    financial problems and, 12
    nationalism and, 84
    population of, 37
    reform of, 39, 43

madhhab/madhahib (legal school/s), 18, 48, 49, 50, 57, 64–65, 66, 68, 69, 72, 74, 90, 91, 96, 100– 103, 104, 105, 106, 133, 134
    decrease in, 49
    definition of, 18, 39
    formation of, 64–65
    Hanafi, *see* Hanafi madhhab
    Hanbali, *see* Hanbali madhhab
    Maliki, *see* Maliki madhhab
    Shafi'i, *see* Shafi'i madhhab
    Shi'i, *see* Shi'a

madrasa. *See* madaris

al-Madrasa al-Sultaniyya, 113, 169

madrasa education, 47, 61, 112, 235
    debates about, 132
    hybridization of, 230
    personal/contractual, 230

Madrasa Organization Code (1887). *See* reform codes

Madrasat al-Qada' (School of
    Jurisprudence). *See* law
    schools
Maghribis (north-west
    Africans), 24, 27, 42, 50,
    56, 90, 145
Al-Mahdi, Muhammad Amin
    (Shaykh al-Azhar), 51–52,
    205
Mahir Pasha, 146, 152
Malik ibn Anas, 64, 101, 102
Maliki madhhab, 39, 50, 66, 89, 91,
    95, 96, 99, 100, 103, 105,
    131, 159, 162, 172, 189, 203,
    214
    defined, 64–65
    errors in Maliki fiqh, 102, 227
Maliki Mufti, 89, 90, 203, 214
Mamluk amirs, 11, 12, 13
al-Manar, 193, 211
    'Abduh and, 170, 194, 196
    Rida and, 172, 194
Mansfield, Mr., 146–147, 153
Maqamat (al-Hariri), 133
maqasid, 155, 160, 207
market competition, 115–116
al-Marsafi, Hasan, 132
Marx, Karl, 57
McIlwraith, Malcolm, 171
Medical School, 26
military, 42, 53, 113
    European-style, 19
    mission of, 149
    organization of, 11–12
military schools, 3, 25, 35, 36, 44,
    80
    collapse of, 38, 56
    competition from, 19–21
    courses at, 40
Ministry of Awqaf, 15

Ministry of Education, 51, 60, 81,
    129, 198, 205, 217
    al-Jinan and, 112
Ministry of Justice, 116
Ministry of Public Education, 218
Ministry of the Interior, 144
Mir'at al-sharq, 82
Misbah al-sharq, 82, 179, 183, 199
Misr, 82
Misr al-fatah, 82, 85
Misr al-qahira, 82
modernists, 5, 6–7, 129, 137, 139,
    144, 163, 206, 233
    conservatives and, 2
    criticism of, 209
    education and, 207–208, 235
    taqlid and, 89
Montesquieu, Charles-Louis de
    Secondat, Baron de, 39
morality, 80, 98, 106, 137, 139,
    159, 165, 167, 168
Mosque of al-Ashraf, 121
Mosque of Sayyida Zaynab, 162
al-Mu'ayyad, 130, 132, 177, 207,
    213, 214, 215, 216, 218, 220,
    222, 225
    on demonstrations, 221, 224
    on reform movement, 208–209
    on Syrian Riwaq Cholera Riot,
    150
    on al-Zawahiri, 208
al-Mu'ayyad mosque, 224
Mubarak, 'Ali, 16, 43–47, 48, 51,
    60, 89, 92, 115, 116
    al-Azhar and, 45, 46
    Delta Barrage and, 45
    education and, 45
    expulsion of, 45
    madrasa education and, 56
al-Mubarrad, 133

Mufti al-Diyar al-Misriyya (Grand
    Mufti of Egypt), 52
muftis, 63, 74, 103, 122, 131, 155,
    163, 182, 219
  duty of, 104, 107
  incorrect rulings and, 106
  See also Grand Mufti, Maliki
    Mufti, Hanafi Mufti, Shafi'i
    Mufti
Mughamiz, Zaki, 177, 179
muhaddithun, 5, 62, 99
Muhammad, 3, 63, 101, 156, 192,
    207
  Night Journey and, 98
Muhammad 'Ali, Viceroy of Egypt,
    29, 43, 46, 47, 51, 90, 157,
    185
  administrative system of, 20, 42
  al-'Attar and, 25–26, 36
  al-Azhar and, 3, 21, 22
  Bentham and, 12
  bureaucratization and, 13
  centralization and, 11–17, 35,
    41, 235
  conscription and, 41
  economic program of, 38
  educational system and, 19, 21,
    22
  land-tenure arrangements and,
    35
  military schools and, 19, 20, 23,
    38, 44, 56, 57
  missions of, 32, 33
  power of, 38
  reform and, 20, 39
  religious institutions and, 13,
    35–36
  successors of, 40
  al-Tahtawi and, 33, 34
  taxation by, 13

'ulama and, 12, 13, 16, 17, 23,
    28, 36, 54
  waqf supervisors and, 14
Muhammadiyya, 99, 100, 102
al-Muhawirat bayna al-muslih wa
    al-muqallid (Muhammad
    Rashid Rida), 172–174
al-Mu'izz, 2
mujtahidun, 65, 66, 67, 68, 69, 70,
    71, 100, 101, 103, 106, 182
Mukhtasar Khalil, 102
Muqaddima (Ibn Khaldun), 80, 122
muqallidun, 70, 79, 80, 173, 174,
    179
al-Muqtataf, 144, 152, 191
murattabat (salaries), 137
al-Musawi, 'Abd al-Husayn Sharaf
    al-Din, 203–204, 228
Mustafa, Ibrahim Bey, 121
Mustafa Pasha, 208
Mu'tazilis, 94, 96, 133, 170, 190
al-Muwailihi, Ibrahim, 82, 202, 203
  'Abduh and, 178, 179
  on Egyptians/Westerners, 183
  al-Muqattam and, 179
al-Muwatta', 102

al-Nabhani, Yusuf (Shaykh), 113, 173
Nadim, 'Abdullah, 85, 87, 105, 112,
    123, 124, 125, 126, 139, 144,
    226
  'Abbas and, 130
  administrative reform program
    by, 128–129
  article by, 154
  Azhari students and, 127
  pedagogical style of, 128
  plea by, 129
  Shaykh Zifti and, 86
  'ulama and, 127

al-Nahj al-qawim, 171, 191
Napoleon, 11, 32, 149
al-Naqqash, Salim, 82, 84, 85
al-Nasafi, 94
nationalism, 5, 84, 178, 218,
    219–220
Nationalist Party, 83, 84, 85, 92
al-Nawawi, Hasuna (Shaykh al-
    Azhar), 130, 145, 148, 151,
    152, 153, 155, 199, 205, 212,
    213, 214, 215, 217, 218
  appointment of, 171, 211
  death of, 69
  demonstrators and, 223
  al-Inbabi and, 132
  natural sciences and, 118
  reforms and, 224
  resignation of, 172, 223–224
  'ulama and, 213
New Order. *See* reform codes
Nietzsche, Friedrich, 4
Night Journey, 98
Nightingale, Florence, 15, 16, 37
al-Nil, 133, 136

On Education (Spencer), 167
One Thousand and One Nights, 34
order, 53–54, 230
Orientalists, 3, 4, 6, 7, 88, 232
Ottoman Empire, 44, 171, 193
  centralization of, 11–17
  control by, 3

Panopticism, 55–56, 57, 153
Paris Exhibition, 181
pedagogy, 21–23, 56, 159, 173
People's Courts, 131, 169
picture scandal, 183–186
population growth, impact of, 55

positivism, 140, 179
Post Office Savings Bank, 175, 177
poverty, 17, 35, 160, 205, 206
Précis de la géographie universelle
    (Malte-Brun), 33
Protestant Reformation, 72–73
public welfare, 106, 113

qadi, 63, 116, 172, 173
Qarawiyyin mosque, 117
al-Qaida, 7, 233
al-Qarabisi, Abu 'Ali al-Husayn, 70
al-Qarafi, Shihab al-Din, 105
Qasr al-Nil Gardens, 93, 218, 221
al-Qawl al-sadid fi al-ijtihad wa al-
    tajdid, 68–71
qiyas (analogy), 63, 64, 65
Qubba Palace, 224
Qur'an, 7, 18, 20, 24, 29, 45, 48, 63,
    64, 67, 68, 72, 73, 94, 96, 99,
    101, 102, 108, 125, 129
  interpreting, 59, 100
  memorization of, 74
  recitation of, 158
  riba' and, 175, 176
  sciences and, 117
  Sunnis and, 2
  teaching, 169
al-Quwaysini, Shaykh, 26, 27–28

al-Rabi', 101
Radi, Shaykh Muhammad, 213
Rafi', Shaykh, 145
al-Ramli, Shihab al-Din, 69
Rashid, Muhammad, 90, 189
Rawdat al-madaris, 68
  Mubarak and, 60
  al-Tahtawi and, 51, 67
al-Razi, Fakhr al-Din, 78

reform, 5, 9, 143, 177, 178, 181,
    197–200, 204, 205–210, 231
  bureaucratic, 47
  criticism of, 163, 172–174
  debate over, 6, 165, 167
  of discipline and morality, 156,
    157, 158, 159–160, 216
  educational, 4, 6, 44, 77, 79, 80,
    84, 112, 232
  of examination procedures
    (faculty), 213, 216, 226
  of examination procedures
    (students), 48–51, 53–54,
    113–114, 125, 131, 214
  European models of, 13
  of holidays, 156, 161
  legitimate, 229
  modernist, 140, 164, 202, 228
  negotiated, 226–227
  opponents of, 139, 140
  of progression through classes,
    155, 159, 214
  proposals for: by 'Abdullah
    Nadim, 123–129; by
    Muhammad 'Abduh, 79–82;
    by Muhammad al-Ahmadi al-
    Zawahiri, 206–208
  of registration procedures and
    student rations, 113,
    114–115, 155, 157
  of salaries and stipends for
    teachers, 131, 154, 157, 161,
    203, 216
  state-sponsored, 144
  of subjects of study, 131, 155,
    160–161, 203, 214, 216
  'ulama and, 82, 167, 203, 229
reform codes, 57, 112–115, 154,
    197, 217, 229, 235

  as cause of financial problems,
    120
  failure of, 115, 205–206
  funding of, 163
  negotiation of, 156–157, 162,
    197, 199–203, 212–213,
    226–230, 235
  opposition to, 49–51, 120, 125,
    162–163, 198, 213, 215–217,
    247 n.61
  support for, 53–54, 162,
    163–164, 205, 216, 217, 222
  1865 code of Shaykh al-'Arusi
    (not implemented), 48–51:
    opposition to, 49–51
  1872 Examination Code of
    Shaykh al-'Abbasi al-Mahdi,
    53–54
  1885 Examination Code of
    Shaykh al-'Abbasi al-Mahdi,
    113–114
  1885 Registration Code of
    Shaykh al-'Abbasi al-Mahdi,
    114–115, 155: provisions not
    implemented until 1898, 115
  1888 Madrasa Organization
    Code, 218
  1888 Code, 125
  1895 Code of the Azhar
    Administrative Council, 131,
    225
  1896 Azhar Organization Code
    of the Azhar Administrative
    Council, 144, 154–162, 169,
    197, 262 n.51, 262 n.55:
    critiqued, 162–163;
    provisions implemented
    1898–1899, 161; supported,
    162

reform codes *(cont.)*
  1908 Azhar Organization Code
    of the Azhar Administrative
    Council, Internal
    Reorganization Code ("New
    Order"), 197, 198, 211–224,
    229–230: creates position of
    inspector, 214;
    demonstrations regarding,
    217–226; Internal
    Organization Plan No. 1,
    214; petition for
    reinstatement of, 225;
    problems with, 215–216,
    218–219, 220–221; reception
    of, 197; temporarily
    suspended, 224–225
  1909 revision of 1908 code,
    225–226: gradualist
    implementation of, 225
  1910 creation of Lajnet Islah
    (government commission to
    study history of reforms),
    225–226
  1911 Reform Program (al-Azhar
    Reorganization Code of 13
    May 1911, Internal
    Organization Code of 26 June
    1911), 226–227, 229:
    creation of shahadat al-
    takhassus, 227
Reformation, Protestant, 72–73, 169
registration code. *See* reform codes
religion, 47, 129
  protection of, 149
  science and, 118–119
  students and, 222
religious education, 47, 127, 206,
    207, 208, 212, 226
  centralization of, 35

changing, 108
ijtihad in, 227
reform of, 228
religious institutions, 14, 47, 144,
    153
religious law, 106, 174. *See also*
    shari'a
religious schools, 108, 135, 208. *See
    also* madaris
religious studies, 119, 207
  brain drain and, 122
  primacy of, 161
  sciences and, 121–122
Revival of the Religious Sciences, The
    (al-Ghazali), 117
revivalists, 2, 88
riba', 175, 176, 182
Rida, Muhammad Rashid, 94, 162,
    172, 194, 196, 200, 201,
    210–211, 228
  on 'Abduh impertinence, 95
  on al-Azhar, 207
  "al-Muhawirat bayna al-muslih
    wa al-muqallid," 172–174
  on Shaykh al-Azhar, 212
Rifa'i, Ahmad, 205
Rifqi Pasha, 83
Risalat al-tawhid ('Abduh), 169, 170,
    171, 210
riwaq (student/scholar residence),
    15, 46, 48, 51, 124, 126, 130,
    134, 137, 139, 154, 155, 157,
    158, 161, 199, 203, 222, 224,
    258 n.41
  'Abbasiya, 206
  Ibtighawiyya, 136
  Maghribi, 27, 42, 205–206
  Sa'idi, 37
  Syrian, 43, 143, 144–145, 148,
    153, 234

Riyad Pasha, 72, 82, 83
Rouiller, M., 129
Rousseau, Jean-Jacques, 29
Rove, Mr., 146
rule of law, 103, 105, 109
Russo-Japanese war (1905), 197

al-Safti, Muhammad Sulayman
    (Shaykh), 139, 141
  on al-Azhar/subjects, 136
  management and, 138
  modernists and, 137
  reform and, 137–138
  Shaykh al-Azhar and, 137
Sa'id, Viceroy of Egypt, 40, 41, 42
  conscription/immigration and,
    56
  expulsion by, 45
  Land Law and, 43
Sa'idis, 43, 46, 50, 90, 143
St. John, James Augustine, 15, 16
salaf, 68, 138, 173
salafis, 251 n.46, 266 n.40
Salim Pasha, 43
Salman, 'Abd al-Karim, 131, 132,
    143, 156, 161, 164, 199, 201,
    203, 210
  Azhar Organization Code and,
    162
Sami, Mahmud, 83, 231
Samir, Ahmad Effendi, 87, 127
  on 'ulama, 84, 85–86
sanctuary, 41–43
Sanu', Ya'qub, 82
Sanusis, 98, 99
al-Sayyadi, Abu al-Huda (Shaykh),
    113, 178–179, 180
  'Abduh and, 178
School of Artillery, 20, 44
School of Engineering, 20, 44

School of Industry, 20
School of Irrigation, 20
School of Islamic Law and
    Jurisprudence, 39, 41, 116
School of Languages and
    Accounting, 38, 39, 41, 46,
    81
School of Maternity, 20
School of Medicine, 20, 26, 33, 34,
    121
School of Music, 20
School of Translation, 20
school systems, European-model,
    81–82
sciences, 77, 98, 131, 140
  empirical, 137
  European, 35
  fatwas on, 116–118
  knowledge of, 129
  law and, 137
  legitimation of, 115–116
  materialist, 118
  mathematical, 119
  natural, 118, 119, 120, 121
  Qur'an and, 117
  religion and, 118–119, 121–122
  religious, 161
  spread of, 87
  teachers and, 160–161
  'ulama and, 79, 119, 137
secularism, 135, 170
al-Shadhili al-Azhari, Ahmad 143,
    153, 164, 210
  scientific subjects and, 136
  on Shaykh al-Azhar, 150, 151,
    152
  Syrian Riwaq Cholera Riot and,
    144, 145, 148, 150, 152
  'ulama and, 149
Shadhili Sufi order, 100, 101, 136

al-Shafi'i (founder of Shafi'i
    madhhab), 39, 63, 64, 101
Shafi'i madhhab, 39, 50, 51, 52, 70,
    71, 89, 91, 101, 105, 117,
    131–132, 152, 159, 199, 214,
    249 n.20, 255 n.48
    defined, 64
Shafi'i Mufti, 89, 214
Shafiq Pasha, Ahmad, 180, 187,
    194, 209, 221–222
    'Abduh and, 178, 195, 197
    on Cromer, 195
    on New Order, 214
    plans by, 214
    Shakir and, 212
Shakir, Muhammad, 211, 212, 214,
    228
Shaltut, Mahmud, 228
al-Sha'rani, 'Abd al-Wahhab, 102
Sharh al-aqa'id al-nasafiyya (al-
    Taftazani), 94
shari'a, 97, 118, 122, 136, 138. See
    also religious law
shari'a courts, 114, 116, 130
al-Shashi, al-Qaffal: fatwa by, 70
al-Shatibi, Abu Ishaq, 99, 103, 104
Shaykh al-Azhar. See al-Azhar,
    Shaykh
shaykhs, 205, 222
    definition of, 17
    stipends for, 161
    students and, 159
    teaching by, 17, 127, 161
Shi'a, 178, 204, 228, 234
    Ja'fari madhhab, 228
al-Shirazi, al-Ustadh Abu Ishaq,
    70–71
al-Shirbini, 'Abd al-Rahman (Shaykh
    al-Azhar, Shafi'i Mufti), 199,
    208, 211

'Abduh and, 132, 209, 210
death of, 211
piety of, 207
resignation from al-Azhar
    Administrative Council, 131
resignation as Shaykh al-Azhar,
    211
al-Shirbitli, Shaykh, 190, 191
al-Shubrawi, 'Abdullah, 71
Shura Council for Legislation, 169,
    210
al-Sinnari, 'Abd al-Rahman, 132,
    139
Sidqi, Isma'il, 226
social change, 4–5, 67, 88
Social Contract (Rousseau), 29
Social Darwinism, 169, 190–191,
    208, 209
social development, 59, 68, 165
social order, 42, 104, 109, 174, 179
social progress, 6, 31, 79
social stability, taqlid and, 99–106
social stagnation, 59, 75, 86, 87,
    229
    halqas and, 76–77
    taqlid and, 82
Spencer, Herbert, 190, 208, 209
    'Abduh and, 167, 168, 191
    practical/civil education and, 168
spirit of inquiry, 72–74, 86
"stagnant ones," 96, 207, 210
state interests, 38–41
strikes, 217–226
students
    conditions for, 123–124, 219
    expulsion of, 222, 223
    graduation of, 125
    payments for, 123
    population of, 37, 123, 124, 125,
    143

regulations for, 158–159
religion and, 222
shaykhs and, 159
soldiers and, 147
strike by, 218, 221, 222, 223
'ulama and, 53, 219, 220
al-Subki, 69, 88
al-Sudfi, Bakr, 224
al-Sudfi, Muhammad 'Ashur, 217
Sufis, 10, 104, 206
Sunna, 68, 69, 99, 100, 211
Sunnis, 100, 102, 204, 234
    Qur'an/hadith and, 2
    Sunnism, 8, 100, 231
al-Surur, 'Abd al-Baqi, 206
surveillance, 56, 229
    bureaucratic, 139
    encoding, 47–53
    normalizing, 48
al-Suyuti, Jalal al-Din, 69, 71, 88,
    101
    al-Tahtawi and, 69
Syrian Catholic Patriarch, 177
Syrian Gate, 145
Syrian Riwaq Cholera Riot (1896),
    144, 148–153, 154, 163, 223,
    234, 235

al-Taftazani, 94
al-Tahtawi, Rifa'a, 28–35, 39, 40,
    41, 44, 46, 51, 56, 60–62, 68,
    72, 78, 79, 81, 84, 85, 86,
    88, 94, 95, 96, 97, 101, 193,
    198
    appointment of, 60
    al-'Attar and, 30, 31, 32
    beneficial knowledge and, 61
    education and, 29, 32–33, 59
    Hanafis and, 69–70
    history of decline and, 33

ijtihad and, 63–71, 98, 232
interpretations and, 74
ittiba' and, 62–63
literacy and, 31
al-Qawl al-sadid fi al-ijtihad wa
    al-tajdid, 68–71
recall from Sudan, 45
Shafi'i definitions and, 70
Taqlid and, 62–71
'ulama and, 34, 61, 62, 87
al-Ta'if, 85
Takhlis al-ibriz fi talkhis Bariz (al-
    Tahtawi), 28, 33, 34, 35
takhrij, 70
"al-Ta'lim," 112
tamaddun, 79–80
al-Tankit wa al-tabkit, 84, 85, 86
Tanta, 128, 154
taqlid, 26, 59, 62–66, 71–72, 80,
    81, 86, 88, 95, 109, 121
    chains of, 87
    challenge to, 84, 103, 104
    defense of, 99
    definition of, 6
    ijtihad and, 227–228
    intellectual laziness/stagnation
        and, 7
    Islamic legal tradition and, 106
    Maliki rulings on, 102–105
    modernist movement and, 89
    practice of, 106
    promotion of, 6, 67
    redefining, 75
    social meaning of, 66–71
    social stability and, 99–106
    social stagnation and, 66, 82
    social values of, 98
Taqwimat al-Sihhiya, 216
tarjih, 69, 70
tartib, 140

Tawfiq, Khedive of Egypt, 90–91,
    92, 107, 122, 129, 264 n.4
'Abduh and, 166
Council of Notables and, 112
Cromer on, 113
opposition to, 83, 90
Tawfiq, Muhammad Effendi,
    176–177, 181–182, 195, 199
and 'Abduh picture, 183–186
criticism by, 185–186
and Humarat Monyati, 176
sentencing for libel of, 186, 271
    n.131
Shaykh Hifni and, 185
similarity to Young Turks, 269
    n.96
worked with Mustafa Kamil, 269
    n.96
taxation, 10, 11
teachers, 37, 116, 215
appointment for, 124–125
qualified, 217
sciences and, 160–161
stipends for, 203, 220
'ulama and, 81
Tharwat, 'Abd al-Khaliq, 226
al-Tijara, 82
Toledano, Ehud: on 'Abbas Pasha, 16
Tolstoy, Leo, 167
transmission, 19, 25, 47, 60, 141
chains of, 54, 74, 76
gaps in, 64
oral, 17, 18, 64, 120, 141
person-to-person, 236
vehicles of, 18
Transvaal fatwa, 188–195
Treaty of London (1840), 40
al-Tuwayrani, Hasan Husni,
    135–136, 140, 163

reform and, 133, 137–138
riwaqs and, 134
subjects and, 134

'ulama/'alim (scholars/scholar), 3, 9,
    14, 16, 17, 18, 24, 25, 26, 33,
    37, 56, 128, 131, 202, 206
authority of, 28, 35, 121, 122
al-Azhar and, 21, 27
bureaucratic, 23
conservatism of, 59
criticism of, 24, 27, 29,
    30–33, 37, 45, 59, 62, 72,
    78–79, 80, 85, 87,
    112–113, 119, 124,
    132–133, 166–167, 168,
    207, 213–214, 231
European/Muslim, 87
function of, 136, 138–139,
    139–140, 229
harmed by reforms, 125
law and, 137
opposition to, 10, 85, 214, 231
reform and, 82, 167, 203, 229
religious knowledge and, 81
responsibility of, 97
as "stagnant ones," 96, 207, 210
stipends for, 123, 161, 219, 220
strike by, 222
students and, 53, 219, 220
teaching by, 22, 49
as transmitters/interpreters, 60,
    108, 114
Utilitarian concepts and, 230
visitations/rituals and, 98
"al-'Ulama wa al-ta'lim" ('Abdullah
    Nadim), 123–129, 144
'Umar, Caliph of Islam, 200
umma, 3, 134, 135

"Universalization of Education, The"
('Ali Yusuf), 119
'Urabi, Ahmad, 83, 91, 93
'Urabi Revolt, 83, 85, 89, 91, 93,
107, 108, 165, 166, 231
'Urabists, 91, 92, 93, 107, 112,
231–232
al-'Urwa al-wuthqa, 112, 178
usul al-fiqh (roots of jurisprudence),
62, 63, 155
Utilitarianism, 23, 47, 55, 61, 139,
144, 198, 207, 230, 235

Veiled Protectorate, 3, 112
Veterinary School, 20
vocational schools, 115, 116

Wahhabis, 98, 99, 178
Wali Allah, Shah, 72
al-Waqa'i' al-Misriyya, 39, 41, 60,
81–82, 131, 229
'Abduh and, 79
al-'Attar and, 26, 28
waqf/awqaf (charitable endowment),
10, 12, 43, 54, 114, 122, 123,
130, 133, 134, 135, 136, 158,
160, 163, 176, 203, 214, 219,
224
centralization, 14–15
charities, 61
control of, 15
funding from, 139
funds, 125, 134, 176
lands, 13, 14, 187, 219
Mamluk warfare and, 10–11
reforms, 21
revenues, 37, 126, 220, 235

revenues, interest on, 177
sequestration of revenues, 16
supervision of, 14
Waqf Administration, 127, 129,
158
War School, 20, 25, 41
al-Watan, 82, 86

Yildiz Palace, 177
Young Egypt, 82
Young Turks, 178, 180, 269 n.96
Yusuf, 'Ali, 122, 138, 141, 187, 209
Arabic style and, 120
on al-Azhar students, 120
campaign by, 140
curriculum and, 119
on Dar al-'Ulum, 119
demonstrations and, 221
on 'ilm, 119
al-Mu'ayyad and, 130
on natural sciences, 121
science/theology and, 118
'ulama and, 119

al-Za'farani, Abu 'Ali, 70
Zaghlul, Ahmad Fathi, 226
al-Zahir, 188, 190, 191, 194
ijtihad and, 193
'ulama and, 193
al-Zawahiri, Ayman, 233
al-Zawahiri, Muhammad al-Ahmadi,
226, 227
on modernists' models, 207–208
on poor morality, 206
reform and, 207
Zaytuna mosque, 117
Zifti, Shaykh, 86